healthy cooking
Taste of Home
annual recipes

76

49

128

EDITORIAL
EDITOR-IN-CHIEF Catherine Cassidy
CREATIVE DIRECTOR Howard Greenberg
EDITORIAL OPERATIONS DIRECTOR
Kerri Balliet

**MANAGING EDITOR/PRINT & DIGITAL
BOOKS** Mark Hagen
ASSOCIATE CREATIVE DIRECTOR
Edwin Robles Jr.

EDITOR Christine Rukavena
ART DIRECTOR Maggie Conners
LAYOUT DESIGNER Catherine Fletcher
EDITORIAL PRODUCTION MANAGER
Dena Ahlers
EDITORIAL PRODUCTION COORDINATOR
Jill Banks
COPY CHIEF Deb Warlaumont Mulvey
COPY EDITORS Dulcie Shoener,
Chris McLaughlin
CONTRIBUTING COPY EDITORS
Kristin Sutter, Valerie Phillips
EDITORIAL INTERN Michael Welch

FOOD EDITORS Gina Nistico; James Schend;
Peggy Woodward, RDN
RECIPE EDITORS Sue Ryon (lead); Mary King;
Irene Yeh
BUSINESS ANALYST, CONTENT TOOLS
Amanda Harmatys
CONTENT OPERATIONS ASSISTANT
Shannon Stroud
EDITORIAL SERVICES ADMINISTRATOR
Marie Brannon

**TEST KITCHEN & FOOD STYLING
MANAGER** Sarah Thompson
TEST COOKS Nicholas Iverson (lead),
Matthew Hass, Lauren Knoelke
FOOD STYLISTS Kathryn Conrad (lead),
Shannon Roum, Leah Rekau
PREP COOKS Bethany Van Jacobson (lead),
Megumi Garcia, Melissa Hansen
CULINARY TEAM ASSISTANT Megan Behr

PHOTOGRAPHY DIRECTOR
Stephanie Marchese
PHOTOGRAPHERS Dan Roberts, Jim Wieland
PHOTOGRAPHER/SET STYLIST
Grace Natoli Sheldon

SET STYLISTS Melissa Franco, Stacey Genaw,
Dee Dee Jacq
CONTRIBUTING SET STYLISTS Pam Stasney,
Karen Ponteri

EDITORIAL BUSINESS MANAGER
Kristy Martin
EDITORIAL BUSINESS ASSOCIATE
Samantha Lea Stoeger

EDITOR, *TASTE OF HOME* Jeanne Ambrose
**ASSOCIATE CREATIVE DIRECTOR,
*TASTE OF HOME*** Erin Burns
ART DIRECTOR, *TASTE OF HOME*
Kristin Bowker

BUSINESS
VICE PRESIDENT, GROUP PUBLISHER
Kirsten Marchioli
PUBLISHER, *TASTE OF HOME* Donna Lindskog
**GENERAL MANAGER, TASTE OF HOME
COOKING SCHOOL** Erin Puariea

TRUSTED MEDIA BRANDS, INC.
**PRESIDENT & CHIEF EXECUTIVE
OFFICER** Bonnie Kintzer
**CHIEF FINANCIAL OFFICER/CHIEF
OPERATING OFFICER** Howard Halligan
CHIEF REVENUE OFFICER Richard Sutton
CHIEF MARKETING OFFICER Alec Casey
CHIEF DIGITAL OFFICER Vince Errico
**SENIOR VICE PRESIDENT, GLOBAL HR
& COMMUNICATIONS** Phyllis E. Gebhardt,
SPHR; SHRM-SCP
**VICE PRESIDENT, DIGITAL CONTENT
& AUDIENCE DEVELOPMENT** Diane Dragan
VICE PRESIDENT, BRAND MARKETING
Beth Gorry
**VICE PRESIDENT, FINANCIAL PLANNING
& ANALYSIS** William Houston
PUBLISHING DIRECTOR, BOOKS
Debra Polansky
CHIEF TECHNOLOGY OFFICER
Aneel Tejwaney
**VICE PRESIDENT, CONSUMER MARKETING
PLANNING** Jim Woods

COVER PHOTOGRAPHY
PHOTOGRAPHER Jim Wieland
FOOD STYLIST Shannon Roum
SET STYLIST Stacey Genaw

PICTURED ON FRONT COVER: Sausage Orecchiette Pasta (p. 141).
PICTURED ON BACK COVER: Chocolate-Glazed Cupcakes (p. 219), Feta Steak Tacos (p. 105),
Mini Barbecue Meat Loaves (p. 100) and Spicy Sweet Potato Kale Soup (p. 31).

healthy cooking

Taste of Home

cooking

annual recipes

Taste of Home

RDA ENTHUSIAST BRANDS, LLC • MILWAUKEE, WI

Contents

Be inspired to try a fabulous new dish today. With hundreds of tempting recipes to choose from, you'll discover everything you need for healthy weeknight dinners, holiday entertaining, golden baked goods and more.

221

Starters & Snacks 6

Soups 20

Side Salads 36

Side Dishes..52

Good Mornings...................................... 66

Slow Cooker.. 82

Beef Entrees 94

Chicken Favorites 108

Turkey Specialties 130

Pork, Ham & More 146

Fish & Seafood 164

Meatless Mains.....................................182

The Bread Basket 198

Cakes & Pies 212

Treat Yourself 228

Indexes 244

Healthy Home-Cooked Meals on Your Timetable

With *Healthy Cooking Annual Recipes,* it's never been easier!

I have a secret: I'm a registered dietitian nutritionist, but I don't really *love* vegetables. I have no problem snacking on deliciously sweet fresh fruit or digging into a sandwich made with hearty whole grain bread. But I'm just not excited by a spoonful of plain green beans on the side of my plate. For me, it's a challenge to get my 2½ cups a day. But, if I make smart choices, getting all the veggies I need isn't all that hard.

I look for recipes that incorporate a serving or two of vegetables right into the dish—that's the way I like veggies best. They aren't hidden, but they're important players in the dish and they taste great—like the carrots, parsnips and mushrooms in **HEARTY BEEF & SWEET POTATO STEW (P. 34).** Not only is it slow-simmered comfort food at its best, but this healthy recipe also makes enough stew for lunchtime leftovers, which is a big plus in my book.

To me, making smart choices is about:
- Incorporating more fruits, vegetables and whole grains into meals.
- Adding only a modest amount of higher-fat, higher-sodium foods for flavor.
- Eating healthy foods most of the time, but not all of the time.

The recipes in this year's *Healthy Cooking Annual Recipes* make it easy for you to make smart choices. They are from home cooks who want to eat more healthfully, just like you. The hardest part will be choosing which tempting recipe to make first!

Happy Cooking,

Peggy

Peggy Woodward, RDN
Food Editor

About Our Nutrition Facts

Healthy Cooking Annual Recipes cookbook provides a variety of recipes that fit into a healthy lifestyle.

FACTS
- Whenever a choice of ingredients is given in a recipe (such as ⅓ cup of sour cream or plain yogurt), the first ingredient listed is always the one calculated in the Nutrition Facts.
- When a range is given for an ingredient (such as 2 to 3 teaspoons), we calculate using the first amount.
- Only the amount of a marinade absorbed during preparation is calculated.
- Optional ingredients are not included in our calculations.

DIABETIC EXCHANGES
All recipes in *Healthy Cooking Annual Recipes* have been reviewed by a registered dietitian nutritionist. Diabetic Exchanges are assigned to recipes in accordance with guidelines from the American Diabetes Association and the Academy of Nutrition and Dietetics.

The majority of recipes in this cookbook are suitable for people with diabetes, but please check the Diabetic Exchanges to make sure the recipe is in accordance with your doctor's instructions and fits your particular dietary guidelines.

SPECIAL INDICATORS
To help those on restricted diets easily find dishes to suit their needs, we clearly mark recipes that are especially low in fat, sodium or carbohydrates, as well as those that contain no meat. You will find these icons, as well as quick-to-prepare recipe indicators, throughout the book:

F One serving contains 3 grams fat or less

S One serving contains 140 milligrams sodium or less

C One serving contains 15 grams carbohydrates or less

M Recipe contains no meat, gelatin, Worcestershire or other animal products

FAST FIX Dish is table-ready in 30 minutes or less.

Smart Choices, Made Easy

Let the recipes in this book help you and your family eat great the whole day through.

A dollop of sweetened Greek yogurt turns fresh fruit into an eye-opening breakfast treat in *Julie Sterchi's* **GRAPES WITH LEMON-HONEY YOGURT.** This creamy, low-fat side is a delicious way to work in a serving of fruit. **P. 71**

Feast on hearty, veggie-packed **QUICK NICOISE SALAD** from St. Louis cook *Valerie Belley.* Besides providing 2 servings of vegetables, this powerhouse dish delivers 21 grams of satisfying protein. **P. 173**

Sneak in more than a half-cup of veggies—and never miss the meat—with flavorful **MUSHROOM BURGERS** from Alberta home cook *Denise Hollebeke.* Whole wheat buns, vegetable toppings and a little cheddar cheese make these burgers not just tasty, but heart-smart, too! **P. 184**

Healthy Makeovers

Get inspired! Use some of Peggy's favorite tricks to make your own recipes more healthy. See how quickly the savings add up!

	ORIGINAL	SUBSTITUTE	SAVE (per serving)
Spaghetti	1 pound Italian turkey sausage; *4 servings*	• ½ pound Italian turkey sausage • ½ pound lean ground turkey • 1 teaspoon Italian seasoning	200 mg sodium
Tacos	1 pound lean ground beef; *4 servings*	• ½ pound lean ground beef • 1 can black beans (rinsed and drained)	5 g fat (2 g sat. fat) (+ 4 g fiber)
Chili	2 cans tomatoes and 1 can tomato sauce; *8 servings*	• no-salt-added versions in the same amounts	400 mg sodium
Cream Soup	2 cups half-and-half cream; *8 servings*	• 2 cups reduced-fat evaporated milk	30 calories, 5 g fat (4 g saturated fat)
Pancakes	4 tablespoons melted butter; *8 servings*	• 2 tablespoons melted butter • 2 tablespoons canola oil	2 g saturated fat
Brunch Bake	12 large eggs; *8 servings*	• 4 large eggs • 2 cups egg substitute	42 calories, 5 g fat (2 g saturated fat)
Quick Breads	1 cup each chocolate chips and chopped pecans; *12 servings*	• ½ cup each in the bread • 1 tablespoon each sprinkled on top	57 calories, 5 g fat
Cupcakes	1 cup canola oil; *24 servings*	• ½ cup canola oil • ½ cup applesauce	36 calories, 5 g fat

9

16

18

Starters & Snacks

❝My strategy to get my picky kids to eat healthy is to let them assemble meals themselves. They love these easy meatball wraps topped with crunchy vegetables and a dollop of creamy yogurt.❞

—JENNIFER BECKMAN FALLS CHURCH, VA
about her recipe, Curried Chicken Meatball Wraps, on page 17

GRILLED LEEK DIP

Grilled Leek Dip F S C

Smoky leeks from the grill add punch to this creamy appetizer with veggies and chips. If baby Vidalia onions are available, I use those.

—**RAMONA PARRIS** MARIETTA, GA

PREP: 10 MIN. • **GRILL:** 10 MIN. + CHILLING
MAKES: 1¼ CUPS

- 2 **medium leeks**
- 2 **teaspoons olive oil**
- ½ **teaspoon salt, divided**
- ¼ **teaspoon pepper**
- 2 **cups (16 ounces) reduced-fat sour cream**
- 2 **tablespoons Worcestershire sauce**
  Assorted fresh vegetables

1. Trim and discard dark green portions of leeks. Brush leeks with oil; sprinkle with ¼ teaspoon salt and the pepper. Grill leeks, covered, over medium-high heat for 8-10 minutes or until lightly charred and tender, turning occasionally. Cool slightly; chop leeks.

2. In a small bowl, combine sour cream, Worcestershire sauce and the remaining salt; stir in leeks. Refrigerate, covered, 2 hours before serving. Serve with vegetables.

PER SERVING *2 tablespoons dip (calculated without vegetables) equals 43 cal., 2 g fat (1 g sat. fat), 8 mg chol., 93 mg sodium, 3 g carb., trace fiber, 2 g pro.*

Sesame-Beef Pot Stickers F C

I enjoy these pot stickers as a late-night snack while I'm watching television. They also work well as a quick appetizer for family parties.

—**CAROLYN TURNER** RENO, NV

PREP: 20 MIN. • **COOK:** 10 MIN./BATCH
MAKES: 2 DOZEN

- ¾ **pound lean ground beef (90% lean)**
- 2 **tablespoons reduced-sodium soy sauce**
- 1 **tablespoon sesame oil**
- 2¼ **teaspoons chili garlic sauce**
- 2 **teaspoons onion powder**
- 1 **teaspoon garlic salt**
- ¼ **teaspoon dried parsley flakes**
- 24 **pot sticker or gyoza wrappers**
- 1 **large egg, lightly beaten**
- 3 **teaspoons sesame or olive oil, divided**
- ½ **cup water, divided**

1. In a large bowl, combine the first seven ingredients. Place 1 tablespoon beef mixture in center of each pot sticker wrapper. (Cover wrappers with a damp towel until ready to use.)

2. Moisten wrapper edges with egg. Fold wrapper over filling; seal edges, pleating the front side several times to form a pleated pouch. Stand pot stickers on a work surface to flatten bottoms; if desired, curve slightly to form crescent shapes.

3. In a large skillet, heat 1½ teaspoons sesame oil over medium-high heat. Arrange half of the pot stickers in concentric circles in pan, flat side down; cook 1-2 minutes or until the bottoms are lightly browned. Carefully add ¼ cup water (water may spatter); reduce the heat to medium. Cook, covered, 3-5 minutes or until water is almost absorbed and the filling is cooked through.

4. Cook, uncovered, 1-2 minutes or until bottoms are crisp and water is completely evaporated. Repeat with remaining pot stickers.

NOTE *Wonton wrappers may be substituted for pot sticker and gyoza wrappers. Stack two or three wonton wrappers on a work surface; cut into circles with a 3½-in. biscuit or round cookie cutter. Fill and cook as directed.*

PER SERVING *1 pot sticker equals 50 cal., 2 g fat (1 g sat. fat), 14 mg chol., 164 mg sodium, 3 g carb., trace fiber, 3 g pro.*

SESAME-BEEF POT STICKERS

Meatballs in Cherry Sauce F C

A ruby red cherry glaze made with pie filling gives homemade meatballs festive color for a special get-together. Everyone will love the zesty, sweet-tart flavors, too.
—RITA CHABOT-SCHULTZ BALLWIN, MO

PREP: 30 MIN. • **BAKE:** 15 MIN.
MAKES: ABOUT 3½ DOZEN

- 1 cup seasoned bread crumbs
- 1 small onion, chopped
- 1 large egg, lightly beaten
- 3 garlic cloves, minced
- 1 teaspoon salt
- ½ teaspoon pepper
- 1 pound lean ground beef (90% lean)
- 1 pound ground pork

SAUCE

- 1 can (21 ounces) cherry pie filling
- ⅓ cup sherry or chicken broth
- ⅓ cup cider vinegar
- ¼ cup steak sauce
- 2 tablespoons brown sugar
- 2 tablespoons reduced-sodium soy sauce
- 1 teaspoon honey

1. Preheat oven to 400°. In a large bowl, combine the first six ingredients. Add beef and pork; mix lightly but thoroughly. Shape into 1-in. balls. Place on a greased rack in a shallow baking pan. Bake for 11-13 minutes or until cooked through. Drain on paper towels.

2. In a large saucepan, combine the sauce ingredients. Bring to a boil over medium heat, stirring constantly. Reduce heat; simmer, uncovered, for 2-3 minutes or until thickened. Add the meatballs; heat through, stirring gently.

PER SERVING *1 meatball equals 76 cal., 3 g fat (1 g sat. fat), 19 mg chol., 169 mg sodium, 7 g carb., trace fiber, 5 g pro.* **Diabetic Exchanges:** *1 lean meat, ½ starch.*

Tropical Island Shrimp Kabobs F S C

PREP: 25 MIN. + MARINATING
COOK: 5 MIN./BATCH • **MAKES:** 2½ DOZEN

- ½ cup coconut milk
- ⅓ cup minced fresh cilantro
- 2 tablespoons lime juice
- 2 garlic cloves, minced
- 2 teaspoons olive oil
- 1½ teaspoons ground coriander
- ¼ teaspoon salt
- ¼ teaspoon coarsely ground pepper
- 30 uncooked shrimp (26-30 per pound size), peeled and deveined
- 30 mango cubes (about 1 large mango)
- 30 fresh pineapple cubes (about 1½ cups)

1. In a large resealable plastic bag, combine the first eight ingredients. Add shrimp; seal bag and turn to coat. Refrigerate 2 hours.

2. Drain shrimp, discarding marinade. On each of 30 metal or soaked wooden appetizer skewers, thread one shrimp, one mango cube and one pineapple cube. Heat a grill pan over medium heat. In batches, cook the kabobs for 2-3 minutes on each side or until shrimp turn pink.

PER SERVING *1 kabob equals 24 cal., trace fat (trace sat. fat), 20 mg chol., 23 mg sodium, 2 g carb., trace fiber, 3 g pro.*

Shrimp, mango and pineapple on skewers make a sunny presentation at parties. To boost flavors, we use a coconut milk, lime juice and cilantro marinade.
—MARY LEVERETTE COLUMBIA, SC

TROPICAL ISLAND SHRIMP KABOBS

Tomato-Squash Appetizer Pizza

F C M FAST FIX ▶

I grow herbs in my windowsill garden and needed new meal ideas to use them up. I created this flatbread pizza, which is also ideal for an appetizer.

—ANDREA TOVAR NEW YORK, NY

START TO FINISH: 30 MIN.
MAKES: 24 PIECES

- 1 loaf (1 pound) frozen bread dough, thawed
- ¼ teaspoon salt
- 1 tablespoon olive oil
- 1½ cups (6 ounces each) shredded part-skim mozzarella cheese
- 1 large yellow summer squash, sliced
- 1 large tomato, sliced
- 4 teaspoons shredded Parmesan cheese
- ¼ teaspoon pepper
- 1 teaspoon each minced fresh basil, oregano and chives

1. Roll dough into a 14x8-in. rectangle. Transfer to a greased baking sheet. Prick dough thoroughly with a fork. Sprinkle with salt. Bake at 425° for 8-10 minutes or until lightly browned.
2. Brush crust with oil. Top with mozzarella cheese, squash, tomato, Parmesan cheese, pepper and herbs. Bake 5-10 minutes longer or until cheese is melted.
PER SERVING *1 piece equals 81 cal., 3 g fat (1 g sat. fat), 4 mg chol., 169 mg sodium, 10 g carb., 1 g fiber, 4 g pro. Diabetic Exchanges: 1 fat, ½ starch.*

TOMATO-SQUASH APPETIZER PIZZA

> I jazz up guacamole by serving it on top of endive leaves. Add red pepper salsa, and you've got a standout appetizer.
> —GILDA LESTER MILLSBORO, DE

Avocado Endive Cups with Salsa F S C M

PREP: 45 MIN. • **MAKES:** 2½ DOZEN

- 1 jar (12 ounces) roasted sweet red peppers, drained and finely chopped
- 1 cup finely chopped fennel bulb
- ¼ cup sliced ripe olives, finely chopped
- 2 tablespoons olive oil
- 1 tablespoon minced fresh cilantro
- ½ teaspoon salt, divided
- ½ teaspoon pepper, divided
- 2 medium ripe avocados, peeled and pitted
- 3 tablespoons lime juice
- 2 tablespoons diced jalapeno pepper
- 1 green onion, finely chopped
- 1 garlic clove, minced
- ½ teaspoon ground cumin
- ¼ teaspoon hot pepper sauce
- 2 plum tomatoes, choppped
- 30 endive leaves
  Chopped fennel fronds

1. In a bowl, combine red peppers, fennel, olives, oil and cilantro; stir in ¼ teaspoon each salt and pepper.
2. In another bowl, mash avocados with a fork. Stir in lime juice, jalapeno, green onion, garlic, cumin, pepper sauce and the remaining salt and pepper. Stir in tomatoes.
3. Spoon about 1 tablespoon avocado mixture onto each endive leaf; top each with about 1 tablespoon pepper mixture. Sprinkle with fennel fronds.
PER SERVING *1 appetizer equals 43 cal., 3 g fat (trace sat. fat), 0 chol., 109 mg sodium, 4 g carb., 3 g fiber, 1 g pro. Diabetic Exchanges: 1 vegetable, ½ fat.*

AVOCADO ENDIVE CUPS WITH SALSA

Crab Rangoon Canapes F S C FAST FIX

I try my best to avoid fried food. This recipe has all the flavor of crab rangoon filling but with fewer calories. It's also a perfect appetizer for summer.

—CHERYL WOODSON LIBERTY, MO

START TO FINISH: 30 MIN.
MAKES: 16 APPETIZERS

- 2 **medium cucumbers**
- 6 **ounces reduced-fat cream cheese**
- ½ **cup lump crabmeat, drained**
- 1 **tablespoon finely chopped green onion**
- ¼ **teaspoon salt**
- ¼ **teaspoon garlic powder**
- ⅛ **teaspoon paprika**
- ½ **cup wonton strips**

1. Cut each cucumber into eight thick slices. Scoop out centers, leaving the bottoms intact.
2. In a small bowl, combine cream cheese, crab, green onion, salt and garlic powder. Spoon 1 tablespoon into each cucumber slice. Sprinkle with paprika; top with wonton strips.

PER SERVING *1 appetizer equals 44 cal., 3 g fat (2 g sat. fat), 11 mg chol., 123 mg sodium, 3 g carb., trace fiber, 2 g pro.*

Grilled Chicken, Mango & Blue Cheese Tortillas F C FAST FIX

Tortillas packed with chicken, mango and blue cheese make a light appetizer to welcome the summer season. We double or triple the ingredients for parties.

—JOSEE LANZI NEW PORT RICHEY, FL

START TO FINISH: 30 MIN.
MAKES: 16 APPETIZERS

- 1 **boneless skinless chicken breast (8 ounces)**
- 1 **teaspoon blackened seasoning**
- ¾ **cup (6 ounces) plain yogurt**
- 1½ **teaspoons grated lime peel**
- 2 **tablespoons lime juice**
- ¼ **teaspoon salt**
- ⅛ **teaspoon pepper**
- 1 **cup finely chopped peeled mango**
- ⅓ **cup finely chopped red onion**
- 4 **flour tortillas (8 inches)**
- ½ **cup crumbled blue cheese**
- 2 **tablespoons minced fresh cilantro**

GRILLED CHICKEN, MANGO & BLUE CHEESE TORTILLAS

1. Moisten a paper towel with cooking oil; using long-handled tongs, rub on grill rack to coat lightly. Sprinkle chicken with blackened seasoning. Grill chicken, covered, over medium heat 6-8 minutes on each side or until a thermometer reads 165°.
2. Meanwhile, in a small bowl, mix yogurt, lime peel, lime juice, salt and pepper. Cool chicken slightly; finely chop and transfer to a small bowl. Stir in mango and onion.
3. Grill tortillas, uncovered, over medium heat 2-3 minutes or until puffed. Turn; top with the chicken mixture and crumbled blue cheese. Grill, covered, for 2-3 minutes longer or until bottoms of tortillas are lightly browned. Drizzle with yogurt mixture; sprinkle with cilantro. Cut each tortilla into four wedges.

PER SERVING *1 wedge equals 85 cal., 3 g fat (1 g sat. fat), 12 mg chol., 165 mg sodium, 10 g carb., 1 g fiber, 5 g pro.* **Diabetic Exchanges:** *1 lean meat, ½ starch.*

HOW TO

NAB THE PERFECT MANGO
❶ Choose plump mangoes with a sweet, fruity fragrance. Avoid those that are bruised or very soft.
❷ Ripe mangoes have green-yellow skin with a pronounced red blush; unripened ones are firm and green with just a hint of red.
❸ To ripen a mango, let it stand at room temperature and out of sunlight. Then refrigerate the ripened mango until ready to use.

Crabbie Phyllo Cups F S C FAST FIX

START TO FINISH: 20 MIN.
MAKES: 2½ DOZEN

- ½ cup reduced-fat spreadable garden vegetable cream cheese
- ½ teaspoon seafood seasoning
- ¾ cup lump crabmeat, drained
- 2 packages (1.9 ounces each) frozen miniature phyllo tart shells
- 5 tablespoons chili sauce

In a small bowl, mix cream cheese and seafood seasoning; gently stir in crab. Spoon 2 teaspoons crab mixture into each tart shell; top with chili sauce.

PER SERVING *1 filled phyllo cup equals 34 cal., 2 g fat (trace sat. fat), 5 mg chol., 103 mg sodium, 3 g carb., 0 fiber, 1 g pro.*

For a nifty way to serve crabmeat as an appetizer, I stuff it in phyllo tart shells. Everyone walks away with them. Also try the recipe with water-packed tuna.
—**JOHNNA JOHNSON** SCOTTSDALE, AZ

CRABBY PHYLLO CUPS

Wicked Deviled Eggs C FAST FIX

My stepdaughter gave me the recipe for this delicious variation on deviled eggs. They make a tasty start to any party or get-together. I think they're even better if made the day before.
—**JANICE L. PARKER** HUMBOLDT, IA

START TO FINISH: 30 MIN.
MAKES: 2 DOZEN

- 12 hard-cooked eggs
- ½ cup Miracle Whip
- 2 tablespoons cider vinegar
- 2 tablespoons prepared mustard
- 1 tablespoon minced fresh parsley or 1 teaspoon dried parsley flakes
- 1 tablespoon butter, melted
- 1 tablespoon sweet pickle relish
- 2 teaspoons Worcestershire sauce
- 1 teaspoon sweet pickle juice
- ½ teaspoon salt
- ½ teaspoon cayenne pepper
- ½ teaspoon pepper
  Paprika

1. Cut eggs in half lengthwise. Remove yolks; set whites aside. In a small bowl, mash yolks. Add the Miracle Whip, vinegar, mustard, parsley, butter, relish, Worcestershire sauce, pickle juice, salt, cayenne and pepper; mix well. Stuff or pipe into egg whites.
2. Refrigerate until serving. Sprinkle with paprika.

PER SERVING *1 stuffed egg half equals 61 cal., 5 g fat (1 g sat. fat), 109 mg chol., 151 mg sodium, 1 g carb., trace fiber, 3 g pro.* **Diabetic Exchange:** *1 fat.*

Blueberry Salsa F S C M FAST FIX

This is a fruity and refreshing twist on salsa. Guests often line up to try it at parties, and they always leave satisfied.
—**KIMBERLY SORENSEN** CARUTHERS, CA

START TO FINISH: 15 MIN.
MAKES: 1½ CUPS

- 1½ cups fresh blueberries
- ¼ cup chopped sweet red pepper
- 2 green onions, finely chopped
- 2 tablespoons minced seeded jalapeno pepper
- 2 tablespoons lemon juice
- 1 to 2 tablespoons minced fresh cilantro
- 1½ teaspoons sugar
- ¼ teaspoon salt
  Dash of pepper

Place blueberries in a food processor; pulse five times or until coarsely chopped. Transfer to a small bowl; stir in the remaining ingredients. Refrigerate until serving.
NOTE *Wear disposable gloves when cutting hot peppers; the oils can burn skin. Avoid touching your face.*
PER SERVING *¼ cup equals 30 cal., trace fat (trace sat. fat), 0 chol., 100 mg sodium, 8 g carb., 1 g fiber, trace pro.* **Diabetic Exchange:** *½ fruit.*

Mocha Pumpkin Seeds S C M FAST FIX ▶

Roasted pumpkin seeds are a classic fall snack. Kick them up a notch with instant coffee and cocoa powder for a mix that's mocha genius.

—**REBEKAH BEYER** SABETHA, KS

START TO FINISH: 25 MIN. • **MAKES:** 3 CUPS

- 6 **tablespoons sugar**
- 2 **tablespoons baking cocoa**
- 1 **tablespoon instant coffee granules**
- 1 **large egg white**
- 2 **cups salted shelled pumpkin seeds (pepitas)**

1. Preheat oven to 325°. Place sugar, cocoa and coffee granules in a small food processor; cover and pulse until finely ground.

2. In a bowl, whisk egg white until frothy. Stir in pumpkin seeds. Sprinkle with sugar mixture and toss to coat. Spread in a single layer in a parchment paper-lined 15x10x1-in. baking pan.

3. Bake 20-25 minutes or until dry and no longer sticky, stirring every 10 minutes. Cool completely in pan. Store in an airtight container.

PER SERVING *¼ cup equals 142 cal., 10 g fat (2 g sat. fat), 0 chol., 55 mg sodium, 10 g carb., 1 g fiber, 6 g pro.* **Diabetic Exchanges:** *2 fat, ½ starch.*

PEA SOUP SHOOTERS

MOCHA PUMPKIN SEEDS

Pea Soup Shooters F S C

Appetizers really don't get any simpler than this. Plus, these shooters can be made ahead, they're colorful, and they won't weigh you down. Top with a dollop of additional yogurt for a little more tang.

—**JACYN SIEBERT** SAN FRANCISCO, CA

PREP: 20 MIN. + CHILLING • **MAKES:** 2 DOZEN

- 1 **package (16 ounces) frozen peas, thawed**
- 1 **cup reduced-sodium chicken broth**
- ¼ **cup minced fresh mint**
- 1 **tablespoon lime juice**
- 1 **teaspoon ground cumin**
- ¼ **teaspoon salt**
- 1½ **cups plain yogurt**
  Fresh mint leaves

1. Place the first six ingredients in a blender; cover and process until smooth. Add yogurt; process until blended. Transfer to a pitcher; refrigerate 1 hour to allow the flavors to blend.

2. To serve, pour soup into shot glasses; top with fresh mint leaves.

PER SERVING *1 serving equals 30 cal., 1 g fat (trace sat. fat), 2 mg chol., 92 mg sodium, 4 g carb., 1 g fiber, 2 g pro.*

Thyme-Sea Salt Crackers F S C M

These homemade crackers are decidedly light and crispy. They are wonderful on their own as a snack or pair well with a sharp white cheddar.

—JESSICA WIRTH CHARLOTTE, NC

PREP: 25 MIN. • **BAKE:** 10 MIN./BATCH • **MAKES:** ABOUT 7 DOZEN

- 2½ cups all-purpose flour
- ½ cup white whole wheat flour
- 1 teaspoon salt
- ¾ cup water
- ¼ cup plus 1 tablespoon olive oil, divided
- 1 to 2 tablespoons minced fresh thyme
- ¾ teaspoon sea or kosher salt

1. Preheat oven to 375°. In a large bowl, whisk flours and salt. Gradually add water and ¼ cup oil, tossing with a fork until dough holds together when pressed. Divide dough into three portions. On a lightly floured surface, roll each portion of dough to ⅛-in. thickness. Cut with a floured 1½-in. round cookie cutter. Place 1 in. apart on ungreased baking sheets. Prick each cracker with a fork; brush lightly with remaining oil. Mix thyme and sea salt; sprinkle over the crackers.

2. Bake 9-11 minutes or until bottoms are lightly browned.

PER SERVING *1 cracker equals 23 cal., 1 g fat (trace sat. fat), 0 chol., 45 mg sodium, 3 g carb., trace fiber, trace pro.*

CILANTRO SHRIMP CUPS

THYME-SEA SALT CRACKERS

Cilantro Shrimp Cups F S C

The crunchy, tangy salad inside these shrimp cups is packed with flavor. Plus, the wonton wrappers make for easy holding.

—RONNA FARLEY ROCKVILLE, MD

PREP: 25 MIN. • **BAKE:** 10 MIN. • **MAKES:** 3 DOZEN

- 36 wonton wrappers
- Cooking spray
- 1¼ pounds peeled and deveined cooked small shrimp, divided
- ½ cup chopped pecans
- ⅓ cup shredded carrot
- ⅓ cup finely chopped celery
- ¼ cup minced fresh cilantro
- 3 tablespoons lime juice
- 3 tablespoons oyster sauce
- 1½ teaspoons reduced-sodium soy sauce

1. Spritz each side of wonton wrappers with cooking spray; gently press into miniature muffin cups. Bake at 350° for 11-13 minutes or until golden brown. Remove to wire racks to cool.

2. Meanwhile, set aside 36 shrimp for garnish; chop remaining shrimp. In a small bowl, combine the chopped shrimp, pecans, carrot, celery, cilantro, lime juice, oyster sauce and soy sauce. Spoon into wonton cups. Garnish each with a reserved shrimp.

PER SERVING *1 appetizer equals 55 cal., 2 g fat (trace sat. fat), 25 mg chol., 135 mg sodium, 6 g carb., trace fiber, 4 g pro.*

ROASTED GRAPE CROSTINI

A trip to Spain introduced me to its culinary treasures, like Manchego cheese and sherry. This appetizer always impresses folks who've never tasted roasted grapes. They're amazing.

—JANICE ELDER CHARLOTTE, NC

Roasted Grape Crostini F S C M

PREP: 25 MIN. • **BAKE:** 30 MIN.
MAKES: 2 DOZEN

- 3 cups seedless red or green grapes, halved lengthwise
- 2 tablespoons sherry vinegar or rice vinegar
- 2 tablespoons olive oil
- ½ teaspoon salt
- ¼ teaspoon freshly ground pepper
- 1 teaspoon grated orange peel
- 24 slices French bread baguette (diagonally cut ½ inch thick)
- ½ cup shaved Manchego cheese or Romano cheese
  Thinly sliced fresh basil leaves

1. Preheat oven to 400°. In a bowl, toss grapes with vinegar, oil, salt and pepper. Place mixture in a greased 15x10x1-in. baking pan. Roast for 30-35 minutes or until softened and lightly browned. Transfer to a small bowl; stir in orange peel.
2. Change oven setting to broil. Place baguette slices on an ungreased baking sheet. Broil 3-4 in. from heat for 1-2 minutes on each side or until light brown. To serve, spoon warm grape mixture over toasts; top with cheese and basil.
PER SERVING *1 appetizer equals 52 cal., 2 g fat (1 g sat. fat), 2 mg chol., 110 mg sodium, 8 g carb., trace fiber, 1 g pro.* **Diabetic Exchanges:** *½ starch, ½ fat.*

Garlicky Herbed Shrimp F S C FAST FIX ▶

I love shrimp. Love garlic. Love herbs. Cook 'em up in butter and what could be better?

—DAVE LEVIN VAN NUYS, CA

START TO FINISH: 25 MIN.
MAKES: ABOUT 3 DOZEN

- 2 pounds uncooked jumbo shrimp, peeled and deveined
- 5 garlic cloves, minced
- 2 green onions, chopped
- ½ teaspoon garlic powder
- ½ teaspoon ground mustard
- ¼ teaspoon seasoned salt
- ¼ teaspoon crushed red pepper flakes
- ⅛ teaspoon pepper
- ½ cup butter, divided
- ¼ cup lemon juice
- 2 tablespoons minced fresh parsley
- 1 tablespoon minced fresh tarragon

1. In a large bowl, combine the first eight ingredients; toss to combine. In a large skillet, heat ¼ cup butter over medium-high heat. Add half of the shrimp mixture; cook and stir for 4-5 minutes or until shrimp turn pink. Transfer to a clean bowl.
2. Repeat with remaining butter and shrimp mixture. Return cooked shrimp to pan. Stir in lemon juice; heat through. Stir in herbs.
PER SERVING *1 shrimp equals 46 cal., 3 g fat (2 g sat. fat), 37 mg chol., 61 mg sodium, 1 g carb., trace fiber, 4 g pro.* **Diabetic Exchange:** *½ fat.*

GARLICKY HERBED SHRIMP

Artichoke Hummus

Whenever I go to a party, the hostess always asks me to bring my hummus. It's a versatile dip that perfectly complements a number of appetizers.

—HOLLY COLE PARRISH, FL

START TO FINISH: 15 MIN.
MAKES: 2 CUPS

- 1 **can (15 ounces) garbanzo beans or chickpeas, rinsed and drained**
- 1 **jar (7½ ounces) marinated quartered artichoke hearts, drained**
- ¼ **cup tahini**
- 1 **tablespoon capers, drained**
- 2 **tablespoons lemon juice**
- 4 **garlic cloves, minced**
- 2 **teaspoons grated lemon peel**
- 1 **teaspoon ground cumin**
- ½ **teaspoon garlic powder**
- ⅛ **teaspoon salt**
  Dash crushed red pepper flakes, optional
  Dash pepper
- 2 **fresh rosemary sprigs, chopped**
  Assorted fresh vegetables or baked pita chips

Place the first 12 ingredients in a food processor; cover and process until smooth. Transfer to a small bowl; stir in rosemary. Serve with vegetables.

PER SERVING *2 tablespoons hummus (calculated without vegetables or chips) equals 75 cal., 5 g fat (1 g sat. fat), 0 chol., 116 mg sodium, 6 g carb., 2 g fiber, 2 g pro.* **Diabetic Exchanges:** *½ starch, ½ fat.*

Curried Chicken Meatball Wraps

My strategy to get my picky kids to eat healthy is to let them assemble meals themselves. They love these easy meatball wraps topped with crunchy vegetables and a dollop of creamy yogurt.

—JENNIFER BECKMAN FALLS CHURCH, VA

PREP: 25 MIN. • **BAKE:** 20 MIN.
MAKES: 2 DOZEN

- 1 **small onion, finely chopped**
- ½ **cup Rice Krispies**
- ¼ **cup golden raisins**
- ¼ **cup minced fresh cilantro**
- 1 **large egg, lightly beaten**

CURRIED CHICKEN MEATBALL WRAPS

- 2 **teaspoons curry powder**
- ½ **teaspoon salt**
- 1 **pound lean ground chicken**
ASSEMBLY
- 1 **cup (8 ounces) plain yogurt**
- ¼ **cup minced fresh cilantro**
- 24 **small Bibb or Boston lettuce leaves**
- ½ **cup golden raisins**
- ½ **cup chopped salted peanuts**
- 1 **medium carrot, shredded**
  Additional minced fresh cilantro

1. Preheat oven to 350°. In a large bowl, combine onion, Rice Krispies, raisins, cilantro, egg, curry powder and salt. Add chicken; mix lightly but thoroughly. With wet hands, shape into 1¼-in. balls. Place meatballs on a rack coated with cooking spray in a 15x10x1-in. baking pan. Bake 18-22 minutes or until lightly browned and cooked through.

2. In a small bowl, mix the yogurt and ¼ cup cilantro. Serve meatballs in lettuce leaves; top with yogurt mixture. Sprinkle with the raisins, peanuts, carrot and additional minced cilantro.

PER SERVING *1 appetizer equals 72 cal., 3 g fat (1 g sat. fat), 22 mg chol., 89 mg sodium, 6 g carb., 1 g fiber, 6 g pro.* **Diabetic Exchanges:** *1 lean meat, ½ starch.*

Festive Cherry Tomatoes F S C M

These red and green delights look so cheery on a holiday buffet. I found a version of this recipe years ago, but I created a lighter version by mixing peas with avocado and adding chipotle peppers for an added kick.

—LORI MERRICK DANVERS, IL

PREP: 45 MIN. • **MAKES:** 4 DOZEN

- 48 **cherry tomatoes**
- 2¼ **cups frozen peas (about 9 ounces), thawed**
- 1 **medium ripe avocado, peeled and pitted**
- ⅓ **cup plain Greek yogurt**
- 3 **tablespoons lime juice**
- 1 **chipotle pepper in adobo sauce, finely chopped**
- ½ **teaspoon salt**
- 2 **tablespoons minced fresh cilantro, divided**

1. Using a sharp knife, cut a thin slice from the top and bottom of each cherry tomato. Scoop out pulp; invert onto paper towels to drain.

2. Place peas in a food processor; cover and process until almost smooth. In a small bowl, mash the avocado with a fork; add pureed peas, yogurt, lime juice, 1 tablespoon cilantro, chipotle pepper and salt.

3. Place pea mixture in a resealable plastic bag; cut a small hole in a corner of bag. Pipe mixture into tomatoes; sprinkle with remaining cilantro. Refrigerate until serving.

PER SERVING *1 appetizer equals 16 cal., 1 g fat (trace sat. fat), trace chol., 35 mg sodium, 2 g carb., 1 g fiber, 1 g pro.* **Diabetic Exchange:** *Free food.*

DID YOU KNOW?

Avocado is high in monounsaturated fat, a so called "good fat" that can lower blood cholesterol along with lowering the risk of stroke and heart disease. Each fruit also contains about 9 grams of healthy fiber.

Homemade Guacamole S C M FAST FIX

My daughters sometimes call this "five-finger" guacamole to remember that it is made with only five ingredients. It's so simple!

—NANETTE HILTON LAS VEGAS, NV

START TO FINISH: 10 MIN.
MAKES: 2 CUPS

- 3 **medium ripe avocados, peeled and cubed**
- ¼ **cup finely chopped onion**
- ¼ **cup minced fresh cilantro**
- 2 **tablespoons lime juice**
- ⅛ **teaspoon salt**
  Tortilla chips

In a small bowl, mash avocados with a fork. Stir in onion, cilantro, lime juice and salt. Serve with chips.

PER SERVING *¼ cup (calculated without chips) equals 111 cal., 10 g fat (1 g sat. fat), 0 chol., 43 mg sodium, 6 g carb., 5 g fiber, 1 g pro.* **Diabetic Exchanges:** *2 fat, ½ starch.*

HOMEMADE GUACAMOLE

Spring Pea Crostini [F] [S] [C] [M] FAST FIX ▶

Peas are an amazing power veggie, full of flavor and nutrients. Combine them with parsley for a colorful and crunchy topping on toast.

—ANA MARIA AVELLAR NEWPORT BEACH, CA

START TO FINISH: 30 MIN.
MAKES: 40 APPETIZERS

- 40 **slices French bread baguette (¼ inch thick)**
- 3 **cups fresh or frozen peas**
- 2 **cups packed fresh parsley sprigs**
- ¾ **cup plain Greek yogurt**
- 5 **tablespoons olive oil, divided**
- 1 **garlic clove, minced**
- ½ **teaspoon salt**
- ½ **teaspoon pepper**
- ½ **cup crumbled goat or feta cheese**
  Thinly sliced fresh basil or whole parsley leaves

1. Preheat broiler. Place baguette slices on ungreased baking sheets. Broil 3-4 in. from the heat 1-2 minutes or until golden brown.
2. In a large saucepan, bring 6 cups salted water to a boil. Add peas; cook, uncovered, 3-4 minutes or just until tender. Drain.
3. Place peas and parsley in a food processor; process until chopped. Add Greek yogurt, 3 tablespoons oil, garlic, salt and pepper; process just until blended.
4. To serve, spread pea mixture over baguette slices. Drizzle with remaining oil; top with cheese and fresh basil.
PER SERVING *1 appetizer equals 43 cal., 3 g fat (1 g sat. fat), 3 mg chol., 65 mg sodium, 4 g carb., 1 g fiber, 1 g pro.*

Balsamic-Cranberry Potato Bites [F] [S] [C]

PREP: 30 MIN. • **BAKE:** 20 MIN.
MAKES: 4 DOZEN (1¼ CUPS SAUCE)

- 12 **small red potatoes, quartered**
- 12 **bacon strips**
- ½ **teaspoon salt**
- ¼ **teaspoon pepper**
- 1 **can (14 ounces) jellied cranberry sauce**
- ¼ **cup balsamic vinegar**

Here's a delicious new twist on rumaki. It's easy to make, and your guests will be delighted with the savory flavors.

—**KELLY BOE** WHITELAND, IN

BALSAMIC-CRANBERRY POTATO BITES

1. Place potatoes in a large saucepan and cover with water. Bring to a boil. Reduce heat; cover and simmer for 3-5 minutes or until almost tender.
2. Meanwhile, cut the bacon strips widthwise into fourths. Drain the potatoes and sprinkle with salt and pepper. Wrap a piece of bacon around each potato quarter; secure with toothpicks. Place in an ungreased 15x10x 1-in. baking pan. Bake at 400° for 20-25 minutes or until the bacon is crisp.
3. In a small saucepan, combine the cranberry sauce and vinegar. Bring to a boil. Reduce heat; simmer, uncovered, until slightly thickened, for about 15 minutes. Serve with appetizers.
PER SERVING *1 appetizer equals 47 cal., 3 g fat (1 g sat. fat), 4 mg chol., 75 mg sodium, 5 g carb., trace fiber, 1 g pro.*

24

27

30

Soups

"This soup is my go-to healthy lunch option.
It's a great way to ensure I get my daily vegetables."

—DAWN DONALD HERRON, MI
about her recipe, Garden Vegetable Beef Soup, on page 29

Spicy Pumpkin & Corn Soup F FAST FIX

A seriously quick dish, it can satisfy a hungry household in 20 minutes. My family loves sharing this soup with a hot pan of corn bread.

—**HEATHER ROREX** WINNEMUCCA, NV

START TO FINISH: 20 MIN.
MAKES: 8 SERVINGS

- 1 **can (15 ounces) solid-pack pumpkin**
- 1 **can (15 ounces) black beans, rinsed and drained**
- 1½ **cups frozen corn**
- 1 **can (10 ounces) diced tomatoes and green chilies**
- 2 **cans (14½ ounces each) reduced-sodium chicken broth**
- ¼ **teaspoon pepper**

In a large saucepan, mix all ingredients. Bring to a boil. Reduce heat; simmer, uncovered, 10-15 minutes or until slightly thickened, stirring occasionally.

FREEZE OPTION *Freeze cooled soup in freezer containers. To use, partially thaw in refrigerator overnight. Heat through in a saucepan, stirring occasionally and adding a little broth if necessary.*

PER SERVING *¾ cup equals 100 cal., trace fat (trace sat. fat), 0 chol., 542 mg sodium, 20 g carb., 5 g fiber, 6 g pro.* **Diabetic Exchange:** *1 starch.*

TURKEY TORTILLA SOUP

SPICY PUMPKIN & CORN SOUP

Turkey Tortilla Soup

My wife created this recipe as a healthy way to use up Thanksgiving leftovers. It's a nice alternative to the typical fare, and it's so easy. Our family looks forward to it every year.

—**MATTHEW SZYNDLER** MAUMEE, OH

PREP: 15 MIN. • **COOK:** 1 HOUR
MAKES: 8 SERVINGS (3 QUARTS)

- 2 **tablespoons canola oil, divided**
- 1 **medium onion, chopped**
- 1 **medium green pepper, chopped**
- 1 **can (28 ounces) no-salt-added crushed tomatoes**
- 1 **can (14½ ounces) diced tomatoes with mild green chilies**
- 2 **cups frozen corn (about 10 ounces)**
- 1 **cup salsa**
- 1 **bay leaf**
- 1 **teaspoon ground cumin**
- 4 **cups chicken stock**
- 1 **cup water**
- 2 **cups cubed cooked turkey**
- 3 **whole wheat tortillas (8 inches)**

Reduced-fat sour cream and shredded Mexican cheese blend, optional

1. In a Dutch oven, heat 1 tablespoon oil. Add onion and pepper; cook and stir 5-7 minutes or until tender. Stir in tomatoes, corn, salsa, bay leaf and cumin. Add stock and water; bring to a boil. Reduce heat; simmer, covered, 45 minutes to let flavors blend. Add turkey; heat through. Remove bay leaf.
2. Meanwhile, cut tortillas into ½-in.-wide strips. In a large skillet, heat 1 teaspoon oil over medium heat. Add tortilla strips in batches; cook and stir 1-2 minutes or until golden brown.
3. Top each serving with tortilla strips and, if desired, sour cream and cheese.

PER SERVING *1½ cups (calculated without optional ingredients) equals 240 cal., 6 g fat (1 g sat. fat), 35 mg chol., 657 mg sodium, 31 g carb., 6 g fiber, 17 g pro.* **Diabetic Exchanges:** *2 lean meat, 1½ starch, 1 vegetable, ½ fat.*

Summer Squash Soup C

Delicate and lemony, my squash soup sets the stage for memorable ladies luncheons. It's the best of late summer in a bowl.
—HEIDI WILCOX LAPEER, MI

PREP: 35 MIN. • **COOK:** 15 MIN.
MAKES: 8 SERVINGS (2 QUARTS)

- 2 large sweet onions, chopped
- 1 medium leek (white portion only), chopped
- 2 tablespoons olive oil
- 6 garlic cloves, minced
- 6 medium yellow summer squash, seeded and cubed (about 6 cups)
- 4 cups reduced-sodium chicken broth
- 4 fresh thyme sprigs
- ¼ teaspoon salt
- 2 tablespoons lemon juice
- ⅛ teaspoon hot pepper sauce
- 1 tablespoon shredded Parmesan cheese
- 2 teaspoons grated lemon peel

1. In a large saucepan, saute onions and leek in oil until tender. Add garlic; cook 1 minute longer. Add squash; saute 5 minutes. Stir in the broth, thyme and salt. Bring to a boil. Reduce heat; cover and simmer for 15-20 minutes or until squash is tender.

2. Discard thyme sprigs. Cool slightly. In a blender, process soup in batches until smooth. Return all to the pan. Stir in lemon juice and hot pepper sauce; heat through. Sprinkle each serving with cheese and lemon peel.

PER SERVING *1 cup equals 90 cal., 4 g fat (1 g sat. fat), trace chol., 377 mg sodium, 12 g carb., 3 g fiber, 4 g pro. Diabetic Exchanges: 1 starch, ½ fat.*

COCONUT CURRY VEGETABLE SOUP

SUMMER SQUASH SOUP

Coconut Curry Vegetable Soup M

I've been a vegetarian since high school, so modifying recipes to fit my meatless requirements is a challenge I enjoy. This soup tastes rich and creamy and is packed with nutrients!
—CARISSA SUMNER WASHINGTON DC

PREP: 15 MIN. • **COOK:** 25 MIN.
MAKES: 6 SERVINGS

- 1 tablespoon canola oil
- 2 celery ribs, chopped
- 2 medium carrots, chopped
- 6 garlic cloves, minced
- 1 tablespoon minced fresh gingerroot
- 2 teaspoons curry powder
- ½ teaspoon ground turmeric
- 1 can (14½ ounces) vegetable broth
- 1 can (13.66 ounces) light coconut milk
- 1 medium potato (about 8 ounces), peeled and chopped
- ½ teaspoon salt
- 1 package (8.8 ounces) ready-to-serve brown rice
  Lime wedges, optional

1. In a large saucepan, heat oil over medium heat. Add celery and carrots; cook and stir 6-8 minutes or until tender. Add the garlic, ginger, curry powder and turmeric; cook 1 minute longer.

2. Add broth, coconut milk, potato and salt; bring to a boil. Reduce heat; cook, uncovered, 10-15 minutes or until potato is tender. Meanwhile, heat rice according to package directions.

3. Stir rice into soup. If desired, serve with lime wedges.

PER SERVING *¾ cup equals 186 cal., 8 g fat (4 g sat. fat), 0 chol., 502 mg sodium, 22 g carb., 2 g fiber, 3 g pro. Diabetic Exchanges: 1½ starch, 1½ fat.*

BROWN RICE MULLIGATAWNY

Brown Rice Mulligatawny Ⓜ

Because this dish freezes well, it's smart to make a double batch. You can also grate the apple and carrots so they melt into the soup.

—SARAH OTT BLANCHARDVILLE, WI

PREP: 20 MIN. • **COOK:** 1 HOUR
MAKES: 5 SERVINGS

- 2 tablespoons butter
- 2 celery ribs, chopped
- 1 small onion, chopped
- 1 medium carrot, finely chopped
- ½ cup chopped fresh mushrooms
- 1 garlic clove, minced
- 2 tablespoons all-purpose flour
- 1½ teaspoons curry powder
- ⅛ teaspoon cayenne pepper
- 1 carton (32 ounces) reduced-sodium chicken broth
- ¼ cup uncooked long grain brown rice
- 2 cups cubed cooked chicken breast
- 2 cups chopped fresh spinach
- ½ cup chopped peeled sweet apple
- ¼ teaspoon salt
- ¼ teaspoon pepper
- ⅛ teaspoon dried thyme
- 5 tablespoons reduced-fat sour cream

1. In a large saucepan, heat butter over medium heat. Add celery, onion and carrot; cook and stir 5-7 minutes or until tender. Add mushrooms and garlic; cook 1 minute longer.
2. Stir in flour, curry powder and cayenne until blended; cook and stir 5 minutes. Gradually whisk in broth.

Bring to a boil, stirring constantly. Add rice. Reduce heat; simmer, covered, 45-50 minutes or until rice is tender.
3. Add chicken, spinach, apple, salt, pepper and thyme; cook, uncovered, 3-5 minutes or until heated through and spinach is wilted. Top each serving with sour cream.
PER SERVING *1 cup with 1 tablespoon sour cream equals 229 cal., 8 g fat (4 g sat. fat), 60 mg chol., 689 mg sodium, 17 g carb., 2 g fiber, 22 g pro. Diabetic Exchanges: 2 lean meat, 1½ fat, 1 vegetable, ½ starch.*

Cioppino-Style Soup

This is an easy, healthy and flavorful soup to make for a light dinner. I prepare it for the family every New Year's Eve as a special meal. I like to include salmon along with the cod, shrimp and crab.

—NANCY HEISHMAN LAS VEGAS, NV

PREP: 20 MIN. • **COOK:** 1¼ HOURS
MAKES: 6 SERVINGS (2½ QUARTS)

- 2 tablespoons olive oil
- 2 medium red onions, chopped
- 3 garlic cloves, minced
- 1 can (28 ounces) no-salt-added crushed tomatoes
- 1 carton (32 ounces) vegetable stock
- 1 cup dry red wine
- 1½ teaspoons Italian seasoning
- ½ teaspoon pepper
- ½ teaspoon crushed red pepper flakes, optional
- 6 ounces uncooked shrimp (31-40 per pound), peeled and deveined
- 1 can (6 ounces) lump crabmeat, drained
- 2 cod fillets (6 ounces each), cut into 1-inch pieces
- ⅓ cup chopped fresh parsley Shredded Parmesan cheese, optional

1. In a 6-qt. stockpot, heat oil over medium heat. Add onions; cook and stir 4-6 minutes or until tender. Add garlic; cook 1 minute longer. Add tomatoes, stock, wine, Italian seasoning and pepper; stir in pepper flakes if desired. Bring to a boil. Reduce heat; simmer, covered, 1 hour to allow flavors to blend.
2. Add shrimp, crab, cod and parsley; cook 3-5 minutes longer or until shrimp turn pink and fish just begins to flake easily with a fork. If desired, top each serving with cheese.
PER SERVING *1¾ cups (calculated without cheese) equals 208 cal., 6 g fat (1 g sat. fat), 83 mg chol., 631 mg sodium, 16 g carb., 4 g fiber, 21 g pro. Diabetic Exchanges: 3 lean meat, 1 vegetable, 1 fat.*

CIOPPINO-STYLE SOUP

Broccoli & Potato Soup **FAST FIX**

If I don't have frozen broccoli on hand,
I toss in some frozen spinach or chopped
carrots and celery instead.

—MARY PRICE YOUNGSTOWN, OH

START TO FINISH: 30 MIN.
MAKES: 3 SERVINGS

- 3 cups cubed peeled potatoes
- 1 medium onion, chopped
- 2 garlic cloves, minced
- 2 cups reduced-sodium chicken
  broth
- 1 cup water
  Dash pepper
- ⅛ teaspoon salt
- 3 cups frozen broccoli florets
- 3 tablespoons all-purpose flour
- ⅓ cup fat-free milk
- ½ cup shredded reduced-fat sharp
  cheddar cheese
  Minced fresh parsley

1. In a large saucepan, combine the
first seven ingredients; bring to a boil.
Reduce heat; simmer, covered, 10-15
minutes or until potatoes are tender.
Stir in broccoli; return to a boil.
2. In a small bowl, whisk flour and
milk until smooth; stir into soup. Cook
and stir 2 minutes or until thickened.
Remove from heat; cool slightly.
3. Process in batches in a blender
until smooth. Return to pan; heat
through. Sprinkle servings with cheese
and parsley.
PER SERVING *2 cups equals 262 cal.,
4 g fat (3 g sat. fat), 14 mg chol., 636 mg
sodium, 44 g carb., 5 g fiber, 14 g pro.
Diabetic Exchanges: 2 starch,
1 medium-fat meat, 1 vegetable.*

TOP TIP

This soup was great and very easy to
make. I sauteed the onions first along
with some diced celery and carrots.
Used my stick blender to blend the
veggies before I added the broccoli,
as we prefer a chunky soup. Then I
diced the broccoli before adding it
and left it chunky, too. My husband
loved it! He thinks this soup will go
perfectly with hamburgers.

—SUZIT TASTEOFHOME.COM

SAUSAGE & GREENS SOUP

Sausage & Greens Soup

I always have an abundance of fresh
vegetables in the fridge, so I wanted to
create a delicious soup to enjoy during the
colder months. I think I found a winner!

—ANGIE PITTS CHARLESTON, SC

PREP: 20 MIN. • **COOK:** 20 MIN.
MAKES: 6 SERVINGS (2¼ QUARTS)

- 1 tablespoon olive oil
- 2 Italian turkey sausage links
  (4 ounces each), casings removed
- 1 medium onion, chopped
- 1 celery rib, chopped
- 1 medium carrot, chopped
- 1 garlic clove, minced
- 6 ounces Swiss chard, stems
  removed, chopped (about 4 cups)
- 1 can (14½ ounces) no-salt-added
  diced tomatoes, undrained
- 1 bay leaf
- 1 teaspoon rubbed sage
- 1 teaspoon Italian seasoning
- ½ teaspoon pepper
- 1 carton (32 ounces) reduced-
  sodium chicken broth
- 1 can (15 ounces) no-salt-added
  white kidney or cannellini beans,
  rinsed and drained
- 1 tablespoon lemon juice

1. In a 6-qt. stockpot, heat oil over
medium-high heat. Add sausage,
onion, celery and carrot; cook
6-8 minutes or until sausage is no
longer pink and vegetables are tender,
breaking up sausage into crumbles.
Add garlic; cook 1 minute longer.
2. Stir in Swiss chard, tomatoes, bay
leaf and seasonings. Add broth; bring
to a boil. Reduce heat; simmer,
covered, 10-12 minutes or until Swiss
chard is tender. Stir in beans and
lemon juice; heat through. Remove
bay leaf.
PER SERVING *1½ cups equals 155 cal.,
5 g fat (1 g sat. fat), 14 mg chol., 658 mg
sodium, 18 g carb., 5 g fiber, 11 g pro.
Diabetic Exchanges: 1 medium-fat
meat, 1 vegetable, ½ starch, ½ fat.*

Garden Vegetable & Herb Soup M

I submitted this recipe to my local newspaper and won first prize. I make the soup whenever my family needs a good dose of veggies.

—JODY SAULNIER N WOODSTOCK, NH

PREP: 20 MIN. • **COOK:** 30 MIN.
MAKES: 8 SERVINGS (2 QUARTS)

- 2 tablespoons olive oil
- 2 medium onions, chopped
- 1 pound red potatoes (about 3 medium), cubed
- 2 large carrots, sliced
- 2 cups water
- 1 can (14½ ounces) diced tomatoes in sauce
- 1½ cups vegetable broth
- 1½ teaspoons garlic powder
- 1 teaspoon dried basil
- ½ teaspoon salt
- ½ teaspoon paprika
- ¼ teaspoon dill weed
- ¼ teaspoon pepper
- 1 medium yellow summer squash, halved and sliced
- 1 medium zucchini, halved and sliced

1. In a large saucepan, heat oil over medium heat. Add onions; cook and stir 4-6 minutes or until tender. Add potatoes and carrots. Stir in water, tomatoes, broth, garlic powder, basil, salt, paprika, dill and pepper.
2. Bring to a boil. Reduce heat; simmer, uncovered, 12-15 minutes or until potatoes and carrots are tender.
3. Add yellow squash and zucchini; cook 8-10 minutes longer or until tender.

PER SERVING *1 cup equals 115 cal., 4 g fat (1 g sat. fat), 0 chol., 525 mg sodium, 19 g carb., 3 g fiber, 2 g pro.* ***Diabetic Exchanges:*** *1 vegetable, 1 fat, ½ starch.*

DID YOU KNOW?

Pure olive oil works better for cooking than virgin or extra-virgin olive oil. These higher grades have a delicate flavor that's ideal for salads and uncooked foods, but they burn more easily than pure oil.

GARDEN VEGETABLE & HERB SOUP

SATISFYING TOMATO SOUP

Satisfying Tomato Soup F C M FAST FIX

I made up my own recipe to satisfy a craving for tomato soup. My sister Joan loves this soup chunky-style, so she doesn't need to use a blender. Maybe you will prefer it that way, too!

—MARIAN BROWN MISSISSAUGA, ON

START TO FINISH: 30 MIN.
MAKES: 4 SERVINGS

- ¼ cup finely chopped onion
- ¼ cup finely chopped celery
- 2 teaspoons canola oil
- 2 cans (14½ ounces each) diced tomatoes, undrained
- 1½ cups water
- 2 teaspoons brown sugar
- ½ teaspoon salt
- ½ teaspoon dried basil
- ¼ teaspoon dried oregano
- ¼ teaspoon coarsely ground pepper

1. In a large saucepan, saute onion and celery in oil for 2-4 minutes or until tender. Add the remaining ingredients. Bring to a boil. Reduce heat; simmer, uncovered, 10 minutes to allow flavors to blend.

2. Puree soup using an immersion blender. Or, cool soup slightly and puree in batches in a blender; return to pan and heat through.

FREEZE OPTION *Freeze cooled soup in freezer containers. To use, partially thaw in refrigerator overnight. Heat through in a saucepan, stirring occasionally and adding a little water if necessary.*

PER SERVING *1¼ cups equals 76 cal., 2 g fat (trace sat. fat), 0 chol., 627 mg sodium, 13 g carb., 4 g fiber, 2 g pro. Diabetic Exchanges: 2 vegetable, ½ fat.*

Cheddar Cauliflower Soup C M

PREP: 20 MIN. • **COOK:** 45 MIN.
MAKES: 8 SERVINGS (2 QUARTS)

- 1 tablespoon olive oil
- 1½ cups thinly sliced leeks (white portion only)
- 1 medium head cauliflower, broken into florets
- 1 tablespoon minced fresh thyme or 1 teaspoon dried thyme
- 2 garlic cloves, minced
- 1 teaspoon Worcestershire sauce
- 1 carton (32 ounces) vegetable broth
- 1 can (12 ounces) reduced-fat evaporated milk
- 1 cup (4 ounces) shredded sharp cheddar cheese
  Additional cheese and fresh thyme, optional

1. In a large saucepan, heat oil over medium heat. Add leeks; cook and stir 3-5 minutes or until tender. Stir in cauliflower, thyme, garlic and Worcestershire sauce. Add broth; bring to a boil. Reduce heat; simmer, covered, 30-35 minutes or until vegetables are very tender.

2. Puree soup using an immersion blender. Or, cool soup slightly and puree in batches in a blender; return to pan. Add evaporated milk and cheese; cook and stir 3-5 minutes or until cheese is melted. If desired, sprinkle with additional cheese and thyme.

PER SERVING *1 cup (calculated without additional cheese) equals 146 cal., 7 g fat (3 g sat. fat), 22 mg chol., 643 mg sodium, 13 g carb., 2 g fiber, 8 g pro. Diabetic Exchanges: 1½ fat, 1 vegetable, ½ reduced-fat milk.*

 Cauliflower is often last on the list of vegetables my family will eat, but they adore this creamy, savory soup with tender leeks and shredded cheddar cheese. Be sure to blend in batches and leave some space between the lid and the jar to allow steam to escape. —KRISTIN RIMKUS SNOHOMISH, WA

CHEDDAR CAULIFLOWER SOUP

Pad thai is one of my favorite foods, but it is often loaded with extra calories. This soup is a healthier option that has all the flavor of traditional pad thai.

—JULIE MERRIMAN SEATTLE, WA

SHRIMP PAD THAI SOUP

Chunky Turkey Soup F

This hearty, chunky soup is the perfect answer to your Turkey Day leftovers. With the earthy flavors of curry and cumin, no one will mistake it for canned soup!

—JANE SCANLON MARCO ISLAND, FL

PREP: 20 MIN. + SIMMERING • **COOK:** 40 MIN.
MAKES: 12 SERVINGS (1⅓ CUPS EACH)

- 1 leftover turkey carcass (from a 12- to 14-pound turkey)
- 4½ quarts water
- 1 medium onion, quartered
- 1 medium carrot, cut into 2-inch pieces
- 1 celery rib, cut into 2-inch pieces

SOUP

- 2 cups shredded cooked turkey
- 4 celery ribs, chopped
- 2 cups frozen corn
- 2 medium carrots, sliced
- 1 large onion, chopped
- 1 cup uncooked orzo pasta
- 2 tablespoons minced fresh parsley
- 4 teaspoons chicken bouillon granules
- 1 teaspoon salt
- 1 teaspoon curry powder
- ½ teaspoon ground cumin
- ½ teaspoon pepper

1. Place the turkey carcass in a stockpot; add the water, onion, carrot and celery. Slowly bring to a boil over low heat; cover and simmer for 1½ hours.
2. Discard the carcass. Strain broth through a cheesecloth-lined colander. If using immediately, skim fat. Or cool, then refrigerate for 8 hours or overnight; remove fat from surface before using. (Broth may be refrigerated for up to 3 days or frozen for 4-6 months.)
3. Place the soup ingredients in a stockpot; add the broth. Bring to a boil. Reduce heat; cover and simmer for 30 minutes or until pasta and vegetables are tender.
PER SERVING *1⅓ cups equals 175 cal., 2 g fat (1 g sat. fat), 19 mg chol., 595 mg sodium, 24 g carb., 2 g fiber, 12 g pro.* **Diabetic Exchanges:** *1½ starch, 1 lean meat.*

Shrimp Pad Thai Soup

PREP: 15 MIN. • **COOK:** 30 MIN.
MAKES: 8 SERVINGS (2¾ QUARTS)

- 1 tablespoon sesame oil
- 2 shallots, thinly sliced
- 1 Thai chili pepper or serrano pepper, seeded and finely chopped
- 1 can (28 ounces) no-salt-added crushed tomatoes
- ¼ cup creamy peanut butter
- 2 tablespoons reduced-sodium soy sauce or fish sauce
- 6 cups reduced-sodium chicken broth
- 1 pound uncooked shrimp (31-40 per pound), peeled and deveined
- 6 ounces uncooked thick rice noodles
- 1 cup bean sprouts
- 4 green onions, sliced
  Chopped peanuts and additional chopped Thai chili pepper, optional
  Lime wedges

1. In a 6-qt. stockpot, heat oil over medium heat. Add shallots and chili pepper; cook and stir 4-6 minutes or until tender. Stir in crushed tomatoes, peanut butter and soy sauce until blended; add broth. Bring to a boil; cook, uncovered, 15 minutes to allow flavors to blend.
2. Add shrimp and noodles; cook 4-6 minutes longer or until shrimp turn pink and noodles are tender. Top each serving with bean sprouts, green onions and, if desired, chopped peanuts and additional chopped chili pepper. Serve with lime wedges.
PER SERVING *1⅓ cups (calculated without optional ingredients) equals 252 cal., 7 g fat (1 g sat. fat), 69 mg chol., 755 mg sodium, 31 g carb., 4 g fiber, 17 g pro.* **Diabetic Exchanges:** *2 lean meat, 1½ starch, 1 vegetable, 1 fat.*

FRESH ASPARAGUS SOUP

Fresh Asparagus Soup C

We have a large asparagus patch and are able to freeze a lot for the year. This recipe highlights all the flavor of the vegetable and is very easy to make. I like to heat some soup up in a coffee mug for an afternoon snack!

—SHERRI MELOTIK OAK CREEK, WI

PREP: 20 MIN. • **COOK:** 20 MIN.
MAKES: 6 SERVINGS

- 1 teaspoon canola oil
- 1 small onion, chopped
- 1 garlic clove, minced
- 2 pounds fresh asparagus, trimmed and cut into 1-inch pieces (about 5 cups)
- 1 can (14½ ounces) reduced-sodium chicken broth
- 4 tablespoons all-purpose flour, divided
- 2½ cups fat-free milk, divided
- 2 tablespoons butter
- ¾ teaspoon salt
- ⅛ teaspoon dried thyme
- ⅛ teaspoon pepper
- ½ cup half-and-half cream
- 2 tablespoons white wine
- 1 tablespoon lemon juice
  Minced fresh chives, optional

1. In a large saucepan, heat oil over medium heat. Add onion; cook and stir 4-6 minutes or until tender. Add garlic; cook 1 minute longer. Add asparagus and chicken broth; bring to a boil. Reduce heat; simmer, uncovered, 8-10 minutes or until the asparagus is tender. Remove from heat; cool slightly. Transfer to a blender; cover and process until smooth.

2. In a small bowl, mix 2 tablespoons flour and ¼ cup milk until smooth; set aside. In same saucepan, heat butter over medium heat. Stir in seasonings and remaining flour until smooth;

cook and stir 45-60 seconds or until light golden brown. Gradually whisk in cream, remaining milk and reserved flour mixture. Bring to a boil, stirring constantly; cook and stir 1-2 minutes or until thickened. Stir in wine, lemon juice and asparagus mixture; heat through. If desired, top with chives.

PER SERVING *1 cup equals 154 cal., 7 g fat (4 g sat. fat), 22 mg chol., 585 mg sodium, 15 g carb., 2 g fiber, 8 g pro.* **Diabetic Exchanges:** *1½ fat, 1 vegetable, ½ fat-free milk.*

Garden Vegetable Beef Soup C

This soup is my go-to healthy lunch option. It's a great way to ensure I get my daily vegetables.

—DAWN DONALD HERRON, MI

PREP: 20 MIN. • **COOK:** 55 MIN.
MAKES: 8 SERVINGS (3½ QUARTS)

- 1½ pounds lean ground beef (90% lean)
- 1 medium onion, chopped
- 2 garlic cloves, minced
- 1 package (10 ounces) julienned carrots
- 2 celery ribs, chopped
- ¼ cup tomato paste
- 1 can (14½ ounces) diced tomatoes, undrained
- 1½ cups shredded cabbage
- 1 medium zucchini, coarsely chopped
- 1 medium red potato (about 5 ounces), finely chopped
- ½ cup fresh or frozen cut green beans
- 1 teaspoon dried basil
- ½ teaspoon dried oregano
- ¼ teaspoon salt
- ¼ teaspoon pepper
- 4 cans (14½ ounces each) reduced-sodium beef broth
  Grated Parmesan cheese, optional

1. In a 6-qt. stockpot, cook beef, onion and garlic over medium heat 6-8 minutes or until beef is no longer pink, breaking up beef into crumbles; drain. Add carrots and celery; cook and stir 6-8 minutes or until tender. Stir in tomato paste; cook 1 minute longer.

2. Add tomatoes, cabbage, zucchini, potato, green beans, seasonings and broth; bring to a boil. Reduce heat; simmer, covered, 35-45 minutes or until vegetables are tender. If desired, top each serving with cheese.

PER SERVING *1¾ cups (calculated without cheese) equals 207 cal., 7 g fat (3 g sat. fat), 57 mg chol., 621 mg sodium, 14 g carb., 3 g fiber, 21 g pro.* **Diabetic Exchanges:** *3 lean meat, 2 vegetable.*

GARDEN VEGETABLE BEEF SOUP

Andouille Sausage Soup

I wanted a soup that is packed with vegetables and hearty flavor. By adding andouille sausage, I made this recipe spicy enough that my sons really enjoy it!
—**STEVEN T. THURNER** JANESVILLE, WI

PREP: 20 MIN. • **COOK:** 35 MIN.
MAKES: 10 SERVINGS (3½ QUARTS)

- 1 **tablespoon canola oil**
- 2 **large onions, chopped**
- 3 **medium carrots, chopped**
- 1 **medium green pepper, chopped**
- 2 **garlic cloves, chopped**
- 1 **package (12 ounces) fully cooked andouille chicken sausage links, cut into ¼-inch slices**
- 1½ **pounds red potatoes (about 5 medium), cut into ½-inch cubes**
- 1 **can (28 ounces) crushed tomatoes in puree**
- 1 **teaspoon Worcestershire sauce**
- ¼ **teaspoon pepper**
- 1 **carton (32 ounces) reduced-sodium beef broth**
- 2 **teaspoons liquid smoke, optional**
- ¼ **teaspoon cayenne pepper, optional**
  Sour cream, optional

1. In a 6-qt. stockpot, heat oil over medium heat. Add the onions, carrots and green pepper; cook and stir for 8-10 minutes or until tender. Add garlic; cook 1 minute longer. Remove from the pot.

2. In same pot, brown sausage over medium heat. Return onion mixture to pot. Add potatoes, tomatoes, Worcestershire sauce, pepper and broth; if desired, stir in liquid smoke and cayenne. Bring to a boil. Reduce heat; simmer, covered, 15-20 minutes or until potatoes are tender. If desired, top servings with sour cream.

PER SERVING *1⅓ cups (calculated without sour cream) equals 168 cal., 5 g fat (1 g sat. fat), 28 mg chol., 540 mg sodium, 23 g carb., 4 g fiber, 10 g pro.* **Diabetic Exchanges:** *1 starch, 1 lean meat, 1 vegetable.*

BLACK BEAN-TOMATO CHILI

Black Bean-Tomato Chili

My daughter Kayla saw a black bean chili while watching a cooking show and called me about it because it looked so good. We messed with our own recipe until we got this easy winner.
—**LISA BELCASTRO** VINEYARD HAVEN, MA

PREP: 10 MIN. • **COOK:** 35 MIN.
MAKES: 6 SERVINGS (2¼ QUARTS)

- 2 **tablespoons olive oil**
- 1 **large onion, chopped**
- 1 **medium green pepper, chopped**
- 3 **garlic cloves, minced**
- 1 **teaspoon ground cinnamon**
- 1 **teaspoon ground cumin**
- 1 **teaspoon chili powder**
- ¼ **teaspoon pepper**
- 3 **cans (14½ ounces each) diced tomatoes, undrained**
- 2 **cans (15 ounces each) black beans, rinsed and drained**
- 1 **cup orange juice or juice from 3 medium oranges**

1. In a Dutch oven, heat oil over medium-high heat. Add the onion and green pepper; cook and stir for 8-10 minutes or until tender. Add the garlic and seasonings; cook 1 minute longer.

2. Stir in remaining ingredients; bring to a boil. Reduce heat; simmer, covered, for 20-25 minutes to allow flavors to blend, stirring occasionally.

PER SERVING *1½ cups equals 232 cal., 5 g fat (1 g sat. fat), 0 chol., 608 mg sodium, 39 g carb., 10 g fiber, 9 g pro.* **Diabetic Exchanges:** *2 vegetable, 1½ starch, 1 lean meat, 1 fat.*

ANDOUILLE SAUSAGE SOUP

Spicy Sweet Potato Kale Soup 🅜

PREP: 25 MIN. • **COOK:** 40 MIN.
MAKES: 12 SERVINGS (3 QUARTS)

- 2 tablespoons olive oil
- 1 medium onion, finely chopped
- 3 garlic cloves, minced
- 3 pounds sweet potatoes (about 5 medium), cubed
- 2 medium Granny Smith apples, peeled and chopped
- 1 teaspoon rubbed sage
- 1 teaspoon honey
- ¾ to 1 teaspoon crushed red pepper flakes
- ½ teaspoon salt
- ¼ teaspoon pepper
- 3 cans (14½ ounces each) vegetable broth
- 2 cans (15 ounces each) white kidney or cannellini beans, rinsed and drained
- 3 cups chopped fresh kale
- ½ cup heavy whipping cream
  Optional toppings: olive oil, giardiniera and shredded Parmesan cheese

I prefer heartier soups in the winter, but sometimes I want a meatless option as opposed to the classic beef stew. This recipe is a healthy choice that keeps me warm on cold days.

—**MARYBETH MANK** MESQUITE, TX

1. In a 6-qt. stockpot, heat oil over medium-high heat. Add onion; cook and stir 6-8 minutes or until tender. Add garlic; cook 1 minute longer. Stir in sweet potatoes, apples, sage, honey, pepper flakes, salt, pepper and broth. Bring to a boil. Reduce heat; simmer, covered, 25-30 minutes or until potatoes are tender.

2. Puree soup using an immersion blender. Or, cool soup slightly and puree in batches in a blender; return to pan. Add beans and kale; cook, uncovered, over medium heat for 10-15 minutes or until kale is tender, stirring occasionally. Stir in cream. Serve with toppings as desired.

PER SERVING *1 cup (calculated without optional toppings) equals 250 cal., 6 g fat (3 g sat. fat), 14 mg chol., 615 mg sodium, 44 g carb., 7 g fiber, 5 g pro.*

SPICY SWEET POTATO KALE SOUP

HEARTY VEGETABLE LENTIL SOUP

Hearty Vegetable Lentil Soup

My mother is diabetic, so I often prepare this nutritious dish for her. I wanted a hearty soup that hits the spot on cold autumn nights, so I paired the lentils with turkey bacon and a handful of spices.
—NICOLE HOPPING PINOLE, CA

PREP: 15 MIN. • **COOK:** 45 MIN.
MAKES: 6 SERVINGS

- 6 bacon strips, chopped
- 1 pound red potatoes (about 3 medium), chopped
- 2 medium carrots, chopped
- 1 medium onion, chopped
- 6 garlic cloves, minced
- ¾ teaspoon ground cumin
- ½ teaspoon salt
- ½ teaspoon rubbed sage
- ½ teaspoon dried thyme
- ¼ teaspoon pepper
- 1½ cups dried lentils, rinsed
- 4 cups chicken stock

1. In a large saucepan, cook bacon over medium heat until crisp, stirring occasionally. Remove with a slotted spoon; drain on paper towels. Discard drippings, reserving 1 tablespoon in pan. Add potatoes, carrots and onion; cook and stir 6-8 minutes or until carrots and onion are tender. Add garlic and seasonings; cook 1 minute longer.
2. Add lentils and stock; bring to a boil. Reduce heat; simmer, covered, 30-35 minutes or until lentils and potatoes are tender. Top each serving with bacon.
PER SERVING *1 cup equals 314 cal., 6 g fat (2 g sat. fat), 10 mg chol., 708 mg sodium, 47 g carb., 17 g fiber, 20 g pro.* **Diabetic Exchanges:** *3 starch, 2 lean meat.*

TOP TIP

To quickly peel fresh garlic, gently crush the clove with the flat side of a large knife blade to loosen the peel. If you don't have a large knife, you can crush the garlic with a small can.

Mediterranean Chicken Orzo Soup

My husband is Greek, so I'm always trying new Mediterranean recipes. This soup is his favorite dish that I make. Serve it with a little feta or Parmesan and a side of toast.
—KRISTINE KOSTUROS OLYMPIA, WA

PREP: 20 MIN. • **COOK:** 25 MIN.
MAKES: 6 SERVINGS (2½ QUARTS)

- 2 tablespoons olive oil, divided
- ¾ pound boneless skinless chicken breasts, cubed
- 2 celery ribs, chopped
- 2 medium carrots, chopped
- 1 small onion, chopped
- ½ teaspoon salt
- ½ teaspoon dried oregano
- ¼ teaspoon pepper
- ¼ cup white wine or additional reduced-sodium chicken broth
- 1 carton (32 ounces) reduced-sodium chicken broth
- 1 teaspoon minced fresh rosemary
- 1 bay leaf
- 1 cup uncooked whole wheat orzo pasta
- 1 teaspoon grated lemon peel
- 1 tablespoon lemon juice
  Minced fresh parsley, optional

1. In large saucepan, heat 1 tablespoon oil over medium-high heat. Add the chicken; cook and stir 6-8 minutes or until no longer pink. Remove chicken from pan.
2. In same pan, heat remaining oil over medium-high heat. Add vegetables, salt, oregano and pepper; cook and stir 4-6 minutes or until vegetables are crisp-tender. Add wine, stirring to loosen browned bits from pan. Stir in broth, rosemary and bay leaf; bring to a boil.
3. Add orzo. Reduce heat; simmer, covered, 15-18 minutes or until orzo is tender, stirring occasionally. Return chicken to pan; heat through. Stir in lemon peel and juice; remove bay leaf. If desired, top each serving with minced parsley.
PER SERVING *1⅔ cups equals 223 cal., 6 g fat (1 g sat. fat), 31 mg chol., 630 mg sodium, 23 g carb., 5 g fiber, 17 g pro.* **Diabetic Exchanges:** *2 lean meat, 1 starch, 1 vegetable, 1 fat.*

MEDITERRANEAN CHICKEN ORZO SOUP

HEARTY BEEF & SWEET POTATO STEW

Hearty Beef & Sweet Potato Stew

I have fond memories of growing up in an Italian/Irish family and learning to cook from my grandparents. This meaty stew reminds me of their contributions to my love of cooking.
—**RENEE GREENE** SMITHTOWN, NY

PREP: 40 MIN. • **BAKE:** 2 HOURS
MAKES: 8 SERVINGS (2½ QUARTS)

- 3 **tablespoons canola oil, divided**
- 1½ **pounds boneless beef chuck steak, cut into 1-inch pieces**
- 2 **medium onions, chopped**
- 2 **garlic cloves, minced**
- 2 **cans (14½ ounces each) reduced-sodium beef broth**
- ⅓ **cup dry red wine or additional reduced-sodium beef broth**
- 1 **tablespoon minced fresh thyme or 1 teaspoon dried thyme**

- 1 **tablespoon Worcestershire sauce**
- 1 **teaspoon salt**
- ¾ **teaspoon pepper**
- 3 **tablespoons cornstarch**
- 3 **tablespoons cold water**
- 1¼ **pounds sweet potatoes (about 2 medium), cut into 1-inch cubes**
- 1 **pound baby portobello mushrooms, halved**
- 4 **medium carrots, sliced**
- 2 **medium parsnips, sliced**
- 1 **medium turnip, cut into ¾-inch cubes**

1. Preheat oven to 325°. In an ovenproof Dutch oven, heat 2 tablespoons oil over medium-high heat. Brown beef in batches. Remove with a slotted spoon.

2. Add remaining oil to pan. Add onions; cook and stir 2-3 minutes or until tender. Add garlic; cook 1 minute longer. Add broth and wine, stirring to remove browned bits from pan. Stir in thyme, Worcestershire sauce, salt and pepper. Return beef to pan; bring to a boil. Bake, covered, 1¼ hours.

3. In a small bowl, mix cornstarch and cold water until smooth; gradually stir into stew. Add the sweet potatoes, mushrooms, carrots, parsnips and turnip to pan. Bake, covered, for 45-60 minutes longer or until beef and vegetables are tender. If desired, strain the cooking juices and skim fat, then return cooking juices to the Dutch oven.

PER SERVING *1¼ cups equals 354 cal., 14 g fat (4 g sat. fat), 57 mg chol., 586 mg sodium, 36 g carb., 6 g fiber, 22 g pro.* **Diabetic Exchanges:** *3 lean meat, 3 vegetable, 1 starch, 1 fat.*

Corn Chowder F

I developed this soup out of two other recipes to create my own low-calorie favorite. It turned out so well that I entered it in my county fair and won a blue ribbon.

—ALYCE WYMAN PEMBINA, ND

PREP: 15 MIN. • **COOK:** 30 MIN.
MAKES: 6 SERVINGS

- 1 small onion, chopped
- 1 garlic clove, minced
- 1½ cups cubed peeled potatoes
- ¼ cup shredded carrot
- 2 cups water
- 2 teaspoons dried parsley flakes
- 2 teaspoons reduced-sodium chicken bouillon granules
- ¼ teaspoon salt
- ⅛ teaspoon pepper
- 1 can (14¾ ounces) cream-style corn
- 1½ cups fat-free milk, divided
- 3 bacon strips, cooked and crumbled
- 3 tablespoons all-purpose flour
- ½ cup cubed reduced-fat process cheese (Velveeta)
- ½ cup beer or nonalcoholic beer
- ½ teaspoon liquid smoke, optional

1. Place a large saucepan coated with cooking spray over medium heat. Add onion and garlic; cook and stir until tender. Add potatoes, carrot, water, parsley and seasonings. Bring to a boil. Reduce the heat; cook, covered, for 15-20 minutes or until the potatoes are tender.

2. Stir in corn, 1¼ cups milk and bacon. In a small bowl, mix flour and remaining milk until smooth; stir into soup. Bring to a boil; cook and stir 2 minutes or until thickened. Add cheese; stir until melted. Stir in the beer and, if desired, liquid smoke; heat through.

PER SERVING *1 cup equals 179 cal., 3 g fat (1 g sat. fat), 9 mg chol., 681 mg sodium, 31 g carb., 2 g fiber, 8 g pro.*

Moroccan Chickpea Stew M

When I served this spicy stew to friends, both vegetarians and meat lovers, they were thrilled with the abundance of squash, potatoes, tomatoes and zucchini.

—CINDY BEBERMAN ORLAND PARK, IL

PREP: 20 MIN. • **COOK:** 30 MIN.
MAKES: 9 SERVINGS (ABOUT 2 QUARTS)

- 1 large onion, finely chopped
- 2 tablespoons olive oil
- 1 tablespoon butter
- 2 garlic cloves, minced
- 2 teaspoons ground cumin
- 1 cinnamon stick (3 inches)
- ½ teaspoon chili powder
- 4 cups vegetable broth
- 2 cups cubed peeled butternut squash
- 1 can (15 ounces) chickpeas or garbanzo beans, rinsed and drained
- 1 can (14½ ounces) diced tomatoes, undrained
- 1 medium red potato, cut into 1-inch cubes
- 1 medium sweet potato, peeled and cut into 1-inch cubes
- 1 medium lemon, thinly sliced
- ¼ teaspoon salt
- 2 small zucchini, cubed
- 3 tablespoons minced fresh cilantro

1. In a Dutch oven, saute onion in oil and butter until tender. Add the garlic, cumin, cinnamon stick and chili powder; saute 1 minute longer.

2. Stir in the broth, squash, chickpeas, tomatoes, potatoes, lemon and salt. Bring to a boil. Reduce heat; cover and simmer for 15-20 minutes or until potatoes and squash are almost tender.

3. Add zucchini; return to a boil. Reduce heat; cover and simmer for 5-8 minutes or until vegetables are tender. Discard cinnamon stick and lemon slices. Stir in cilantro.

PER SERVING *1 cup equals 152 cal., 5 g fat (1 g sat. fat), 3 mg chol., 621 mg sodium, 24 g carb., 5 g fiber, 4 g pro.* **Diabetic Exchanges:** *1 starch, 1 vegetable, 1 fat.*

CORN CHOWDER

41

46

42

Side Salads

"As the cook of the family, I appreciate how simple this dish is to make on abusy weeknight, and it's versatile enough to include ingredients that you have onhand. My favorite variation is to substitute diced mango for the cranberries."

—MARY SHENK DEKALB, IL
about her recipe, Lemon Cranberry Quinoa Salad, on page 42

Layered Grilled Corn Salad M

This has been a go-to dish for me for many years. It's a lovely side or it can be served for a light lunch in lettuce cups with warm slices of bread.

—ANGELA SMITH BLUFFTON, SC

PREP: 25 MIN. + CHILLING
MAKES: 10 SERVINGS

- 10 medium ears sweet corn, husks removed
- ¼ cup olive oil
- 1 teaspoon salt
- ¾ teaspoon coarsely ground pepper
- ¾ teaspoon crushed red pepper flakes
- 2 large tomatoes, finely chopped
- 1 medium red onion, thinly sliced
- 12 fresh basil leaves, thinly sliced
- 1 cup zesty Italian salad dressing

1. Brush corn with olive oil. Grill corn, covered, over medium heat for 10-12 minutes or until lightly browned and tender, turning occasionally. Cool slightly.

2. Cut corn from cobs; transfer to a small bowl. Stir in salt, pepper and pepper flakes. In a 2-qt. glass bowl, layer a third of each of the following: corn, tomatoes, onion and basil. Repeat layers twice. Pour dressing over top; refrigerate at least 1 hour.

PER SERVING ¾ cup equals 224 cal., 15 g fat (2 g sat. fat), 0 chol., 656 mg sodium, 21 g carb., 3 g fiber, 3 g pro.

LAYERED GRILLED CORN SALAD

I still think there's no better combo than sweet potatoes with pork, or prosciutto in this case. As a retired physician I'm glad that sweet potatoes are being given their due as nutritional powerhouses.

—HELEN CONWELL PORTLAND, OR

ROASTED SWEET POTATO & PROSCIUTTO SALAD

Roasted Sweet Potato & Prosciutto Salad C

PREP: 20 MIN. • **BAKE:** 40 MIN. + COOLING
MAKES: 8 SERVINGS (¾ CUP EACH)

- 3 medium sweet potatoes (about 2½ pounds), peeled and cut into 1-inch pieces
- 4 tablespoons olive oil, divided
- ½ teaspoon salt, divided
- ⅛ teaspoon pepper
- 3 ounces thinly sliced prosciutto, julienned
- ½ cup sliced radishes
- ⅓ cup chopped pecans, toasted
- ¼ cup finely chopped sweet red pepper
- 2 green onions, sliced, divided
- 1 tablespoon lemon juice
- 1 teaspoon honey

1. Preheat oven to 400°. Place sweet potatoes in a greased 15x10x1-in. baking pan. Drizzle with 2 tablespoons oil and sprinkle with ¼ teaspoon salt and the pepper; toss to coat. Roast 30 minutes, stirring occasionally.

2. Sprinkle prosciutto over sweet potatoes; roast 10-15 minutes longer or until potatoes are tender and the prosciutto is crisp. Transfer to a large bowl; cool slightly.

3. Add radishes, pecans, red pepper and half of the green onions. In a small bowl, whisk lemon juice, honey, and remaining oil and salt until blended. Drizzle over salad; toss to combine. Sprinkle with remaining green onion.

NOTE To toast nuts, bake in a shallow pan in a 350° oven for 5-10 minutes or cook in a skillet over low heat until lightly browned, stirring occasionally.

PER SERVING ¾ cup equals 167 cal., 12 g fat (2 g sat. fat), 9 mg chol., 360 mg sodium, 13 g carb., 2 g fiber, 4 g pro.
Diabetic Exchanges: 2 fat, 1 starch.

Rainbow Veggie Salad F C M FAST FIX ▶

Every salad should be colorful and crunchy like this one, with its bright tomatoes, carrots, peppers and sassy greens. Toss with your best dressing.

—LIZ BELLVILLE HAVELOCK, NC

START TO FINISH: 25 MIN.
MAKES: 8 SERVINGS

- ½ **English cucumber, cut lengthwise in half and sliced**
- 2 **medium carrots, thinly sliced**
- 1 **cup each red and yellow cherry tomatoes, halved**
- ¾ **cup pitted ripe olives, halved**
- 1 **celery rib, thinly sliced**
- ¼ **cup each chopped sweet yellow, orange and red pepper**
- ¼ **cup thinly sliced red onion**
- ⅛ **teaspoon garlic salt**
   Dash coarsely ground pepper
- 1 **package (5 ounces) spring mix salad greens**
- ⅔ **cup reduced-fat buttermilk ranch salad dressing**

1. Place the vegetables, garlic salt and pepper in a large bowl; toss to combine.

2. Just before serving, add salad greens. Drizzle with dressing and toss gently to combine.

PER SERVING *1 cup equals 64 cal., 3 g fat (1 g sat. fat), trace chol., 232 mg sodium, 7 g carb., 2 g fiber, 2 g pro.* **Diabetic Exchanges:** *1 vegetable, ½ fat.*

Balsamic Three-Bean Salad F M

Here's my little girl's favorite salad. She eats it just about as fast as I can make it. Prepare it ahead so the flavors have plenty of time to get to know each other.

—STACEY FEATHER JAY, OK

PREP: 25 MIN. + CHILLING
MAKES: 12 SERVINGS (¾ CUP EACH)

- 2 **pounds fresh green beans, trimmed and cut into 2-inch pieces**
- ½ **cup balsamic vinaigrette**
- ¼ **cup sugar**
- 1 **garlic clove, minced**
- ¾ **teaspoon salt**
- 2 **cans (16 ounces each) kidney beans, rinsed and drained**
- 2 **cans (15 ounces each) white kidney or cannellini beans, rinsed and drained**
- 4 **fresh basil leaves, torn**

1. Fill a Dutch oven three-fourths full with water; bring to a boil. Add green beans; cook, uncovered, 3-6 minutes or until beans are crisp-tender. Drain and immediately drop into ice water. Drain and pat dry.

2. In a large bowl, whisk vinaigrette, sugar, garlic and salt until sugar is dissolved. Add canned beans and green beans; toss to coat. Refrigerate, covered, for at least 4 hours. Stir in basil just before serving.

PER SERVING *¾ cup equals 190 cal., 3 g fat (trace sat. fat), 0 chol., 462 mg sodium, 33 g carb., 9 g fiber, 9 g pro.* **Diabetic Exchanges:** *1½ starch, 1 very lean meat, 1 vegetable, ½ fat.*

BALSAMIC THREE-BEAN SALAD

Fresh Sugar Snap Pea Salad C M

We found fresh sugar snap peas at the local produce market, the start of a cheerful salad with a quick and tasty onion dressing.
—**COURTNEY STULTZ** COLUMBUS, KS

PREP: 15 MIN. + CHILLING • **MAKES:** 6 SERVINGS

- 2 **tablespoons olive oil**
- 2 **tablespoons white wine vinegar**
- 2 **teaspoons honey**
- ½ **teaspoon salt**
- ½ **teaspoon pepper**
- ¼ **teaspoon dried thyme**
- ½ **cup chopped onion**
- ½ **teaspoon poppy seeds**
- 1 **pound fresh sugar snap peas, trimmed and halved (about 4 cups)**

1. Place the first seven ingredients in a blender; cover and process until blended. Transfer to a large bowl; stir in poppy seeds.
2. Add peas to dressing and toss to coat. Refrigerate, covered, 30 minutes before serving.
PER SERVING ⅔ cup equals 86 cal., 5 g fat (1 g sat. fat), 0 chol., 201 mg sodium, 9 g carb., 2 g fiber, 3 g pro.
Diabetic Exchanges: 1 vegetable, 1 fat.

Mixed Greens with Orange-Ginger Vinaigrette C M FAST FIX ▶

Zingy vinaigrette starts with orange juice, ginger and a flick of cayenne. Just whisk, toss with greens and top the salad your way.
—**JOY ZACHARIA** CLEARWATER, FL

START TO FINISH: 20 MIN. • **MAKES:** 8 SERVINGS

- ¼ **cup orange juice**
- ¼ **cup canola oil**
- 2 **tablespoons white vinegar**
- 2 **tablespoons honey**
- 2 **teaspoons grated fresh gingerroot**
- ½ **teaspoon salt**
- ¼ **teaspoon cayenne pepper**
- 12 **cups torn mixed salad greens**
- 2 **medium navel oranges, peeled and sliced crosswise**
- 1 **cup thinly sliced red onion**

In a small bowl, whisk the first seven ingredients until blended. In a large bowl, toss the greens with ¼ cup vinaigrette; transfer to a serving dish. Top with oranges and onion. Serve immediately with remaining vinaigrette.
PER SERVING 1½ cups salad with 1 tablespoon vinaigrette equals 119 cal., 7 g fat (1 g sat. fat), 0 chol., 202 mg sodium, 15 g carb., 3 g fiber, 2 g pro. **Diabetic Exchanges:** 1½ fat, 1 vegetable, ½ starch.

Sunny Strawberry & Cantaloupe Salad S C M FAST FIX

My little ones absolutely love this salad and ask me to serve it all the time. Fruit and cheese taste delish together, and the kids like the crunch of the sunflower seeds.
—AYSHA SCHURMAN AMMON, ID

START TO FINISH: 15 MIN. • **MAKES:** 4 SERVINGS

- 1 cup sliced fresh strawberries
- 1 cup cubed cantaloupe
- ½ cup (about 2 ounces) cubed part-skim mozzarella cheese
- 2 tablespoons raspberry vinaigrette
- ½ cup fresh raspberries
- 1 tablespoon sunflower kernels
  Thinly sliced fresh mint leaves, optional

In a large bowl, combine the strawberries, cantaloupe and cheese. Drizzle with vinaigrette and toss to coat. Just before serving, gently stir in raspberries; top with the sunflower kernels. If desired, sprinkle with mint.
PER SERVING ¾ cup equals 105 cal., 7 g fat (2 g sat. fat), 4 mg chol., 113 mg sodium, 10 g carb., 2 g fiber, 3 g pro.
Diabetic Exchanges: 1½ fat, ½ fruit.

Broccoli & Apple Salad F S FAST FIX

Creamy yogurt dressing and crunchy veggies contrast nicely in a cool salad. Even my picky daughter can't get enough!
—LYNN CLUFF LITTLEFIELD, AZ

START TO FINISH: 15 MIN. • **MAKES:** 6 SERVINGS

- 3 cups small fresh broccoli florets
- 3 medium apples, chopped
- ½ cup chopped mixed dried fruit
- 1 tablespoon chopped red onion
- ½ cup reduced-fat plain yogurt
- 4 bacon strips, cooked and crumbled

In a large bowl, combine broccoli, apples, dried fruit and onion. Add yogurt; toss to coat. Sprinkle with bacon. Refrigerate until serving.
PER SERVING 1 cup equals 124 cal., 3 g fat (1 g sat. fat), 7 mg chol., 134 mg sodium, 22 g carb., 3 g fiber, 4 g pro.
Diabetic Exchanges: 1½ starch, ½ fat.

Lemon Cranberry Quinoa Salad FAST FIX ▶

START TO FINISH: 30 MIN.
MAKES: 8 SERVINGS

- 2 cups reduced-sodium chicken broth
- 1 cup quinoa, rinsed
- 1 cup chopped peeled jicama
- 1 cup chopped seeded cucumber
- 1 cup chopped avocado
- ¾ cup dried cranberries
- ½ cup minced fresh parsley
- 1 green onion, thinly sliced

DRESSING

- ¼ cup olive oil
- 2 teaspoons grated lemon peel
- 2 tablespoons lemon juice
- 2 teaspoons minced fresh gingerroot
- ¾ teaspoon salt

1. In a small saucepan, bring broth to a boil. Add quinoa. Reduce heat; simmer, covered, 12-15 minutes or until liquid is absorbed. Remove from heat; fluff with a fork.

2. In a large bowl, combine cooked quinoa, jicama, cucumber, avocado, cranberries, parsley and green onion. In a small bowl, whisk the dressing ingredients until blended. Pour over quinoa mixture; gently toss to coat. Serve warm or cold.

NOTE *Look for quinoa in the cereal, rice or organic food aisle.*

PER SERVING *¾ cup equals 218 cal., 11 g fat (2 g sat. fat), 0 chol., 370 mg sodium, 27 g carb., 5 g fiber, 5 g pro. Diabetic Exchanges: 2 starch, 2 fat.*

As the cook of the family, I appreciate how simple this dish is to make on a busy weeknight, and it's versatile enough to include ingredients that you have on hand. My favorite variation is to substitute diced mango for the cranberries.
—**MARY SHENK** DEKALB, IL

LEMON CRANBERRY QUINOA SALAD

CHILLED SHRIMP PASTA SALAD

Chilled Shrimp Pasta Salad FAST FIX ▶

This chilled salad is just the thing for a hot summer day. It's also a tasty side dish for sharing anytime.
—**MARY PRICE** YOUNGSTOWN, OH

START TO FINISH: 30 MIN.
MAKES: 12 SERVINGS (¾ CUP EACH)

- 3 cups uncooked small pasta shells
- ½ cup sour cream
- ½ cup mayonnaise
- ¼ cup horseradish sauce
- 2 tablespoons grated onion
- 1½ teaspoons seasoned salt
- ¾ teaspoon pepper
- 1 pound peeled and deveined cooked small shrimp
- 1 large cucumber, seeded and chopped
- 3 celery ribs, thinly sliced
  Red lettuce leaves, optional

1. Cook pasta according to package directions. Drain the pasta; rinse with cold water.

2. In a large bowl, mix sour cream, mayonnaise, horseradish sauce, onion, seasoned salt and pepper. Stir in shrimp, cucumber, celery and pasta. Refrigerate until serving. If desired, serve on lettuce.

PER SERVING *¾ cup (calculated without lettuce) equals 239 cal., 12 g fat (2 g sat. fat), 72 mg chol., 344 mg sodium, 20 g carb., 1 g fiber, 11 g pro. Diabetic Exchanges: 2 fat, 1 starch, 1 lean meat.*

Brown Rice, Tomato & Basil Salad Ⓜ

I like to take this delicious, satisfying and light salad to office potlucks and family get-togethers. You can also prepare it ahead and refrigerate until ready to serve.

—**ANN CRAWFORD** GOODYEAR, AZ

PREP: 20 MIN. • **COOK:** 30 MIN.
MAKES: 10 SERVINGS

- 2 cups uncooked brown basmati rice
- 2 tablespoons olive oil
- 1 medium onion, finely chopped
- 3 cups grape tomatoes, halved
- 3 garlic cloves, minced
- 1 tablespoon balsamic vinegar
- 6 ounces feta cheese, cut into ½-inch cubes
- ½ cup fresh basil leaves, thinly sliced
- ¼ cup pitted Greek olives, coarsely chopped
- 1 teaspoon salt
- ½ teaspoon pepper

1. Cook rice according to package directions. Meanwhile, in a large skillet, heat oil over medium heat. Add onion; cook and stir until tender. Add tomatoes and garlic; cook 1 minute longer. Remove from heat; stir in balsamic vinegar.

2. Place rice in a large bowl. Add tomato mixture, cheese, basil, olives, salt and pepper; toss gently to coat. Serve warm or at room temperature.

PER SERVING ¾ cup equals 256 cal., 11 g fat (3 g sat. fat), 15 mg chol., 516 mg sodium, 34 g carb., 2 g fiber, 6 g pro.

Spring Greek Pasta Salad Ⓜ FAST FIX ▶

For a springtime meal, we toss rotini pasta with cucumber, zucchini and sweet red peppers. Turn it into a heartier main dish by adding grilled chicken.

—**CHRISTINE SCHENHER** EXETER, CA

START TO FINISH: 30 MIN.
MAKES: 16 SERVINGS (¾ CUP EACH)

- 4 cups veggie rotini or other spiral pasta (about 12 ounces)

VINAIGRETTE

- ¼ cup olive oil
- 3 tablespoons lemon juice
- 2 tablespoons balsamic vinegar
- 1 tablespoon water
- 3 garlic cloves, minced
- 1 teaspoon salt
- ¼ teaspoon pepper
- 3 tablespoons minced fresh oregano or 1 tablespoon dried oregano

SALAD

- 3 large tomatoes, seeded and chopped
- 1 medium sweet red pepper, chopped
- 1 small cucumber, seeded and chopped
- 1 small zucchini, chopped
- 1 small red onion, halved and thinly sliced
- ⅓ cup sliced pitted Greek olives, optional
- 1 cup (4 ounces) crumbled feta cheese

1. Cook pasta according to package directions. Drain; rinse with cold water and drain well.

2. In a small bowl, whisk oil, lemon juice, vinegar, water, garlic, salt and pepper until blended. Stir in oregano.

3. In a large bowl, combine pasta, vegetables and, if desired, olives. Add vinaigrette and feta cheese; toss to combine. Refrigerate, covered, until serving.

PER SERVING ¾ cup (calculated without olives) equals 142 cal., 5 g fat (1 g sat. fat), 4 mg chol., 219 mg sodium, 20 g carb., 2 g fiber, 5 g pro. **Diabetic Exchanges:** 1 starch, 1 fat.

SPRING GREEK PASTA SALAD

Crisp & Spicy Cucumber Salad F S M

Sweet-hot Asian flavors from rice vinegar, sesame oil and cayenne will light up your taste buds!

—ALIVIA DOCKERY JENSEN BEACH, FL

PREP: 25 MIN. + MARINATING
MAKES: 6 SERVINGS

- 2 **small English cucumbers, thinly sliced**
- 2 **medium carrots, thinly sliced**
- 1 **large sweet red pepper, julienned**
- ½ **medium red onion, thinly sliced**
- 2 **green onions, sliced**
- ½ **serrano or jalapeno pepper, seeded and thinly sliced, optional**

MARINADE

- ⅓ **cup sugar**
- ⅓ **cup rice vinegar**
- ⅓ **cup water**
- 1 **teaspoon each salt, garlic powder and pepper**
- 1 **teaspoon sesame oil**
- 1 **teaspoon reduced-sodium soy sauce**
- 1 **small garlic clove, minced**
- ½ **teaspoon minced fresh gingerroot**
- ¼ **teaspoon cayenne pepper, optional**
 Optional toppings: minced fresh cilantro, chopped peanuts and additional sliced green onion

1. In a large bowl, combine the first six ingredients. In a small bowl, mix marinade ingredients, stirring to dissolve sugar. Pour over vegetables; toss to combine. Refrigerate, covered, 30 minutes or overnight.

2. Serve with a slotted spoon. If desired, sprinkle with toppings.

NOTE *Wear disposable gloves when cutting hot peppers; the oils can burn skin. Avoid touching your face.*

PER SERVING ¾ *cup (calculated without toppings) equals 96 cal., 1 g fat (trace sat. fat), 0 chol., 51 mg sodium, 22 g carb., 3 g fiber, 2 g pro.* **Diabetic Exchanges:** *1 starch, 1 vegetable.*

I'm a real believer in clean eating and a healthy lifestyle, which includes eating your veggies. This salad is loaded with the summer's finest, plus a little extra heat.

—IETEF VITA DENVER, CO

Chipotle Lime Avocado Salad S M FAST FIX ▶

START TO FINISH: 15 MIN.
MAKES: 4 SERVINGS

- ¼ **cup lime juice**
- ¼ **cup maple syrup**
- ½ **teaspoon ground chipotle pepper**
- ¼ **teaspoon cayenne pepper, optional**
- 2 **medium ripe avocados, peeled and cubed**
- ½ **medium cucumber, peeled and chopped**
- 1 **tablespoon minced fresh chives**
- 2 **large tomatoes, cut into ½-inch slices**

In a small bowl, whisk lime juice, maple syrup, chipotle pepper and, if desired, cayenne until blended. In another bowl, combine avocados, cucumber and chives. Drizzle with dressing; toss gently to coat. Serve over tomatoes.

PER SERVING *1 serving equals 191 cal., 11 g fat (1 g sat. fat), 0 chol., 26 mg sodium, 25 g carb., 6 g fiber, 3 g pro.*

DID YOU KNOW?

Many grocery store cucumbers are coated with protective wax to prolong freshness. They should be peeled before eating. There is no need to peel English cucumbers that are wrapped in plastic instead. Ditto for cukes from the farmers market or your own garden. Whether or not to peel is a taste preference.

CRISP & SPICY CUCUMBER SALAD

CHIPOTLE LIME AVOCADO SALAD

Cherry Tomato Salad C M

This recipe evolved from a need to use the bumper crops of cherry tomatoes that we regularly grow. It's become a summer favorite, especially at cookouts.

—**SALLY SIBLEY** ST. AUGUSTINE, FL

PREP: 15 MIN. + MARINATING • **MAKES:** 6 SERVINGS

- 1 **quart cherry tomatoes, halved**
- ¼ **cup canola oil**
- 3 **tablespoons white vinegar**
- ½ **teaspoon salt**
- ½ **teaspoon sugar**
- ¼ **cup minced fresh parsley**
- 1 **to 2 teaspoons minced fresh basil**
- 1 **to 2 teaspoons minced fresh oregano**

Place tomatoes in a shallow bowl. In a small bowl, whisk oil, vinegar, salt and sugar until blended; stir in the herbs. Pour over the tomatoes; gently toss to coat. Refrigerate, covered, overnight.

PER SERVING *¾ cup equals 103 cal., 10 g fat (1 g sat. fat), 0 chol., 203 mg sodium, 4 g carb., 1 g fiber, 1 g pro.* **Diabetic Exchanges:** *2 fat, 1 vegetable.*

ARUGULA SALAD WITH SHAVED PARMESAN

Arugula Salad with Shaved Parmesan C M FAST FIX

Fresh peppery arugula, golden raisins, crunchy almonds and shredded Parmesan combine to make this perfect dinner salad. I first put it together for my mom, and the whole family ended up loving it!

—**NICOLE RASH** BOISE, ID

START TO FINISH: 15 MIN. • **MAKES:** 4 SERVINGS

- 6 **cups fresh arugula**
- ¼ **cup golden raisins**
- ¼ **cup sliced almonds, toasted**
- 3 **tablespoons olive oil**
- 1 **tablespoon lemon juice**
- ¼ **teaspoon salt**
- ¼ **teaspoon freshly ground pepper**
- ⅓ **cup shaved Parmesan cheese**

In a large bowl, combine the arugula, raisins and almonds. Drizzle with oil and lemon juice. Sprinkle with salt and pepper; toss to coat. Divide salad among four plates; top with cheese.

NOTE *To toast nuts, bake in a shallow pan in a 350° oven for 5-10 minutes or cook in a skillet over low heat until lightly browned, stirring occasionally.*

PER SERVING *1 cup equals 181 cal., 15 g fat (3 g sat. fat), 4 mg chol., 242 mg sodium, 10 g carb., 2 g fiber, 4 g pro.* **Diabetic Exchanges:** *3 fat, ½ starch.*

CHERRY TOMATO SALAD

- cider vinegar
- spoon seasoned salt
- spoon pepper
- spoon celery seed
- packages (14 ounces each) coleslaw mix
- 1 small sweet red pepper, chopped
- ½ cup thinly sliced sweet onion

In a large bowl, mix the first six ingredients. Add coleslaw mix, red pepper and onion; toss to coat. Refrigerate at least 1 hour before serving.

PER SERVING *⅔ cup equals 180 cal., 15 g fat (2 g sat. fat), 7 mg chol., 247 mg sodium, 11 g carb., 2 g fiber, 1 g pro.*

> This simple slaw tastes best when it's refrigerated for at least an hour. The mixture seems to get creamier as it sits.
>
> —**MICHELLE GAUER** SPICER, MN

ZESTY COLESLAW

MINTED FRUIT SALAD

Minted Fruit Salad F S M

Filled with the season's best and freshest fruit, this salad shouts "summer." The hint of mint adds a refreshing note to the sweet fruit combo.

—**EDIE DESPAIN** LOGAN, UT

PREP: 20 MIN. + COOLING • **MAKES:** 6 SERVINGS

- 1 cup unsweetened apple juice
- 2 tablespoons honey
- 4 teaspoons finely chopped crystallized ginger
- 4 teaspoons lemon juice
- 4 cups cantaloupe balls
- 1 cup sliced fresh strawberries
- 1 cup fresh blueberries
- 2 teaspoons chopped fresh mint leaves

1. In a small saucepan, combine the apple juice, honey, ginger and lemon juice. Bring to a boil over medium-high heat. Cook and stir for 2 minutes or until mixture is reduced to ¾ cup. Remove from the heat. Cool.
2. In a serving bowl, combine the cantaloupe, strawberries, blueberries and mint. Drizzle with cooled apple juice mixture; gently toss to coat.

PER SERVING *1 cup equals 113 cal., 1 g fat (trace sat. fat), 0 chol., 14 mg sodium, 28 g carb., 2 g fiber, 1 g pro.*
Diabetic Exchanges: 1 fruit, ½ starch.

GARDEN BOUNTY POTATO SALAD

Garden Bounty Potato Salad C M

A parent from a school where I previously taught gave me this recipe, and I think of that parent and child every time I recreate this potato salad. The salad looks beautiful, and the basil vinaigrette keeps it light and bright.

—DEE DEE CALOW WARREN, IL

PREP: 35 MIN. • **COOK:** 25 MIN. + CHILLING
MAKES: 20 SERVINGS (¾ CUP EACH)

- 3 **pounds small red potatoes, quartered**
- 1 **pound fresh green beans, trimmed and cut in half**
- ⅓ **cup olive oil**
- ¼ **cup red wine vinegar**
- ¼ **cup minced fresh basil**
- 2 **tablespoons minced fresh parsley**
- 1½ **teaspoons salt**
- ½ **teaspoon pepper**
- 6 **hard-cooked large eggs, sliced**
- 1 **cup grape tomatoes**

1. Place potatoes in a large saucepan and cover with water. Bring to a boil. Reduce heat; cover and cook for 4 minutes. Stir in beans; cover and cook 10-12 minutes longer or until vegetables are tender. Drain. Transfer to a large bowl.

2. In a small bowl, whisk oil, vinegar, basil, parsley, salt and pepper. Pour over vegetables; toss to coat. Cover and refrigerate for at least 1 hour.

3. Stir before serving; top with eggs and tomatoes.

PER SERVING *¾ cup equals 113 cal., 5 g fat (1 g sat. fat), 64 mg chol., 202 mg sodium, 13 g carb., 2 g fiber, 4 g pro. Diabetic Exchanges: 1 starch, 1 fat.*

All-Spiced Up Raspberry and Mushroom Salad S C M FAST FIX

START TO FINISH: 30 MIN.
MAKES: 4 SERVINGS

- 2 **tablespoons raspberry vinegar**
- 2 **tablespoons olive oil, divided**
- 1 **tablespoon red jalapeno pepper jelly**
- ¼ **teaspoon ground allspice**
- 1 **pound small fresh mushrooms, halved**
- 4 **cups spring mix salad greens**
- 1 **cup fresh raspberries**
- 2 **tablespoons chopped red onion**
- 2 **tablespoons minced fresh mint**
- 2 **tablespoons sliced almonds, toasted**
- ¼ **cup crumbled goat cheese**

1. In a small bowl, whisk vinegar, 1 tablespoon oil, pepper jelly and allspice until blended. In a large skillet, heat remaining oil over medium-high heat. Add mushrooms; cook and stir until tender; cool slightly.

2. In a large bowl, combine salad greens, raspberries, onion, mint and almonds. Just before serving, add mushrooms and vinaigrette; toss to combine. Top with cheese.

NOTE *To toast nuts, bake in a shallow pan in a 350° oven for 5-10 minutes or cook in a skillet over low heat until lightly browned, stirring occasionally.*

PER SERVING *1 serving equals 168 cal., 11 g fat (2 g sat. fat), 9 mg chol., 54 mg sodium, 15 g carb., 6 g fiber, 6 g pro. Diabetic Exchanges: 2 fat, 1 starch.*

Here's a refreshing salad for summertime or any time. Make a tasty homemade vinaigrette with just raspberry vinegar, olive oil, jalapeno jelly and allspice.

—ROXANNE CHAN ALBANY, CA

ALL-SPICED UP RASPBERRY AND MUSHROOM SALAD

Wendy's Apple Pomegranate Salad C M FAST FIX ▶

My grandparents grew pomegranates, pecans and walnuts. Some of my best memories are of learning to cook with my grandmother. Whenever I prepare it, I feel like I'm having lunch with her again.

—**WENDY BALL** BATTLE CREEK, MI

START TO FINISH: 20 MIN.
MAKES: 8 SERVINGS

- 1 **bunch romaine, torn (about 8 cups)**
- ½ **cup pomegranate seeds**
- ½ **cup chopped pecans or walnuts, toasted**
- ½ **cup shredded Parmesan cheese**
- 1 **large Granny Smith apple, chopped**
- 1 **tablespoon lemon juice**
- ¼ **cup olive oil**
- ¼ **cup white wine vinegar**
- 2 **tablespoons sugar**
- ¼ **teaspoon salt**

1. In a large bowl, combine romaine, pomegranate seeds, pecans and cheese. Toss apple with lemon juice and add to salad.

2. Whisk remaining ingredients until blended. Drizzle over salad; toss to coat. Serve immediately.

PER SERVING *1 cup equals 165 cal., 13 g fat (2 g sat. fat), 4 mg chol., 163 mg sodium, 10 g carb., 2 g fiber, 3 g pro.* ***Diabetic Exchanges:** 2½ fat, 1 vegetable.*

HOW TO

PREPARE POMEGRANATE

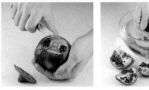

❶ Cut off the crown. Score the fruit into quarters, taking care not to cut into the red juice sacs (arils).
❷ Soak sections in a bowl of water 5 minutes. With your fingers, break sections open and gently remove the seed clusters. Discard skin and membrane. Drain, reserving arils; dry arils on paper towels. The arils may be eaten whole, seeds and all.

WENDY'S APPLE POMEGRANATE SALAD

Heirloom Tomato & Zucchini Salad C M FAST FIX

Tomato wedges give this salad a juicy bite. It's a great way to use up fresh herbs and vegetables from your own garden or the farmers market.

—**MATTHEW HASS** FRANKLIN, WI

START TO FINISH: 25 MIN.
MAKES: 12 SERVINGS (¾ CUP EACH)

- 7 large heirloom tomatoes (about 2½ pounds), cut into wedges
- 3 medium zucchini, halved lengthwise and thinly sliced
- 2 medium sweet yellow peppers, thinly sliced
- ⅓ cup cider vinegar
- 3 tablespoons olive oil
- 1 tablespoon sugar
- 1½ teaspoons salt
- 1 tablespoon each minced fresh basil, parsley and tarragon

1. In a large bowl, combine tomatoes, zucchini and peppers. In a small bowl, whisk vinegar, oil, sugar and salt until blended. Stir in herbs.
2. Just before serving, drizzle dressing over salad; toss gently to coat.

PER SERVING *1 cup equals 68 cal., 4 g fat (1 g sat. fat), 0 chol., 306 mg sodium, 8 g carb., 2 g fiber, 2 g pro. Diabetic Exchanges: 1 vegetable, ½ fat.*

VIBRANT BLACK-EYED PEA SALAD

HEIRLOOM TOMATO & ZUCCHINI SALAD

Vibrant Black-Eyed Pea Salad C M

My black-eyed pea salad reminds me of a Southern cooking class my husband and I took while visiting Savannah, Georgia. People go nuts for it at picnics.

—**DANIELLE ULAM** HOOKSTOWN, PA

PREP: 25 MIN. + CHILLING
MAKES: 10 SERVINGS

- 2 cans (15½ ounces each) black-eyed peas, rinsed and drained
- 2 cups grape tomatoes, halved
- 1 each small green, yellow and red peppers, finely chopped
- 1 small red onion, chopped
- 1 celery rib, chopped
- 2 tablespoons minced fresh basil

DRESSING
- ¼ cup red wine vinegar or balsamic vinegar
- 1 tablespoon stone-ground mustard
- 1 teaspoon minced fresh oregano or ¼ teaspoon dried oregano
- ¾ teaspoon salt
- ½ teaspoon freshly ground pepper
- ¼ cup olive oil

1. In a large bowl, combine black-eyed peas, tomatoes, peppers, onion, celery and basil.
2. For dressing, in a small bowl, whisk vinegar, mustard, oregano, salt and pepper. Gradually whisk in oil until blended. Drizzle over salad; toss to coat. Refrigerate, covered, at least 3 hours before serving.

PER SERVING *¾ cup equals 130 cal., 6 g fat (1 g sat. fat), 0 chol., 319 mg sodium, 15 g carb., 3 g fiber, 5 g pro. Diabetic Exchanges: 1 starch, 1 fat.*

Summer Squash & Watermelon Salad F C M FAST FIX ▶

I always like to take a healthy option to parties and potlucks, and people seem to really appreciate that. No oil is necessary for this salad: the lemon juice and feta cheese combine to lightly coat the bright, fresh ingredients.

—CAMILLE PARKER CHICAGO, IL

START TO FINISH: 20 MIN.
MAKES: 12 SERVINGS (¾ CUP EACH)

- 6 cups cubed seedless watermelon
- 2 medium yellow summer squash, chopped
- 2 medium zucchini, chopped
- ½ cup lemon juice
- 12 fresh mint leaves, torn
- 1 teaspoon salt
- 8 cups fresh arugula or baby spinach
- 1 cup (4 ounces) crumbled feta cheese

In a large bowl, combine the first six ingredients. Just before serving, add arugula and cheese; toss gently to combine.
PER SERVING *1 cup equals 60 cal., 2 g fat (1 g sat. fat), 5 mg chol., 297 mg sodium, 11 g carb., 2 g fiber, 3 g pro. Diabetic Exchanges: 1 vegetable, ½ fruit.*

SUMMER SQUASH & WATERMELON SALAD

FAUX POTATO SALAD

Make your potato salad super healthy by taking out the potatoes. It may sound crazy, but cauliflower is a tasty alternative to spuds.
—MIKE SCHULZ TAWAS CITY, MI

Faux Potato Salad F C M FAST FIX ▶

START TO FINISH: 30 MIN.
MAKES: 8 SERVINGS

- 1 medium head cauliflower, broken into florets
- 1 medium carrot, chopped
- 2 hard-cooked large eggs, chopped
- 4 green onions, chopped
- 1 celery rib, chopped
- ¼ cup pitted green olives, halved lengthwise
- ¼ cup thinly sliced radishes
- ¼ cup chopped dill pickle
- ¼ cup fat-free mayonnaise
- 1 tablespoon Dijon mustard
- ¼ teaspoon salt
- ⅛ teaspoon pepper

1. In a large saucepan, bring 1 in. of water to a boil. Add cauliflower florets; cook, covered, 5-8 minutes or until tender. Drain and rinse in cold water. Pat dry and place in a large bowl. Add carrot, eggs, green onions, celery, olives, radishes and pickle.
2. In a small bowl, mix the remaining ingredients. Add to the cauliflower mixture and toss to coat. Refrigerate until serving.
PER SERVING *¾ cup equals 61 cal., 2 g fat (trace sat. fat), 54 mg chol., 375 mg sodium, 7 g carb., 3 g fiber, 3 g pro. Diabetic Exchanges: 1 vegetable, ½ starch.*

57

63

62

Side Dishes

"I wanted to add Brussels sprouts to our holiday feast, so I created this dish I knew my family would enjoy. The recipe has been a Thanksgiving tradition ever since."

—BRENDA WASHNOCK NEGAUNEE, MI
about her recipe, Roasted Balsamic Brussels Sprouts with Pancetta, on page 59

CHEESY CHIVE POTATOES

Cheesy Chive Potatoes M FAST FIX

These potatoes are a speedy side dish that complements most any entree. Feta cheese adds a rich, zesty flavor. A neighbor supplies me with fresh chives, but you can use frozen or dried for convenience.

—**JEAN KOMLOS** PLYMOUTH, MI

START TO FINISH: 30 MIN.
MAKES: 6 SERVINGS

- 6 **medium potatoes, peeled and cubed**
- ½ **cup fat-free milk**
- ½ **cup crumbled feta cheese**
- 1 **tablespoon butter**
- ½ **teaspoon salt**
- ⅛ **teaspoon pepper**
- 2 **tablespoons minced chives**

1. Place potatoes in a large saucepan and cover with water. Bring to a boil. Reduce heat; cover and cook for 10-15 minutes or until tender.
2. Drain potatoes. Add the milk, cheese, butter, salt and pepper; mash. Stir in chives.
PER SERVING *¾ cup equals 171 cal., 4 g fat (2 g sat. fat), 10 mg chol., 313 mg sodium, 30 g carb., 2 g fiber, 5 g pro. Diabetic Exchanges: 2 starch, 1 fat.*

HOW TO

MASTER MASHED POATOES
❶ Choose russet potatoes or another starchy variety.
❷ Let steam evaporate from drained potatoes before mashing.
❸ For fluffy results, heat milk and butter before adding to potatoes. Mash just until done.

Honey & Ginger Glazed Carrots M FAST FIX

For weeknights and special events alike, we make sweet and tangy carrots flavored with ginger, lemon and honey. You could substitute pecans for the almonds or opt to leave the nuts out. The dish is also tasty made ahead and reheated in the oven.

—**LAURA MIMS** LITTLE ELM, TX

START TO FINISH: 25 MIN.
MAKES: 6 SERVINGS

- 1½ **pounds fresh carrots, sliced**
- ½ **cup golden raisins**
- 3 **tablespoons honey**
- 2 **tablespoons butter**
- 2 **tablespoons lemon juice**
- 1½ **teaspoons ground ginger**
- ½ **teaspoon salt**
- ½ **cup slivered almonds, toasted**

1. Place carrots in a large saucepan; add water to cover. Bring to a boil. Cook, covered, 6-8 minutes or until crisp-tender. Drain and return to pan.
2. Add raisins, honey, butter, lemon juice, ginger and salt; cook and stir for 4-5 minutes longer or until carrots are tender. Just before serving, sprinkle with almonds.
NOTE *To toast nuts, bake in a shallow pan in a 350° oven for 5-10 minutes or cook in a skillet over low heat until lightly browned, stirring occasionally.*
PER SERVING *⅔ cup equals 204 cal., 9 g fat (3 g sat. fat), 10 mg chol., 307 mg sodium, 32 g carb., 5 g fiber, 4 g pro. Diabetic Exchanges: 2 vegetable, 1½ fat, 1 starch.*

HONEY & GINGER GLAZED CARROTS

Two-Tone Potato Wedges Ⓜ

Better than french fries, these tasty potatoes have just the right touch of garlic and Parmesan cheese. This is the only way my daughter will eat sweet potatoes, and she loves 'em!

—MARIA NICOLAU SCHUMACHER
LARCHMONT, NY

PREP: 10 MIN. • **BAKE:** 40 MIN.
MAKES: 4 SERVINGS

- 2 **medium potatoes**
- 1 **medium sweet potato**
- 1 **tablespoon olive oil**
- ¼ **teaspoon salt**
- ¼ **teaspoon pepper**
- 1 **tablespoon grated Parmesan cheese**
- 2 **garlic cloves, minced**

1. Cut each potato and the sweet potato into eight wedges; place in a large resealable plastic bag. Add the oil, salt and pepper; seal bag and shake to coat. Arrange in a single layer in a 15x10x1-in. baking pan coated with cooking spray.

2. Bake, uncovered, at 425° for 20 minutes. Turn potatoes; sprinkle with cheese and garlic. Bake for 20-25 minutes or until golden brown.

PER SERVING *6 potato wedges equals 151 cal., 4 g fat (1 g sat. fat), 1 mg chol., 176 mg sodium, 27 g carb., 3 g fiber, 3 g pro.* **Diabetic Exchanges:** *1½ starch, 1 fat.*

> I've heard radishes are the only vegetable you don't cook, but a cookbook from the 1950s disagrees. Green beans or wax beans round out this dish.
>
> —PAMELA JANE KAISER MANSFIELD, MO

SAUTEED RADISHES WITH GREEN BEANS

Sauteed Radishes with Green Beans Ⓒ Ⓜ FAST FIX

START TO FINISH: 20 MIN.
MAKES: 4 SERVINGS

- 1 **tablespoon butter**
- ½ **pound fresh green or wax beans, trimmed**
- 1 **cup thinly sliced radishes**
- ½ **teaspoon sugar**
- ¼ **teaspoon salt**
- 2 **tablespoons pine nuts, toasted**

1. In a large skillet, heat butter over medium-high heat. Add green beans; cook and stir 3-4 minutes or until crisp-tender.

2. Add radishes; cook 2-3 minutes longer or until vegetables are tender, stirring occasionally. Stir in sugar and salt; sprinkle with nuts.

NOTE *To toast nuts, bake in a shallow pan in a 350° oven for 5-10 minutes or cook in a skillet over low heat until lightly browned, stirring occasionally.*

PER SERVING *½ cup equals 75 cal., 6 g fat (2 g sat. fat), 8 mg chol., 177 mg sodium, 5 g carb., 2 g fiber, 2 g pro.* **Diabetic Exchanges:** *1 vegetable, 1 fat.*

TWO-TONE POTATO WEDGES

Kasha Varnishkes

This is one of the great Jewish comfort foods. It's easy to put together, and leftovers make a surprisingly delicious breakfast. Find kasha with other grains or in the kosher foods section.
—**JOANNE WEINTRAUB** MILWAUKEE, WI

PREP: 10 MIN. • **COOK:** 25 MIN. • **MAKES:** 8 SERVINGS

- 4 **cups uncooked bow tie pasta**
- 2 **large onions, chopped**
- 1 **cup sliced fresh mushrooms**
- 2 **tablespoons canola oil**
- 1 **cup roasted whole grain buckwheat groats (kasha)**
- 1 **large egg, lightly beaten**
- 2 **cups chicken broth, heated**
- ½ **teaspoon salt**
  Dash pepper
  Minced fresh parsley

1. Cook pasta according to package directions. Meanwhile, saute onions and mushrooms in oil in a large skillet until lightly browned, about 9 minutes. Remove from pan and set aside.

2. Combine buckwheat groats and egg in a small bowl; add to the pan. Cook and stir over high heat for 2-4 minutes or until buckwheat is browned, separating grains with the back of a spoon. Add the hot broth, salt and pepper.

3. Bring to a boil; stir in the onion mixture. Reduce heat; cover and simmer for 10-12 minutes or until the liquid is absorbed. Drain pasta; add to the pan and heat through. Sprinkle with parsley.

PER SERVING ¾ cup equals 270 cal., 6 g fat (1 g sat. fat), 28 mg chol., 408 mg sodium, 47 g carb., 4 g fiber, 9 g pro.

KASHA VARNISHKES

GARLIC-SESAME GREEN BEANS

Garlic-Sesame Green Beans F C M

Sauteed bits of garlic and shallot, plus a sprinkling of toasted sesame seeds, turn ordinary beans into something special. Keep the recipe in mind for your garden crop in summer, too.
—**DEIRDRE COX** KANSAS CITY, MO

PREP: 25 MIN. • **COOK:** 10 MIN. • **MAKES:** 12 SERVINGS

- 3 **pounds fresh green beans, trimmed**
- 1 **tablespoon sesame oil**
- 1 **tablespoon canola oil**
- 1 **shallot, finely chopped**
- 6 **garlic cloves, minced**
- 1½ **teaspoons salt**
- ½ **teaspoon pepper**
- 2 **tablespoons sesame seeds, toasted**

1. In a Dutch oven, bring 10 cups water to a boil. Add green beans; cook, uncovered, 6-8 minutes or until tender.

2. Meanwhile, in a small skillet, heat the oils over medium heat. Add shallot, garlic, salt and pepper; cook and stir for 2-3 minutes or until tender.

3. Drain green beans and return to Dutch oven. Add shallot mixture; toss to coat. Sprinkle with sesame seeds.

PER SERVING 1 serving equals 67 cal., 3 g fat (trace sat. fat), 0 chol., 305 mg sodium, 9 g carb., 4 g fiber, 3 g pro. **Diabetic Exchanges:** 2 vegetable, ½ fat.

Herbed Potato Packet C M

PREP: 15 MIN. • **GRILL:** 25 MIN. • **MAKES:** 4 SERVINGS

- 1 **pound baby red potatoes (about 16), halved**
- ¼ **cup cranberry juice**
- 2 **tablespoons butter, cubed**
- 1 **teaspoon each minced fresh dill, oregano, rosemary and thyme**
- ½ **teaspoon salt**
- ⅛ **teaspoon pepper**

1. In a large bowl, combine all ingredients; place mixture on a piece of heavy-duty foil (about 18x12-in. rectangle). Fold foil around mixture, sealing tightly.

2. Grill, covered, over medium heat 25-30 minutes or until potatoes are tender. Open foil carefully to allow steam to escape.

PER SERVING *¾ cup equals 117 cal., 6 g fat (4 g sat. fat), 15 mg chol., 351 mg sodium, 15 g carb., 1 g fiber, 2 g pro. Diabetic Exchanges: 1 starch, 1 fat.*

Every year, my father and I plant a garden together. We like to use fresh herbs from our garden, but you could use ⅓ teaspoon of each dried herb that you don't have available fresh. —**BERNADETTE BENNETT** WACO, TX

HERBED POTATO PACKETS

HONEY-TARRAGON GRILLED ASPARAGUS

Honey-Tarragon Grilled Asparagus C M FAST FIX ▶

I grow purple asparagus, so I'm always looking for new ways to prepare it. Recently, my husband and I discovered how wonderful any color of asparagus tastes when it's grilled.

—**SUE GRONHOLZ** BEAVER DAM, WI

START TO FINISH: 15 MIN. • **MAKES:** 8 SERVINGS

- 2 **pounds fresh asparagus, trimmed**
- 2 **tablespoons olive oil**
- 1 **teaspoon salt**
- ½ **teaspoon pepper**
- ¼ **cup honey**
- 2 **to 4 tablespoons minced fresh tarragon**

On a large plate, toss asparagus with oil, salt and pepper. Grill, covered, over medium heat 6-8 minutes or until crisp-tender, turning spears occasionally and basting frequently with honey during the last 3 minutes. Sprinkle with tarragon.

PER SERVING *1 serving equals 76 cal., 4 g fat (1 g sat. fat), 0 chol., 302 mg sodium, 11 g carb., 1 g fiber, 2 g pro. Diabetic Exchanges: 1 vegetable, ½ starch, ½ fat.*

Anything goes in a rice pilaf, so add peas and baby portobello mushrooms for a springlike burst of color and a variety of textures. —STACY MULLENS GRESHAM, OR

MUSHROOM & PEA RICE PILAF

Mushroom & Pea Rice Pilaf M FAST FIX ▶

START TO FINISH: 25 MIN.
MAKES: 6 SERVINGS

- 1 package (6.6 ounces) rice pilaf mix with toasted almonds
- 1 tablespoon butter
- 1½ cups fresh or frozen peas
- 1 cup sliced baby portobello mushrooms

1. Prepare pilaf according to package directions.
2. In a large skillet, heat butter over medium heat. Add the peas and the mushrooms; cook and stir 6-8 minutes or until tender. Stir in rice.
PER SERVING ⅔ cup equals 177 cal., 6 g fat (2 g sat. fat), 10 mg chol., 352 mg sodium, 28 g carb., 3 g fiber, 5 g pro. *Diabetic Exchanges: 2 starch, ½ fat.*

Roasted Green Vegetable Medley S C M

I have cooked a lot of things—from family favorites to gourmet meals—but I'd never roasted vegetables until lately. Now, it's my preferred way to cook them! I've adapted this recipe to use my favorite veggies, but almost any kind can be prepared this way.
—SUZAN CROUCH GRAND PRAIRIE, TX

PREP: 15 MIN. • **BAKE:** 20 MIN.
MAKES: 12 SERVINGS (¾ CUP EACH)

- 2 cups fresh broccoli florets
- 1 pound thin fresh green beans, trimmed and cut into 2-inch pieces
- 10 small fresh mushrooms, halved
- 8 fresh Brussels sprouts, halved
- 2 medium carrots, cut into ¼-inch slices
- 1 medium onion, sliced
- 3 to 5 garlic cloves, thinly sliced
- 4 tablespoons olive oil, divided
- ½ cup grated Parmesan cheese
- 3 tablespoons julienned fresh basil leaves, optional
- 2 tablespoons minced fresh parsley
- 2 tablespoons lemon juice
- 1 tablespoon grated lemon peel
- ¼ teaspoon salt
- ¼ teaspoon pepper

1. Place first seven ingredients in a large bowl; drizzle with 2 tablespoons oil and toss to coat. Divide between two 15x10x1-in. baking pans coated with cooking spray. Bake at 425° for 20-25 minutes or until vegetables are tender, stirring occasionally.
2. Transfer to a large bowl. Mix the remaining oil with the remaining ingredients; add to vegetables and toss to coat.
PER SERVING ¾ cup equals 80 cal., 5 g fat (1 g sat. fat), 3 mg chol., 63 mg sodium, 7 g carb., 2 g fiber, 3 g pro. *Diabetic Exchanges: 1 vegetable, 1 fat.*

Roasted Balsamic Brussels Sprouts with Pancetta

I wanted to add Brussels sprouts to our holiday feast, so I created this dish I knew my family would enjoy. The recipe has been a Thanksgiving tradition ever since.

—**BRENDA WASHNOCK** NEGAUNEE, MI

PREP: 15 MIN. • **BAKE:** 30 MIN.
MAKES: 6 SERVINGS

- 2 **pounds fresh Brussels sprouts, trimmed and halved**
- 3 **tablespoons olive oil, divided**
- ½ **teaspoon salt**
- ¼ **teaspoon pepper**
- 2 **ounces sliced pancetta or bacon strips, chopped**
- 2 **garlic cloves, minced**
- 1 **tablespoon balsamic vinegar**
- ⅓ **cup dried cranberries**
- ½ **cup pine nuts**

1. Preheat oven to 400°. In a large bowl, toss Brussels sprouts with 2 tablespoons oil, salt and pepper. Transfer to a 15x10x1-in. baking pan. Roast 30-35 minutes or until tender and lightly charred, stirring halfway through cooking. Place in a large bowl.

2. Meanwhile, in a large skillet, heat remaining oil over medium-high heat. Add the pancetta; cook and stir for 4-6 minutes or until crisp. Add the garlic; cook 1 minute longer. Remove from heat; stir in vinegar. Add dried cranberries and pancetta mixture; toss to combine. Sprinkle with pine nuts.

PER SERVING *¾ cup equals 253 cal., 18 g fat (3 g sat. fat), 8 mg chol., 407 mg sodium, 20 g carb., 6 g fiber, 8 g pro.*

DID YOU KNOW?

Balsamic vinegar is made from sweet white grapes and gets its dark color from aging in wooden barrels. The longer it ages, the more thick and sweet it becomes. Highly aged vinegars are expensive and best enjoyed drizzled over cheese or used for dipping with oil and bread. Moderately priced vinegar works fine for preparing sauces and reductions. If needed, add a little sugar to taste.

ROASTED BALSAMIC BRUSSELS SPROUTS WITH PANCETTA

ROSEMARY ROASTED POTATOES AND ASPARAGUS

Rosemary Roasted Potatoes and Asparagus C M

Dress up asparagus with fresh rosemary and heritage potatoes as an earthy counterpoint to the fresh green spears. Add minced garlic and you get a more than impressive side dish.

—TRISHA KRUSE EAGLE, ID

PREP: 10 MIN. • **BAKE:** 35 MIN.
MAKES: 4 SERVINGS

- ½ **pound fingerling potatoes, cut into 1-inch pieces**
- ¼ **cup olive oil, divided**
- 2 **tablespoons minced fresh rosemary or 2 teaspoons dried rosemary, crushed**
- 2 **garlic cloves, minced**
- 1 **pound fresh asparagus, trimmed**
- ¼ **teaspoon salt**
- ¼ **teaspoon freshly ground pepper**

1. In a small bowl, combine potatoes, 2 tablespoons oil, rosemary and garlic; toss to coat. Place mixture in a greased 15x10x1-in. baking pan. Roast at 400° for 20 minutes, stirring once.
2. Drizzle asparagus with remaining oil; add to the pan. Bake 15-20 minutes longer or until vegetables are tender, stirring occasionally. Sprinkle with salt and pepper.
PER SERVING 1 serving equals 175 cal., 14 g fat (2 g sat. fat), 0 chol., 156 mg sodium, 11 g carb., 2 g fiber, 3 g pro. *Diabetic Exchanges: 3 fat, 1 vegetable, ½ starch.*

Creamy Roasted Garlic & Spinach Orzo

This side dish brings instant comfort. I first made it without spinach so my husband and daughter would like it. The next time, I added spinach for all the extra health benefits. They still devoured it, and that makes it a win-win in my book.

—DAWN MOORE WARREN, PA

PREP: 35 MIN. • **COOK:** 20 MIN.
MAKES: 6 SERVINGS

- 1 **whole garlic bulb**
- 1 **teaspoon plus 1 tablespoon olive oil, divided**
- 1¾ **cups uncooked whole wheat orzo pasta**
- 2½ **cups chicken stock**
- 3 **ounces reduced-fat cream cheese, cubed**
- 1 **package (9 ounces) fresh spinach, trimmed and chopped**
- ¼ **cup shredded Asiago cheese**
- ¼ **cup fat-free milk**
- 1 **teaspoon salt-free garlic pepper seasoning blend**
- ¼ **teaspoon salt**
- 2 **tablespoons minced fresh parsley**

1. Preheat oven to 425°. Remove papery outer skin from garlic bulb, but do not peel or separate the cloves. Cut off top of garlic bulb, exposing the individual cloves. Drizzle cut cloves with 1 teaspoon oil. Wrap in foil. Bake 30-35 minutes or until cloves are soft. Unwrap. When cool enough to handle, squeeze garlic from skins.
2. In a Dutch oven, heat remaining oil over medium-high heat. Add pasta; cook and stir over medium-high heat 2-3 minutes or until lightly browned. Add stock; bring to a boil. Reduce heat; simmer, covered, 10-12 minutes or until pasta is tender and the liquid is absorbed.
3. Stir in cream cheese until melted. Add spinach, Asiago cheese, milk, seasoning blend, salt and roasted garlic; cook and stir until spinach is wilted. Sprinkle with parsley.

PER SERVING ⅔ cup equals 271 cal., 8 g fat (3 g sat. fat), 14 mg chol., 422 mg sodium, 37 g carb., 9 g fiber, 12 g pro. *Diabetic Exchanges: 2 starch, 1½ fat, 1 vegetable.*

Squash Saute F C M FAST FIX

Italian seasonings are a nice accent for summer squash. They give this versatile side dish a fresh Mediterranean taste.

—VICKI SCHURK HAMDEN, CT

START TO FINISH: 15 MIN.
MAKES: 2 SERVINGS

- 1 **cup sliced zucchini**
- 1 **cup sliced yellow summer squash**
- 2 **tablespoons finely chopped onion**
- ½ **teaspoon olive oil**
- ¼ **teaspoon dried basil**
- ¼ **teaspoon dried oregano**
- ⅛ **teaspoon salt**
  Dash garlic powder
  Dash pepper

In a large skillet, saute the zucchini, squash and onion in oil 4-6 minutes or until crisp-tender. Add the remaining ingredients; cook 1 minute longer.
PER SERVING ⅔ cup equals 37 cal., 1 g fat (trace sat. fat), 0 chol., 155 mg sodium, 6 g carb., 2 g fiber, 1 g pro. *Diabetic Exchange: 1 vegetable.*

CREAMY ROASTED GARLIC & SPINACH ORZO

![ROASTED CAULIFLOWER WITH TAHINI YOGURT SAUCE]

ROASTED CAULIFLOWER WITH TAHINI YOGURT SAUCE

Roasted Cauliflower with Tahini Yogurt Sauce C M

This dish reminds me of a meal that my grandmother, who loved cauliflower, used to serve. I think she'd want to add it to her recipe collection.

—LIDIA HADDADIAN PASADENA, CA

PREP: 15 MIN. • **BAKE:** 40 MIN.
MAKES: 4 SERVINGS

- ¼ cup grated Parmesan cheese
- 3 tablespoons olive oil
- 2 garlic cloves, minced
- 1 small head cauliflower (about 1½ pounds), cut into 4 wedges
- ¼ teaspoon salt
- ¼ teaspoon pepper

SAUCE

- ½ cup fat-free plain Greek yogurt
- 1 tablespoon lemon juice
- 1 tablespoon tahini
- ¼ teaspoon salt
- Dash paprika
- Dash cayenne pepper
- Minced fresh parsley

1. Preheat oven to 375°. In a small bowl, mix cheese, oil and garlic. Rub cheese mixture over cauliflower; place in a foil-lined 15x10x1-in. baking pan coated with cooking spray, cut sides up. Sprinkle with salt and pepper. Roast for 40-45 minutes or until golden brown.

2. Meanwhile, in a small bowl, combine yogurt, lemon juice, tahini, salt, paprika and cayenne. Serve with cauliflower; sprinkle with parsley.
PER SERVING *1 serving equals 177 cal., 14 g fat (3 g sat. fat), 4 mg chol., 421 mg sodium, 7 g carb., 2 g fiber, 7 g pro.* **Diabetic Exchanges:** *2 fat, 1 vegetable.*

Green Beans with Shallots C M FAST FIX

Using frozen green beans means this recipe is ultra-quick for a busy night. It's a simple, nutritious solution for any meal.

—LINDA RABBITT CHARLES CITY, IA

START TO FINISH: 15 MIN.
MAKES: 4 SERVINGS

- 1 package (12 ounces) frozen Steamfresh whole green beans
- 1¾ cups sliced fresh mushrooms
- 2 shallots, chopped
- 1 tablespoon olive oil
- ½ teaspoon salt
- ½ teaspoon dill weed
- ½ teaspoon pepper

1. Cook the green beans according to package directions.

2. Meanwhile, in a large skillet, saute mushrooms and shallots in oil until tender. Remove from the heat. Add the green beans, salt, dill and pepper; toss to coat.
PER SERVING *¾ cup equals 83 cal., 4 g fat (trace sat. fat), 0 chol., 299 mg sodium, 10 g carb., 3 g fiber, 2 g pro.* **Diabetic Exchanges:** *2 vegetable, ½ fat.*

Confetti Corn S M FAST FIX

This easy corn dish is sure to dress up almost any entree. You have the tender corn paired with the crunch of water chestnuts, red pepper and chopped carrot in this healthy side.

—GLENDA WATTS CHARLESTON, IL

START TO FINISH: 15 MIN.
MAKES: 4 SERVINGS

- ¼ cup chopped carrot
- 1 tablespoon olive oil
- 2¾ cups fresh or frozen corn, thawed
- ¼ cup chopped water chestnuts
- ¼ cup chopped sweet red pepper

In a large skillet, saute carrot in oil until crisp-tender. Stir in the corn, water chestnuts and red pepper; heat through.
PER SERVING *¾ cup equals 140 cal., 4 g fat (1 g sat. fat), 0 chol., 7 mg sodium, 26 g carb., 3 g fiber, 4 g pro.* **Diabetic Exchanges:** *1½ starch, ½ fat.*

CONFETTI CORN

PARMESAN-BUTTERNUT SQUASH

Potato Kugel M

PREP: 20 MIN. • **BAKE:** 40 MIN.
MAKES: 12 SERVINGS

- 2 **large eggs**
- ¼ **cup matzo meal**
- 2 **teaspoons kosher salt**
  Dash pepper
- 6 **large potatoes (about 4¾ pounds), peeled**
- 1 **large onion, cut into 6 wedges**
- ¼ **cup canola oil**

1. Preheat the oven to 375°. In a large bowl, whisk the eggs, matzo meal, salt and pepper.
2. In a food processor fitted with the grating attachment, alternately grate potatoes and onion. Add to the egg mixture and toss to coat. In a small saucepan, heat oil over medium heat until warmed. Stir into potato mixture. Transfer to a greased 13x9-in. baking dish. Bake for 40-50 minutes or until golden brown.
PER SERVING *1 serving equals 210 cal., 6 g fat (1 g sat. fat), 35 mg chol., 515 mg sodium, 36 g carb., 3 g fiber, 5 g pro.*

Parmesan-Butternut Squash F M FAST FIX ▶

Butternut squash sprinkled with Parmesan and bread crumbs makes a superb side dish we like to share. By using the microwave oven you cut down on long roasting time.
—JACKIE O'CALLAGHAN
WEST LAFAYETTE, IN

START TO FINISH: 25 MIN.
MAKES: 8 SERVINGS

- 1 **medium butternut squash (about 3 pounds), peeled and cut into 1-inch cubes**
- 2 **tablespoons water**
- ½ **cup panko (Japanese) bread crumbs**
- ½ **cup grated Parmesan cheese**
- ¼ **teaspoon salt**
- ⅛ **teaspoon pepper**

1. Place squash and water in a large microwave-safe bowl. Microwave, covered, on high 15-17 minutes or until tender; drain.
2. Preheat broiler. Transfer squash to a greased 15x10x1-in. baking pan. Toss bread crumbs with cheese, salt and pepper; sprinkle over squash. Broil 3-4 in. from heat 1-2 minutes or until topping is golden brown.
NOTE *This recipe was tested in a 1,100-watt microwave.*
PER SERVING *¾ cup equals 112 cal., 2 g fat (1 g sat. fat), 4 mg chol., 168 mg sodium, 23 g carb., 6 g fiber, 4 g pro. Diabetic Exchange: 1½ starch.*

The secret to keeping your potatoes their whitest is to switch back and forth when grating the potatoes and onion in your food processor or box grater.
—ELLEN RUZINSKY YORKTOWN HEIGHTS, NY

POTATO KUGEL

Shredded Gingered Brussels Sprouts F C M FAST FIX

Even people who normally don't care for Brussels sprouts will ask for a second helping of these.

—JAMES SCHEND PLEASANT PRAIRIE, WI

START TO FINISH: 25 MIN.
MAKES: 6 SERVINGS

- 1 pound fresh Brussels sprouts
- 1 tablespoon olive oil
- 1 small onion, finely chopped
- 1 tablespoon minced fresh gingerroot
- 1 garlic clove, minced
- ½ teaspoon salt
- 2 tablespoons water
- ¼ teaspoon pepper

1. Trim Brussels sprouts. Cut sprouts lengthwise in half; cut crosswise into thin slices.

2. Place a large skillet over medium-high heat. Add Brussels sprouts; cook and stir 2-3 minutes or until sprouts begin to brown lightly. Add oil and toss to coat. Stir in the onion, ginger, garlic and salt. Add the water; reduce heat to medium and cook, covered, for 1-2 minutes or until the vegetables are tender. Stir in pepper.

PER SERVING *¾ cup equals 56 cal., 2 g fat (trace sat. fat), 0 chol., 214 mg sodium, 8 g carb., 3 g fiber, 2 g pro.* **Diabetic Exchanges:** *1 vegetable, ½ fat.*

Broccoli with Garlic, Bacon & Parmesan C FAST FIX

START TO FINISH: 30 MIN.
MAKES: 8 SERVINGS

- 1 teaspoon salt
- 2 bunches broccoli (about 3 pounds), stems removed, cut into florets
- 6 thick-sliced bacon strips, chopped
- 2 tablespoons olive oil
- 6 to 8 garlic cloves, thinly sliced
- ½ teaspoon crushed red pepper flakes
- ¼ cup shredded Parmesan cheese

1. Fill a 6-qt. stockpot two-thirds full with water; add salt and bring to a boil.

My approach to broccoli is to cook it slowly in broth so the garlic blends with smoky bacon. A few simple ingredients make ordinary broccoli irresistible.

—ERIN CHILCOAT CENTRAL ISLIP, NY

BROCCOLI WITH GARLIC, BACON & PARMESAN

In batches, add broccoli and cook 2-3 minutes or until broccoli turns bright green; remove with a slotted spoon.

2. In a large skillet, cook bacon over medium heat until crisp, stirring often. Remove with a slotted spoon; drain on paper towels. Discard drippings, reserving 1 tablespoon in pan.

3. Add oil to drippings; heat over medium heat. Add garlic and pepper flakes; cook and stir 2-3 minutes or until garlic is fragrant (do not allow to brown). Add broccoli; cook until broccoli is tender, stirring often. Stir in bacon; sprinkle with cheese.

PER SERVING *¾ cup equals 155 cal., 10 g fat (3 g sat. fat), 11 mg chol., 371 mg sodium, 11 g carb., 4 g fiber, 8 g pro.* **Diabetic Exchanges:** *2 fat, 1 vegetable.*

Confetti Succotash M FAST FIX

This veggie dish perks up any meal with its vibrant, varied ingredients and its refreshing blend of flavors.
—NICOLE WILLIS LAS VEGAS, NV

START TO FINISH: 20 MIN.
MAKES: 4 SERVINGS

- ¼ cup chopped sweet red pepper
- ¼ cup chopped green pepper
- 2 tablespoons thinly sliced green onion
- 1 tablespoon butter
- 2 cups frozen corn, thawed
- 1 cup frozen lima beans, thawed
- ¼ cup half-and-half cream
- 2 teaspoons minced fresh marjoram or ½ teaspoon dried marjoram
- ¼ teaspoon salt
- ⅛ teaspoon pepper

In a large skillet, saute peppers and onion in butter until crisp-tender. Add the remaining ingredients. Bring to a gentle boil. Reduce heat; cover and simmer for 5-6 minutes or until tender, stirring occasionally.
PER SERVING ¾ cup equals 171 cal., 5 g fat (3 g sat. fat), 15 mg chol., 192 mg sodium, 28 g carb., 5 g fiber, 6 g pro. *Diabetic Exchanges: 2 starch, 1 fat.*

Roasted Asparagus with Feta M FAST FIX

Pretty and festive, this simple-to-do side dish is delicious right out of the oven.
—PHYLLIS SCHMALZ KANSAS CITY, KS

START TO FINISH: 25 MIN.
MAKES: 6 SERVINGS

- 2 pounds fresh asparagus, trimmed
- 1 tablespoon olive oil
  Kosher salt to taste
- 2 medium tomatoes, seeded and chopped
- ½ cup crumbled feta cheese

1. Arrange asparagus in an ungreased 13x9-in. baking dish. Drizzle with oil and sprinkle with salt.
2. Bake dish, uncovered, at 400° for 15-20 minutes or until tender.
3. Transfer asparagus to a serving dish; sprinkle with tomatoes and feta cheese. Serve immediately.
PER SERVING 1 serving (calculated without salt) equals 72 cal., 4 g fat (1 g sat. fat), 5 mg chol., 103 mg sodium, 6 g carb., 2 g fiber, 4 g pro. *Diabetic Exchanges: 1 vegetable, 1 fat.*

PUMPKIN & CAULIFLOWER GARLIC MASH

Pumpkin & Cauliflower Garlic Mash C M FAST FIX

I wanted healthy alternatives to my family's favorite recipes. Pumpkin, cauliflower and thyme turn into an amazing dish—you'll never miss plain old mashed potatoes.
—KARI WHEATON SOUTH BELOIT, IL

START TO FINISH: 25 MIN.
MAKES: 6 SERVINGS

- 1 medium head cauliflower, broken into florets (about 6 cups)
- 3 garlic cloves
- ⅓ cup spreadable cream cheese
- 1 can (15 ounces) solid-pack pumpkin
- 1 tablespoon minced fresh thyme
- 1 teaspoon salt
- ¼ teaspoon cayenne pepper
- ¼ teaspoon pepper

1. Place 1 in. of water in a large saucepan; bring to a boil. Add the cauliflower and garlic cloves; cook, covered, 8-10 minutes or until tender. Drain; transfer to a food processor.
2. Add remaining ingredients; process until smooth. Return to pan; heat through, stirring occasionally.
PER SERVING ⅔ cup equals 87 cal., 4 g fat (2 g sat. fat), 9 mg chol., 482 mg sodium, 12 g carb., 4 g fiber, 4 g pro. *Diabetic Exchanges: 1 vegetable, ½ starch, ½ fat.*

TOP TIP

Awesome! I sprinkled in dried thyme instead of using fresh. I also cut the cayenne and black pepper down to a sprinkle for my super-sensitive kid, and I added more salt.
—KEVERWANN TASTEOFHOME.COM

CONFETTI SUCCOTASH

71

74

79

Good Mornings

"I've been cooking this strata for years, and my family just can't get enough! The fresh basil gives this healthy brunch dish an added flavor boost."

—JEAN ECOS HARTLAND, WI
about her recipe, Basil Vegetable Strata, on page 75

Cool Summertime Oatmeal S M

Start this breakfast the night before so you can get a few extra zzzs in the morning. My husband adds coconut to his, and I stir in dried fruit.

—JUNE THOMAS CHESTERTON, IN

PREP: 10 MIN. + CHILLING
MAKES: 4 SERVINGS

- 1⅓ cups old-fashioned oats
- ¾ cup fat-free milk
- ¾ cup (6 ounces) reduced-fat plain yogurt
- ¼ cup honey
- 1 cup pitted fresh or frozen dark sweet cherries, thawed
- 1 cup fresh or frozen blueberries, thawed
- ½ cup chopped walnuts, toasted

1. In a small bowl, combine the oats, milk, yogurt and honey. Refrigerate, covered, overnight.
2. Top each serving with cherries, blueberries and walnuts.

NOTE *To toast nuts, bake in a shallow pan in a 350° oven for 5-10 minutes or cook in a skillet over low heat until lightly browned, stirring occasionally.*

PER SERVING *1 serving equals 350 cal., 12 g fat (2 g sat. fat), 4 mg chol., 53 mg sodium, 55 g carb., 5 g fiber, 10 g pro.*

SAUSAGE-SWEET POTATO HASH & EGGS

COOL SUMMERTIME OATMEAL

Sausage-Sweet Potato Hash & Eggs FAST FIX

When I first began making this dish for breakfast, I served it with fried eggs on top. Now I sometimes even make it for supper and serve it without eggs—especially when I want a quick-to-make dish with easy cleanup.

—NANCY MURPHY MOUNT DORA, FL

START TO FINISH: 25 MIN.
MAKES: 4 SERVINGS

- ½ pound Italian turkey sausage links, casings removed
- 2 medium sweet potatoes, peeled and cut into ¼-inch cubes
- 2 medium Granny Smith apples, chopped
- ¼ cup dried cranberries
- ¼ cup chopped pecans
- ¼ teaspoon salt
- 4 green onions, sliced
- 4 large eggs

1. In a large nonstick skillet coated with cooking spray, cook sausage and sweet potatoes over medium-high heat 8-10 minutes or until sausage is no longer pink, breaking up sausage into crumbles.
2. Add apples, cranberries, pecans and salt; cook and stir 4-6 minutes longer or until potatoes are tender. Remove from pan; sprinkle with green onions. Keep warm.
3. Wipe skillet clean and coat with cooking spray; place skillet over medium-high heat. Break eggs, one at a time, into pan. Reduce heat to low. Cook to desired doneness, turning after whites are set if desired. Serve with hash.

PER SERVING *1 serving equals 338 cal., 14 g fat (3 g sat. fat), 207 mg chol., 465 mg sodium, 42 g carb., 6 g fiber, 15 g pro. Diabetic Exchanges: 2 starch, 2 medium-fat meat, ½ fruit.*

Fluffy Banana Pancakes M FAST FIX ▸

I love to make pancakes for my family on Saturday mornings. Since we often have ripe bananas, I decided to add them to a batch of pancake batter. The results were delicious!

—LORI STEVENS RIVERTON, UT

START TO FINISH: 30 MIN.
MAKES: 14 PANCAKES

- 1 **cup all-purpose flour**
- 1 **cup whole wheat flour**
- 3 **tablespoons brown sugar**
- 1 **teaspoon baking powder**
- 1 **teaspoon baking soda**
- 1 **teaspoon ground cinnamon**
- ½ **teaspoon salt**
- 2 **large eggs**
- 2 **cups buttermilk**
- 2 **tablespoons canola oil**
- 1 **teaspoon vanilla extract**
- 1 **ripe medium banana, finely chopped**
- ⅓ **cup finely chopped walnuts**

1. In a large bowl, combine the first seven ingredients. In another bowl, whisk eggs, buttermilk, oil and vanilla until blended. Add to dry ingredients, stirring just until moistened. Fold in banana and walnuts.

2. Pour batter by ¼ cupfuls onto a hot griddle coated with cooking spray. Cook until bubbles begin to form on top and bottoms are golden brown. Turn; cook pancakes until second side is golden brown.

FREEZE OPTION *Freeze cooled pancakes between layers of waxed paper in a resealable plastic freezer bag. To use, place pancakes on an ungreased baking sheet, cover with foil and reheat in a preheated 375° oven 5-10 minutes. Or, place two pancakes on a microwave-safe plate and microwave on high for 40-50 seconds or until heated through.*

PER SERVING *2 pancakes equals 283 cal., 10 g fat (2 g sat. fat), 63 mg chol., 503 mg sodium, 40 g carb., 4 g fiber, 9 g pro.* **Diabetic Exchanges:** *2½ starch, 1½ fat.*

Cinnamon-Sugar Coffee Cake M

PREP: 20 MIN. • **BAKE:** 25 MIN.
MAKES: 15 SERVINGS

- 2 **large eggs**
- ⅓ **cup canola oil**
- ¼ **cup sugar**
- ¼ **cup honey**
- 1 **teaspoon vanilla extract**
- 1 **cup all-purpose flour**
- 1 **cup whole wheat flour**
- 1 **teaspoon baking powder**
- 1 **teaspoon baking soda**
- ½ **teaspoon salt**
- 1 **cup fat-free plain Greek yogurt**

TOPPING
- ⅓ **cup packed brown sugar**
- ¼ **cup sugar**
- 1 **teaspoon ground cinnamon**
- 1 **teaspoon vanilla extract**
- ½ **cup chopped pecans**

1. Preheat the oven to 350°. Coat a 13x9-in. baking pan with cooking spray.

2. In a large bowl, beat eggs, oil, sugar, honey and vanilla until well blended. In another bowl, whisk flours, baking powder, baking soda and salt; add to egg mixture alternately with yogurt, beating well after each addition.

3. Transfer batter to prepared pan. In a small bowl, mix sugars, cinnamon and vanilla until blended. Stir in the pecans; sprinkle over batter. Bake for 25-30 minutes or until a toothpick inserted into center comes out clean. Cool in pan on a wire rack.

PER SERVING *1 piece equals 211 cal., 9 g fat (1 g sat. fat), 25 mg chol., 209 mg sodium, 30 g carb., 2 g fiber, 5 g pro.* **Diabetic Exchanges:** *2 starch, 2 fat.*

I'm a big fan of coffee cake, but I wanted to come up with a lighter version. This version has less fat and sugar, but still tastes great. It's a wonderful addition to breakfast! **—LISA VARNER** EL PASO, TX

CINNAMON-SUGAR COFFEE CAKE

APPLE SPICED TEA

Apple Spiced Tea F S M FAST FIX

Treat yourself to a steaming cup of homemade tea. After you try this sweetly spiced drink, you'll make it a regular event.
—**SUSAN WESTERFIELD** ALBUQUERQUE, NM

START TO FINISH: 10 MIN.
MAKES: 1 SERVING

- ½ cup apple cider or juice
- ¼ teaspoon minced fresh gingerroot
- 2 whole allspice
- 2 whole cloves
- 1 black tea bag
- ½ cup boiling water
- 1 tablespoon brown sugar

In a small bowl, combine the first five ingredients. Add boiling water. Cover and steep for 5 minutes. Strain, discarding tea bag and spices. Stir in sugar. Serve immediately.
PER SERVING *1 cup equals 112 cal., trace fat (trace sat. fat), 0 chol., 12 mg sodium, 28 g carb., trace fiber, trace pro.* **Diabetic Exchanges:** *1 starch, 1 fruit.*

DID YOU KNOW?

Dark brown sugar contains more molasses than light or golden brown sugar. The types are generally interchangeable in recipes. But if you prefer a bolder flavor, choose dark brown sugar.

English Muffin Egg Sandwich M FAST FIX

You can't beat the delicious combination of mushrooms, onions, peppers and cream cheese! Leave out the red pepper flakes for a less spicy taste.
—**AMY LLOYD** MADISON, WI

START TO FINISH: 25 MIN.
MAKES: 8 SERVINGS

- ½ pound sliced fresh mushrooms
- 1 small sweet red pepper, chopped
- 1 small sweet onion, chopped
- ½ teaspoon garlic salt
- ¼ teaspoon pepper
- ¼ teaspoon crushed red pepper flakes, optional
- 7 large eggs, lightly beaten
- 8 whole wheat English muffins, split and toasted
- 4 ounces reduced-fat cream cheese

1. Place a large nonstick skillet coated with cooking spray over medium-high heat. Add mushrooms, red pepper, onion and seasonings; cook and stir 5-7 minutes or until mushrooms are tender. Remove from pan.
2. Wipe skillet clean and coat with cooking spray; place skillet over medium heat. Add eggs; cook and stir just until eggs are thickened and no liquid egg remains. Add vegetables; heat through, stirring gently.
3. Spread muffin bottoms with cream cheese; top with egg mixture. Replace muffin tops.
PER SERVING *1 sandwich equals 244 cal., 9 g fat (4 g sat. fat), 173 mg chol., 425 mg sodium, 30 g carb., 5 g fiber, 14 g pro.* **Diabetic Exchanges:** *2 starch, 1 medium-fat meat, ½ fat.*

ENGLISH MUFFIN EGG SANDWICH

Grapes with Lemon-Honey Yogurt F S M FAST FIX

I like to sweeten up Greek yogurt with honey, cinnamon and vanilla. It's a tasty counterpoint to plump grapes and crunchy nuts.

—**JULIE STERCHI** CAMPBELLSVILLE, KY

START TO FINISH: 10 MIN.
MAKES: 8 SERVINGS

- 1 cup fat-free plain Greek yogurt
- 2 tablespoons honey
- 1 teaspoon vanilla extract
- ½ teaspoon grated lemon peel
- ⅛ teaspoon ground cinnamon
- 3 cups seedless red grapes
- 3 cups green grapes
- 3 tablespoons sliced almonds, toasted

In a small bowl, combine the first five ingredients. Divide grapes among eight serving bowls. Top with yogurt mixture; sprinkle with almonds.

NOTE *To toast nuts, bake in a shallow pan in a 350° oven for 5-10 minutes or cook in a skillet over low heat until lightly browned, stirring occasionally.*

PER SERVING *¾ cup grapes with 2 tablespoons yogurt mixture and about 1 teaspoon almonds equals 138 cal., 2 g fat (trace sat. fat), 0 chol., 20 mg sodium, 28 g carb., 2 g fiber, 6 g pro.* **Diabetic Exchanges:** *1½ fruit, ½ starch.*

Caramel Apple Coffee Cake with Walnuts M

I created this recipe after a trip to an orchard with my family. This moist cake is full of hearty apples and nuts, while the caramel frosting adds a delectable finish.

—**SHARON CABLE** DYERSVILLE, IA

PREP: 25 MIN. • **BAKE:** 45 MIN. + COOLING
MAKES: 16 SERVINGS

- 3 large eggs
- 1½ cups sugar
- 1 cup unsweetened applesauce
- ⅓ cup canola oil
- 2 teaspoons vanilla extract
- 3 cups all-purpose flour
- 1 teaspoon salt
- 1 teaspoon baking soda
- 3 cups chopped peeled apples (about 3 medium)

CARAMEL APPLE COFFEE CAKE WITH WALNUTS

TOPPING

- ⅓ cup packed brown sugar
- 3 tablespoons butter
- 1 tablespoon fat-free milk
  Dash salt
- ¼ cup chopped walnuts or pecans, toasted

1. Preheat oven to 350°. Coat a 10-in. fluted tube pan with cooking spray; dust with flour, tapping out extra.
2. In a large bowl, beat eggs, sugar, applesauce, oil and vanilla until well blended. In another bowl, whisk flour, salt and baking soda; gradually beat into sugar mixture. Stir in apples.
3. Transfer to prepared pan. Bake 45-55 minutes or until a toothpick inserted into center comes out clean.

Cool coffee cake in pan 10 minutes before removing to a wire rack to cool completely.

4. In a small saucepan, combine brown sugar, butter, milk and salt. Bring to a boil, stirring constantly; cook 2 minutes. Remove from heat; let stand to thicken slightly. Spoon slowly over cake. Sprinkle with nuts.

EDITOR'S NOTES *To remove cakes easily, use solid shortening to grease plain and fluted tube pans. To toast nuts, spread in a 15x10x1-in. baking pan. Bake at 350° for 5-10 minutes or until lightly browned, stirring occasionally.*

PER SERVING *1 piece equals 280 cal., 9 g fat (2 g sat. fat), 41 mg chol., 268 mg sodium, 46 g carb., 1 g fiber, 4 g pro.*

Sausage-Egg Burritos FAST FIX

My husband and I try to eat healthy, but finding new meals for breakfast is a challenge. By adding tomatoes, spinach and garlic to traditional egg whites, we can have a dish that is both light and satisfying.

—WENDY BALL BATTLE CREEK, MI

START TO FINISH: 20 MIN.
MAKES: 6 SERVINGS

- ½ **pound bulk lean turkey breakfast sausage**
- 3 **large eggs**
- 4 **large egg whites**
- 1 **tablespoon olive oil**
- 2 **cups chopped fresh spinach**
- 2 **plum tomatoes, seeded and chopped**
- 1 **garlic clove, minced**
- ¼ **teaspoon pepper**
- 6 **whole wheat tortillas (8 inches), warmed**
  Salsa, optional

1. In a large nonstick skillet coated with cooking spray, cook sausage over medium heat 4-6 minutes or until no longer pink, breaking into crumbles. Remove from pan.

2. In a small bowl, whisk eggs and egg whites until blended. In same pan, add eggs; cook and stir over medium heat until eggs are thickened and no liquid egg remains. Remove from pan; wipe skillet clean if necessary.

3. In skillet, heat oil over medium-high heat. Add spinach, tomatoes and garlic; cook and stir 2-3 minutes or until spinach is wilted. Stir in sausage and eggs; heat through. Sprinkle with pepper.

4. To serve, spoon ⅔ cup filling across center of each tortilla. Fold bottom and sides of tortilla over filling and roll up. If desired, serve with salsa.

PER SERVING *1 burrito equals 258 cal., 10 g fat (2 g sat. fat), 134 mg chol., 596 mg sodium, 24 g carb., 4 g fiber,* 20 *g pro.* **Diabetic Exchanges:** *2 medium-fat meat, 1½ starch, ½ fat.*

Raspberry Peach Puff Pancake M

Here's a simple, satisfying treat that's perfect for when you have company for brunch. It's elegant enough that you can even serve it for dessert at other meals.

—*TASTE OF HOME* TEST KITCHEN

PREP: 15 MIN. • **BAKE:** 20 MIN.
MAKES: 4 SERVINGS

- 2 **medium peaches, peeled and sliced**
- ½ **teaspoon sugar**
- ½ **cup fresh raspberries**
- 1 **tablespoon butter**
- 3 **large eggs**
- ½ **cup fat-free milk**
- ⅛ **teaspoon salt**
- ½ **cup all-purpose flour**
- ¼ **cup vanilla yogurt**

1. Preheat oven to 400°. In a small bowl, toss peaches with sugar; gently stir in raspberries.

2. Place butter in a 9-in. pie plate; heat in oven 2-3 minutes or until butter is melted. Meanwhile, in a small bowl, whisk eggs, milk and salt until blended; gradually whisk in flour. Remove pie plate from oven; tilt carefully to coat the bottom and sides with butter. Immediately pour in egg mixture.

3. Bake 18-22 minutes or until puffed and browned. Remove pancake from oven. Serve immediately with the fruit and yogurt.

PER SERVING *1 piece with ½ cup fruit and 1 tablespoon yogurt equals 199 cal., 7 g fat (3 g sat. fat), 149 mg chol., 173 mg sodium, 25 g carb., 3 g fiber, 9 g pro.* **Diabetic Exchanges:** *1 medium-fat meat, 1 fruit, ½ starch, ½ fat.*

TOP TIP

For an easy, classic variation, squeeze some fresh lemon juice over the puff pancake and dust it generously with confectioners' sugar.

SAUSAGE-EGG BURRITOS

RASPBERRY PEACH PUFF PANCAKE

I got this recipe from my favorite bagel shop in New York City. Now I make this every time I'm craving a quick and healthy breakfast. I like to add chopped pitted green olives to the schmear.

—JULIE MERRIMAN SEATTLE, WA

BAGEL WITH A VEGGIE SCHMEAR

Bagel with a Veggie Schmear M FAST FIX

START TO FINISH: 20 MIN.
MAKES: 4 SERVINGS

- 4 ounces fat-free cream cheese
- 4 ounces fresh goat cheese
- ½ teaspoon grated lime peel
- 1 tablespoon lime juice
- ⅔ cup finely chopped cucumber
- ¼ cup finely chopped celery
- 3 tablespoons finely chopped carrot
- 1 radish, finely chopped
- 2 tablespoons finely chopped red onion
- 2 tablespoons thinly sliced fresh basil
- 4 whole wheat bagels, split and toasted
- 8 slices tomato
  Coarsely ground pepper, optional

1. In a bowl, beat cheeses, lime peel and lime juice until blended. Fold in vegetables and basil.
2. Serve on bagels with tomato slices. If desired, sprinkle with pepper.
PER SERVING *2 open-faced sandwiches equals 341 cal., 6 g fat (3 g sat. fat), 22 mg chol., 756 mg sodium, 56 g carb., 10 g fiber, 20 g pro.*

Curry Scramble C M FAST FIX

I have eggs every morning, and this is a great change from the classic scrambled egg meal. I like to add sliced peppers on top if I have them on hand.

—VALERIE BELLEY ST. LOUIS, MO

START TO FINISH: 15 MIN.
MAKES: 4 SERVINGS

- 8 large eggs
- ¼ cup fat-free milk
- ½ teaspoon curry powder
- ¼ teaspoon salt
- ⅛ teaspoon pepper
- ⅛ teaspoon ground cardamom, optional
- 2 medium tomatoes, sliced or chopped

1. In a large bowl, whisk eggs, milk, curry powder, salt, pepper and, if desired, cardamom until blended.
2. Place a large nonstick skillet coated with cooking spray over medium heat. Pour in egg mixture; cook and stir until eggs are thickened and no liquid egg remains. Serve with tomatoes.
PER SERVING *1 serving equals 160 cal., 10 g fat (3 g sat. fat), 372 mg chol., 299 mg sodium, 4 g carb., 1 g fiber, 14 g pro.* **Diabetic Exchange:** *2 medium-fat meat.*

CURRY SCRAMBLE

Basil Vegetable Strata M

I've been cooking this strata for years, and my family just can't get enough! The fresh basil gives this healthy brunch dish an added flavor boost.

—**JEAN ECOS** HARTLAND, WI

PREP: 40 MIN. + CHILLING
BAKE: 1 HOUR + STANDING
MAKES: 8 SERVINGS

- 3 **teaspoons canola oil, divided**
- ¾ **pound sliced fresh mushrooms**
- 1 **cup finely chopped sweet onion**
- 1 **large sweet red pepper, cut into thin strips**
- 1 **large sweet yellow pepper, cut into thin strips**
- 1 **medium leek (white portion only), chopped**
- ½ **teaspoon salt**
- ½ **teaspoon pepper**
- 10 **slices whole wheat bread, cut into 1-inch pieces**
- 1½ **cups (6 ounces) shredded part-skim mozzarella cheese**
- ¼ **cup grated Parmesan cheese**
- 8 **large eggs**
- 4 **large egg whites**
- 2½ **cups fat-free milk**
- ¼ **cup chopped fresh basil**

1. In a large skillet, heat 1 teaspoon canola oil over medium-high heat. Add mushrooms; cook and stir for 8-10 minutes or until tender. Remove from pan.

2. In same pan, heat 1 teaspoon oil over medium heat. Add onion; cook and stir 6-8 minutes or until golden brown. Add onion to mushrooms.

3. Add remaining oil to pan. Add the peppers, leek, salt and pepper; cook and stir 6-8 minutes or until leek is tender. Stir in sauteed mushrooms and onion.

4. In a greased 13x9-in. baking dish, layer half of each of the following: bread cubes, vegetable mixture, mozzarella cheese and Parmesan cheese. Repeat layers. In a large bowl, whisk eggs, egg whites and milk until blended; pour over layers. Sprinkle with basil. Refrigerate the strata, covered, overnight.

5. Preheat oven to 350°. Remove strata from refrigerator while the oven heats.

6. Bake, covered, 50 minutes. Bake, uncovered, 10-15 minutes longer or until lightly browned and a knife inserted near the center comes out clean. Let strata stand 10 minutes before serving.

PER SERVING *1 piece equals 322 cal., 13 g fat (5 g sat. fat), 201 mg chol., 620 mg sodium, 28 g carb., 4 g fiber, 24 g pro.* **Diabetic Exchanges:** *2 medium-fat meat, 1½ starch, 1 vegetable, ½ fat.*

Crunchy French Toast M FAST FIX

I like to eat healthy, and I don't want to skip breakfast. This light version of classic French toast is perfect for quick meals or Sunday brunches. My kids love it...and so do I!

—**BARBARA ARNOLD** SPOKANE, WA

START TO FINISH: 20 MIN.
MAKES: 4 SERVINGS

- 6 **large eggs**
- ⅓ **cup fat-free milk**
- 2 **teaspoons vanilla extract**
- ⅛ **teaspoon salt**
- 1 **cup frosted cornflakes, crushed**
- ½ **cup old-fashioned oats**
- ¼ **cup sliced almonds**
- 8 **slices whole wheat bread**
  Maple syrup

1. In a shallow bowl, whisk the eggs, milk, vanilla and salt until blended. In another shallow bowl, toss cornflakes with oats and almonds.

2. Heat a griddle coated with cooking spray over medium heat. Dip both sides of bread in egg mixture, then in cereal mixture, patting to help the coating adhere. Place on the griddle; toast 3-4 minutes on each side or until golden brown. Serve with syrup.

PER SERVING *2 slices French toast (calculated without syrup) equals 335 cal., 11 g fat (2 g sat. fat), 196 mg chol., 436 mg sodium, 43 g carb., 5 g fiber, 17 g pro.* **Diabetic Exchanges:** *3 starch, 1 medium-fat meat, ½ fat.*

CRUNCHY FRENCH TOAST

Maple Apple Baked Oatmeal M

I've tried different types of fruit for this recipe, but apples seem to be my family's favorite. I mix the dry and wet ingredients in separate bowls the night before and combine them the next morning when it's ready to be baked.

—MEGAN BROOKS SAINT LAZARE, QC

PREP: 20 MIN. • **BAKE:** 25 MIN.
MAKES: 8 SERVINGS

- 3 **cups old-fashioned oats**
- 2 **teaspoons baking powder**
- 1¼ **teaspoons ground cinnamon**
- ½ **teaspoon salt**
- ¼ **teaspoon ground nutmeg**
- 2 **large eggs**
- 2 **cups fat-free milk**
- ½ **cup maple syrup**
- ¼ **cup canola oil**
- 1 **teaspoon vanilla extract**
- 1 **large apple, chopped**
- ¼ **cup sunflower kernels or pepitas**

1. Preheat oven to 350°. In a large bowl, mix the first five ingredients. In a small bowl, whisk eggs, milk, syrup, oil and vanilla until blended; stir into dry ingredients. Let stand 5 minutes. Stir in apple.

2. Transfer to an 11x7-in. baking dish coated with cooking spray. Sprinkle with the sunflower kernels. Bake, uncovered, 25-30 minutes or until set and edges are lightly browned.

PER SERVING *1 piece equals 305 cal., 13 g fat (2 g sat. fat), 48 mg chol., 325 mg sodium, 41 g carb., 4 g fiber, 8 g pro. Diabetic Exchanges: 3 starch, 1½ fat.*

FIESTA TIME OMELET

MAPLE APPLE BAKED OATMEAL

Fiesta Time Omelet C M FAST FIX

I came up with this dish when I needed to use some black olives and jalapenos. With their abundance of vegetables, two of these large omelets can feed four people if served with side dishes.

—JENNINE VICTORY BEE BRANCH, AR

START TO FINISH: 15 MIN.
MAKES: 2 SERVINGS

- 4 **large eggs**
- ¼ **cup fat-free milk**
- ¼ **teaspoon salt**
- ¼ **cup queso fresco**
- ¼ **cup canned diced jalapeno peppers or chopped green chilies**
- 2 **tablespoons finely chopped sweet red pepper**
- 2 **tablespoons sliced ripe olives**
- 2 **teaspoons chopped fresh cilantro**
- ¼ **medium ripe avocado, peeled and sliced**

1. In a small bowl, whisk the eggs, milk and salt until blended.

2. Place a 10-in. nonstick skillet coated with cooking spray over medium-high heat. Pour in the egg mixture. Mixture should set immediately at edges. As the eggs set, push cooked portions toward the center, letting uncooked eggs flow underneath. When eggs are thickened and no liquid egg remains, spoon the cheese, peppers, olives and cilantro on one side. Fold omelet in half. Cut in half; slide onto two plates. Top with the avocado.

PER SERVING *½ omelet equals 242 cal., 16 g fat (5 g sat. fat), 383 mg chol., 601 mg sodium, 7 g carb., 2 g fiber, 18 g pro. Diabetic Exchanges: 2 medium-fat meat, 1 fat, ½ starch.*

Mini Italian Frittatas ☒ Ⓜ

I created this recipe when my friends and I had a picnic breakfast. I wanted an egg meal that was portable and easy to make. The result was this crowd-pleasing frittata!
—JESSIE APFE BERKELEY, CA

PREP: 20 MIN. • **BAKE:** 20 MIN.
MAKES: 1 DOZEN

- ½ cup boiling water
- ¼ cup sun-dried tomatoes (not packed in oil)
- ¾ cup shredded part-skim mozzarella cheese, divided
- ½ cup chopped fresh spinach
- ⅓ cup water-packed artichoke hearts, rinsed, drained and chopped
- ⅓ cup chopped roasted sweet red peppers
- ¼ cup grated Parmesan cheese
- ¼ cup ricotta cheese
- 2 tablespoons minced fresh basil
- 1 tablespoon prepared pesto
- 2 teaspoons Italian seasoning
- ¼ teaspoon garlic powder
- 8 large eggs
- ½ teaspoon pepper
- ¼ teaspoon salt

1. Preheat oven to 350°. Pour boiling water over tomatoes in a small bowl; let stand 5 minutes. Drain and chop the tomatoes.
2. In a small bowl, combine ½ cup mozzarella cheese, spinach, artichoke hearts, red peppers, Parmesan cheese, ricotta cheese, basil, pesto, Italian seasoning, garlic powder and the tomatoes. In a large bowl, whisk eggs, salt and pepper until blended; stir in cheese mixture.
3. Fill greased or foil-lined muffin cups three-fourths full. Sprinkle with remaining mozzarella cheese. Bake 18-22 minutes or until set. Cool for 5 minutes before removing from pan. Serve warm.

PER SERVING *1 mini frittata equals 95 cal., 6 g fat (3 g sat. fat), 149 mg chol., 233 mg sodium, 2 g carb., trace fiber, 8 g pro.* **Diabetic Exchanges:** *1 lean meat, 1 fat.*

Poached Eggs with Tarragon Asparagus ☒ Ⓜ FAST FIX ▶

START TO FINISH: 30 MIN.
MAKES: 4 SERVINGS

- 1 pound fresh asparagus, trimmed
- 1 tablespoon olive oil
- 1 garlic clove, minced
- 1 tablespoon minced fresh tarragon
- ½ teaspoon salt
- ¼ teaspoon pepper
- 1 tablespoon butter
- ¼ cup seasoned bread crumbs
- 4 large eggs

1. Place 3 in. of water in a large skillet with high sides; bring to a boil. Add the asparagus; cook, uncovered, for 2-4 minutes or until asparagus turns bright green. Remove asparagus and immediately drop into ice water. Drain and pat dry.
2. In a separate large skillet, heat oil over medium heat. Add garlic; cook and stir 1 minute. Add asparagus, tarragon, salt and pepper; cook the asparagus for 2-3 minutes or until crisp-tender, turning occasionally. Remove from pan; keep warm. In same skillet, melt butter over medium heat. Add bread crumbs; cook and stir for 1-2 minutes or until toasted. Remove from heat.
3. Add 2-3 in. fresh water to skillet used to cook asparagus. Bring to a boil; adjust the heat to maintain a gentle simmer. Break cold eggs, one at a time, into a small bowl; holding bowl close to surface of water, slip egg into water.
4. Cook eggs, uncovered, 3-4 minutes or until whites are completely set and yolks begin to thicken but are not hard. Using a slotted spoon, lift eggs out of water; serve over asparagus. Sprinkle with toasted bread crumbs.

PER SERVING *1 serving equals 170 cal., 12 g fat (4 g sat. fat), 194 mg chol., 513 mg sodium, 8 g carb., 1 g fiber, 9 g pro.* **Diabetic Exchanges:** *1½ fat, 1 medium-fat meat, 1 vegetable.*

I adapted this recipe from a dish I had in Napa Valley. I decided to add toasted bread crumbs as a garnish. The result was a breakfast option that everyone loves. —JENNIFER TIDWELL FAIR OAKS, CA

POACHED EGGS WITH TARRAGON ASPARAGUS

¼ cup flaxseed
¼ cup canola oil
¼ cup honey
1 tablespoon maple syrup
1 teaspoon apple pie spice
½ teaspoon salt
½ teaspoon vanilla extract
½ cup dried cranberries
½ cup raisins

1. Preheat oven to 300°. In a large bowl, combine oats, almonds, brown sugar and flax. In a microwave-safe dish, whisk oil, honey, maple syrup, pie spice and salt. Microwave on high for 30-45 seconds or until heated through, stirring once. Stir in vanilla. Pour over oat mixture; toss to coat.

2. Spread evenly in a 15x10x1-in. baking pan coated with cooking spray. Bake 30-40 minutes or until golden brown, stirring every 10 minutes. Cool completely on a wire rack. Stir in the cranberries and raisins. Store in an airtight container.

NOTE *This recipe was tested in a 1,100-watt microwave.*

PER SERVING *½ cup equals 255 cal., 10 g fat (1 g sat. fat), 0 chol., 84 mg sodium, 40 g carb., 5 g fiber, 7 g pro.*

GET-UP-AND-GO GRANOLA

Whenever I take this eye-catching fruit salad to a party or gathering, people ask for the recipe. The blueberries and cherries give the salad its distinctive flavor. **—JULIE STERCHI** CAMPBELLSVILLE, KY

FRESH FRUIT COMBO

Fresh Fruit Combo F S M

START TO FINISH: 20 MIN.
MAKES: 14 SERVINGS

2 cups cubed fresh pineapple
2 medium oranges, peeled and chopped
3 kiwifruit, peeled and sliced
1 cup sliced fresh strawberries
1 cup halved seedless red grapes
2 medium firm bananas, sliced
1 large red apple, cubed
1 cup fresh or frozen blueberries
1 cup fresh or canned pitted dark sweet cherries

In a large bowl, combine the first five ingredients; refrigerate until serving. To serve, fold in the bananas, apple, blueberries and cherries.

PER SERVING *¾ cup equals 78 cal., trace fat (trace sat. fat), 0 chol., 3 mg sodium, 20 g carb., 3 g fiber, 1 g pro. Diabetic Exchange: 1 fruit.*

Get-Up-and-Go Granola S M

My family loves to have this soul-warming granola before hiking, biking or even when camping. It smells delicious while baking, and you can easily make it in large batches to share with family and friends.

—SABRINA OLSON OTSEGO, MN

PREP: 15 MIN. • **BAKE:** 30 MIN. + COOLING
MAKES: 7½ CUPS

6 cups old-fashioned oats
½ cup unblanched almonds, coarsely chopped
¼ cup packed brown sugar

Mango-Peach Smoothies F S M FAST FIX ▶

This is my son's favorite breakfast—he'll take one of these over pancakes any day! Get creative when mixing fruits and fruit-flavored yogurts; we love peach yogurt with mango, strawberry yogurt with blueberries or pina colada yogurt with mango and banana.

—DANA HERRA DEKALB, IL

START TO FINISH: 5 MIN.
MAKES: 4 SERVINGS

- 1 cup fat-free milk
- 12 ounces peach yogurt (about 1¼ cups)
- 2½ cups frozen mango chunks

Place all ingredients in a blender; cover and process until smooth. Serve immediately.

PER SERVING 1 cup equals 180 cal., 1 g fat (1 g sat. fat), 5 mg chol., 71 mg sodium, 39 g carb., 3 g fiber, 6 g pro.

Crisp Chocolate Chip Waffles M

This variation on classic waffles is a great choice when you're in a rush. The recipe makes a big batch, so I usually freeze what I don't eat.

—LAUREN REIFF EAST EARL, PA

PREP: 15 MIN. • **COOK:** 5 MIN./BATCH
MAKES: 12 WAFFLES

- 1¼ cups all-purpose flour
- ¾ cup whole wheat flour
- ¼ cup quick-cooking oats
- 2 teaspoons baking powder
- 1 teaspoon sugar
- ¼ teaspoon salt
- 2 large eggs
- 1⅓ cups fat-free milk
- 2 tablespoons olive oil
- 1 tablespoon butter, melted
- 1 tablespoon honey
- ½ cup miniature semisweet chocolate chips

1. In a large bowl, whisk the first six ingredients. In another bowl, whisk eggs, milk, oil, butter and honey until blended. Add to dry ingredients; stir just until moistened. Stir in chips.
2. Bake in a preheated waffle iron according to manufacturer's directions until golden brown.

PER SERVING 2 waffles equals 339 cal., 13 g fat (5 g sat. fat), 77 mg chol., 361 mg sodium, 49 g carb., 4 g fiber, 10 g pro.

Beef, Potato & Egg Bake C

To keep my family going all morning, I start with lean ground beef and spices, then sneak some spinach into this protein-packed dish.

—JENNIFER FISHER AUSTIN, TX

PREP: 25 MIN. • **BAKE:** 45 MIN.
MAKES: 12 SERVINGS

- 1 pound lean ground beef (90% lean)
- 2 teaspoons onion powder
- 1½ teaspoons salt, divided
- 1 teaspoon garlic powder
- ½ teaspoon rubbed sage
- ½ teaspoon crushed red pepper flakes
- 1 package (10 ounces) frozen chopped spinach, thawed and squeezed dry
- 4 cups frozen shredded hash brown potatoes
- 14 large eggs
- 1 cup fat-free ricotta cheese
- ⅓ cup fat-free milk
- ¾ to 1 teaspoon pepper
- ¾ cup shredded Colby-Monterey Jack cheese
- 1⅓ cups grape tomatoes, halved

1. Preheat oven to 350°. In a large skillet, cook beef with onion powder, ½ teaspoon salt, garlic powder, sage and pepper flakes over medium heat 6-8 minutes or until no longer pink, breaking up beef into crumbles; drain. Stir in spinach. Remove from heat.
2. Spread potatoes in a greased 13x9-in. baking dish; top with beef mixture. In a large bowl, whisk eggs, ricotta cheese, milk, pepper and remaining salt; pour over top. Sprinkle with cheese. Top with tomatoes.
3. Bake, uncovered, for 45-50 minutes or until a knife inserted near the center comes out clean. Let stand for 5-10 minutes before serving.

PER SERVING 1 piece equals 218 cal., 11 g fat (5 g sat. fat), 250 mg chol., 489 mg sodium, 9 g carb., 1 g fiber, 20 g pro. **Diabetic Exchanges:** 3 lean meat, ½ starch.

BEEF, POTATO & EGG BAKE

GINGER-KALE SMOOTHIES

Ginger-Kale Smoothies F S M FAST FIX

Since I started drinking these spicy smoothies for breakfast every day, I honestly feel better! Substitute any fruit and juice you like to make this recipe your own healthy blend.

—**LINDA GREEN** KILAUEA, HI

START TO FINISH: 15 MIN.
MAKES: 2 SERVINGS

- 1¼ cups orange juice
- 1 teaspoon lemon juice
- 2 cups torn fresh kale
- 1 medium apple, peeled and coarsely chopped
- 1 tablespoon minced fresh gingerroot
- 4 ice cubes
- ⅛ teaspoon ground cinnamon
- ⅛ teaspoon ground turmeric or ¼-inch piece fresh turmeric, peeled and finely chopped
  Dash cayenne pepper

Place all ingredients in a blender; cover and process until blended. Serve immediately.
PER SERVING 1 cup equals 121 cal., trace fat (trace sat. fat), 0 chol., 22 mg sodium, 29 g carb., 2 g fiber, 1 g pro. **Diabetic Exchanges:** 1½ fruit, 1 vegetable.

Potato-Cheddar Frittata C M FAST FIX

I like to serve this protein-packed frittata with toasted rustic bread. You can also use leftovers instead of the refrigerated potatoes with onions.

—**DONNA MARIE RYAN** TOPSFIELD, MA

START TO FINISH: 30 MIN.
MAKES: 4 SERVINGS

- 8 large egg whites
- 4 large eggs
- ½ cup shredded cheddar cheese
- ½ cup fat-free milk
- 2 green onions, chopped
- 2 teaspoons minced fresh parsley
- ¼ teaspoon salt
- ¼ teaspoon pepper
- 1 tablespoon canola oil
- 1½ cups refrigerated diced potatoes with onion

1. Preheat broiler. In a large bowl, whisk the first eight ingredients. In a 10-in. ovenproof skillet, heat oil over medium-high heat. Add potatoes with onion; cook and stir 3-4 minutes or until tender. Reduce heat; pour in egg mixture. Cook, covered, 5-7 minutes or until nearly set.
2. Broil 3-4 in. from the heat for 2-3 minutes or until the eggs are set. Let stand 5 minutes. Cut into wedges.

PER SERVING 1 wedge equals 241 cal., 13 g fat (5 g sat. fat), 201 mg chol., 555 mg sodium, 11 g carb., 1 g fiber, 19 g pro. **Diabetic Exchanges:** 2 medium-fat meat, 1 starch, 1 fat.

Blackberry Smoothies F S M FAST FIX

Smoothies are a creamy treat and will get you going in the morning, too. I like to combine assorted berries, yogurt, orange juice and honey.

—**VALERIE BELLEY** ST. LOUIS, MO

START TO FINISH: 10 MIN.
MAKES: 4 SERVINGS

- 1 cup orange juice
- 1 cup (8 ounces) plain yogurt
- 2 to 3 tablespoons honey
- 1½ cups fresh or frozen blackberries
- ½ cup frozen unsweetened mixed berries

In a blender, combine the first five ingredients; cover and process for about 15 seconds or until smooth. Pour into chilled glasses; serve immediately. Top with additional blackberries and yogurt if desired.
PER SERVING 1 cup equals 130 cal., 2 g fat (1 g sat. fat), 8 mg chol., 29 mg sodium, 26 g carb., 3 g fiber, 3 g pro. **Diabetic Exchanges:** 1 starch, 1 fruit.

POTATO-CHEDDAR FRITTATA

Turkey Sausage Patties C

I developed this recipe as a way to keep my husband from eating pork sausage. It also makes great meatballs and burgers.

—YVONNE WOODRUFF SACRAMENTO, CA

PREP: 20 MIN. • **COOK:** 20 MIN.
MAKES: 2½ DOZEN

- 2 large eggs
- ⅔ cup seasoned bread crumbs
- 1 small onion, finely chopped
- 2 tablespoons Worcestershire sauce
- 3 garlic cloves, minced
- 2 teaspoons garlic salt
- 2 teaspoons dried thyme
- 2 teaspoons ground cumin
- ½ teaspoon crushed red pepper flakes
- ½ teaspoon pepper
- ⅛ teaspoon ground nutmeg
- 2 pounds lean ground turkey
- 5 teaspoons canola oil, divided

1. In a large bowl, combine the first 11 ingredients. Crumble turkey over mixture and mix well. Shape into thirty 2½-in. patties.

2. Heat 1 teaspoon oil in a large skillet over medium heat. Cook the sausage patties in batches over medium heat 2-3 minutes on each side or until meat is no longer pink, using remaining oil as needed.

PER SERVING *1 patty equals 70 cal., 4 g fat (1 g sat. fat), 38 mg chol., 204 mg sodium, 3 g carb., trace fiber, 6 g pro. Diabetic Exchange: 1 lean meat.*

Brown Sugar & Banana Oatmeal F S M FAST FIX

Oatmeal is a classic breakfast food—quick, easy and satisfying. I came up with this version by using some of the same ingredients from my favorite breakfast smoothie.

—JESSI RIZZI ODENTON, MD

START TO FINISH: 15 MIN.
MAKES: 3 SERVINGS

- 2 cups fat-free milk
- 1 cup quick-cooking oats
- 1 large ripe banana, sliced
- 2 teaspoons brown sugar
- 1 teaspoon honey
- ½ teaspoon ground cinnamon
  Additional fat-free milk or ground cinnamon, optional

1. In a small saucepan, bring milk to a boil; stir in oats. Cook over medium heat for 1-2 minutes or until thickened, stirring occasionally.

2. Stir in banana, brown sugar, honey and cinnamon. Serve with additional milk and cinnamon if desired.

PER SERVING *1 cup (calculated without additional milk) equals 215 cal., 2 g fat (trace sat. fat), 3 mg chol., 71 mg sodium, 42 g carb., 4 g fiber, 10 g pro.*

Cocoa Pancakes F M FAST FIX

We love these chocolaty whole wheat pancakes that taste like a treat. The yogurt and raspberries are a delicious and good-for-you accent. Use one egg if you don't have egg substitute on hand.

—LISA DEMARSH MT SOLON, VA

START TO FINISH: 25 MIN.
MAKES: 8 PANCAKES

- ¾ cup whole wheat flour
- ¼ cup sugar
- 2 tablespoons baking cocoa
- 1 teaspoon baking powder

COCOA PANCAKES

- ⅛ teaspoon salt
- ⅛ teaspoon ground nutmeg
- ¾ cup fat-free milk
- ¼ cup egg substitute
- 1 tablespoon reduced-fat butter, melted
- 1 cup fresh raspberries
- ½ cup fat-free vanilla yogurt

1. In a small bowl, combine the first six ingredients. Combine the milk, egg substitute and butter; add to dry ingredients just until moistened.

2. Pour batter by scant ¼ cupfuls onto a hot griddle coated with cooking spray; turn when bubbles form on top. Cook until the second side is lightly browned. Serve with raspberries and vanilla yogurt.

NOTE *This recipe was tested with Land O'Lakes light stick butter.*

PER SERVING *2 pancakes with ¼ cup raspberries and 2 tablespoons yogurt equals 201 cal., 2 g fat (1 g sat. fat), 6 mg chol., 249 mg sodium, 40 g carb., 5 g fiber, 8 g pro. Diabetic Exchanges: 2 starch, ½ fruit.*

88

91

90

Slow Cooker

"The first time I served these wraps was at the party following my son's baptism. I made a double batch and fed a crowd of 20!"

—AMY LENTS GRAND FORKS, ND
about her recipe, Mexican Shredded Beef Wraps, on page 90

SLOW-COOKED PEACH SALSA

Turkey with Cranberry Sauce F C

Here's a tasty and easy way to cook turkey breast in the slow cooker. Ideal for holiday potlucks, the sweet cranberry sauce complements the turkey nicely.

—MARIE RAMSDEN FAIRGROVE, MI

PREP: 15 MIN. • **COOK:** 4 HOURS
MAKES: 15 SERVINGS

- 2 **boneless skinless turkey breast halves (3 pounds each)**
- 1 **can (14 ounces) jellied cranberry sauce**
- ½ **cup plus 2 tablespoons water, divided**
- 1 **envelope onion soup mix**
- 2 **tablespoons cornstarch**

1. Place turkey breasts in a 5-qt. slow cooker. In a large bowl, combine the cranberry sauce, ½ cup water and soup mix. Pour over the turkey. Cover and cook on low for 4-6 hours or until meat is tender. Remove turkey and keep warm.

2. Transfer cooking juices to a large saucepan. Combine the cornstarch and remaining water until smooth. Bring cranberry mixture to a boil; gradually stir in cornstarch mixture until smooth. Cook and stir for 2 minutes or until thickened. Serve sauce with turkey.

PER SERVING *1 serving equals 248 cal., 1 g fat (trace sat. fat), 112 mg chol., 259 mg sodium, 12 g carb., trace fiber, 45 g pro.* **Diabetic Exchanges:** *5 lean meat, ½ starch.*

TURKEY WITH CRANBERRY SAUCE

Slow-Cooked Peach Salsa F S C M

Fresh peaches and tomatoes make my salsa a hands-down winner over store versions. As a treat, I give my co-workers several jars throughout the year.

—PEGGI STAHNKE CLEVELAND, OH

PREP: 20 MIN. • **COOK:** 3 HOURS
MAKES: 11 CUPS

- 4 **pounds tomatoes (about 12 medium), chopped**
- 1 **medium onion, chopped**
- 4 **jalapeno peppers, seeded and finely chopped**
- ½ **to ⅔ cup packed brown sugar**
- ¼ **cup minced fresh cilantro**
- 4 **garlic cloves, minced**
- 1 **teaspoon salt**
- 4 **cups chopped peeled fresh peaches (about 4 medium), divided**
- 1 **can (6 ounces) tomato paste**

1. In a 5-qt. slow cooker, combine the first seven ingredients; stir in 2 cups peaches. Cook, covered, on low for 3-4 hours or until onion is tender.

2. Stir tomato paste and remaining peaches into slow cooker. Transfer to covered containers. (If freezing salsa, use freezer-safe containers and fill to within ½ in. of tops.) Refrigerate up to 1 week or freeze up to 12 months. Thaw frozen salsa in the refrigerator before serving.

NOTE *Wear disposable gloves when cutting hot peppers; the oils can burn skin. Avoid touching your face.*

PER SERVING *¼ cup equals 28 cal., trace fat (trace sat. fat), 0 chol., 59 mg sodium, 7 g carb., 1 g fiber, 1 g pro.* **Diabetic Exchange:** *½ starch.*

Slow Cooker Lava Cake M

Because I love chocolate, this decadent slow cooker cake has long been a family favorite. This cake can also be served cold.

—ELIZABETH FARRELL HAMILTON, MT

PREP: 15 MIN.
COOK: 2 HOURS + STANDING
MAKES: 8 SERVINGS

- 1 cup all-purpose flour
- 1 cup packed brown sugar, divided
- 5 tablespoons baking cocoa, divided
- 2 teaspoons baking powder
- ¼ teaspoon salt
- ½ cup fat-free milk
- 2 tablespoons canola oil
- ½ teaspoon vanilla extract
- ⅛ teaspoon ground cinnamon
- 1¼ cups hot water

1. In a large bowl, whisk flour, ½ cup brown sugar, 3 tablespoons cocoa, baking powder and salt. In another bowl, whisk milk, oil and vanilla until blended. Add to flour mixture; stir just until moistened.

2. Spread mixture into a 3-qt. slow cooker coated with cooking spray. In a small bowl, mix cinnamon and the remaining brown sugar and cocoa; stir in the hot water. Pour over batter (do not stir).

3. Cook, covered, on high for 2-2½ hours or until a toothpick inserted in cake portion comes out clean. Turn off slow cooker; let stand 15 minutes before serving.

PER SERVING *1 serving equals 207 cal., 4 g fat (trace sat. fat), trace chol., 191 mg sodium, 41 g carb., 1 g fiber, 3 g pro.*

Spring Herb Roast C

PREP: 20 MIN.
COOK: 4 HOURS + STANDING
MAKES: 8 SERVINGS

- 2 large onions, halved and sliced (about 3 cups)
- ½ pound sliced fresh mushrooms
- 1 beef rump roast or bottom round roast (3 to 4 pounds)
- 2 teaspoons salt
- ½ teaspoon pepper
- 1 tablespoon canola oil
- 1½ cups water
- 2 tablespoons tomato paste
- 3 garlic cloves, minced
- ½ teaspoon each dried basil, marjoram and thyme
  Minced fresh parsley

1. Place onions and mushrooms in a 5- or 6-qt. slow cooker. Sprinkle roast with salt and pepper. In a large skillet, heat oil over medium-high heat; brown roast on all sides. Transfer to slow cooker.

2. In a small bowl, mix water, tomato paste, garlic, basil, marjoram and thyme; pour over roast. Cook, covered, on low 4-5 hours or until meat is tender (a thermometer should read at least 145°).

3. Remove roast from slow cooker; tent with foil. Let stand 15 minutes before slicing. Serve with onion mixture; sprinkle with parsley.

PER SERVING *5 ounces cooked beef with ¼ cup vegetable mixture equals 257 cal., 10 g fat (3 g sat. fat), 101 mg chol., 650 mg sodium, 6 g carb., 1 g fiber, 35 g pro.* **Diabetic Exchanges:** *5 lean meat, 1 vegetable, ½ fat.*

This is a wonderful roast that you can forget about while it's cooking (though the aroma will remind you). It's great served with brown rice or mashed potatoes.

—DONNA ROBERTS MANHATTAN, KS

SPRING HERB ROAST

This knockout shredded pork makes a healthy, delicious and hearty salad with black beans, corn, cotija cheese and plenty of fresh greens.
—MARY SHIVERS ADA, OK

SOUTHWEST SHREDDED PORK SALAD

Southwest Shredded Pork Salad [c]

PREP: 20 MIN. • **COOK:** 6 HOURS
MAKES: 12 SERVINGS

- 1 boneless pork loin roast (3 to 4 pounds)
- 1½ cups apple cider or juice
- 1 can (4 ounces) chopped green chilies, drained
- 3 garlic cloves, minced
- 1½ teaspoons salt
- 1½ teaspoons hot pepper sauce
- 1 teaspoon chili powder
- 1 teaspoon pepper
- ½ teaspoon ground cumin
- ½ teaspoon dried oregano
- 12 cups torn mixed salad greens
- 1 can (15 ounces) black beans, rinsed and drained
- 2 medium tomatoes, chopped
- 1 small red onion, chopped
- 1 cup fresh or frozen corn
- 1 cup (4 ounces) crumbled cotija or shredded part-skim mozzarella cheese
  Salad dressing of your choice

1. Place pork in a 5- or 6-qt. slow cooker. In a small bowl, mix cider, green chilies, garlic, salt, pepper sauce, chili powder, pepper, cumin and oregano; pour over pork. Cook, covered, on low 6-8 hours or until meat is tender.

2. Remove roast from slow cooker; discard cooking juices. Shred pork with two forks. Arrange salad greens on a large serving platter. Top with pork, black beans, tomatoes, onion, corn and cheese. Serve with salad dressing of your choice.

FREEZE OPTION *Place shredded pork in a freezer container; top with cooking juices. Cool and freeze. To use, partially thaw in refrigerator overnight. Heat through in a small saucepan, stirring occasionally.*

PER SERVING *1 serving equals 233 cal., 8 g fat (4 g sat. fat), 67 mg chol., 321 mg sodium, 12 g carb., 3 g fiber, 28 g pro.* **Diabetic Exchanges:** *4 lean meat, 1 vegetable, ½ starch.*

Slow-Cooked Chicken Chili

Lime juice gives this chili a zesty twist, while canned tomatoes and beans make preparation a breeze. It's fun to serve with toasted tortilla strips.

—DIANE RANDAZZO SINKING SPRING, PA

PREP: 25 MIN. • **COOK:** 4 HOURS
MAKES: 6 SERVINGS (2 QUARTS)

- 1 medium onion, chopped
- 1 each medium sweet yellow, red and green peppers, chopped
- 2 tablespoons olive oil
- 3 garlic cloves, minced
- 1 pound ground chicken
- 2 cans (14½ ounces each) diced tomatoes, undrained
- 1 can (15 ounces) white kidney or cannellini beans, rinsed and drained
- ¼ cup lime juice
- 1 tablespoon all-purpose flour
- 1 tablespoon baking cocoa
- 1 tablespoon ground cumin
- 1 tablespoon chili powder
- 2 teaspoons ground coriander
- 1 teaspoon grated lime peel
- ½ teaspoon salt
- ½ teaspoon garlic pepper blend
- ¼ teaspoon pepper
- 2 flour tortillas (8 inches), cut into ¼-inch strips
- 6 tablespoons reduced-fat sour cream

1. In a large skillet, saute onion and peppers in oil for 7-8 minutes or until crisp-tender. Add garlic; cook 1 minute longer. Add chicken; cook and stir over medium heat for 8-9 minutes or until meat is no longer pink.

2. Transfer to a 3-qt. slow cooker. Stir in the tomatoes, beans, lime juice, flour, cocoa, cumin, chili powder, coriander, lime peel, salt, garlic pepper and pepper.

3. Cover chili and cook on low for 4-5 hours or until heated through.

4. Place tortilla strips on a baking sheet coated with cooking spray. Bake at 400° for 8-10 minutes or until crisp. Serve chili with sour cream and tortilla strips.

PER SERVING *1¼ cups with 10 tortilla strips and 1 tablespoon sour cream equals 356 cal., 14 g fat (3 g sat. fat), 55 mg chol., 644 mg sodium, 39 g carb., 8 g fiber, 21 g pro.*

SLOW-COOKED CHICKEN CHILI

Slow Cooker Split Pea Soup F

When I have leftover ham in the fridge, I always like to make this soup. Just throw the ingredients in the slow cooker, turn it on and dinner is done.

—**PAMELA CHAMBERS** WEST COLUMBIA, SC

PREP: 15 MIN. • COOK: 8 HOURS
MAKES: 8 SERVINGS

- 1 package (16 ounces) dried green split peas, rinsed
- 2 cups cubed fully cooked ham
- 1 large onion, chopped
- 1 cup julienned or chopped carrots
- 3 garlic cloves, minced
- ½ teaspoon dried rosemary, crushed
- ½ teaspoon dried thyme
- 1 carton (32 ounces) reduced-sodium chicken broth
- 2 cups water

In a 4- or 5-qt. slow cooker, combine all ingredients. Cover and cook on low for 8-10 hours or until peas are tender.

FREEZE OPTION *Freeze cooled soup in freezer containers. To use, thaw overnight in the refrigerator. Heat through in a saucepan over medium heat, stirring occasionally.*

PER SERVING *1 cup equals 260 cal., 2 g fat (1 g sat. fat), 21 mg chol., 728 mg sodium, 39 g carb., 15 g fiber, 23 g pro. **Diabetic Exchanges:** 2½ starch, 2 lean meat.*

All-Day Brisket with Potatoes

I think the slow cooker was invented with brisket in mind. And this sweet and savory version just melts in your mouth. I always buy "first-cut" or "flat-cut" brisket, which has far less fat than other cuts.

—**LANA GRYGA** GLEN FLORA, WI

PREP: 30 MIN. • COOK: 8 HOURS
MAKES: 8 SERVINGS

- 2 medium potatoes, peeled and cut into ¼-inch slices
- 2 celery ribs, sliced
- 1 fresh beef brisket (3 pounds)
- 1 tablespoon canola oil
- 1 large onion, sliced
- 2 garlic cloves, minced
- 1 can (12 ounces) beer
- ½ teaspoon beef bouillon granules
- ¾ cup stewed tomatoes
- ⅓ cup tomato paste
- ¼ cup red wine vinegar
- 3 tablespoons brown sugar
- 3 tablespoons Dijon mustard
- 3 tablespoons soy sauce
- 2 tablespoons molasses
- ½ teaspoon paprika
- ¼ teaspoon salt
- ⅛ teaspoon pepper
- 1 bay leaf

1. Place potatoes and celery in a 5-qt. slow cooker. Cut brisket in half. In a large skillet, brown beef in oil on all sides; transfer to slow cooker. In the same pan, saute onion until tender. Add garlic; cook 1 minute longer. Add to slow cooker.

2. Add beer and bouillon granules to skillet, stirring to loosen browned bits from pan; pour over meat. In a large bowl, combine the remaining ingredients; add to slow cooker.

3. Cover and cook on low 8-10 hours or until meat and vegetables are tender. Discard bay leaf. To serve, thinly slice across the grain.

NOTE *This is a fresh beef brisket, not corned beef.*

PER SERVING *1 serving equals 352 cal., 9 g fat (3 g sat. fat), 72 mg chol., 722 mg sodium, 25 g carb., 2 g fiber, 38 g pro. **Diabetic Exchanges:** 5 lean meat, 1 starch, 1 vegetable, ½ fat.*

ALL-DAY BRISKET WITH POTATOES

Tangy Orange Chicken Thighs C

This is a quick dish that results in tender, flavorful chicken in a tangy tomato-based sauce. The recipe can easily be doubled or tripled depending on the size of your slow cooker.

—DAHLIA ABRAMS DETROIT, MI

PREP: 20 MIN. • **COOK:** 5 HOURS
MAKES: 8 SERVINGS

- 2 cups sliced fresh carrots
- 1 can (14½ ounces) diced tomatoes, undrained
- 1 medium onion, chopped
- 1 can (6 ounces) tomato paste
- ½ cup orange juice
- 2 garlic cloves, minced
- 2 teaspoons dried basil
- 1½ teaspoons sugar
- ½ teaspoon dried oregano
- ½ teaspoon dried thyme
- ½ teaspoon dried rosemary, crushed
- ½ teaspoon pepper
- 2 teaspoons grated orange peel, divided
- 8 boneless skinless chicken thighs (about 2 pounds)
- 2 tablespoons lemon juice
- 4 bacon strips, cooked and crumbled

1. In a 3-qt. slow cooker, combine the first 12 ingredients. Stir in 1 teaspoon orange peel. Add chicken; spoon sauce over top. Cover and cook on low for 5-6 hours or until chicken is tender.
2. Remove to a serving platter. Stir lemon juice and remaining orange peel into sauce; pour over chicken. Sprinkle with bacon.

PER SERVING *1 chicken thigh with ½ cup sauce equals 248 cal., 10 g fat (3 g sat. fat), 80 mg chol., 236 mg sodium, 15 g carb., 3 g fiber, 25 g pro. Diabetic Exchanges: 3 lean meat, 1 starch.*

TOP TIP

I bake bacon strips at 350° until crisp, then drain on paper towels and store in single layers in a freezer container. It's easy to remove the number of strips I need for a quick breakfast, sandwich or salad.

—DALE H. HOLLAND, MI

Teriyaki Beef Stew

In the spirit of the old saying "Necessity is the mother of invention," I created this sweet-tangy beef recipe because I had a package of stew meat that needed to be used. After I spotted the ginger beer in the fridge, the rest is history. It's nice to have a new way to serve an affordable cut of meat.

—LESLIE SIMMS SHERMAN OAKS, CA

PREP: 20 MIN. • **COOK:** 6½ HOURS
MAKES: 8 SERVINGS

- 2 pounds beef stew meat
- 1 bottle (12 ounces) ginger beer or ginger ale
- ¼ cup teriyaki sauce
- 2 garlic cloves, minced
- 2 tablespoons sesame seeds
- 2 tablespoons cornstarch
- 2 tablespoons cold water
- 2 cups frozen peas, thawed
  Hot cooked rice, optional

1. In a large nonstick skillet, brown beef stew meat in batches. Transfer to a 3-qt. slow cooker.
2. In a small bowl, combine the ginger beer, teriyaki sauce, garlic and sesame seeds; pour over beef. Cover and cook on low for 6-8 hours or until the meat is tender.
3. Combine cornstarch and cold water until smooth; gradually stir into stew. Stir in peas. Cover and cook on high for 30 minutes or until thickened. Serve with rice if desired.

PER SERVING *1 cup stew (calculated without rice) equals 310 cal., 12 g fat (4 g sat. fat), 94 mg chol., 528 mg sodium, 17 g carb., 2 g fiber, 33 g pro. Diabetic Exchanges: 4 lean meat, 1 starch.*

TERIYAKI BEEF STEW

The first time I served these wraps was at the party following my son's baptism. I made a double batch and fed a crowd of 20!

—AMY LENTS GRAND FORKS, ND

Mexican Shredded Beef Wraps

PREP: 20 MIN. • **COOK:** 6 HOURS
MAKES: 6 SERVINGS

- 1 small onion, finely chopped
- 1 jalapeno pepper, seeded and minced
- 3 garlic cloves, minced
- 1 boneless beef chuck roast (2 to 3 pounds)
- ½ teaspoon salt
- ½ teaspoon pepper
- 1 can (8 ounces) tomato sauce
- ¼ cup lime juice
- 1 tablespoon chili powder
- 1 teaspoon ground cumin
- ¼ teaspoon cayenne pepper
- 6 flour or whole wheat tortillas (8 inches)
  Optional toppings: torn romaine, chopped tomatoes and sliced avocado

1. Place onion, jalapeno and garlic in a 4-qt. slow cooker. Sprinkle roast with salt and pepper; place over vegetables. In a small bowl, mix tomato sauce, lime juice, chili powder, cumin and cayenne; pour over roast.

2. Cook, covered, on low 6-8 hours or until meat is tender. Remove roast; cool slightly. Shred meat with two forks; return to slow cooker. Serve on tortillas with toppings of your choice.

NOTE *Wear disposable gloves when cutting hot peppers; the oils can burn skin. Avoid touching your face.*

PER SERVING *1 wrap (calculated without optional toppings) equals 428 cal., 18 g fat (6 g sat. fat), 98 mg*
chol., 696 mg sodium, 31 g carb., 1 g fiber, 35 g pro. ***Diabetic Exchanges:*** *5 lean meat, 2 starch.*

Slow Cooker French Dip Sandwiches

These sandwiches make a standout addition to any buffet line. Make sure to have plenty of small cups of broth for everyone to grab. Dipping perfection!
—**HOLLY NEUHARTH** MESA, AZ

PREP: 15 MIN. • **COOK:** 8 HOURS
MAKES: 12 SERVINGS

- 1 beef rump or bottom round roast (3 pounds)
- 1½ teaspoons onion powder
- 1½ teaspoons garlic powder
- ½ teaspoon Creole seasoning
- 1 carton (26 ounces) beef stock
- 12 whole wheat hoagie buns, split
- 6 ounces Havarti cheese, cut into 12 slices

1. Cut roast in half. Mix onion powder, garlic powder and Creole seasoning; rub onto beef. Place in a 5-qt. slow cooker; add stock. Cook, covered, on low 8-10 hours or until meat is tender.

2. Remove beef; cool slightly. Skim fat from cooking juices. When cool enough to handle, shred beef with two forks and return to slow cooker.

3. Place buns on ungreased baking sheets, cut side up. Using tongs, place beef on bun bottoms. Place cheese on the bun tops. Broil 3-4 in. from heat for 1-2 minutes or until cheese is melted. Close the sandwiches; serve with cooking juices.

NOTE *The following spices may be substituted for 1 teaspoon Creole seasoning: ¼ teaspoon each salt, garlic powder and paprika; and a pinch each of dried thyme, ground cumin and cayenne pepper.*

PER SERVING *1 sandwich with ⅓ cup au jus equals 456 cal., 14 g fat (5 g sat. fat), 81 mg chol., 722 mg sodium, 50 g carb., 7 g fiber, 35 g pro.*

SLOW COOKER FRENCH DIP SANDWICHES

Sweet Onion & Red Bell Pepper Topping F S C M

When the spring Vidalia onions hit the market, this is one of the first recipes I make. I use it on hot dogs, bruschetta, cream cheese and crackers. It is so tasty and versatile.

—**PAT HOCKETT** OCALA, FL

PREP: 20 MIN. • **COOK:** 4 HOURS
MAKES: 4 CUPS

- 4 **large sweet onions, thinly sliced (about 8 cups)**
- 4 **large sweet red peppers, thinly sliced (about 6 cups)**
- ½ **cup cider vinegar**
- ¼ **cup packed brown sugar**
- 2 **tablespoons canola oil**
- 2 **tablespoons honey**
- 2 **teaspoons celery seed**
- ¾ **teaspoon crushed red pepper flakes**
- ½ **teaspoon salt**

In a 5- or 6-qt. slow cooker, combine all ingredients. Cook, covered, on low for 4-5 hours or until vegetables are tender. Serve with a slotted spoon.
PER SERVING *¼ cup equals 76 cal., 2 g fat (trace sat. fat), 0 chol., 84 mg sodium, 14 g carb., 2 g fiber, 1 g pro. Diabetic Exchange: 1 starch.*

Butternut Squash with Whole Grain Pilaf F M

Fresh thyme really shines in this hearty slow-cooked side dish featuring tender butternut squash, nutritious whole grain pilaf and vitamin-packed baby spinach.

—*TASTE OF HOME TEST KITCHEN*

PREP: 15 MIN. • **COOK:** 4 HOURS
MAKES: 12 SERVINGS (¾ CUP EACH)

- 1 **medium butternut squash (about 3 pounds), cut into ½-inch cubes**
- 1 **cup uncooked whole grain brown and red rice blend**
- 1 **medium onion, chopped**
- ½ **cup water**
- 3 **garlic cloves, minced**
- 2 **teaspoons minced fresh thyme or ½ teaspoon dried thyme**
- ½ **teaspoon salt**
- ¼ **teaspoon pepper**
- 1 **can (14½ ounces) vegetable broth**
- 1 **package (6 ounces) fresh baby spinach**

APPLE PIE OATMEAL DESSERT

1. In a 4-qt. slow cooker, combine the first eight ingredients. Stir in broth.
2. Cook, covered, on low 4-5 hours or until grains are tender. Stir in spinach before serving.
NOTE *This recipe was tested with RiceSelect Royal Blend Whole Grain Texmati Brown & Red Rice with Barley and Rye. Look for it in the rice aisle.*
PER SERVING *¾ cup equals 97 cal., 1 g fat (trace sat. fat), 0 chol., 252 mg sodium, 22 g carb., 4 g fiber, 3 g pro. Diabetic Exchange: 1½ starch.*

Apple Pie Oatmeal Dessert M

This warm and comforting dessert brings back memories of time spent with my family around the kitchen table. I serve this dish with sweetened whipped cream or vanilla ice cream as a topper.

—**CAROL GREER** EARLVILLE, IL

PREP: 15 MIN. • **COOK:** 4 HOURS
MAKES: 6 SERVINGS

- 1 **cup quick-cooking oats**
- ½ **cup all-purpose flour**
- ⅓ **cup packed brown sugar**
- 2 **teaspoons baking powder**
- 1½ **teaspoons apple pie spice**
- ¼ **teaspoon salt**
- 3 **large eggs**
- 1⅔ **cups 2% milk, divided**
- 1½ **teaspoons vanilla extract**
- 3 **medium apples, peeled and finely chopped**
  Vanilla ice cream, optional

1. In a large bowl, whisk oats, flour, brown sugar, baking powder, pie spice and salt. In a small bowl, whisk eggs, 1 cup milk and vanilla until blended. Add to oat mixture, stirring just until moistened. Fold in apples.
2. Transfer to a greased 3-qt. slow cooker. Cook, covered, on low for 4-5 hours or until apples are tender and top is set.
3. Stir in remaining milk. Serve warm or cold, with ice cream if desired.
PER SERVING *¾ cup (calculated without ice cream) equals 238 cal., 5 g fat (2 g sat. fat), 111 mg chol., 306 mg sodium, 41 g carb., 3 g fiber, 8 g pro.*

TANGY LAMB TAGINE

Tangy Lamb Tagine

I love lamb stew but wanted to try something a bit different. So I created this recipe that uses Moroccan spices. It's a wonderful way to use lamb, and it's easy to make in the slow cooker. The stew tastes even better a day or two later, when the flavors have had a chance to meld.

—**BRIDGET KLUSMAN** OTSEGO, MI

PREP: 40 MIN. • **COOK:** 8 HOURS
MAKES: 8 SERVINGS

- 3 **pounds lamb stew meat, cut into 1½-inch cubes**
- 1 **teaspoon salt**
- 1 **teaspoon pepper**
- 4 **tablespoons olive oil, divided**
- 6 **medium carrots, sliced**
- 2 **medium onions, chopped**
- 6 **garlic cloves, minced**
- 2 **teaspoons grated lemon peel**
- ¼ **cup lemon juice**
- 1 **tablespoon minced fresh gingerroot**
- 1½ **teaspoons ground cinnamon**
- 1½ **teaspoons ground cumin**
- 1½ **teaspoons paprika**
- 2½ **cups reduced-sodium chicken broth**
- ¼ **cup sweet vermouth**
- ¼ **cup honey**
- ½ **cup pitted dates, chopped**
- ½ **cup sliced almonds, toasted**

1. Sprinkle lamb with salt and pepper. In a Dutch oven, brown meat in 2 tablespoons oil in batches. Using a slotted spoon, transfer to a 4- or 5-qt. slow cooker.

2. In the same pan, saute the carrots, onions, garlic and lemon peel in remaining oil until crisp-tender. Add lemon juice, ginger, cinnamon, cumin and paprika; cook and stir 2 minutes longer. Add to slow cooker.

3. Stir in the broth, vermouth, honey and dates. Cover and cook on low for

8-10 hours or until lamb is tender. Sprinkle with almonds.
PER SERVING *1¼ cups equals 440 cal., 19 g fat (4 g sat. fat), 111 mg chol., 620 mg sodium, 28 g carb., 4 g fiber, 38 g pro.*

Slow Cooker Mushroom Chicken & Peas

Some amazingly fresh mushrooms I found at our local farmers market inspired this recipe. When you start with the best ingredients, you can't go wrong.

—**JENNIFER TIDWELL** FAIR OAKS, CA

PREP: 10 MIN. • **COOK:** 3 HOURS 10 MIN.
MAKES: 4 SERVINGS

- 4 **boneless skinless chicken breast halves (6 ounces each)**
- 1 **envelope onion mushroom soup mix**
- 1 **cup water**
- ½ **pound sliced baby portobello mushrooms**
- 1 **medium onion, chopped**
- 4 **garlic cloves, minced**
- 2 **cups frozen peas, thawed**

1. Place chicken in a 3-qt. slow cooker. Sprinkle with soup mix, pressing to help seasonings adhere. Add water, mushrooms, onion and garlic.

2. Cook, covered, on low 3-4 hours or until chicken is tender (a thermometer inserted in chicken should read at least 165°). Stir in the peas; cook, covered, 10 minutes longer or until heated through.

PER SERVING *1 chicken breast half with ¾ cup vegetable mixture equals 292 cal., 5 g fat (1 g sat. fat), 94 mg chol., 566 mg sodium, 20 g carb., 5 g fiber, 41 g pro.* **Diabetic Exchanges:** *5 lean meat, 1 starch, 1 vegetable.*

SLOW COOKER MUSHROOM CHICKEN & PEAS

This is one of my favorite soup recipes to serve in the winter because it's super easy to make and fills the whole house with a wonderful aroma. My entire family loves it! —**BRANDY STANSBURY** EDNA, TX

GINGER CHICKEN NOODLE SOUP

Ginger Chicken Noodle Soup **F C**

PREP: 15 MIN. • **COOK:** 3½ HOURS
MAKES: 8 SERVINGS (2½ QUARTS)

- 1 **pound boneless skinless chicken breasts, cubed**
- 2 **medium carrots, shredded**
- 3 **tablespoons sherry or reduced-sodium chicken broth**
- 2 **tablespoons rice vinegar**
- 1 **tablespoon reduced-sodium soy sauce**
- 2 **to 3 teaspoons minced fresh gingerroot**
- ¼ **teaspoon pepper**
- 6 **cups reduced-sodium chicken broth**
- 1 **cup water**
- 2 **cups fresh snow peas, halved**
- 2 **ounces uncooked angel hair pasta, broken into thirds**

1. In a 5-qt. slow cooker, combine the first seven ingredients; stir in broth and water. Cook, covered, on low for 3-4 hours or until chicken is tender.
2. Stir in snow peas and pasta. Cook, covered, on low 30 minutes longer or until snow peas and pasta are tender.
PER SERVING *1¼ cups equals 126 cal., 2 g fat (trace sat. fat), 31 mg chol., 543 mg sodium, 11 g carb., 2 g fiber, 16 g pro.* **Diabetic Exchanges:** *2 lean meat, 1 starch.*

Parsley Smashed Potatoes **F**

I love potatoes, but I don't like the work involved in making mashed potatoes from scratch. I came up with this side dish that's really easy thanks to my slow cooker.
—**KATIE HAGY** BLACKSBURG, SC

PREP: 20 MIN. • **COOK:** 6 HOURS
MAKES: 8 SERVINGS

- 16 **small red potatoes (about 2 pounds)**
- 1 **celery rib, sliced**
- 1 **medium carrot, sliced**
- ¼ **cup finely chopped onion**
- 2 **cups chicken broth**
- 1 **tablespoon minced fresh parsley**
- 1½ **teaspoons salt, divided**
- 1 **teaspoon pepper, divided**
- 1 **garlic clove, minced**
- 2 **tablespoons butter, melted**
  Additional minced fresh parsley

1. Place potatoes, celery, carrot and onion in a 4-qt. slow cooker. In a small bowl, mix broth, parsley, 1 teaspoon salt, ½ teaspoon pepper and garlic; pour over vegetables. Cook, covered, on low for 6-8 hours or until potatoes are tender.
2. Transfer potatoes from slow cooker to a 15x10x1-in. pan; discard cooking liquid and vegetables. Using the bottom of a measuring cup, flatten potatoes slightly. Transfer to a large bowl; drizzle with butter. Sprinkle with remaining salt and pepper; toss to coat. Sprinkle with additional parsley.
PER SERVING *2 smashed potatoes equals 114 cal., 3 g fat (2 g sat. fat), 8 mg chol., 190 mg sodium, 20 g carb., 2 g fiber, 2 g pro.* **Diabetic Exchanges:** *1 starch, ½ fat.*

PARSLEY SMASHED POTATOES

99

105

103

Beef Entrees

❝My mom often cooked giant zucchini that she grew in her garden. I adapted this recipe from one of her favorite weeknight meals. Although I love fresh-picked zucchini, ones from the grocery store work great, too.❞

—**SUSAN PETERSON** BLAINE, MN
about her recipe, Beef & Bulgur-Stuffed Zucchini Boats, on page 97

Easy & Elegant Tenderloin Roast ⓒ

A friend of mine served this tenderloin several years ago and passed along the recipe to me. The trick is not to skimp on the seasonings. You'll get predictably delicious results every time.

—**MARY KANDELL** HURON, OH

PREP: 10 MIN. • **BAKE:** 50 MIN. + STANDING
MAKES: 12 SERVINGS

- 1 beef tenderloin (5 pounds)
- 2 tablespoons olive oil
- 4 garlic cloves, minced
- 2 teaspoons sea salt
- 1½ teaspoons coarsely ground pepper

1. Preheat oven to 425°. Place roast on a rack in a shallow roasting pan. In a small bowl, mix the oil, garlic, salt and pepper; rub over roast.
2. Roast for 50-70 minutes or until meat reaches desired doneness (for medium-rare, a thermometer should read 145°; medium, 160°; well-done, 170°). Remove from oven; tent with foil. Let the meat stand 15 minutes before slicing.

PER SERVING *5 ounces cooked beef equals 294 cal., 13 g fat (5 g sat. fat), 82 mg chol., 394 mg sodium, 1 g carb., trace fiber, 40 g pro.* **Diabetic Exchanges:** *5 lean meat, ½ fat.*

Tasty Tacos FAST FIX ▶

I use taco seasoning made from scratch with pantry staples to turn my dinners into all-out fiestas. Add your favorite toppings, and dinner is served!

—**REBECCA LEVESQUE** ST. GEORGE, NB

START TO FINISH: 30 MIN.
MAKES: 4 SERVINGS

- 1 pound lean ground beef (90% lean)
- 1 medium onion, finely chopped
- 1 garlic clove, minced
- ½ cup water
- 1 tablespoon chili powder
- 1½ teaspoons ground cumin
- ½ teaspoon salt
- ½ teaspoon paprika
- ½ teaspoon pepper
- ¼ teaspoon dried oregano
- ¼ teaspoon crushed red pepper flakes
- 8 taco shells, warmed

KOREAN BEEF AND RICE

Optional toppings: shredded lettuce, chopped tomatoes, sliced green onions and shredded cheddar cheese

1. In a large skillet, cook beef, onion and garlic over medium heat until meat is no longer pink; drain. Stir in the water and seasonings. Bring to a boil. Reduce heat; simmer, uncovered, for 5-10 minutes or until thickened.
2. Spoon beef mixture into taco shells. Serve with toppings of your choice.

PER SERVING *2 tacos (calculated without optional toppings) equals 306 cal., 15 g fat (5 g sat. fat), 71 mg chol., 468 mg sodium, 19 g carb., 3 g fiber, 24 g pro.* **Diabetic Exchanges:** *3 lean meat, 1 starch, 1 fat.*

Korean Beef and Rice FAST FIX ▶

A friend raved about beef cooked in soy sauce and ginger, so I tried it. It's delicious! Dazzle the table with this tasty version of beef and rice.

—**BETSY KING** DULUTH, MN

START TO FINISH: 15 MIN.
MAKES: 4 SERVINGS

- 1 pound lean ground beef (90% lean)
- 3 garlic cloves, minced
- ¼ cup packed brown sugar
- ¼ cup reduced-sodium soy sauce
- 2 teaspoons sesame oil
- ¼ teaspoon ground ginger
- ¼ teaspoon crushed red pepper flakes
- ¼ teaspoon pepper
- 2⅔ cups hot cooked brown rice
- 3 green onions, thinly sliced

1. In a large skillet, cook beef and garlic over medium heat 6-8 minutes or until the meat is no longer pink, breaking up beef into crumbles. Meanwhile, in a small bowl, mix brown sugar, soy sauce, oil and seasonings.
2. Stir sauce into beef; heat through. Serve with rice. Sprinkle with sliced green onions.

FREEZE OPTION *Freeze the cooled meat mixture in freezer containers. To use, partially thaw in refrigerator overnight. Heat through in a saucepan, stirring occasionally.*

PER SERVING *½ cup beef mixture with ⅔ cup rice equals 413 cal., 13 g fat (4 g sat. fat), 71 mg chol., 647 mg sodium, 46 g carb., 3 g fiber, 27 g pro.* **Diabetic Exchanges:** *3 starch, 3 lean meat, ½ fat.*

Beef & Bulgur-Stuffed Zucchini Boats

My Mom often cooked giant zucchini that she grew in her garden. I adapted this recipe from one of her favorite weeknight meals. Although I love fresh-picked zucchini, ones from the grocery store work great, too.

—SUSAN PETERSON BLAINE, MN

PREP: 35 MIN. • **BAKE:** 30 MIN.
MAKES: 4 SERVINGS

- 4 medium zucchini
- 1 pound lean ground beef (90% lean)
- 1 large onion, finely chopped
- 1 small sweet red pepper, chopped
- 1½ cups tomato sauce
- ½ cup bulgur
- ¼ teaspoon pepper
- ½ cup salsa
- ½ cup shredded reduced-fat cheddar cheese

1. Preheat oven to 350°. Cut each zucchini lengthwise in half. Scoop out pulp, leaving a ¼-in. shell; chop pulp.
2. In a large skillet, cook beef, onion and red pepper over medium heat for 6-8 minutes or until meat is no longer pink, breaking into crumbles; drain. Stir in the tomato sauce, bulgur, pepper and zucchini pulp. Bring to a boil. Reduce the heat and simmer, uncovered, for 12-15 minutes or until bulgur is tender. Stir in salsa. Spoon into zucchini shells.
3. Place in a 13x9-in. baking dish coated with cooking spray. Bake, covered, 20 minutes. Sprinkle with cheddar cheese. Bake, uncovered, for 10-15 minutes longer or until zucchini is tender and filling is heated through.
PER SERVING *2 stuffed zucchini halves equals 361 cal., 13 g fat (6 g sat. fat), 81 mg chol., 714 mg sodium, 31 g carb., 7 g fiber, 32 g pro.* **Diabetic Exchanges:** *4 lean meat, 2 vegetable, 1 starch.*

TOP TIP

Using lean ground beef in the zucchini boats instead of beef that's 80% lean saves 45 calories per 4-ounce serving of beef. Lean ground beef is also 29% lower in saturated fat.

Orange Beef Lettuce Wraps

Here's a lighter version of a restaurant favorite. I also recommend trying these wraps with ground chicken or turkey.

—ROBIN HAAS CRANSTON, RI

PREP: 20 MIN. • **COOK:** 20 MIN.
MAKES: 8 SERVINGS

SAUCE
- ¼ cup rice vinegar
- 3 tablespoons water
- 3 tablespoons orange marmalade
- 1 tablespoon sugar
- 1 tablespoon reduced-sodium soy sauce
- 2 garlic cloves, minced
- 1 teaspoon Sriracha Asian hot chili sauce

WRAPS
- 1½ pounds lean ground beef (90% lean)
- 2 garlic cloves, minced
- 2 teaspoons minced fresh gingerroot
- ¼ cup reduced-sodium soy sauce
- 2 tablespoons orange juice
- 1 tablespoon sugar
- 1 tablespoon orange marmalade
- ¼ teaspoon crushed red pepper flakes
- 2 teaspoons cornstarch
- ¼ cup cold water
- 2 cups cooked brown rice
- 8 Bibb or Boston lettuce leaves
- 1 cup shredded carrots
- 3 green onions, thinly sliced

1. In a small bowl, combine sauce ingredients; set aside.
2. In a large skillet, cook beef, garlic and ginger over medium heat for 8-10 minutes or until no longer pink, breaking into crumbles; drain. Stir in the soy sauce, orange juice, sugar, marmalade and pepper flakes. Mix cornstarch and water; stir into pan. Cook and stir for 1-2 minutes or until sauce is thickened.
3. Serve with rice in lettuce leaves. Top with carrots and green onions; drizzle with sauce.
PER SERVING *1 wrap equals 250 cal., 8 g fat (3 g sat. fat), 53 mg chol., 462 mg sodium, 26 g carb., 2 g fiber, 19 g pro.* **Diabetic Exchanges:** *2 starch, 2 lean meat.*

ORANGE BEEF LETTUCE WRAPS

SUBLIME LIME BEEF

Sublime Lime Beef **FAST FIX** ▶

It's fun to watch the happy reactions of others when they try my lime beef kabobs for the first time. They're so good it's hard not to smile.

—**DIEP NGUYEN** HANFORD, CA

START TO FINISH: 25 MIN.
MAKES: 4 SERVINGS

- ⅓ cup lime juice
- 2 teaspoons sugar
- 2 garlic cloves, minced
- 1 beef top sirloin steak (1 inch thick and 1 pound)
- 1½ teaspoons pepper
- ¾ teaspoon salt
- 2 tablespoons unsalted dry roasted peanuts, chopped
- 3 cups hot cooked brown rice

1. In a small bowl, mix the lime juice, sugar and garlic until blended; set aside. Cut steak into 2x1x¾-in. pieces; toss with pepper and salt. Thread beef onto four metal or soaked wooden skewers.

2. Grill kabobs, covered, over medium heat or broil 4 in. from heat for 2-4 minutes on each side or until the beef reaches desired doneness. Add the peanuts to sauce; serve with kabobs and rice.

PER SERVING *1 kabob with ¾ cup rice and 1 tablespoon sauce equals 352 cal., 8 g fat (2 g sat. fat), 46 mg chol., 502 mg sodium, 39 g carb., 3 g fiber, 29 g pro.* **Diabetic Exchanges:** *3 lean meat, 2½ starch.*

Spinach & Feta Burgers

Turkey burgers have their fans, but we prefer burgers of ground beef, spinach and feta. We serve them on toasted buns with lettuce, tomato and tzatziki.

—**SUSAN STETZEL** GAINESVILLE, NY

PREP: 25 MIN. • **GRILL:** 15 MIN.
MAKES: 8 SERVINGS

- 1 tablespoon olive oil
- 2 shallots, chopped
- 2½ cups fresh baby spinach, coarsely chopped
- 3 garlic cloves, minced
- ⅔ cup crumbled feta cheese
- ¾ teaspoon Greek seasoning
- ½ teaspoon salt
- ¼ teaspoon pepper
- 2 pounds lean ground beef (90% lean)
- 8 whole wheat hamburger buns, split
    Optional toppings: refrigerated tzatziki sauce, fresh baby spinach and tomato slices

1. In a large skillet, heat the oil over medium-high heat. Add shallots; cook and stir 1-2 minutes or until tender. Add the spinach and garlic; cook for 30-45 seconds or until the spinach is wilted. Transfer to a large bowl and cool slightly.

2. Stir feta cheese and seasonings into the spinach. Add beef; mix lightly but thoroughly. Shape into eight ½-in.-thick patties.

3. Grill burgers, covered, over medium heat 6-8 minutes on each side or until a thermometer reads 160°. Grill buns over medium heat, cut side down, for 30-60 seconds or until toasted. Serve burgers on buns with toppings if desired.

FREEZE OPTION *Place patties on a plastic wrap-lined baking sheet; wrap and freeze until firm. Remove from pan and transfer to a resealable plastic freezer bag; return to freezer. To use, cook fthe rozen patties as directed, increasing time as necessary for a thermometer to read 160°.*

PER SERVING *1 burger (calculated without optional toppings) equals 343 cal., 15 g fat (5 g sat. fat), 76 mg chol., 636 mg sodium, 25 g carb., 4 g fiber, 28 g pro.* **Diabetic Exchanges:** *3 lean meat, 2 fat, 1½ starch.*

SPINACH & FETA BURGERS

> Dirty rice from a restaurant or box can have a lot of sodium and fat. Here's a hearty, healthy way I like to trim it.
> —RAQUEL HAGGARD EDMOND, OK

CAJUN BEEF & RICE

Cajun Beef & Rice FAST FIX

START TO FINISH: 30 MIN.
MAKES: 4 SERVINGS

- 1 **pound lean ground beef (90% lean)**
- 3 **celery ribs, chopped**
- 1 **small green pepper, chopped**
- 1 **small sweet red pepper, chopped**
- ¼ **cup chopped onion**
- 2 **cups water**
- 1 **cup instant brown rice**
- 1 **tablespoon minced fresh parsley**
- 1 **tablespoon Worcestershire sauce**
- 2 **teaspoons reduced-sodium beef bouillon granules**
- 1 **teaspoon Cajun seasoning**
- ¼ **teaspoon crushed red pepper flakes**
- ¼ **teaspoon pepper**
- ⅛ **teaspoon garlic powder**

1. In a large skillet, cook beef, celery, green and red peppers and onion over medium heat 8-10 minutes or until beef is no longer pink, breaking up beef into crumbles; drain.
2. Stir in the remaining ingredients. Bring to a boil. Reduce heat; simmer, covered, for 12-15 minutes or until rice is tender.
PER SERVING *1½ cups equals 291 cal., 10 g fat (4 g sat. fat), 71 mg chol., 422 mg sodium, 23 g carb., 2 g fiber, 25 g pro.* **Diabetic Exchanges:** *3 lean meat, 1 starch, 1 vegetable.*

Spicy Beef & Pepper Stir-Fry C

Think of this stir-fry as your chance to play with heat and spice. I balance the beef with coconut milk and a spritz of lime.
—JOY ZACHARIA CLEARWATER, FL

PREP: 20 MIN. + STANDING
COOK: 10 MIN.
MAKES: 4 SERVINGS

- 1 **pound beef top sirloin steak, cut into thin strips**
- 1 **tablespoon minced fresh gingerroot**
- 3 **garlic cloves, minced, divided**
- ¼ **teaspoon pepper**
- ¾ **teaspoon salt, divided**
- 1 **cup light coconut milk**
- 2 **tablespoons sugar**
- 1 **tablespoon Sriracha Asian hot chili sauce**
- ½ **teaspoon grated lime peel**
- 2 **tablespoons lime juice**
- 2 **tablespoons canola oil, divided**
- 1 **large sweet red pepper, cut into thin strips**
- ½ **medium red onion, thinly sliced**
- 1 **jalapeno pepper, seeded and thinly sliced**
- 4 **cups fresh baby spinach**
- 2 **green onions, thinly sliced**
- 2 **tablespoons chopped fresh cilantro**

1. In a large bowl, toss the beef with ginger, 2 cloves garlic, pepper and ½ teaspoon salt; let stand 15 minutes. In a small bowl, whisk coconut milk, sugar, chili sauce, lime peel, lime juice and remaining salt until blended.
2. In a large skillet, heat 1 tablespoon oil over medium-high heat. Add beef; stir-fry 2-3 minutes or until no longer pink. Remove from pan.
3. Stir-fry red pepper, red onion, jalapeno and remaining garlic in remaining oil just until vegetables are crisp-tender. Stir in coconut milk mixture; heat through. Stir in spinach and beef; cook until spinach is wilted and beef is heated through. Sprinkle with onions and cilantro.
PER SERVING *¾ cup equals 312 cal., 16 g fat (5 g sat. fat), 46 mg chol., 641 mg sodium, 15 g carb., 2 g fiber, 26 g pro.* **Diabetic Exchanges:** *3 lean meat, 2 fat, 1 vegetable, ½ starch.*

Open-Faced Roast Beef Sandwiches C FAST FIX

Arugula brings the zing to this sandwich. I usually make extras because most people who taste them want seconds.
—MARY PRICE YOUNGSTOWN, OH

START TO FINISH: 15 MIN.
MAKES: 8 SERVINGS

- 1 **pound sliced deli roast beef**
- 8 **slices ciabatta bread (½ inch thick)**
- 2 **cups fresh arugula**
- 2 **cups torn romaine**
- 4 **teaspoons olive oil**
- 1 **tablespoon lemon juice**
- 1 **tablespoon white wine vinegar**
- 1½ **teaspoons prepared horseradish**

Place roast beef on ciabatta slices. In a large bowl, combine the arugula and romaine. Whisk the remaining ingredients; drizzle over greens and toss to coat. Arrange over the beef; serve immediately.
PER SERVING *1 open-faced sandwich equals 150 cal., 5 g fat (1 g sat. fat), 32 mg chol., 422 mg sodium, 14 g carb., 1 g fiber, 14 g pro.* **Diabetic Exchanges:** *2 lean meat, 1 starch, ½ fat.*

MINI BARBECUE MEAT LOAVES

Mini Barbecue Meat Loaves C

I gave classic meat loaf a tasty twist by adding barbecue sauce. My kids usually get bored with beef entrees, but they keep asking for this dish. It's become a staple.
—VICKI SMITH OKEECHOBEE, FL

PREP: 15 MIN. • **BAKE:** 25 MIN.
MAKES: 1 DOZEN

- ⅔ cup barbecue sauce
- ⅓ cup salsa
- 2 teaspoons Worcestershire sauce
- 1 cup dry bread crumbs
- 1 small onion, finely chopped
- 1 small green pepper, finely chopped
- 1 large egg, lightly beaten
- 2 tablespoons Montreal steak seasoning
- 1½ pounds lean ground beef (90% lean)

1. Preheat oven to 400°. In a large bowl, mix the barbecue sauce, salsa and Worcestershire sauce; reserve ½ cup mixture for topping. Add the bread crumbs, onion, pepper, egg and steak seasoning to remaining sauce mixture. Add ground beef; mix lightly but thoroughly.

2. Place ⅓ cup beef mixture into each of 12 greased muffin cups. Spoon reserved sauce mixture over tops.

3. Bake 25-30 minutes or until a thermometer reads 160°. Let stand 5 minutes before removing from pan.
PER SERVING *1 mini meat loaf equals 163 calories, 6 g fat (2 g sat. fat), 51 mg chol., 633 mg sodium, 14 g carb., 1 g fiber, 13 g pro.* **Diabetic Exchanges:** *2 lean meat, 1 starch.*

Italian Beef and Shells FAST FIX

I fix this supper when I'm pressed for time. It's as tasty as it is fast. Team it with salad, bread and fresh fruit for a healthy meal.
—MIKE TCHOU PEPPER PIKE, OH

START TO FINISH: 30 MIN.
MAKES: 4 SERVINGS

- 1½ cups uncooked medium pasta shells
- 1 pound lean ground beef (90% lean)
- 1 small onion, chopped
- 1 garlic clove, minced
- 1 jar (24 ounces) marinara sauce
- 1 small yellow summer squash, quartered and sliced
- 1 small zucchini, quartered and sliced
- ¼ cup dry red wine or reduced-sodium beef broth
- ½ teaspoon salt
- ½ teaspoon Italian seasoning
- ½ teaspoon pepper

1. Cook pasta according to package directions.

2. Meanwhile, in a Dutch oven, cook the beef, onion and garlic over medium heat until meat is no longer pink; drain. Stir in marinara sauce, squash, zucchini, wine and seasonings. Bring to a boil. Reduce heat; simmer, uncovered, for 10-15 minutes or until thickened. Drain pasta; stir into beef mixture and heat through.
PER SERVING *1¾ cups equals 396 cal., 10 g fat (4 g sat. fat), 71 mg chol., 644 mg sodium, 45 g carb., 5 g fiber, 29 g pro.* **Diabetic Exchanges:** *3 starch, 3 lean meat.*

Grilled Beef Chimichangas

I created this recipe when I didn't have the ingredients on hand for my go-to dish. After I made these chimis on the grill, they became my new favorite!
—JACKIE BURNS KETTLE FALLS, WA

PREP: 25 MIN. • **GRILL:** 10 MIN.
MAKES: 6 SERVINGS

- 1 pound lean ground beef (90% lean)
- 1 small onion, chopped
- 2 garlic cloves, minced
- 1 can (4 ounces) chopped green chilies
- ¼ cup salsa
- ¼ teaspoon ground cumin
- 6 whole wheat tortillas (8 inches)
- ¾ cup shredded Monterey Jack cheese
    Reduced-fat sour cream and guacamole, optional

1. In a large skillet, cook beef, onion and garlic over medium heat for 6-8 minutes or until meat is no longer pink and onion is tender, breaking up beef into crumbles; drain. Stir in chilies, salsa and cumin.

2. Spoon ½ cup beef mixture across the center of each tortilla; top with 2 tablespoons cheese. Fold bottom and sides of tortilla over filling and roll up.

3. Place chimichangas on grill rack, seam side down. Grill, covered, over medium-low heat 10-12 minutes or until crisp and browned, turning once. If desired, serve chimichangas with sour cream and guacamole.
PER SERVING *1 chimichanga (calculated without sour cream and guacamole) equals 295 cal., 12 g fat (5 g sat. fat), 60 mg chol., 370 mg sodium, 25 g carb., 4 g fiber, 22 g pro.* **Diabetic Exchanges:** *2 lean meat, 1½ starch, 1 fat.*

GRILLED BEEF CHIMICHANGAS

Steaks with Poblano Relish S C

Spice up mealtime with these juicy beef tenderloin steaks topped with a zippy Southwest-style poblano pepper and garlic relish.

—BILLIE MOSS WALNUT CREEK, CA

PREP: 10 MIN. + STANDING • **COOK:** 10 MIN.
MAKES: 2 SERVINGS

- ½ poblano or Anaheim pepper, stem and seeds removed
- 1 unpeeled garlic clove
- 1 teaspoon minced fresh cilantro
- ½ teaspoon ground cumin, divided
- ⅛ teaspoon plus ¼ teaspoon chili powder, divided
- 2 beef tenderloin steaks (4 ounces each)
- 1 teaspoon olive oil
  Dash salt and pepper

1. Broil the pepper half and garlic clove 4 in. from heat until skin on the pepper blisters, about 10-12 minutes. Immediately place in a bowl; cover and let stand for 15-20 minutes.

2. Peel pepper and garlic skin; finely chop and place in a small bowl. Stir in the cilantro, ¼ teaspoon cumin and ⅛ teaspoon chili powder; set aside.

3. Rub steaks with oil. Combine the salt, pepper and remaining cumin and chili powder; rub over steaks.

4. In a nonstick skillet, cook steaks over medium-high heat for 5-7 minutes on each side or until meat reaches desired doneness (for medium-rare, a meat thermometer should read 145°; medium, 160°; well-done, 170°). Let stand for 5 minutes. Serve with poblano relish.

NOTE *Wear disposable gloves when cutting hot peppers; the oils can burn skin. Avoid touching your face.*

PER SERVING *1 steak with 2 tablespoons relish equals 208 cal., 11 g fat (3 g sat. fat), 71 mg chol., 133 mg sodium, 3 g carb., 1 g fiber, 24 g pro.* **Diabetic Exchanges:** *3 lean meat, ½ fat.*

POWER LASAGNA

Power Lasagna

When my husband and I wanted to live healthier, our first step was to eat more power foods, such as whole grains, fresh veggies and protein. Combined with our love for Italian food, this tasty lasagna is one of the nutritious results.

—JENNIFER YADEN RICHMOND, KY

PREP: 30 MIN. • **BAKE:** 40 MIN. + STANDING
MAKES: 8 SERVINGS

- 9 whole wheat lasagna noodles
- 1 pound lean ground beef (90% lean)
- 1 medium zucchini, finely chopped
- 1 medium onion, finely chopped
- 1 medium green pepper, finely chopped
- 3 garlic cloves, minced
- 1 jar (24 ounces) meatless pasta sauce
- 1 can (14½ ounces) no-salt-added diced tomatoes, drained
- ½ cup loosely packed basil leaves, chopped
- 2 tablespoons ground flaxseed
- 5 teaspoons Italian seasoning
- ¼ teaspoon pepper
- 1 carton (15 ounces) fat-free ricotta cheese
- 1 package (10 ounces) frozen chopped spinach, thawed and squeezed dry
- 1 large egg, lightly beaten
- 2 tablespoons white balsamic vinegar
- 2 cups (8 ounces) shredded part-skim mozzarella cheese
- ¼ cup grated Parmesan cheese

1. Preheat oven to 350°. Cook noodles according to package directions. Meanwhile, in a 6-qt. stockpot, cook beef, zucchini, onion and green pepper over medium heat until the beef is no longer pink, breaking up beef into crumbles. Add garlic; cook 1 minute longer. Drain.

2. Stir in pasta sauce, diced tomatoes, basil, flax, Italian seasoning and pepper; heat though. Drain noodles and rinse in cold water.

3. In a small bowl, mix ricotta cheese, spinach, egg and vinegar. Spread 1 cup meat mixture into a 13x9-in. baking dish coated with cooking spray. Layer with three noodles, 2 cups of meat mixture, 1¼ cups of ricotta cheese mixture and ⅔ cup mozzarella cheese. Repeat layers. Top with the remaining noodles, meat mixture and mozzarella cheese; sprinkle with Parmesan cheese.

4. Bake, covered, for 30 minutes. Uncover; bake 10-15 minutes longer or until cheese is melted. Let stand for 10 minutes before serving.

PER SERVING *1 piece equals 392 cal., 12 g fat (5 g sat. fat), 89 mg chol., 691 mg sodium, 39 g carb., 8 g fiber, 32 g pro.* **Diabetic Exchanges:** *3 lean meat, 2 starch, 1 vegetable, 1 fat.*

Easy Marinated Flank Steak [C]

I got this recipe from a friend 15 years ago. Even now, when my family makes steak on the grill, this is the recipe we use. It's a must when we're having company.

—**DEBBIE BONCZEK** TARIFFVILLE, CT

PREP: 10 MIN. + MARINATING
GRILL: 15 MIN. • **MAKES:** 8 SERVINGS

- 3 tablespoons ketchup
- 1 tablespoon chopped onion
- 1 tablespoon canola oil
- 1 teaspoon brown sugar
- 1 teaspoon Worcestershire sauce
- 1 garlic clove, minced
- ⅛ teaspoon pepper
- 1 beef flank steak (about 2 pounds)

1. In a large resealable plastic bag, combine the first seven ingredients. Add beef; seal bag and turn to coat. Refrigerate 8 hours or overnight.

2. Drain beef, discarding marinade. Moisten a paper towel with cooking oil; using long-handled tongs, rub on grill rack to coat lightly.

3. Grill beef, covered, over medium heat or broil 4 in. from heat for 6-8 minutes on each side or until meat reaches desired doneness (for medium-rare, a thermometer should read 145°; medium, 160°; well-done, 170°). To serve, thinly slice across the grain.

FREEZE OPTION *Freeze beef with marinade in a resealable plastic freezer bag. To use, thaw in refrigerator overnight. Drain beef, discarding marinade. Grill as directed.*
PER SERVING *3 ounces cooked beef equals 192 cal., 10 g fat (4 g sat. fat), 54 mg chol., 145 mg sodium, 2 g carb., trace fiber, 22 g pro.* **Diabetic Exchange:** *3 lean meat.*

Pepper Steak with Potatoes [FAST FIX]

I added potatoes to an Asian pepper steak recipe. Now this meaty skillet dish is a favorite in my house full of hungry guys.

—**KRISTINE MARRA** CLIFTON PARK, NY

START TO FINISH: 30 MIN.
MAKES: 6 SERVINGS

- 1½ pounds red potatoes (about 5 medium), sliced

- ½ cup water
- 1 cup beef broth
- 4 teaspoons cornstarch
- ⅛ teaspoon pepper
- 2 tablespoons olive oil, divided
- 1 beef top sirloin steak (1 pound), thinly sliced
- 1 garlic clove, minced
- 1 medium green pepper, julienned
- 1 small onion, chopped

1. Place potatoes and water in a large microwave-safe dish. Microwave, covered, on high for 5-7 minutes or until tender.

2. Meanwhile, in a small bowl, mix the broth, cornstarch and pepper until smooth. In a large skillet, heat 1 tablespoon oil over medium-high heat. Add beef; cook and stir for 2-3 minutes or until no longer pink. Add garlic; cook 1 minute longer. Remove beef from pan.

3. In same pan, heat remaining oil. Add green pepper and onion; cook and stir until vegetables are crisp-tender. Stir cornstarch mixture and add to pan. Bring to a boil; cook and stir 1-2 minutes or until sauce is thickened. Add potatoes and beef to pan; heat through.

NOTE *This recipe was tested in a 1,100-watt microwave.*
PER SERVING *1 cup equals 277 cal., 10 g fat (2 g sat. fat), 55 mg chol., 179 mg sodium, 27 g carb., 3 g fiber, 23 g pro.* **Diabetic Exchanges:** *2 meat, 2 vegetable, 1 starch.*

Italian Crumb-Crusted Beef Roast [C]

Italian-style panko crumbs and seasoning give this roast beef a special touch—it's a nice, effortless weeknight meal. That way, you can put your energy into relaxing.

—**MARIA REGAKIS** SAUGUS, MA

PREP: 10 MIN.
BAKE: 1¾ HOURS + STANDING
MAKES: 8 SERVINGS

- 1 beef sirloin tip roast (3 pounds)
- ¼ teaspoon salt
- ¾ cup Italian-style panko (Japanese) bread crumbs
- ¼ cup mayonnaise
- 3 tablespoons dried minced onion
- ½ teaspoon Italian seasoning
- ¼ teaspoon pepper

1. Preheat oven to 325°. Place roast on a rack in a shallow roasting pan; sprinkle with salt. In a small bowl, mix remaining ingredients; press onto top and sides of roast.

2. Roast for 1¾-2¼ hours or until meat reaches desired doneness (for medium-rare, a thermometer should read 145°; medium, 160°; well-done, 170°). Remove roast from oven; tent with foil. Let stand for 10 minutes before slicing.

PER SERVING *5 ounces of cooked beef equals 319 cal., 15 g fat (3 g sat. fat), 111 mg chol., 311 mg sodium, 7 g carb., trace fiber, 35 g pro.* **Diabetic Exchanges:** *5 lean meat, 1 fat, ½ starch.*

ITALIAN CRUMB-CRUSTED BEEF ROAST

GLUTEN-FREE SKILLET PASTA

Gluten-Free Skillet Pasta

This is always a good recipe to make when short on time. Lovely herb accents enhance this easy stovetop spaghetti.
—**MARV SALTER** WEST HILLS, CA

PREP: 15 MIN. • **COOK:** 20 MIN.
MAKES: 2 SERVINGS

- ½ **pound lean ground beef (90% lean)**
- 1 **cup sliced fresh mushrooms**
- ⅓ **cup chopped onion**
- 1 **garlic clove, minced**
- 1 **cup gluten-free reduced-sodium beef broth**
- ⅔ **cup water**
- ⅓ **cup tomato paste**
- ½ **teaspoon dried basil**
- ½ **teaspoon dried oregano**
- ⅛ **teaspoon pepper**
- 3 **ounces uncooked gluten-free spaghetti, broken in half**
- 2 **teaspoons grated Parmesan cheese**

1. In a large skillet, cook the beef, mushrooms, onion and garlic over medium heat until meat is no longer pink and vegetables are tender; drain.
2. Stir in the broth, water, tomato paste, seasonings and spaghetti. Bring to a boil. Reduce heat; cover and simmer for 15-20 minutes or until the spaghetti is tender. Sprinkle with grated cheese.
NOTE *Read all ingredient labels for possible gluten content prior to use. Ingredient formulas can change, and production facilities vary among brands. If you're concerned that your brand may contain gluten, contact the company.*
PER SERVING *1½ cups equals 412 cal., 11 g fat (4 g sat. fat), 75 mg chol., 335 mg sodium, 46 g carb., 4 g fiber, 31 g pro.* **Diabetic Exchanges:** *3 lean meat, 2½ starch, 2 vegetable.*

Fajita Skillet FAST FIX ▶

This amazing recipe gives you authentic fajita flavor in 30 minutes without using a mix! It's a real treat that's sure to have everyone coming back for seconds.
—***TASTE OF HOME*** **TEST KITCHEN**

START TO FINISH: 30 MIN.
MAKES: 4 SERVINGS

- 2 **flour tortillas (10 inches), cut into ½-inch strips**
- 3 **tablespoons olive oil, divided**
- ½ **pound boneless skinless chicken breasts, cut into strips**
- ½ **pound beef top sirloin steak, cut into thin strips**
- 1 **medium green pepper, sliced**
- 1 **small onion, sliced**
- 2 **tablespoons soy sauce**
- 2 **teaspoons brown sugar**
- ½ **teaspoon chili powder**
- ½ **teaspoon ground cumin**
- ¼ **teaspoon pepper**
- 1 **teaspoon cornstarch**
- 2 **tablespoons lime juice**
- 1 **cup cubed fresh pineapple**
- 1 **medium tomato, coarsely chopped**

1. In a large skillet, fry tortilla strips in 2 tablespoons of oil on both sides until golden brown. Drain on paper towels.
2. In the same skillet, cook chicken, beef, green pepper, onion, soy sauce, brown sugar, chili powder, cumin and pepper in remaining oil 3-4 minutes or until chicken is no longer pink.
3. In a small bowl, combine the cornstarch and lime juice until smooth; add to the pan. Bring liquid to a boil; cook and stir for 1 minute or until thickened. Stir in the pineapple and tomato; heat through. Serve with tortilla strips.
PER SERVING *1¾ cup equals 390 cal., 17 g fat (3 g sat. fat), 63 mg chol., 717 mg sodium, 29 g carb., 5 g fiber, 27 g pro.* **Diabetic Exchanges:** *3 lean meat, 2 fat, 1½ starch, 1 vegetable.*

FAJITA SKILLET

FETA STEAK TACOS

Feta Steak Tacos FAST FIX

These tacos have the perfect combination of Mexican and Mediterranean flavors. They're always a big hit with my family!
—**DEBBIE REID** CLEARWATER, FL

START TO FINISH: 30 MIN.
MAKES: 8 SERVINGS

- 1¼ **pounds beef flat iron steak or top sirloin steak, cut into thin strips**
- ¼ **cup Greek vinaigrette**
- ½ **cup fat-free plain Greek yogurt**
- 2 **teaspoons lime juice**
- 1 **tablespoon oil from sun-dried tomatoes**
- 1 **small onion, cut into thin strips**
- 1 **small green pepper, cut into thin strips**
- ¼ **cup chopped oil-packed sun-dried tomatoes**
- ¼ **cup sliced Greek olives**
- 8 **whole wheat tortillas (8 inches), warmed**

- ¼ **cup crumbled garlic and herb feta cheese**
- 8 **lime wedges**

1. In a large bowl, toss beef with the vinaigrette; let stand 15 minutes. In a small bowl, mix yogurt and lime juice.
2. Meanwhile, in a large skillet, heat the oil from sun-dried tomatoes over medium-high heat. Add onion and pepper; cook and stir 3-4 minutes or until crisp-tender. Remove to a bowl; stir in sun-dried tomatoes and olives.
3. Add beef to the same pan; cook and stir over medium-high heat for 2-3 minutes or until browned. Remove from pan. Serve steak in tortillas with the pepper mixture, cheese and yogurt mixture. Squeeze lime wedges over the tacos.
PER SERVING *1 taco with 1 tablespoon yogurt sauce equals 317 cal., 15 g fat (4 g sat. fat), 48 mg chol., 372 mg*

sodium, 25 g carb., 3 g fiber, 20 g pro.
Diabetic Exchanges: *3 lean meat, 2 fat, 1½ starch.*

BBQ Yumburgers FAST FIX

My husband can't resist these barbecued delights. I freeze patties ahead of time so I'm ready whenever a craving hits.
—**ALAN HOYE** WHITMORE LAKE, MI

START TO FINISH: 30 MIN.
MAKES: 4 SERVINGS

- 2 **teaspoons canola oil**
- 1 **large onion, halved and sliced**
- 1 **pound lean ground beef (90% lean)**
- 2 **tablespoons finely chopped onion**
- 2 **tablespoons barbecue sauce**
- 2 **garlic cloves, minced**
- 1 **teaspoon onion powder**
- ½ **teaspoon salt**
- ¼ **teaspoon pepper**
- 4 **whole wheat hamburger buns, split**
  Optional toppings: tomato slices, lettuce leaves and additional barbecue sauce

1. In a small skillet, heat the oil over medium-high heat. Add the sliced onion; cook and stir 4-6 minutes or until tender.
2. In a large bowl, combine the beef, chopped onion, barbecue sauce, garlic, onion powder, salt and pepper, mixing lightly but thoroughly. Shape into four ½-in.-thick patties.
3. Grill the burgers, covered, over medium heat or broil 4 in. from heat for 4-6 minutes on each side or until a thermometer reads 160°. Serve on buns with cooked onions and, if desired, optional toppings.
FREEZE OPTION *Place patties on a plastic wrap-lined baking sheet; wrap and freeze until firm. Remove from pan and transfer to a resealable plastic freezer bag; return to freezer. To use, prepare sliced onions. Grill frozen patties as directed, increasing time as necessary for a thermometer to read 160°. Serve on buns with toppings.*
PER SERVING *1 burger (calculated without optional toppings) equals 341 cal., 14 g fat (4 g sat. fat), 71 mg chol., 634 mg sodium, 28 g carb., 4 g fiber, 26 g pro.* ***Diabetic Exchanges:*** *3 lean meat, 2 starch, ½ fat.*

VEGETABLE STEAK KABOBS

West Coast Snappy Joes FAST FIX

Meet my California-inspired sloppy joe. Load it up with whatever taco toppings you like. The meat filling is also incredible served over mac and cheese.
—DEVON DELANEY WESTPORT, CT

START TO FINISH: 30 MIN.
MAKES: 6 SERVINGS

- 1 pound lean ground beef (90% lean)
- 1 medium onion, chopped
- 1 garlic clove, minced
- 1 can (8 ounces) tomato sauce
- ⅓ cup soft sun-dried tomato halves (not packed in oil), chopped
- ⅓ cup chopped roasted sweet red peppers
- 2 tablespoons chopped pickled jalapeno peppers
- 2 tablespoons tomato paste
- 1 tablespoon brown sugar
- 1 tablespoon balsamic vinegar
- ½ teaspoon Montreal steak seasoning
- ½ teaspoon pepper
- 6 hamburger buns, split
  Optional toppings: chopped avocado, sour cream, shredded cheddar cheese and chopped green onions

1. In a large skillet, cook the beef, onion and garlic over medium heat for 6-8 minutes or until the meat is no longer pink, breaking up beef into crumbles; drain.

2. Stir in tomato sauce, sun-dried tomatoes, roasted peppers, jalapenos, tomato paste, brown sugar, vinegar, steak seasoning and pepper. Bring to a boil. Reduce heat; simmer, uncovered, 4-6 minutes or until thickened, stirring occasionally. Serve on buns with toppings as desired.

FREEZE OPTION *Freeze cooled meat mixture in freezer containers. To use, partially thaw in the refrigerator overnight. Heat through in a saucepan, stirring occasionally and adding a little water if necessary.*

EDITOR'S NOTE *This recipe was tested with sun-dried tomatoes that are ready to use without soaking. When using other sun-dried tomatoes that are not oil-packed, cover with boiling water and let stand until soft. Drain tomatoes before using.*

PER SERVING *1 sandwich (calculated without optional toppings) equals 288 cal., 8 g fat (3 g sat. fat), 47 mg chol., 575 mg sodium, 32 g carb., 3 g fiber, 20 g pro.* **Diabetic Exchanges:** *2 starch, 2 lean meat.*

Vegetable Steak Kabobs S C

The marinade for this steak and vegetable skewer is the best one I've ever found. I use it on chicken and pork, too.
—NORMA HARDER WEYAKWIN, SK

PREP: 20 MIN. + MARINATING
GRILL: 10 MIN. • **MAKES:** 6 SERVINGS

- ½ cup olive oil
- ⅓ cup red wine vinegar
- 2 tablespoons ketchup
- 2 to 3 garlic cloves, minced
- 1 teaspoon Worcestershire sauce
- ½ teaspoon each dried marjoram, basil and oregano
- ½ teaspoon dried rosemary, crushed
- 1 beef top sirloin steak (1½ pounds), cut into 1-inch cubes
- ½ pound whole fresh mushrooms
- 2 medium onions, cut into wedges
- 1½ cups cherry tomatoes
- 2 small green peppers, cut into 1-inch pieces

1. In a small bowl, whisk oil, vinegar, ketchup, garlic, Worcestershire sauce and seasonings. Pour ½ cup marinade into a large resealable plastic bag. Add beef; seal bag and turn to coat. Pour the remaining marinade into another large resealable plastic bag. Add the mushrooms, onions, tomatoes and peppers; seal bag and turn to coat. Refrigerate beef and vegetables for 8 hours or overnight.

2. Drain beef, discarding marinade. Drain vegetables, reserving marinade for basting. On six metal or soaked wooden skewers, alternately thread beef and vegetables.

3. Grill kabobs, covered, over medium heat for 10-15 minutes or until beef reaches desired doneness and the vegetables are crisp-tender, turning occasionally. Baste with reserved marinade during the last 5 minutes.

PER SERVING *1 kabob equals 234 cal., 10 g fat (2 g sat. fat), 69 mg chol., 99 mg sodium, 10 g carb., 2 g fiber, 26 g pro.* **Diabetic Exchanges:** *3 lean meat, 2 vegetable.*

WEST COAST SNAPPY JOES

Salisbury Steak Supreme c

When I was running late one night, a go-to recipe of my mom's popped into my head. Now it's one of my husband's favorites. It's a fast answer to unexpected company.

—PATRICIA SWART GALLOWAY, NJ

PREP: 20 MIN. • **COOK:** 15 MIN.
MAKES: 4 SERVINGS

- 2 medium red onions, divided
- ½ cup soft bread crumbs
- ¾ teaspoon salt-free seasoning blend
- ½ teaspoon pepper
  Dash ground nutmeg
- 1 pound lean ground beef (90% lean)
- 1 teaspoon cornstarch
- 1 teaspoon reduced-sodium beef bouillon granules
- ½ cup cold water
- 2 teaspoons butter
- 1½ cups sliced fresh mushrooms

1. Thinly slice 1½ onions; finely chop remaining onion half. In a large bowl, toss bread crumbs with chopped onion and seasonings. Add beef; mix lightly but thoroughly. Shape into four ½-in.-thick oval patties.

2. Place a large nonstick skillet coated with cooking spray over medium heat. Add patties; cook 5-6 minutes on each side or until a thermometer reads 160°. Remove from pan. Discard the drippings from pan.

3. In a small bowl, mix cornstarch, bouillon and water until smooth. In same skillet, heat butter over medium-high heat. Add mushrooms and sliced onions; cook and stir 5-7 minutes or until onions are tender.

4. Stir in cornstarch mixture. Bring to a boil; cook and stir 1-2 minutes or until thickened. Return Salisbury steaks to pan, turning to coat with sauce; heat through.

NOTE *To make soft bread crumbs, tear bread into pieces and place in a food processor or blender. Cover and pulse until crumbs form. One slice of bread yields ½ to ¾ cup crumbs.*

PER SERVING *1 serving equals 244 cal., 12 g fat (5 g sat. fat), 76 mg chol., 192 mg sodium, 10 g carb., 1 g fiber, 24 g pro.* **Diabetic Exchanges:** *3 lean meat, 1 starch, ½ fat.*

Grilled Southwestern Steak Salad

I am always trying to get my boyfriend to eat more salad. This dish of steak, peppers and onions is the only salad that he can't get enough of.

—YVONNE STARLIN HERMITAGE, TN

PREP: 25 MIN. • **GRILL:** 20 MIN.
MAKES: 4 SERVINGS

- 1 beef top sirloin steak (1-inch thick and ¾ pound)
- ¼ teaspoon salt
- ¼ teaspoon ground cumin
- ¼ teaspoon pepper
- 3 poblano peppers, halved and seeded
- 2 large ears sweet corn, husks removed
- 1 large sweet onion, cut into ½-inch rings
- 1 tablespoon olive oil
- 2 cups uncooked multigrain bow tie pasta
- 2 large tomatoes

DRESSING
- ¼ cup lime juice
- 1 tablespoon olive oil
- ¼ teaspoon salt
- ¼ teaspoon ground cumin
- ¼ teaspoon pepper
- ⅓ cup chopped fresh cilantro

1. Rub steak with salt, cumin and pepper. Brush poblano peppers, corn and onion with oil. Grill steak, covered, over medium heat or broil 4 in. from heat 6-8 minutes on each side or until meat reaches desired doneness (for medium-rare, a thermometer should read 145°; medium, 160°; well-done, 170°). Grill vegetables, covered, 8-10 minutes or until crisp-tender, turning occasionally.

2. Cook pasta according to package directions. Meanwhile, cut corn from cob; coarsely chop peppers, onion and tomatoes. Transfer vegetables to a large bowl. In a small bowl, whisk lime juice, oil, salt, cumin and pepper until blended; stir in cilantro.

3. Drain pasta; add to the vegetable mixture. Drizzle with dressing; toss to coat. Cut steak into thin slices; add to salad.

PER SERVING *2 cups pasta mixture with 2 ounces cooked beef equals 456 cal., 13 g fat (3 g sat. fat), 34 mg chol., 378 mg sodium, 58 g carb., 8 g fiber, 30 g pro.*

GRILLED SOUTHWESTERN STEAK SALAD

112

117

129

Chicken Favorites

“This delicious chicken proves that comfort food doesn't have to be full of unwanted calories. Mixed with orange and lemon juice, my roast chicken is both flavorful and healthy.”

—ROBIN HAAS CRANSTON, RI
about her recipe, Sunday Roast Chicken, on page 111

Skillet Chicken with Olives C FAST FIX

While I was visiting my cousin in Italy, she made this heavenly chicken for lunch. Now it's a family favorite stateside, too.
—**JOSEPH PISANO** REVERE, MA

START TO FINISH: 20 MIN.
MAKES: 4 SERVINGS

- 4 **boneless skinless chicken thighs (about 1 pound)**
- 1 **teaspoon dried rosemary, crushed**
- ½ **teaspoon pepper**
- ¼ **teaspoon salt**
- 1 **tablespoon olive oil**
- ½ **cup pimiento-stuffed olives, coarsely chopped**
- ¼ **cup white wine or chicken broth**
- 1 **tablespoon drained capers, optional**

1. Sprinkle chicken with rosemary, pepper and salt. In a large skillet, heat oil over medium-high heat. Brown chicken on both sides.

2. Add olives, wine and, if desired, capers. Reduce heat; simmer, covered, 2-3 minutes or until a thermometer inserted into chicken reads 170°.

PER SERVING *1 serving (calculated without capers) equals 237 cal., 15 g fat (3 g sat. fat), 76 mg chol., 571 mg sodium, 2 g carb., trace fiber, 21 g pro. Diabetic Exchanges: 3 lean meat, 2 fat.*

SKILLET CHICKEN WITH OLIVES

SPEEDY CHICKEN MARSALA

Speedy Chicken Marsala FAST FIX

This is one of my favorite dishes to order in restaurants, so I created a version that I could make in a flash on a weeknight at home.
—**TRISHA KRUSE** EAGLE, ID

START TO FINISH: 30 MIN.
MAKES: 4 SERVINGS

- 8 **ounces uncooked whole wheat or multigrain angel hair pasta**
- 4 **boneless skinless chicken breast halves (5 ounces each)**
- ¼ **cup all-purpose flour**
- 1 **teaspoon lemon-pepper seasoning**
- ½ **teaspoon salt**
- 2 **tablespoons olive oil, divided**
- 4 **cups sliced fresh mushrooms**
- 1 **garlic clove, minced**
- 1 **cup dry Marsala wine**

1. Cook pasta according to package directions. Pound chicken with a meat mallet to ¼-in. thickness. In a large resealable plastic bag, mix the flour, lemon-pepper and salt. Add chicken, one piece at a time; close bag and shake to coat.

2. In a large skillet, heat 1 tablespoon oil over medium heat. Add chicken; cook for 4-5 minutes on each side or until no longer pink. Remove from the pan.

3. In the same skillet, heat remaining oil over medium-high heat. Add the mushrooms; cook and stir until tender. Add the garlic; cook 1 minute longer. Add the wine; bring to a boil. Cook for 5-6 minutes or until liquid is reduced by half, stirring to loosen browned bits from pan. Return the chicken to pan, turning to coat with sauce; heat through.

4. Drain the pasta; serve with the chicken mixture.

PER SERVING *1 serving equals 493 cal., 11 g fat (2 g sat. fat), 78 mg chol., 279 mg sodium, 50 g carb., 7 g fiber, 40 g pro.*

TOP TIP

Marsala is a fortified (higher alcohol) wine from Sicily that's popular in Italian cooking. It's made in dry and sweet styles. Use dry Marsala or cooking Marsala in this recipe. You could also prepare it with sherry if you don't have Marsala.

Sunday Roast Chicken

This delicious chicken proves that comfort food doesn't have to be full of unwanted calories. Mixed with orange and lemon juice, my roast chicken is both flavorful and healthy.

—**ROBIN HAAS** CRANSTON, RI

PREP: 30 MIN. • **BAKE:** 1¾ HOURS + RESTING
MAKES: 6 SERVINGS

- 1 medium fennel bulb
- 5 large carrots, cut into 1½-inch pieces
- 1 large white onion, quartered, divided
- 1 medium lemon
- 3 garlic cloves, minced
- 1 tablespoon honey
- 1 teaspoon kosher salt
- 1 teaspoon crushed red pepper flakes
- 1 teaspoon pepper
- 1 broiler/fryer chicken (4 pounds)
- 2 garlic cloves
- 1 cup orange juice

1. Preheat oven to 350°. Using a sharp knife, trim the stalks and root end of fennel bulb. Cut bulb lengthwise into quarters; cut and remove core. Cut fennel into 1-in. wedges. Spread the fennel, carrots and three of the onion quarters in a shallow roasting pan.

2. Cut lemon in half; squeeze juice into a small bowl, reserving lemon halves. Stir minced garlic, honey, salt, pepper flakes and pepper into juice.

3. Place chicken on a work surface, neck side down. With fingers, carefully loosen skin from the tail end of the chicken breast. Spoon juice mixture under skin of breast; secure skin with toothpicks. Place garlic cloves, lemon halves and the remaining onion inside chicken cavity. Tuck wings under chicken; tie drumsticks together. Place over vegetables, breast side up.

4. Pour the orange juice over chicken. Roast for 1½-2 hours or until a thermometer inserted in thickest part of thigh reads 170°-175°. (Cover the chicken loosely with foil if it browns too quickly.)

5. Remove roasting pan from oven; increase oven setting to 450°. Remove chicken from pan; tent with foil and let stand 15 minutes before carving.

6. Meanwhile, return roasting pan to oven; roast vegetables 10-15 minutes longer or until vegetables are tender and lightly browned. Using a slotted spoon, remove vegetables from pan. If desired, skim fat from pan juices and serve with chicken and vegetables.
PER SERVING *4 ounces cooked chicken (skin removed) with ½ cup vegetables equals 292 cal., 8 g fat (2 g sat. fat), 98 mg chol., 470 mg sodium, 20 g carb., 4 g fiber, 34 g pro.* **Diabetic Exchanges:** *4 lean meat, 1 starch, 1 vegetable.*

Chicken with Peach-Cucumber Salsa FAST FIX ▶

START TO FINISH: 25 MIN.
MAKES: 4 SERVINGS

- 1½ cups chopped peeled fresh peaches (about 2 medium)
- ¾ cup chopped cucumber
- 4 tablespoons peach preserves, divided
- 3 tablespoons finely chopped red onion
- 1 teaspoon minced fresh mint
- ¾ teaspoon salt, divided
- 4 boneless skinless chicken breast halves (6 ounces each)
- ¼ teaspoon pepper

1. For salsa, in a small bowl, combine peaches, cucumber, 2 tablespoons peach preserves, onion, mint and ¼ teaspoon salt.

2. Sprinkle chicken with pepper and remaining salt. Moisten a paper towel with cooking oil; using long-handled tongs, rub on grill rack to coat lightly. Grill chicken, covered, over medium heat 5 minutes. Turn; grill 7-9 minutes longer or until a thermometer reads 165°, brushing tops occasionally with remaining preserves. Serve with salsa.
PER SERVING *1 chicken breast half with ½ cup salsa equals 261 cal., 4 g fat (1 g sat. fat), 94 mg chol., 525 mg sodium, 20 g carb., 1 g fiber, 35 g pro.* **Diabetic Exchanges:** *5 lean meat, ½ starch, ½ fruit.*

To keep our kitchen cool, we grill chicken outdoors and pass it with a minty peach salsa that can easily be made ahead.
—**JANIE COLLE** HUTCHINSON, KS

CHICKEN WITH PEACH-CUCUMBER SALSA

Spicy Barbecued Chicken C FAST FIX

This zesty chicken is great served with basil-buttered grilled corn on the cob and fresh coleslaw.

—RITA WINTRODE CORRYTON, TN

START TO FINISH: 30 MIN.
MAKES: 8 SERVINGS

- 1 tablespoon canola oil
- 2 garlic cloves, minced
- ½ cup chili sauce
- 3 tablespoons brown sugar
- 2 teaspoons salt-free seasoning blend, divided
- ¾ teaspoon cayenne pepper, divided
- 2 teaspoons ground mustard
- 2 teaspoons chili powder
- 8 boneless skinless chicken breast halves (4 ounces each)

1. In a small pan, heat oil; add garlic and cook over medium heat 1 minute. Add the chili sauce, brown sugar, 1 teaspoon seasoning and ¼ teaspoon cayenne. Bring to a boil; cook and stir 1 minute. Remove from heat.
2. Mix mustard, chili powder and the remaining seasoning blend and cayenne; rub over chicken. Moisten a paper towel with cooking oil; using long-handled tongs, lightly coat the grill rack. Grill chicken, covered, over medium heat for 4 minutes. Turn; grill 4-6 minutes longer or until a thermometer reads 165°, brushing the tops occasionally with the chili sauce mixture.
PER SERVING *1 chicken breast half equals 179 cal., 5 g fat (1 g sat. fat), 63 mg chol., 293 mg sodium, 10 g carb., trace fiber, 23 g pro.* **Diabetic Exchanges:** *3 lean meat, ½ starch, ½ fat.*

HOW TO

OIL A GRILL GRATE

Fold a paper towel into a small pad and moisten it with cooking oil. Holding the pad with long-handled tongs, rub it over the grate.

Oven-Fried Chicken Drumsticks C

Greek yogurt creates an amazing marinade that makes the chicken incredibly moist. No one will guess that it's been lightened up and not even fried!

—KIMBERLY WALLACE DENNISON, OH

PREP: 20 MIN. + MARINATING
BAKE: 40 MIN. • **MAKES:** 4 SERVINGS

- 1 cup fat-free plain Greek yogurt
- 1 tablespoon Dijon mustard
- 2 garlic cloves, minced
- 8 chicken drumsticks (4 ounces each), skin removed
- ½ cup whole wheat flour
- 1½ teaspoons paprika
- 1 teaspoon baking powder
- 1 teaspoon salt
- 1 teaspoon pepper
  Olive oil-flavored cooking spray

1. In a large resealable plastic bag, combine yogurt, mustard and garlic. Add chicken; seal bag and turn to coat. Refrigerate 8 hours or overnight.
2. Preheat oven to 425°. In another plastic bag, mix flour, paprika, baking powder, salt and pepper. Remove the chicken from marinade and add, one piece at a time, to flour mixture; close bag and shake to coat. Place on a wire rack over a baking sheet; spritz with cooking spray. Bake 40-45 minutes or until a thermometer reads 180°.
PER SERVING *2 chicken drumsticks equals 227 cal., 7 g fat (1 g sat. fat), 81 mg chol., 498 mg sodium, 9 g carb., 1 g fiber, 31 g pro.* **Diabetic Exchanges:** *4 lean meat, ½ starch.*

OVEN-FRIED CHICKEN DRUMSTICKS

Pan-Roasted Chicken and Vegetables

This simple meal tastes like it needs hours of hands-on time to put together, but it takes just minutes to prep the simple ingredients. So easy.

—SHERRI MELOTIK OAK CREEK, WI

PREP: 15 MIN. • **BAKE:** 45 MIN.
MAKES: 6 SERVINGS

- 2 **pounds red potatoes (about 6 medium), cut into ¾-inch pieces**
- 1 **large onion, coarsely chopped**
- 2 **tablespoons olive oil**
- 3 **garlic cloves, minced**
- 1¼ **teaspoons salt, divided**
- 1 **teaspoon dried rosemary, crushed, divided**
- ¾ **teaspoon pepper, divided**
- ½ **teaspoon paprika**
- 6 **bone-in chicken thighs (about 2¼ pounds), skin removed**
- 6 **cups fresh baby spinach (about 6 ounces)**

1. Preheat oven to 425°. In a large bowl, combine potatoes, onion, oil, garlic, ¾ teaspoon salt, ½ teaspoon rosemary and ½ teaspoon pepper; toss to coat. Transfer to a 15x10x1-in. baking pan coated with cooking spray.

2. In a small bowl, mix paprika and remaining salt, rosemary and pepper. Sprinkle the chicken with paprika mixture and place over vegetables. Roast for 35-40 minutes or until a thermometer inserted into chicken reads 170°-175° and vegetables are just tender.

3. Remove chicken to a serving platter; keep warm. Top vegetables with spinach. Roast 8-10 minutes longer or until vegetables are tender and spinach is wilted. Stir vegetables to combine; serve with chicken.

PER SERVING *1 chicken thigh with 1 cup vegetables equals 357 cal., 14 g fat (3 g sat. fat), 87 mg chol., 597 mg sodium, 28 g carb., 4 g fiber, 28 g pro.*
***Diabetic Exchanges:** 4 lean meat, 1½ starch, 1 vegetable, 1 fat.*

PAN-ROASTED CHICKEN AND VEGETABLES

Caribbean Delight **C**

When hot summer nights drive me out of the kitchen, I head for the grill with this recipe. My family enjoys this spicy chicken accompanied with a salad.
—**LEIGH ANN GRADY** MURRAY, KY

PREP: 5 MIN. + MARINATING • **GRILL:** 10 MIN.
MAKES: 6 SERVINGS

- 2 tablespoons finely chopped onion
- ¼ cup butter, cubed
- 2 garlic cloves, minced
- ⅓ cup white vinegar
- ⅓ cup lime juice
- ¼ cup sugar
- 2 tablespoons curry powder
- 1 teaspoon salt
- ¼ to ½ teaspoon cayenne pepper
- 6 boneless skinless chicken breast halves (4 ounces each)

1. In a small saucepan, saute onion in butter until tender. Add garlic; cook 1 minute longer. Stir in the vinegar, lime juice, sugar, curry, salt and cayenne. Place chicken in a large resealable plastic bag; add the onion mixture. Seal bag and turn to coat. Refrigerate for at least 2 hours.
2. Drain and discard marinade. Grill chicken, uncovered, over medium heat, for 5-7 minutes on each side or until a thermometer reads 170°.
PER SERVING *1 chicken breast half equals 162 cal., 5 g fat (2 g sat. fat), 70 mg chol., 224 mg sodium, 4 g carb., trace fiber, 23 g pro. Diabetic Exchanges: 3 lean meat, ½ fat.*

GARLIC CHICKEN RIGATONI

Garlic Chicken Rigatoni **FAST FIX** ▶

My family loves the scampi-inspired combination of garlic and olive oil in this delicious pasta. I love that it's guilt-free!
—**JUDY CRAWFORD** DEMING, NM

START TO FINISH: 30 MIN.
MAKES: 4 SERVINGS

- 8 ounces uncooked rigatoni or large tube pasta
- ¼ cup sun-dried tomatoes (not packed in oil)
- ½ cup boiling water
- ½ pound boneless skinless chicken breasts, cut into 1-inch cubes
- ¼ teaspoon garlic salt
- 2 tablespoons all-purpose flour
- 2 tablespoons olive oil, divided
- 1½ cups sliced fresh mushrooms
- 3 garlic cloves, minced
- ¼ cup reduced-sodium chicken broth
- ¼ cup white wine or additional reduced-sodium chicken broth
- 2 tablespoons minced fresh parsley
- ¼ teaspoon dried basil
- ⅛ teaspoon salt
- ⅛ teaspoon pepper
- ⅛ teaspoon crushed red pepper flakes
- ¼ cup grated Parmesan cheese

1. Cook rigatoni according to package directions. In a small bowl, combine tomatoes and boiling water; let stand 5 minutes. Drain; chop tomatoes.
2. Sprinkle chicken with garlic salt; add flour and toss to coat. In a large skillet, heat 1 tablespoon oil over medium-high heat. Add chicken; cook and stir 4-5 minutes or until no longer pink. Remove from pan.
3. In the same skillet, heat remaining oil over medium-high heat. Add the mushrooms and garlic; cook and stir until tender. Add broth, wine, parsley, seasonings and chopped tomatoes; bring to a boil. Stir in the chicken and heat through.
4. Drain rigatoni; add to chicken mixture. Sprinkle with cheese and toss to coat.
PER SERVING *1½ cups pasta with 1 tablespoon cheese equals 398 cal., 11 g fat (2 g sat. fat), 36 mg chol., 290 mg sodium, 50 g carb., 3 g fiber, 23 g pro.*

CARIBBEAN DELIGHT

Apple-Marinated Chicken & Vegetables

PREP: 20 MIN. + MARINATING
GRILL: 25 MIN. • **MAKES:** 6 SERVINGS

- 1 **cup apple juice**
- ½ **cup canola oil**
- ¼ **cup packed brown sugar**
- ¼ **cup reduced-sodium soy sauce**
- 3 **tablespoons lemon juice**
- 2 **tablespoons minced fresh parsley**
- 3 **garlic cloves, minced**
- 6 **boneless skinless chicken breast halves (6 ounces each)**
- 4 **large carrots**
- 2 **medium zucchini**
- 2 **medium yellow summer squash**

1. In a small bowl, whisk the first seven ingredients until blended. Place 1 cup marinade and chicken in a large resealable plastic bag; seal bag and turn to coat. Refrigerate 6 hours or overnight. Cover and refrigerate remaining marinade.

2. Cut carrots, zucchini and squash lengthwise into quarters; cut crosswise into 2-in. pieces. Toss with ½ cup reserved marinade.

3. Drain chicken, discarding marinade in bag. Grill chicken, covered, over medium heat or broil 4 in. from heat 6-8 minutes on each side or until a thermometer reads 165°, basting frequently with remaining marinade during the last 5 minutes. Keep warm.

4. Transfer vegetables to a grill wok or basket; place on grill rack. Grill vegetables, covered, over medium heat 10-12 minutes or until crisp-tender, stirring frequently. Serve with chicken.

NOTE *If you do not have a grill wok or basket, use a disposable foil pan. Poke holes in the bottom of the pan with a meat fork to allow liquid to drain.*

PER SERVING *1 chicken breast half with 1 cup vegetables equals 367 cal., 16 g fat (2 g sat. fat), 94 mg chol., 378 mg sodium, 19 g carb., 3 g fiber, 37 g pro.*

MEDITERRANEAN ORZO CHICKEN SALAD

Mediterranean Orzo Chicken Salad FAST FIX ▶

In the summer, I pull out this recipe for a cool supper. The lemon dressing is so refreshing. If you have leftover grilled chicken, use it here.
—**SUSAN KIEBOAM** STREETSBORO, OH

START TO FINISH: 25 MIN.
MAKES: 6 SERVINGS

- 2 **cups uncooked whole wheat orzo pasta**
- 2 **cups shredded rotisserie chicken**
- 10 **cherry tomatoes, halved**
- ½ **cup crumbled tomato and basil feta cheese**
- 1 **can (2¼ ounces) sliced ripe olives, drained**
- ¼ **cup chopped sweet onion**
- ¼ **cup olive oil**
- 2 **tablespoons lemon juice**
- ½ **teaspoon salt**
- ¼ **teaspoon dried oregano**

1. Cook pasta according to package directions. Drain pasta; rinse with cold water and drain well.

2. In a large bowl, combine the pasta, chicken, tomatoes, cheese, olives and onion. In a small bowl, whisk the remaining ingredients until blended. Drizzle over salad; toss to coat.

PER SERVING *1 cup equals 397 cal., 16 g fat (3 g sat. fat), 47 mg chol., 407 mg sodium, 40 g carb., 10 g fiber, 22 g pro.* **Diabetic Exchanges:** *3 lean meat, 2½ starch, 2 fat.*

I actually created this at a campground, so you know it's easy. Using the same marinade for the chicken and veggies keeps it simple so we can spend more time outside and less making dinner.
—**JAYME SCHERTZ** CLINTONVILLE, WI

APPLE-MARINATED CHICKEN & VEGETABLES

Sausage Chicken Jambalaya

If you enjoy entertaining, this jambalaya is a terrific one-pot meal for feeding a hungry crowd. It has all the classic flavor but is easy on the waistline.

—BETTY BENTHIN GRASS VALLEY, CA

PREP: 20 MIN. • **COOK:** 30 MIN.
MAKES: 9 SERVINGS

- 6 **fully cooked spicy chicken sausage links (3 ounces each), cut into ½-inch slices**
- ½ **pound chicken tenderloins, cut into ½-inch slices**
- 1 **tablespoon olive oil**
- 3 **celery ribs, chopped**
- 1 **large onion, chopped**
- 2¾ **cups chicken broth**
- 1 **can (14½ ounces) diced tomatoes, undrained**
- 1½ **cups uncooked long grain rice**
- 1 **teaspoon dried thyme**
- 1 **teaspoon Cajun seasoning**

1. In a large saucepan, saute sausage and chicken in oil for 5 minutes. Add celery and onion; saute 6-8 minutes longer or until vegetables are tender. Stir in remaining ingredients.

2. Bring to a boil. Reduce heat; cover and simmer for 15-20 minutes or until rice is tender. Let stand for 5 minutes.

PER SERVING *1 cup equals 259 cal., 7 g fat (2 g sat. fat), 60 mg chol., 761 mg sodium, 31 g carb., 2 g fiber, 19 g pro.* ***Diabetic Exchanges:*** *2 lean meat, 1½ starch, 1 vegetable, ½ fat.*

SAUSAGE CHICKEN JAMBALAYA

I enjoy beef Stroganoff but wanted a version with chicken. For a French twist, I added ham, Swiss and Dijon. It quickly became a family favorite.

—JEANNE HOLT MENDOTA HEIGHTS, MN

CHICKEN CORDON BLEU STROGANOFF

Chicken Cordon Bleu Stroganoff

PREP: 15 MIN. • **COOK:** 25 MIN.
MAKES: 6 SERVINGS

- 1 **tablespoon canola oil**
- ½ **pound sliced fresh mushrooms**
- 1 **large onion, chopped**
- 2 **tablespoons all-purpose flour**
- 3 **cups reduced-sodium chicken broth**
- ⅓ **cup white wine or additional chicken broth**
- 1 **tablespoon Dijon mustard**
- 4 **cups uncooked whole wheat egg noodles**
- 2 **cups cubed cooked chicken breast**
- ¾ **cup cubed fully cooked ham**
- ½ **cup shredded Swiss cheese, divided**
- ½ **cup reduced-fat sour cream**
- ¼ **teaspoon salt**
- ¼ **teaspoon pepper**
- 1 **green onion, thinly sliced**

1. In a 6-qt. stockpot, heat oil over medium-high heat. Add mushrooms and onion; cook and stir 6-8 minutes or until tender. Stir in the flour until blended; gradually stir in broth, wine and mustard. Bring to a boil.

2. Add the noodles; return to a boil. Reduce heat; simmer, uncovered, for 10-12 minutes or until noodles are tender, stirring occasionally. Stir in chicken, ham and ¼ cup cheese until cheese is melted.

3. Remove from heat; stir in the sour cream, salt and pepper. Sprinkle with green onion and remaining cheese.

PER SERVING *1⅓ cups equals 308 cal., 9 g fat (3 g sat. fat), 61 mg chol., 732 mg sodium, 29 g carb., 4 g fiber, 28 g pro.* ***Diabetic Exchanges:*** *3 lean meat, 1½ starch, 1 vegetable, ½ fat.*

Artichoke Ratatouille Chicken **C**

I loaded all the fresh produce I could find into this speedy chicken dinner. Serve it on its own or over pasta.

—JUDY ARMSTRONG PRAIRIEVILLE, LA

PREP: 25 MIN. • **BAKE:** 1 HOUR
MAKES: 6 SERVINGS

- 3 **Japanese eggplants (about 1 pound)**
- 4 **plum tomatoes**
- 1 **medium sweet yellow pepper**
- 1 **medium sweet red pepper**
- 1 **medium onion**
- 1 **can (14 ounces) water-packed artichoke hearts, drained and quartered**
- 2 **tablespoons minced fresh thyme**
- 2 **tablespoons capers, drained**
- 2 **tablespoons olive oil**
- 2 **garlic cloves, minced**
- 1 **teaspoon Creole seasoning, divided**
- 1½ **pounds boneless skinless chicken breasts, cubed**
- 1 **cup white wine or chicken broth**
- ¼ **cup grated Asiago cheese**
  Hot cooked pasta, optional

1. Preheat the oven to 350°. Cut the eggplants, tomatoes, peppers and onion into ¾-in. pieces; place in a large bowl. Stir in artichokes, thyme, capers, oil, garlic and ½ teaspoon Creole seasoning.
2. Sprinkle chicken with remaining Creole seasoning. Transfer chicken to a 13x9-in. baking dish coated with cooking spray; spoon the vegetable mixture over top. Drizzle with wine.
3. Bake, covered, for 30 minutes. Uncover; bake 30-45 minutes longer or until chicken is no longer pink and vegetables are tender. Sprinkle with cheese. If desired, serve with pasta.
PER SERVING *1⅔ cups (calculated without pasta) equals 252 cal., 9 g fat (2 g sat. fat), 67 mg chol., 468 mg sodium, 15 g carb., 4 g fiber, 28 g pro. Diabetic Exchanges: 3 lean meat, 1 starch, 1 fat.*

Tapenade-Stuffed Chicken Breasts **C** FAST FIX ▶

I created this recipe for my husband, who absolutely loves olives. I usually make a larger batch of the olive tapenade and serve it with bread or crackers as a snack or appetizer.

—JESSICA LEVINSON NYACK, NY

START TO FINISH: 30 MIN.
MAKES: 4 SERVINGS

- 4 **oil-packed sun-dried tomatoes**
- 4 **pitted Greek olives**
- 4 **pitted Spanish olives**
- 4 **pitted ripe olives**
- ¼ **cup roasted sweet red peppers, drained**
- 4 **garlic cloves, minced**
- 1 **tablespoon olive oil**
- 2 **teaspoons balsamic vinegar**
- 4 **boneless skinless chicken breast halves (6 ounces each)**
  Grated Parmesan cheese

1. Place the first eight ingredients in a food processor; pulse until tomatoes and olives are coarsely chopped. Cut a pocket horizontally in the thickest part of each chicken breast. Fill with olive mixture; secure with toothpicks.
2. Moisten a paper towel with cooking oil; using long-handled tongs, rub on grill rack to coat lightly. Grill chicken, covered, over medium heat or broil 4 in. from heat 8-10 minutes on each side or until a thermometer inserted into stuffing reads 165°. Sprinkle with Parmesan cheese. Discard toothpicks before serving.
PER SERVING *1 stuffed chicken breast half (calculated without cheese) equals 264 cal., 11 g fat (2 g sat. fat), 94 mg chol., 367 mg sodium, 5 g carb., 1 g fiber, 35 g pro. Diabetic Exchanges: 5 lean meat, 1 fat.*

TAPENADE-STUFFED CHICKEN BREASTS

BALSAMIC CHICKEN WITH ROASTED TOMATOES

Balsamic Chicken with Roasted Tomatoes FAST FIX

This entree is a great way to savor fresh tomatoes, especially during the warm summer months. It's quite simple, but the sweet, tangy tomato glaze is just so good.

—KAREN GEHRIG CONCORD, NC

START TO FINISH: 25 MIN.
MAKES: 4 SERVINGS

- 2 tablespoons honey
- 2 tablespoons olive oil, divided
- 2 cups grape tomatoes
- 4 boneless skinless chicken breast halves (6 ounces each)
- ½ teaspoon salt
- ½ teaspoon pepper
- 2 tablespoons balsamic glaze

1. Preheat oven to 400°. Mix honey and 1 tablespoon oil. Add tomatoes and toss to coat. Transfer to a greased 15x10x1-in. baking pan. Bake for 5-7 minutes or until softened.
2. Pound chicken breasts with a meat mallet to ½-in. thickness; sprinkle with salt and pepper. In a large skillet, heat remaining oil over medium heat. Add the chicken; cook 5-6 minutes on each side or until no longer pink. Serve with roasted tomatoes; drizzle with balsamic glaze.

NOTE *To make your own balsamic glaze, bring ½ cup balsamic vinegar to a boil in a small saucepan. Reduce the heat to medium; simmer the vinegar for 10-12 minutes or until thickened to a glaze consistency.* **Makes:** *about 2 tablespoons.*
PER SERVING *1 chicken breast half with ½ cup of tomatoes and 1½ teaspoons glaze equals 306 cal., 11 g fat (2 g sat. fat), 94 mg chol., 384 mg sodium, 16 g carb., 1 g fiber, 35 g pro.* **Diabetic Exchanges:** *5 lean meat, 1½ fat, 1 starch.*

Thai Chicken and Slaw

Because of the hint of sweetness from the honey, this recipe has become very popular with my friends and family. I make it whenever I have visitors.

—KAREN NORRIS PHILADELPHIA, PA

PREP: 25 MIN. + MARINATING
COOK: 30 MIN. • **MAKES:** 8 SERVINGS

- ½ cup honey
- ½ cup canola oil
- ½ cup white wine vinegar
- 2 tablespoons minced fresh gingerroot
- 2 tablespoons reduced-sodium soy sauce
- 2 garlic cloves, minced
- 1 teaspoon sesame oil
- 8 boneless skinless chicken thighs (about 2 pounds)
- SLAW
- 6 cups coleslaw mix
- 1 cup frozen shelled edamame, thawed
- 1 medium sweet pepper, chopped
- 1 tablespoon creamy peanut butter
- ½ teaspoon salt
- 4 green onions, sliced

1. In a small bowl, whisk the first seven ingredients until blended. Pour 1 cup marinade into a large resealable plastic bag. Add chicken; seal bag and turn to coat. Refrigerate overnight. Cover and refrigerate the remaining marinade.
2. Preheat oven to 350°. Drain the chicken, discarding marinade in bag. Place in a 13x9-in. baking dish coated with cooking spray. Bake, uncovered, 30-40 minutes or until temperature reads 170°.
3. Meanwhile, place coleslaw mix, edamame and pepper in a large bowl. Add peanut butter and salt to reserved marinade; whisk until blended. Pour over coleslaw mixture; toss to coat. Refrigerate until serving.
4. Serve chicken with slaw; sprinkle with green onions.
PER SERVING *1 chicken thigh with ⅔ cup slaw equals 326 cal., 18 g fat (3 g sat. fat), 76 mg chol., 171 mg sodium, 16 g carb., 2 g fiber, 24 g pro.* **Diabetic Exchanges:** *3 lean meat, 2 fat, 1 vegetable, ½ starch.*

THAI CHICKEN AND SLAW

Grilled Tomatillo Chicken for Two [C]

This winning chicken gets its flavorful kick from a tomatillo mixture jazzed up with lime juice, cilantro and jalapeno. Dollop with sour cream and serve over rice for a memorable meal.

—AUDREY KINNE ELKHART, IN

PREP: 25 MIN. • **GRILL:** 10 MIN.
MAKES: 2 SERVINGS

- 2 **boneless skinless chicken breast halves (6 ounces each)**
- 2 **slices provolone cheese**
- 1 **small onion, chopped**
- 1½ **teaspoons olive oil**
- 3 **tomatillos, husks removed, chopped**
- 2 **tablespoons lime juice**
- 3 **pickled jalapeno slices, chopped**
- 1 **garlic clove, minced**
- 2 **tablespoons minced fresh cilantro**
- ½ **teaspoon ground cumin**
- ¼ **teaspoon salt**
- ⅛ **teaspoon pepper**
  Hot cooked rice
  Sour cream, optional

1. Moisten a paper towel with cooking oil; using long-handled tongs, lightly coat the grill rack. Grill the chicken, covered, over medium heat or broil 4 in. from the heat for 4-7 minutes on each side or until a thermometer reads 170°. Top with cheese; cook 1 minute longer or until cheese is melted.

2. In a large skillet, saute onion in oil until tender. Add the tomatillos, lime juice, jalapenos and garlic; cook 3 minutes longer. Stir in the cilantro, cumin, salt and pepper. Serve the tomatillo mixture and chicken with rice; dollop with sour cream if desired.

PER SERVING *1 chicken breast half with ½ cup tomatillo mixture (calculated without rice and sour cream) equals 324 cal., 14 g fat (5 g sat. fat), 109 mg chol., 596 mg sodium, 9 g carb., 2 g fiber, 40 g pro.* **Diabetic Exchanges:** *5 lean meat, 1½ fat, 1 vegetable.*

CHICKEN SAUSAGES WITH POLENTA

Chicken Sausages with Polenta [FAST FIX]

I get a kick out of serving this savory dish—everyone's always on time for dinner when they know it's on the menu.

—ANGELA SPENGLER TAMPA, FL

START TO FINISH: 30 MIN.
MAKES: 6 SERVINGS

- 4 **teaspoons olive oil, divided**
- 1 **tube (1 pound) polenta, cut into ½-inch slices**
- 1 **each medium green, sweet red and yellow peppers, thinly sliced**
- 1 **medium onion, thinly sliced**
- 1 **package (12 ounces) fully cooked Italian chicken sausage links, thinly sliced**
- ¼ **cup grated Parmesan cheese**
- 1 **tablespoon minced fresh basil**

1. In a large nonstick skillet, heat 2 teaspoons oil over medium heat. Add the polenta; cook 9-11 minutes on each side or until golden brown. Keep warm.

2. Meanwhile, in another large skillet, heat remaining oil over medium-high heat. Add peppers and onion; cook and stir until tender. Remove from pan.

3. Add sausages to the same pan; cook and stir 4-5 minutes or until browned. Return pepper mixture to pan; heat through. Serve with polenta; sprinkle with cheese and basil.

PER SERVING *⅔ cup sausage mixture with 2 slices polenta equals 212 cal., 9 g fat (2 g sat. fat), 46 mg chol., 628 mg sodium, 19 g carb., 2 g fiber, 13 g pro.* **Diabetic Exchanges:** *2 lean meat, 1 starch, 1 vegetable, ½ fat.*

HONEY-LEMON CHICKEN ENCHILADAS

Honey-Lemon Chicken Enchiladas FAST FIX

Honey, lemon and chili flavors blend wonderfully in enchiladas. My family devours this dish. I also use the chicken filling for soft tacos with toppings.
—**KRISTI MOAK** GILBERT, AZ

START TO FINISH: 30 MIN.
MAKES: 6 SERVINGS

- ¼ cup honey
- 2 tablespoons lemon or lime juice
- 1 tablespoon canola oil
- 2 teaspoons chili powder
- ¼ teaspoon garlic powder
- 3 cups shredded cooked chicken breast
- 2 cans (10 ounces each) green enchilada sauce
- 12 corn tortillas (6 inches), warmed
- ¾ cup shredded reduced-fat cheddar cheese
  Sliced green onions and chopped tomatoes, optional

1. In a large bowl, whisk the first five ingredients. Add chicken and toss to coat. Pour 1 can enchilada sauce into a greased microwave-safe 11x7-in. dish. Place ¼ cup chicken mixture off center on each tortilla. Roll up and place in prepared dish, seam side down. Top tortillas with remaining enchilada sauce.
2. Microwave, covered, on high for 11-13 minutes or until heated through. Sprinkle with cheese. If desired, top with green onions and tomatoes.
NOTE *This recipe was tested in a full-size 1,100-watt microwave. If your microwave does not accommodate an 11x7-in. dish, bake casserole, covered, in a preheated 400° oven for 25-30 minutes or until heated through. Sprinkle with cheese and toppings as directed.*
PER SERVING *2 enchiladas (calculated without optional toppings) equals 349 cal., 11 g fat (3 g sat. fat), 64 mg chol., 698 mg sodium, 39 g carb., 3 g fiber, 27 g pro.* **Diabetic Exchanges:** *3 lean meat, 2½ starch.*

> My family goes back to this one-bowl meal again and again. The zing comes from our favorite sesame ginger dressing.
> —MELISSA JELINEK APPLE VALLEY, MN

CHINESE CHICKEN SALAD

Chinese Chicken Salad FAST FIX

START TO FINISH: 20 MIN.
MAKES: 4 SERVINGS

- 2 cups cubed fresh pineapple
- 2 cups sliced bok choy
- 2 cups shredded red cabbage
- ⅓ cup plus ¼ cup sesame ginger salad dressing, divided
- 4 boneless skinless chicken breast halves (4 ounces each)

1. Preheat broiler. In a large bowl, combine pineapple, bok choy, cabbage and ⅓ cup salad dressing; toss to coat.
2. Place the chicken in a 15x10x1-in. baking pan. Brush both sides of the chicken with the remaining salad dressing. Broil 3-4 in. from heat for 4-5 minutes on each side or until a thermometer reads 165°.
3. Divide the salad among four bowls. Slice the chicken; arrange over salad. Serve immediately.
PER SERVING *1 serving equals 302 cal., 13 g fat (3 g sat. fat), 63 mg chol., 433 mg sodium, 21 g carb., 2 g fiber, 24 g pro.* **Diabetic Exchanges:** *3 lean meat, 1½ fat, 1 starch, 1 vegetable, ½ fruit.*

Spring Chicken and Pea Salad **C** FAST FIX ▶

My endive, radicchio and chicken salad makes a wonderful luncheon or light dinner to welcome in spring.
—**ROXANNE CHAN** ALBANY, CA

START TO FINISH: 20 MIN.
MAKES: 4 SERVINGS

- 1 **cup fresh peas**
- 2 **cups torn curly or Belgian endive**
- 2 **cups torn radicchio**
- 2 **cups chopped rotisserie chicken**
- ½ **cup sliced radishes**
- 2 **tablespoons chopped red onion**
- 2 **tablespoons fresh mint leaves, torn**

DRESSING
- 2 **tablespoons olive oil**
- ¼ **teaspoon grated lemon peel**
- 1 **tablespoon lemon juice**
- 1 **tablespoon mint jelly**
- 1 **garlic clove, minced**
- ¼ **teaspoon salt**
- ¼ **teaspoon pepper**
  Toasted pine nuts, optional

1. In a large saucepan, bring ½ in. of water to a boil. Add peas; cover and cook 5-8 minutes or until tender.

2. Drain peas; place in a large bowl. Add the endive, radicchio, chicken, radishes, onion and mint. In a small saucepan, combine oil, lemon peel, juice, jelly, garlic, salt and pepper; cook and stir over medium-low heat for 4-6 minutes or until jelly is melted. Drizzle over the salad; toss to coat. If desired, sprinkle with pine nuts.

PER SERVING *1½ cups equals 250 cal., 12 g fat (2 g sat. fat), 62 mg chol., 225 mg sodium, 12 g carb., 3 g fiber, 23 g pro.* **Diabetic Exchanges:** *3 lean meat, 1½ fat, 1 vegetable, ½ starch.*

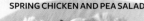

SPRING CHICKEN AND PEA SALAD

CHICKEN STRIPS MILANO

Chicken Strips Milano FAST FIX ▶

A dear friend shared this recipe a few years ago. Since then, I've prepared the garlicky chicken pasta for both family dinners and get-togethers.
—**LARA PRIEST** GANSEVOORT, NY

START TO FINISH: 20 MIN.
MAKES: 6 SERVINGS

- 12 **ounces linguine**
- 1 **tablespoon minced garlic**
- 4½ **teaspoons plus 2 tablespoons olive oil, divided**
- ¾ **teaspoon dried parsley flakes**
- ¾ **teaspoon pepper, divided**
- ¼ **cup all-purpose flour**
- 1 **teaspoon dried basil**
- ½ **teaspoon salt**
- 2 **large eggs**
- 1½ **pounds boneless skinless chicken breasts, cut into strips**

1. Cook the linguine according to package directions.

2. Meanwhile, in a large skillet, saute garlic in 4½ teaspoons oil for 1 minute. Stir in parsley and ½ teaspoon pepper. Remove to a small bowl and set aside.

3. In a shallow bowl, combine the flour, basil, salt and remaining pepper. In another shallow bowl, whisk eggs. Dredge chicken strips in flour mixture, then dip in eggs.

4. In the same skillet, cook and stir chicken in remaining oil over medium-high heat for 8-10 minutes or until no longer pink.

5. Drain linguine; place on a serving platter. Pour the garlic mixture over linguine and toss to coat; top with chicken strips.

PER SERVING *3 ounces cooked chicken with ¾ cup linguine equals 441 cal., 14 g fat (3 g sat. fat), 133 mg chol., 278 mg sodium, 46 g carb., 2 g fiber, 33 g pro.* **Diabetic Exchanges:** *3 starch, 3 lean meat, 1½ fat.*

Mediterranean Baked Chicken with Lemon ⓒ

While visiting our daughters in Ohio, we celebrated by cooking a wonderful Lebanese dinner. We served this chicken with garlic-roasted potatoes and finished with our homemade baklava.

—SHIRLEY GLAAB HATTIESBURG, MS

PREP: 20 MIN. + MARINATING
BAKE: 35 MIN. • **MAKES:** 8 SERVINGS

- 1 cup olive oil
- ½ cup lemon juice
- 6 garlic cloves, minced
- 1 teaspoon salt
- 1 teaspoon dried thyme
- ½ teaspoon pepper
- ¼ teaspoon ground allspice
- ¼ teaspoon ground nutmeg
- 8 boneless skinless chicken breast halves (6 ounces each)
- 3 medium lemons, thinly sliced

SPICE BLEND
- 2 teaspoons paprika
- ½ teaspoon garlic salt
- ½ teaspoon lemon-pepper seasoning
- ¼ teaspoon ground allspice
- ⅛ teaspoon ground cinnamon

1. In a small bowl, whisk the first eight ingredients until blended. Pour 1 cup of marinade into a large resealable plastic bag. Add chicken; seal bag and turn to coat. Refrigerate 1 hour. Cover and refrigerate remaining marinade.
2. Preheat oven to 350°. Arrange the lemon slices in two greased 11x7-in. baking dishes. Drain the chicken, discarding marinade in bag. Place the chicken over lemon slices. Mix spice blend ingredients; sprinkle over the chicken. Drizzle with the reserved marinade. Bake chicken, covered, for 35-40 minutes or until a thermometer reads 165°.

PER SERVING *1 chicken breast half equals 385 cal., 26 g fat (4 g sat. fat), 94 mg chol., 469 mg sodium, 4 g carb., 1 g fiber, 34 g pro.*

Chicken & Garlic with Fresh Herbs ⓒ `FAST FIX` ▶

The key to this savory chicken is the combination of garlic and fresh rosemary and thyme. I like to serve it with mashed potatoes or fresh Italian bread.

—JAN VALDEZ LOMBARD, IL

START TO FINISH: 30 MIN.
MAKES: 6 SERVINGS

- 6 boneless skinless chicken thighs (about 1½ pounds)
- ½ teaspoon salt
- ¼ teaspoon pepper
- 1 tablespoon olive oil
- 10 garlic cloves, peeled and halved
- 2 tablespoons brandy or chicken stock
- 1 cup chicken stock
- 1 teaspoon minced fresh rosemary or ¼ teaspoon dried rosemary, crushed
- ½ teaspoon minced fresh thyme or ⅛ teaspoon dried thyme
- 1 tablespoon minced fresh chives

1. Sprinkle the chicken with salt and pepper. In a large skillet, heat oil over medium-high heat. Brown chicken on both sides. Remove from pan.
2. Remove skillet from heat; add garlic and brandy. Return to heat; cook and stir over medium heat 1-2 minutes or until liquid is almost evaporated.
3. Stir in stock, rosemary and thyme; return chicken to pan. Bring to a boil. Reduce heat; simmer, uncovered, for 6-8 minutes or until a thermometer reads 170°. Sprinkle with chives.

PER SERVING *1 chicken thigh with 2 tablespoons cooking juices equals 203 cal., 11 g fat (3 g sat. fat), 76 mg chol., 346 mg sodium, 2 g carb., trace fiber, 22 g pro.* ***Diabetic Exchanges:*** *3 lean meat, ½ fat.*

CHICKEN & GARLIC WITH FRESH HERBS

BASIL CHICKEN

Chicken with Mandarin Salsa FAST FIX ▶

When I have leftover veggies, I dress up the salsa a little bit with some finely chopped green onions and sweet red peppers. If you like a more spicy salsa, toss in a little cayenne pepper.

—AYSHA SCHURMAN AMMON, ID

START TO FINISH: 20 MIN.
MAKES: 4 SERVINGS

- 1 can (11 ounces) mandarin oranges
- ½ cup chopped pecans
- ¼ cup finely chopped red onion
- 2 tablespoons minced fresh cilantro
- 1 pound boneless skinless chicken breasts, cut into 1-inch cubes
- ½ teaspoon salt
- ½ teaspoon pepper
- 1 tablespoon olive oil
- 2 garlic cloves, minced
- 2⅔ cups hot cooked brown rice

1. Drain the oranges, reserving ¼ cup juice. For the salsa, in a large bowl, combine the oranges, pecans, onion and cilantro.
2. Sprinkle the chicken with salt and pepper. In a large skillet, heat oil over medium-high heat. Add chicken; cook and stir 4 minutes. Add garlic; cook 1 minute longer. Stir in reserved juice. Bring to a boil. Reduce heat; simmer, uncovered, for 4-6 minutes or until chicken is no longer pink. Top with salsa; serve with rice.
PER SERVING *⅔ cup chicken mixture with ⅔ cup cooked rice equals 453 cal., 18 g fat (2 g sat. fat), 63 mg chol., 362 mg sodium, 46 g carb., 5 g fiber, 28 g pro.*

CHICKEN WITH MANDARIN SALSA

Basil Chicken C

This cinch of a marinade gives chicken breast lots of Italian flavor. Serve the chicken with a tossed green salad and garlic breadsticks, or put slices on a ciabatta roll along with lettuce, tomato and mozzarella for a zesty sandwich.

—LISA MORIARTY WILTON, NH

PREP: 10 MIN. + MARINATING
GRILL: 10 MIN. • **MAKES:** 4 SERVINGS

- 3 tablespoons red wine vinegar
- 3 tablespoons olive oil
- 2 tablespoons chopped red onion
- 2 tablespoons minced fresh basil
- 1 garlic clove, minced
- ¼ teaspoon salt
- ¼ teaspoon pepper
- 4 boneless skinless chicken breast halves (6 ounces each)
  Grilled romaine, optional

1. In a large resealable plastic bag, combine the first seven ingredients. Add chicken; seal bag and turn to coat. Refrigerate 8 hours or overnight.
2. Drain chicken, discarding the marinade. Grill chicken, covered, over medium heat or broil 4 in. from heat 5-7 minutes on each side or until a thermometer reads 165°. If desired, serve over grilled romaine.
FREEZE OPTION *Freeze chicken with marinade in a resealable plastic freezer bag. To use, thaw in the refrigerator overnight. Drain chicken, discarding marinade. Grill as directed.*
PER SERVING *1 chicken breast half equals 231 cal., 9 g fat (2 g sat. fat), 94 mg chol., 156 mg sodium, 1 g carb., trace fiber, 34 g pro.* **Diabetic Exchanges:** *5 lean meat, 1 fat.*

Asian Chicken Thighs

A sweet-tangy sauce coats juicy chicken thighs in this simple skillet dish. I like to serve it with rice or ramen noodle slaw.
—**DAVE FARRINGTON** MIDWEST CITY, OK

PREP: 15 MIN. • **COOK:** 50 MIN.
MAKES: 5 SERVINGS

- 5 teaspoons olive oil
- 5 bone-in chicken thighs (about 1¾ pounds), skin removed
- ⅓ cup water
- ¼ cup packed brown sugar
- 2 tablespoons orange juice
- 2 tablespoons reduced-sodium soy sauce
- 2 tablespoons ketchup
- 1 tablespoon white vinegar
- 4 garlic cloves, minced
- ½ teaspoon crushed red pepper flakes
- ¼ teaspoon Chinese five-spice powder
- 2 teaspoons cornstarch
- 2 tablespoons cold water
  Sliced green onions
  Hot cooked rice, optional

1. In a large skillet, heat oil over medium heat. Add the chicken; cook 8-10 minutes on each side or until golden brown. In a small bowl, whisk water, brown sugar, orange juice, soy sauce, ketchup, vinegar, garlic, pepper flakes and five-spice powder. Pour over chicken. Bring to a boil. Reduce heat; simmer, uncovered, for 30-35 minutes or until chicken is tender, turning chicken occasionally.
2. Mix cornstarch and cold water until smooth; stir into pan. Bring to a boil; cook and stir 1 minute or until sauce is thickened. Sprinkle with green onions. If desired, serve with rice.
FREEZE OPTION *Cool chicken. Freeze in freezer containers. To use, partially thaw chicken in refrigerator overnight. Heat slowly in a covered skillet until a thermometer inserted into chicken reads 165°, stirring occasionally and adding a little water if necessary.*
PER SERVING *1 chicken thigh (calculated without rice) equals 292 cal., 14 g fat (3 g sat. fat), 87 mg chol., 396 mg sodium, 15 g carb., trace fiber, 25 g pro. Diabetic Exchanges: 3 lean meat, 1 starch, 1 fat.*

I love to share my cooking, and this hearty meal has gotten a tasty reputation around town. Acquaintances have actually approached me in public to ask for the recipe. —**LAURIE SLEDGE** BRANDON, MS

SPICY ROASTED SAUSAGE, POTATOES AND PEPPERS

Spicy Roasted Sausage, Potatoes and Peppers

PREP: 20 MIN. • **BAKE:** 30 MIN.
MAKES: 4 SERVINGS

- 1 pound potatoes (about 2 medium), peeled and cut into ½-inch cubes
- 1 package (12 ounces) fully cooked andouille chicken sausage links or flavor of your choice, cut into 1-inch pieces
- 1 medium red onion, cut into wedges
- 1 medium sweet red pepper, cut into 1-inch pieces
- 1 medium green pepper, cut into 1-inch pieces
- ½ cup pickled pepper rings
- 1 tablespoon olive oil
- ½ to 1 teaspoon Creole seasoning
- ¼ teaspoon pepper

1. Preheat oven to 400°. In a large bowl, combine the potatoes, sausage, onion, red pepper, green pepper and pepper rings. Mix oil, Creole seasoning and pepper; drizzle over the potato mixture and toss to coat.
2. Transfer to a 15x10x1-in. baking pan coated with cooking spray. Roast 30-35 minutes or until vegetables are tender, stirring occasionally.
PER SERVING *1½ cups equals 257 cal., 11 g fat (3 g sat. fat), 65 mg chol., 759 mg sodium, 24 g carb., 3 g fiber, 17 g pro. Diabetic Exchanges: 3 lean meat, 1 starch, 1 vegetable, 1 fat.*

In-a-Pinch Chicken & Spinach C FAST FIX

I needed a fast supper while baby-sitting my grandchild. I used what my daughter-in-law had in the fridge and turned it into what's now one of our favorite recipes.
—**SANDRA ELLIS** STOCKBRIDGE, GA

START TO FINISH: 25 MIN.
MAKES: 4 SERVINGS

- 4 **boneless skinless chicken breast halves (6 ounces each)**
- 2 **tablespoons olive oil**
- 1 **tablespoon butter**
- 1 **package (6 ounces) fresh baby spinach**
- 1 **cup salsa**

1. Pound chicken with a meat mallet to ½-in. thickness. In a large skillet, heat oil and butter over medium heat. Cook chicken 5-6 minutes on each side or until no longer pink. Remove and keep warm.
2. Add the spinach and salsa to pan; cook and stir 3-4 minutes or just until spinach is wilted. Serve with chicken.

PER SERVING *1 chicken breast half with ⅓ cup spinach mixture equals 297 cal., 14 g fat (4 g sat. fat), 102 mg chol., 376 mg sodium, 6 g carb., 1 g fiber, 36 g pro.* **Diabetic Exchanges:** *5 lean meat, 2 fat, 1 vegetable.*

STOVETOP TARRAGON CHICKEN

IN-A-PINCH CHICKEN & SPINACH

Stovetop Tarragon Chicken

My oldest daughter can't get enough of the tarragon sauce. She uses biscuits to soak up every drop. My husband and I like it over mashed potatoes.
—**TINA WESTOVER** LA MESA, CA

PREP: 10 MIN. • **COOK:** 30 MIN.
MAKES: 4 SERVINGS

- 4 **boneless skinless chicken breast halves (5 ounces each)**
- 2 **teaspoons paprika**
- 1 **tablespoon olive oil**
- 1 **package (10 ounces) julienned carrots**
- ½ **pound sliced fresh mushrooms**
- 2 **cans (10¾ ounces each) reduced-fat reduced-sodium condensed cream of chicken soup, undiluted**
- 3 **teaspoons dried tarragon**
- 1 **tablespoon lemon juice**
- 3 **small zucchini, thinly sliced**

1. Sprinkle chicken with paprika. In a Dutch oven, heat oil over medium heat. Cook chicken 2 minutes on each side or until lightly browned; remove from pan.
2. Add carrots and mushrooms to same pan; cook, covered, 6-8 minutes or until the carrots are crisp-tender, stirring occasionally. In a small bowl, mix soup, tarragon and lemon juice until blended; pour over vegetables. Return chicken to pan. Bring to a boil; reduce heat to low. Cook, covered, for 8 minutes. Top with zucchini; cook, covered, 6-8 minutes longer or until a thermometer inserted into chicken reads 165° and vegetables are tender.

PER SERVING *1 chicken breast with 1 cup vegetables equals 345 cal., 11 g fat (3 g sat. fat), 85 mg chol., 649 mg sodium, 28 g carb., 5 g fiber, 35 g pro.* **Diabetic Exchanges:** *4 lean meat, 2 vegetable, 1 starch, 1 fat.*

Chicken with Three-Citrus Topping F

Honey sweetens up the citrusy fruit salad that makes this chicken such a pretty dish. Add fresh bakery bread and you have something delightful for company.

—**MOLLY SLOSSON** WESTPORT, WA

PREP: 30 MIN. • **BROIL:** 10 MIN.
MAKES: 8 SERVINGS (7⅓ CUPS TOPPING)

- ¼ cup lime juice
- 1 tablespoon honey
- 1 teaspoon grated lime peel
- ½ teaspoon cayenne pepper
- 4 cups sweet red grapefruit sections
- 2⅔ cups orange sections
- ⅔ cup lemon sections
- 1 tablespoon rotisserie chicken seasoning
- 8 boneless skinless chicken breast halves (4 ounces each)

1. Preheat broiler. In a large bowl, mix the lime juice, honey, lime peel and cayenne. Add citrus sections; toss to coat. Sprinkle seasoning over chicken.
2. Place chicken on greased rack of a broiler pan. Broil 4 in. from the heat 5-6 minutes on each side or until a thermometer reads 165°. Serve with the citrus topping.

PER SERVING *1 chicken breast half with about ¾ cup topping equals 201 cal., 3 g fat (1 g sat. fat), 63 mg chol., 446 mg sodium, 21 g carb., 3 g fiber, 24 g pro. **Diabetic Exchanges:** 3 lean meat, 1½ fruit.*

LIME CHICKEN WITH SALSA VERDE SOUR CREAM

CHICKEN WITH THREE-CITRUS TOPPING

Lime Chicken with Salsa Verde Sour Cream C FAST FIX

Whenever I'm in a time crunch, this dish comes to the rescue. Mexican spices and salsa verde give broiled chicken a big pick-me-up. My friends are always asking me for the recipe.

—**ELLEN FOWLER** SEATTLE, WA

START TO FINISH: 20 MIN.
MAKES: 4 SERVINGS

- ¾ teaspoon ground coriander
- ¼ teaspoon salt
- ¼ teaspoon ground cumin
- ¼ teaspoon pepper
- 4 boneless skinless chicken thighs (about 1 pound)
- ⅓ cup reduced-fat sour cream
- 2 tablespoons salsa verde
- 2 tablespoons minced fresh cilantro, divided
- 1 medium lime

1. Preheat broiler. Mix seasonings; sprinkle over chicken. Place chicken on a broiler pan. Broil 4 in. from heat for 6-8 minutes on each side or until a thermometer reads 170°.
2. Meanwhile, in a small bowl, mix the sour cream, salsa and 1 tablespoon cilantro. Cut lime in half. Squeeze juice from one lime half into sour cream mixture; stir to combine. Cut the remaining lime half into four wedges. Serve chicken with sauce and the lime wedges. Sprinkle chicken with the remaining cilantro.

PER SERVING *1 chicken thigh with 1½ tablespoons sour cream equals 199 cal., 10 g fat (3 g sat. fat), 82 mg chol., 267 mg sodium, 4 g carb., 1 g fiber, 23 g pro. **Diabetic Exchanges:** 3 lean meat, 1 fat.*

SAUSAGE & PEPPER PIZZA

Italian Sausage and Provolone Skewers C FAST FIX

START TO FINISH: 30 MIN.
MAKES: 8 SERVINGS

- 1 large onion
- 1 large sweet red pepper
- 1 large green pepper
- 2 cups cherry tomatoes
- 1 tablespoon olive oil
- ½ teaspoon pepper
- ¼ teaspoon salt
- 2 packages (12 ounces each) fully cooked Italian chicken sausage links, cut into 1¼-inch slices
- 16 cubes provolone cheese (¾ inch each)

1. Cut onion and peppers into 1-in. pieces; place in a large bowl. Add the tomatoes, oil, pepper and salt; toss to coat. On 16 metal or soaked wooden skewers, alternately thread sausage and vegetables.

2. Grill, covered, over medium heat 8-10 minutes or until sausage is heated through and vegetables are tender, turning occasionally. Remove kabobs from grill; thread one cheese cube onto each kabob.

PER SERVING *2 kabobs equals 220 cal., 13 g fat (5 g sat. fat), 75 mg chol., 682 mg sodium, 7 g carb., 2 g fiber, 20 g pro.* **Diabetic Exchanges:** *3 medium-fat meat, 1 vegetable.*

Sausage & Pepper Pizza

All pizza should satisfy a craving. This one easily beats delivery service to your table.
—**JAMES SCHEND** PLEASANT PRAIRIE, WI

PREP: 25 MIN. • **BAKE:** 20 MIN.
MAKES: 6 SERVINGS

- 1 package (6½ ounces) pizza crust mix
- 1 can (8 ounces) pizza sauce
- 1¼ cups (5 ounces) shredded pizza cheese blend
- 1 medium onion, sliced
- 1 medium green pepper, sliced
- 2 fully cooked Italian chicken sausage links, sliced
  Grated Parmesan cheese, optional

1. Preheat oven to 425°. Prepare the pizza dough according to package directions. Press dough onto bottom and ½ in. up sides of a greased 13x9-in. baking pan.

2. Spread with pizza sauce. Top with 1 cup cheese blend, onion, pepper and sausage; sprinkle with the remaining cheese blend.

3. Bake 17-20 minutes or until crust is golden brown. If desired, sprinkle with Parmesan cheese.

PER SERVING *1 piece (calculated without Parmesan cheese) equals 257 cal., 9 g fat (5 g sat. fat), 39 mg chol., 565 mg sodium, 28 g carb., 2 g fiber, 15 g pro.* **Diabetic Exchanges:** *2 starch, 2 medium-fat meat.*

My husband made sausage and veggie kabobs when we didn't have buns to make classic sausage bombers. Grill 'em up, then add cheese cubes.
—**CINDY HILLIARD** KENOSHA, WI

ITALIAN SAUSAGE AND PROVOLONE SKEWERS

Mushroom & Herb Chicken C FAST FIX

My easy skillet dish is a comfort food classic. It's also delicious with rice instead of noodles. No one will guess they're eating healthy with this one.

—BETSY KING DULUTH, MN

START TO FINISH: 30 MIN.
MAKES: 4 SERVINGS

- 4 boneless skinless chicken breast halves (5 ounces each)
- 1 tablespoon butter
- 1 can (10¾ ounces) reduced-fat reduced-sodium condensed cream of mushroom soup, undiluted
- 1 cup sliced fresh mushrooms
- ½ cup water
- 1 teaspoon minced chives
- 1 teaspoon Dijon mustard
- ½ teaspoon lemon-pepper seasoning
- ¼ teaspoon salt
- ¼ teaspoon garlic salt
- ¼ teaspoon dried rosemary, crushed
- ¼ teaspoon dried thyme
  Hot cooked egg noodles

1. Flatten chicken to ½-in. thickness. In a large skillet, brown chicken in butter. In a small bowl, combine the soup, mushrooms, water, chives, mustard, lemon-pepper, salt, garlic salt, rosemary and thyme; pour over the chicken.

2. Bring to a boil. Reduce heat; cover and simmer for 8-10 minutes or until a thermometer reads 170°. Serve with egg noodles.

PER SERVING *1 chicken breast with ⅓ cup sauce (calculated without noodles) equals 228 cal., 7 g fat (3 g sat. fat), 89 mg chol., 698 mg sodium, 8 g carb., 1 g fiber, 30 g pro.* **Diabetic Exchanges:** *4 lean meat, ½ starch.*

Summer Splash Chicken Salad FAST FIX

When it's too hot to eat inside, I head out to the patio. Shred some rotisserie chicken and toss with mango, watermelon and grapes for an ooh-ahh summer salad.

—BARBARA SPITZER LODI, CA

START TO FINISH: 20 MIN.
MAKES: 4 SERVINGS

- ½ cup plain yogurt
- 4½ teaspoons brown sugar

SUMMER SPLASH CHICKEN SALAD

- ½ teaspoon grated lime peel
- 1 tablespoon lime juice
- ¼ teaspoon salt
- 2 cups cubed cooked chicken breast
- 1 cup green grapes, halved
- 1 cup chopped peeled mango
- 1 cup chopped seedless watermelon
- 4 cups torn Bibb or Boston lettuce
- ¼ cup chopped pistachios, toasted

1. In a bowl, mix first five ingredients until blended. Add chicken, grapes, mango and watermelon; toss gently to combine.

2. Divide lettuce among four plates; top with chicken mixture. Sprinkle with pistachios.

NOTE *To toast nuts, bake in a shallow pan in a 350° oven for 5-10 minutes or cook in a skillet over low heat until lightly browned, stirring occasionally.*

PER SERVING *1 cup chicken mixture with 1 cup lettuce and 1 tablespoon pistachios equals 262 cal., 7 g fat (2 g sat. fat), 58 mg chol., 249 mg sodium, 27 g carb., 3 g fiber, 24 g pro.* **Diabetic Exchanges:** *3 lean meat, 1 vegetable, 1 fruit, 1 fat, ½ starch.*

136

138

143

Turkey Specialties

"My fiance and I love Greek food. I recently made a few changes to a meat loaf recipe in order to create burgers. This is the perfect meal on a hot summer day."

—MELISSA BEYER UTICA, NY
about her recipe, Sun-Dried Tomato Burgers, on page 133

Waldorf Turkey Salad FAST FIX

Crisp apples, celery and walnuts teamed with lean poultry turn any meal into a picnic. The combination of tastes and textures makes this Waldorf Turkey Salad a cool classic.

—MITZI SENTIFF ANNAPOLIS, MD

START TO FINISH: 25 MIN.
MAKES: 4 SERVINGS

- 1 cup (8 ounces) plain yogurt
- 2 tablespoons honey
- ⅛ to ¼ teaspoon ground ginger
- ¼ teaspoon salt
- 2 cups cubed cooked turkey breast
- 1 cup cubed apple
- 1 cup seedless red grapes, halved
- ½ cup thinly sliced celery
- ½ cup raisins
- 4 lettuce leaves
- 2 tablespoons chopped walnuts

1. In a small bowl, whisk the yogurt, honey, ginger and salt. In a large bowl, combine the turkey, apple, grapes, celery and raisins; add yogurt mixture and toss to coat.

2. Serve the turkey salad on lettuce; sprinkle with walnuts.

PER SERVING *1¼ cups equals 294 cal., 5 g fat (2 g sat. fat), 68 mg chol., 233 mg sodium, 39 g carb., 2 g fiber, 25 g pro.* ***Diabetic Exchanges:*** *3 lean meat, 1½ fruit, 1 starch, ½ fat.*

TURKEY & APRICOT WRAPS

For these wraps, I combined the traditional Southern appetizer of jam and cream cheese on crackers with the turkey sandwiches we ate at my bridal luncheon. I like to sneak fresh baby spinach into all sorts of recipes because it has such a nice crunch and fresh flavor. —KIM BEAVERS NORTH AUGUSTA, SC

WALDORF TURKEY SALAD

Turkey & Apricot Wraps FAST FIX

START TO FINISH: 15 MIN.
MAKES: 4 SERVINGS

- ½ cup reduced-fat cream cheese
- 3 tablespoons apricot preserves
- 4 whole wheat tortillas (8 inches), room temperature
- ½ pound sliced reduced-sodium deli turkey
- 2 cups fresh baby spinach or arugula

In a small bowl, mix cream cheese and preserves. Spread about 2 tablespoons over each tortilla to within ½ in. of edges. Layer with turkey and spinach. Roll up tightly. Serve immediately or wrap in plastic wrap and refrigerate until serving.

PER SERVING *1 wrap equals 312 cal., 10 g fat (4 g sat. fat), 41 mg chol., 655 mg sodium, 33 g carb., 2 g fiber, 20 g pro.* ***Diabetic Exchanges:*** *2 starch, 2 lean meat, 1 fat.*

Sun-Dried Tomato Burgers

My fiance and I love Greek food. I recently made a few changes to a meat loaf recipe in order to create burgers. This is the perfect meal on a hot summer day.

—MELISSA BEYER UTICA, NY

PREP: 30 MIN. • **GRILL:** 10 MIN.
MAKES: 4 SERVINGS

- ½ **cup reduced-fat sour cream**
- 2 **teaspoons lemon juice**
- 1 **garlic clove, minced**
- ¼ **teaspoon dried oregano**
- ¼ **teaspoon pepper**

BURGERS

- 1 **pound lean ground turkey**
- ¼ **cup crumbled feta cheese**
- ¼ **cup oil-packed sun-dried tomatoes, chopped**
- ¼ **cup sun-dried tomato pesto**
- 1 **tablespoon salt-free Greek seasoning**
- 4 **whole wheat hamburger buns, split**
- ¼ **cup chopped water-packed artichoke hearts**
- ¼ **cup julienned roasted sweet red peppers**

1. For sauce, in a small bowl, mix the first five ingredients. Refrigerate until serving.

2. In a large bowl, combine turkey, feta cheese, tomatoes, pesto and Greek seasoning, mixing lightly but thoroughly. Shape into four ½-in.-thick patties.

3. Moisten a paper towel with cooking oil; using long-handled tongs, rub on grill rack to coat lightly. Grill burgers, covered, over medium heat or broil 4 in. from heat for 4-6 minutes on each side or until a thermometer reads 165°. Serve burgers on buns with the sauce, artichoke hearts and peppers.

PER SERVING *1 burger equals 391 cal., 17 g fat (5 g sat. fat), 92 mg chol., 640 mg sodium, 30 g carb., 5 g fiber, 31 g pro.* **Diabetic Exchanges:** *3 lean meat, 2 starch, 2 fat.*

Broccoli, Rice and Sausage Dinner `FAST FIX`

The first recipe my kids requested when they left home was broccoli with sausage and rice. If fresh zucchini or summer squash is available, add it to the mix.

—JOANN PARMENTIER BRANCH, MI

START TO FINISH: 25 MIN.
MAKES: 6 SERVINGS

- 1 **tablespoon canola oil**
- 1 **package (13 ounces) smoked turkey sausage, sliced**
- 4 **cups small fresh broccoli florets**
- 2 **cups water**
- 1 **can (14½ ounces) diced tomatoes, drained**
- ¼ **teaspoon seasoned salt**
- ¼ **teaspoon garlic powder**
- ¼ **teaspoon dried oregano**
- 2 **cups uncooked instant brown rice**
- ½ **cup shredded sharp cheddar cheese**

  Reduced-fat sour cream and Louisiana-style hot sauce, optional

1. In a large skillet, heat the oil over medium-high heat. Add the sausage; cook and stir for 2-3 minutes or until browned. Add broccoli; cook and stir 2 minutes longer.

2. Add the water, tomatoes and seasonings; bring to a boil. Stir in the rice. Reduce heat; simmer, covered, 5 minutes.

3. Remove from heat; stir rice mixture and sprinkle with cheese. Let stand, covered, for 5 minutes or until liquid is almost absorbed and cheese is melted. If desired, serve with sour cream and hot sauce.

PER SERVING *1 cup (calculated without sour cream and hot sauce) equals 276 cal., 10 g fat (3 g sat. fat), 48 mg chol., 853 mg sodium, 30 g carb., 4 g fiber, 17 g pro.* **Diabetic Exchanges:** *2 lean meat, 1½ starch, 1 vegetable, ½ fat.*

BROCCOLI, RICE AND SAUSAGE DINNER

TURKEY LO MEIN

Turkey Lo Mein FAST FIX >

I love Chinese dishes but not the required veggie chopping. Using presliced mushrooms and ready-made sauce, I came up with a quick, easy and versatile meal. I sometimes add peanuts or cashews for extra crunch and flavor.
—**CHRISTI PAULTON** PHELPS, WI

START TO FINISH: 30 MIN.
MAKES: 8 SERVINGS

- 8 **ounces uncooked linguine**
- 2 **pounds turkey breast tenderloins, cut into ¼-inch strips**
- 2 **tablespoons canola oil, divided**
- ½ **pound sliced fresh mushrooms**
- 1⅔ **cups julienned sweet red, yellow and/or green peppers**
- ⅓ **cup chopped onion**
- ⅔ **cup stir-fry sauce**

1. Cook linguine according to package directions. Meanwhile, in a large skillet or wok, stir-fry turkey in batches in 1 tablespoon hot oil for 5-6 minutes or until no longer pink. Remove and keep warm.
2. In the same pan, stir-fry peppers and onion in remaining oil for 4-5 minutes or until crisp-tender. Add mushrooms; stir-fry 3-4 minutes or until vegetables are tender. Add turkey and stir-fry sauce; cook and stir for 2-3 minutes or until heated through. Drain linguine; add to turkey mixture and toss to coat.
PER SERVING *1 cup equals 287 cal., 6 g fat (1 g sat. fat), 56 mg chol., 771 mg sodium, 28 g carb., 2 g fiber, 33 g pro.* **Diabetic Exchanges:** *3 lean meat, 2 starch.*

Curry-Roasted Turkey and Potatoes FAST FIX

Honey mustard is the top condiment around here, so I wanted a healthy recipe to serve it with. Roasted turkey with a dash of curry is the perfect match.
—**CAROL WITCZAK** TINLEY PARK, IL

START TO FINISH: 30 MIN.
MAKES: 4 SERVINGS

- 1 **pound Yukon Gold potatoes (about 3 medium), cut into ½-inch cubes**
- 2 **medium leeks (white portion only), thinly sliced**
- 2 **tablespoons canola oil, divided**
- ½ **teaspoon pepper, divided**
- ¼ **teaspoon salt, divided**
- 3 **tablespoons Dijon mustard**
- 3 **tablespoons honey**
- ¾ **teaspoon curry powder**
- 1 **package (17.6 ounces) turkey breast cutlets**
  Minced fresh cilantro or thinly sliced green onions, optional

1. Preheat oven to 450°. Place the potatoes and leeks in a 15x10x1-in. baking pan coated with cooking spray. Drizzle vegetables with 1 tablespoon oil; sprinkle with ¼ teaspoon pepper and ⅛ teaspoon salt. Stir to coat. Roast 15 minutes, stirring once.
2. Meanwhile, in a small bowl, combine the mustard, honey, curry powder and remaining oil. Sprinkle turkey with remaining salt and pepper.
3. Drizzle 2 tablespoons mustard mixture over potatoes; stir to coat. Place turkey over potato mixture; drizzle with remaining mustard mixture. Roast 6-8 minutes or until turkey is no longer pink and potatoes are tender. If desired, sprinkle with minced cilantro.
PER SERVING *3 ounces cooked turkey with ¾ cup potato mixture equals 393 cal., 9 g fat (1 g sat. fat), 71 mg chol., 582 mg sodium, 44 g carb., 3 g fiber, 33 g pro.* **Diabetic Exchanges:** *4 lean meat, 3 starch, 1½ fat.*

CURRY-ROASTED TURKEY AND POTATOES

Gluten-Free Turkey Spaghetti

My family never tires of this versatile entree. I sometimes omit the turkey for a meatless meal, change up the veggies or use my own tomato sauce.
—**MARY LOU MOELLER** WOOSTER, OH

PREP: 15 MIN. • **COOK:** 25 MIN.
MAKES: 4 SERVINGS

- 1 **pound lean ground turkey**
- 1 **small green pepper, chopped**
- ½ **cup sliced fresh mushrooms**
- ¼ **cup chopped onion**
- 1 **can (15 ounces) tomato sauce**
- 6 **ounces uncooked gluten-free spaghetti, broken into 2-inch pieces**
- ¾ **cup water**
- ¼ **teaspoon garlic salt**
   Grated Parmesan cheese, optional

1. In a large nonstick skillet coated with cooking spray, cook the turkey, pepper, mushrooms and onion over medium heat until meat is no longer pink and vegetables are crisp-tender.
2. Stir in the tomato sauce, spaghetti, water and garlic salt. Bring to a boil. Reduce heat; cover and simmer for 15-20 minutes or until spaghetti and vegetables are tender. Garnish with cheese if desired.
NOTE *Read all ingredient labels for possible gluten content prior to use. Ingredient formulas can change, and production facilities vary among brands. If you're concerned that your brand may contain gluten, contact the company.*
PER SERVING *1¼ cups (calculated without cheese) equals 361 cal., 10 g fat (3 g sat. fat), 90 mg chol., 709 mg sodium, 40 g carb., 3 g fiber, 26 g pro. **Diabetic Exchanges:** 3 lean meat, 2 starch, 1 vegetable.*

DID YOU KNOW?

Lean ground turkey (93% lean) contains 53% less fat and 38% less saturated fat than turkey that's 85% lean. It's good in casseroles, tacos and other dishes that use crumbled meat. Higher-fat meat works better for burgers or meat loaf.

When we were first married and poor college students, I found this simple recipe and adjusted it to our tastes. The fresh bell pepper and red onion give it a wonderful flavor. —**KALLEE TWINER** MARYVILLE, TN

QUICK & EASY TURKEY SLOPPY JOES

Quick & Easy Turkey Sloppy Joes FAST FIX

START TO FINISH: 30 MIN.
MAKES: 8 SERVINGS

- 1 **pound lean ground turkey**
- 1 **large red onion, chopped**
- 1 **large green pepper, chopped**
- 1 **can (8 ounces) tomato sauce**
- ½ **cup barbecue sauce**
- 1 **teaspoon dried oregano**
- 1 **teaspoon ground cumin**
- 1 **teaspoon chili powder**
- ¼ **teaspoon salt**
- 8 **hamburger buns, split**

1. In a large skillet, cook the turkey, onion and pepper over medium heat for 6-8 minutes or until turkey is no longer pink and vegetables are tender, breaking up turkey into crumbles.
2. Stir in tomato sauce, barbecue sauce and seasonings. Bring to a boil. Reduce heat; simmer, uncovered, for 10 minutes to allow flavors to blend, stirring occasionally. Serve on buns.
PER SERVING *1 sandwich equals 251 cal., 6 g fat (2 g sat. fat), 39 mg chol., 629 mg sodium, 32 g carb., 2 g fiber, 16 g pro. **Diabetic Exchanges:** 2 lean meat, 1½ starch, 1 vegetable.*

Turkey Sausage Zucchini Boats C

PREP: 30 MIN. • **BAKE:** 35 MIN.
MAKES: 6 SERVINGS

- 6 **medium zucchini**
- 1 **pound lean ground turkey**
- 1 **small onion, chopped**
- 1 **celery rib, chopped**
- 1 **garlic clove, minced**
- 1½ **teaspoons Italian seasoning**
- ¾ **teaspoon salt**
- ¼ **teaspoon cayenne pepper**
- ¼ **teaspoon paprika**
- 1 **cup salad croutons, coarsely crushed**
- 1 **cup (4 ounces) shredded part-skim mozzarella cheese, divided**

1. Preheat oven to 350°. Cut each zucchini lengthwise in half. Scoop out pulp, leaving a ¼-in. shell; chop pulp.

2. In a large skillet, cook turkey, onion, celery, garlic and seasonings over medium heat for 6-8 minutes or until turkey is no longer pink, breaking up turkey into crumbles. Stir in croutons, ½ cup cheese and the zucchini pulp. Spoon into zucchini shells.

3. Place in two ungreased 13x9-in. baking dishes; add ¼ in. water. Bake, covered, 30-35 minutes or until the zucchini is tender. Sprinkle with the remaining cheese. Bake, uncovered, about 5 minutes or until the cheese is melted.

PER SERVING *2 zucchini halves equals 240 cal., 11 g fat (4 g sat. fat), 63 mg chol., 556 mg sodium, 13 g carb., 2 g fiber, 23 g pro.* **Diabetic Exchanges:** *3 lean meat, 1 vegetable, ½ starch.*

HOW TO

QUICKLY CHOP ONIONS

Peel onion; cut in half vertically. Leave root end intact. Place onion half flat side down on cutting board. Make several slices parallel to board into the onion, leaving root uncut. Then slice perpendicularly to chop the onion.

When I worked in the school library, my co-workers were my taste-testers. They approved this healthy and happy spin on stuffed zucchini.
—**STEPHANIE COTTERMAN** WEST ALEXANDRIA, OH

TURKEY SAUSAGE ZUCCHINI BOATS

Turkey Chop Suey FAST FIX

I use leftover turkey for my fast-to-fix chop suey. Canned bean sprouts and water chestnuts add a nice crunch to the mix.

—RUTH PETERSON JENISON, MI

START TO FINISH: 20 MIN.
MAKES: 4 SERVINGS

- 1 small onion, sliced
- 2 celery ribs, sliced
- 1 tablespoon butter
- 2 cups cubed cooked turkey breast
- 1 can (8 ounces) sliced water chestnuts, drained
- 1¼ cups reduced-sodium chicken broth
- 2 tablespoons cornstarch
- ¼ cup cold water
- 3 tablespoons reduced-sodium soy sauce
- 1 can (14 ounces) bean sprouts, drained
  Hot cooked rice

1. In a large skillet, saute onion and celery in butter until tender. Add the turkey, water chestnuts and broth; bring to a boil. Reduce heat.
2. In a small bowl, combine the cornstarch, water and soy sauce until smooth; add to turkey mixture. Bring to a boil; cook and stir for 2 minutes or until thickened. Add bean sprouts. Serve with rice.

PER SERVING *1¼ cups (calculated without rice) equals 204 cal., 4 g fat (2 g sat. fat), 68 mg chol., 762 mg sodium, 17 g carb., 3 g fiber, 25 g pro. Diabetic Exchanges: 3 lean meat, 2 vegetable, ½ starch.*

Black Bean Turkey Enchiladas

My best friend and I created this recipe together because we wanted a meal that's easy to prepare, affordable and nutritious. We both have hectic schedules, so when we're feeling crunched for time, it's a relief to have these wholesome enchiladas waiting for us in the freezer.

—HOLLY BABER SEATTLE, WA

PREP: 35 MIN. • **BAKE:** 15 MIN.
MAKES: 14 SERVINGS

- 1¼ pounds lean ground turkey
- 1 small onion, chopped
- 1 teaspoon reduced-sodium taco seasoning
- ½ teaspoon ground cumin
- ¼ teaspoon pepper
- 1 package (8 ounces) reduced-fat cream cheese, cubed
- 1 cup (4 ounces) shredded Mexican cheese blend, divided
- 1 can (15 ounces) black beans, rinsed and drained
- 1½ cups frozen corn, thawed
- 1 can (14½ ounces) fire-roasted diced tomatoes, drained
- 2 cans (4 ounces each) chopped green chilies
- ¼ cup salsa
- 14 whole wheat tortillas (8 inches), warmed
- 2 cans (10 ounces each) enchilada sauce
  Minced fresh cilantro
- ¾ cup reduced-fat plain Greek yogurt

1. Preheat oven to 375°. In a large nonstick skillet, cook turkey, onion and seasonings over medium heat for 6-8 minutes or until the turkey is no longer pink and onion is tender. Stir in the cream cheese and ½ cup Mexican cheese blend until melted. Add beans, corn, tomatoes, chilies and salsa.
2. Place ½ cup of turkey mixture off center on each tortilla. Roll up and place seam side down in two 13x9-in. baking dishes coated with cooking spray. Top with the enchilada sauce; sprinkle with remaining cheese.
3. Bake casseroles, uncovered, for 15-20 minutes or until heated through. Sprinkle with cilantro; serve with Greek yogurt.

FREEZE OPTION *Cool unbaked casseroles; cover and freeze. To use, partially thaw in the refrigerator overnight. Remove from refrigerator 30 minutes before baking. Preheat oven to 375°. Bake the casseroles as directed, increasing bake time to 20-25 minutes or until heated through and a thermometer inserted into center reads 165°.*

PER SERVING *1 enchilada equals 343 cal., 13 g fat (5 g sat. fat), 51 mg chol., 795 mg sodium, 37 g carb., 5 g fiber, 19 g pro. Diabetic Exchanges: 3 lean meat, 2½ starch.*

BLACK BEAN TURKEY ENCHILADAS

ITALIAN TURKEY SKILLET

Italian Turkey Skillet FAST FIX

I try to find imaginative ways to use leftovers, especially turkey. This pasta toss is lightly coated with tomato sauce and accented with fresh mushrooms.

—**PATRICIA KILE** ELIZABETHTOWN, PA

START TO FINISH: 20 MIN.
MAKES: 8 SERVINGS

- 1 package (16 ounces) linguine
- 2 tablespoons canola oil
- ¾ cup sliced fresh mushrooms
- 1 medium onion, chopped
- 1 celery rib, chopped
- 1 small green pepper, chopped
- 2 cups cubed cooked turkey
- 1 can (14½ ounces) diced tomatoes, drained
- 1 can (10¾ ounces) condensed tomato soup, undiluted
- 1 tablespoon Italian seasoning
- 1 tablespoon minced fresh parsley
- ¼ teaspoon pepper
- ⅛ teaspoon salt
- 1 cup (4 ounces) shredded cheddar cheese, optional

1. Cook linguine according to package directions. Meanwhile, in a large skillet, heat oil over medium-high heat. Add mushrooms, onion, celery and green pepper; cook and stir until tender. Stir in turkey, tomatoes, soup, Italian seasoning, parsley, pepper and salt; heat through.

2. Drain linguine; add to the turkey mixture and toss to combine. If desired, sprinkle pasta with cheddar cheese and let stand, covered, until the cheese is melted.

PER SERVING *1 cup pasta (calculated without cheese) equals 338 cal., 7 g fat (1 g sat. fat), 27 mg chol., 362 mg sodium, 51 g carb., 4 g fiber, 19 g pro.*

Herb-Rubbed Turkey S C

If you're looking for a new twist on turkey, this recipe may just be the one. I prepare a salt-free rub that goes under the turkey skin. Then I remove the skin before eating, which makes the dish low in fat. This seasoning blend proves that you don't need to add a lot of salt for good flavor!

—**RUBY BERGSCHNEIDER** JACKSONVILLE, IL

PREP: 30 MIN.
BAKE: 2 HOURS + STANDING
MAKES: 28 SERVINGS

- 6 garlic cloves, minced
- 2 tablespoons plus 2 teaspoons rubbed sage
- 1 tablespoon minced fresh thyme or 1 teaspoon dried thyme
- 2 teaspoons pepper
- ½ teaspoon each ground allspice, ginger and mustard
- ¼ teaspoon cayenne pepper
- 1 tablespoon all-purpose flour
- 1 turkey-size oven roasting bag
- 2 celery ribs, chopped
- 2 small carrots, chopped
- 1 small onion, chopped
- 1 small potato, sliced
- 1 turkey (14 pounds)
- 1 tablespoon cornstarch
- 2 tablespoons cold water

1. Preheat oven to 350°. In a small bowl, mix garlic, herbs and spices until blended. Sprinkle flour into oven bag; shake to coat. Place bag in a roasting pan; add vegetables to bag and sprinkle with 5 teaspoons herb mixture.

2. Pat the turkey dry. With fingers, carefully loosen the skin from turkey breast; rub half of the remaining herb mixture under the skin. Secure skin to underside of breast with toothpicks. Rub the remaining herb mixture over inside of turkey. Tuck wings under the turkey; tie drumsticks together.

3. Place turkey in bag over vegetables, breast side up; close bag with nylon tie. Cut six ½-in. slits in top of bag; close with tie provided. Bake 2-2½ hours or until a thermometer inserted into thickest part of thigh reads 170°-175°.

4. Remove turkey from oven bag to a serving platter; tent with foil. Let stand for 20 minutes before carving. Strain the contents of oven bag into a small saucepan, discarding vegetables; skim fat from the cooking juices. In a small bowl, mix cornstarch and water until smooth; gradually whisk into cooking juices. Bring to a boil; cook and stir for 2 minutes or until thickened. Serve with turkey.

PER SERVING *4 ounces cooked turkey (calculated without skin) equals 198 cal., 6 g fat (2 g sat. fat), 86 mg chol., 80 mg sodium, 1 g carb., trace fiber, 33 g pro.* **Diabetic Exchange:** *4 lean meat.*

Honey-Ginger Turkey Kabobs

Lime juice and fresh pineapple lend an island flair to these fun kabobs, served with well-seasoned rice.

—**PAM THOMAS** MARION, IA

PREP: 30 MIN. + MARINATING
GRILL: 10 MIN. • **MAKES:** 4 SERVINGS

- 2 **tablespoons chopped green onion**
- 2 **tablespoons soy sauce**
- 1 **tablespoon honey**
- 1 **tablespoon minced fresh gingerroot**
- 1 **teaspoon lime juice**
- 2 **garlic cloves, minced**
- 1 **pound turkey breast tenderloins, cut into 1-inch cubes**
- 2 **cups cubed fresh pineapple**
- 1 **medium sweet red pepper, chopped**
- 1 **medium red onion, cut into chunks**
- 1 **medium lime, cut into wedges**

PINEAPPLE RICE

- 2½ **cups water**
- 1 **cup uncooked long grain rice**
- ½ **cup chopped dried pineapple**
- 2 **teaspoons butter**
- ½ **teaspoon grated lime peel**
- ¼ **teaspoon salt**
- ¼ **cup minced fresh cilantro**
- ¼ **cup chopped green onions**
- 2 **tablespoons lime juice**

1. In a large resealable plastic bag, combine the first six ingredients; add the turkey. Seal bag and turn to coat; refrigerate for at least 2 hours.
2. Drain and discard marinade. On eight metal or soaked wooden skewers, alternately thread the turkey, fresh pineapple, red pepper, red onion and lime wedges; set aside.
3. In a large saucepan, bring water to a boil. Stir in the rice, dried pineapple, butter, lime peel and salt. Reduce heat; cover and simmer for 15-20 minutes or until tender.
4. Meanwhile, grill kabobs, covered, over medium heat or broil 4-6 in. from the heat for 4-6 minutes on each side or until turkey is no longer pink and vegetables are tender. Stir the cilantro, onions and lime juice into the rice. Serve with kabobs.

PER SERVING *2 kabobs with ¾ cup rice equals 437 cal., 4 g fat (2 g sat. fat), 61 mg chol., 543 mg sodium, 71 g carb., 4 g fiber, 32 g pro.*

Chloe, my 3-year-old, is a big fan of these healthy peppers, which have a great thyme flavor. She likes to help mix the ingredients and make meals with me.
—**JENNIFER KENT** PHILADELPHIA, PA

TURKEY-THYME STUFFED PEPPERS

Turkey-Thyme Stuffed Peppers

PREP: 30 MIN. • **COOK:** 10 MIN.
MAKES: 4 SERVINGS

- 1 **pound lean ground turkey**
- 1 **medium onion, finely chopped**
- 3 **garlic cloves, minced**
- ½ **teaspoon dried thyme**
- ¼ **teaspoon salt**
- ¼ **teaspoon dried rosemary, crushed**
- ⅛ **teaspoon pepper**
- 1 **can (14½ ounces) diced tomatoes, undrained**
- 1 **package (8.8 ounces) ready-to-serve brown rice**
- ½ **cup seasoned bread crumbs**
- 4 **medium sweet yellow or orange peppers**
- ¼ **cup shredded part-skim mozzarella cheese**

1. In a large skillet, cook turkey and onion over medium heat 8-10 minutes or until turkey is no longer pink and onion is tender, breaking up turkey into crumbles. Add the garlic and seasonings; cook 1 minute longer. Stir in tomatoes, rice and bread crumbs.
2. Cut sweet peppers lengthwise in half; remove seeds. Arrange pepper halves in a 13x9-in. microwave-safe dish; fill with turkey mixture. Sprinkle with cheese. Microwave, covered, on high for 7-9 minutes or until peppers are crisp-tender.

NOTE *This recipe was tested in a full-size 1,100-watt microwave. If your microwave does not accommodate a 13x9-in. dish, microwave stuffed peppers, half at a time, in an 8-in. square dish for 6-8 minutes or until peppers are crisp-tender.*

PER SERVING *2 stuffed pepper halves equals 423 cal., 13 g fat (3 g sat. fat), 82 mg chol., 670 mg sodium, 43 g carb., 6 g fiber, 31 g pro.* **Diabetic Exchanges:** *3 medium-fat meat, 2 starch, 2 vegetable.*

SAUSAGE ORECCHIETTE PASTA

I adapted this pasta to be like my favorite Italian restaurant version, only lighter— and tastier. I often use spicy sausage and broccoli rabe.

—MELANIE C. TRITTEN
CHARLOTTE, NC

Sausage Orecchiette Pasta FAST FIX

START TO FINISH: 25 MIN.
MAKES: 6 SERVINGS

- 4 cups uncooked orecchiette or small tube pasta
- 1 package (19½ ounces) Italian turkey sausage links, casings removed
- 3 garlic cloves, minced
- 1 cup white wine or chicken broth
- 4 cups small fresh broccoli florets
- 1 can (14½ ounces) diced tomatoes, drained
- ⅓ cup grated Parmesan cheese

1. Cook pasta according to package directions. Meanwhile, in a large skillet, cook sausage over medium heat 6-8 minutes or until no longer pink, breaking into crumbles. Add garlic; cook 1 minute longer. Add the wine, stirring to loosen browned bits from pan. Bring to a boil; cook 1-2 minutes or until liquid is reduced by half.

2. Stir in the broccoli and tomatoes. Reduce heat; simmer, covered, for 4-6 minutes or until the broccoli is crisp-tender. Drain pasta; add to skillet and toss to coat. Serve with cheese.

PER SERVING *1⅔ cups equals 363 cal., 8 g fat (2 g sat. fat), 38 mg chol., 571 mg sodium, 48 g carb., 5 g fiber, 20 g pro. Diabetic Exchanges: 3 lean meat, 2½ starch, 1 vegetable.*

Turkey Burgers with Peach Mayo FAST FIX

The unique fruit and mayo combination puts this burger over the top. You can also substitute nectarines for the peaches. They're both delicious!

—CHARLENE CHAMBERS
ORMOND BEACH, FL

START TO FINISH: 25 MIN.
MAKES: 6 SERVINGS

- 1½ teaspoons canola oil
- 2 small peaches, peeled and chopped
- ½ teaspoon minced fresh gingerroot
- 4 teaspoons reduced-sodium teriyaki sauce, divided
- ¼ cup chopped red onion
- ½ teaspoon pepper
- ¼ teaspoon salt
- 1½ pounds lean ground turkey
- ⅓ cup fat-free mayonnaise
- 6 multigrain hamburger buns, split and toasted
  Optional toppings: lettuce leaves and slices of peaches, red onion and tomatoes

1. In a skillet, heat oil over medium-high heat. Add peaches and ginger; cook and stir until peaches are tender. Stir in 1 teaspoon teriyaki sauce; cook 1 minute longer. Transfer to a small bowl; cool slightly.

2. In a large bowl, combine onion, pepper, salt and remaining teriyaki sauce. Add the turkey and mix lightly but thoroughly. Shape into six ½-in.-thick patties.

3. Moisten a paper towel with cooking oil; using long-handled tongs, rub on grill rack to coat lightly. Grill burgers, covered, over medium heat or broil 4 in. from heat for 5-6 minutes on each side or until a thermometer reads 165°.

4. Stir mayonnaise into the peach mixture. Serve burgers on buns with peach mayo and toppings as desired.

PER SERVING *1 burger (calculated without optional toppings) equals 319 cal., 14 g fat (3 g sat. fat), 91 mg chol., 580 mg sodium, 25 g carb., 2 g fiber, 25 g pro. Diabetic Exchanges: 3 lean meat, 2 starch, 1 fat.*

TURKEY BURGERS WITH PEACH MAYO

Spiced Turkey Tenderloin

Here's an easy turkey dish sure to really wake up your taste buds. It's the perfect choice for a weeknight dinner, or you can easily increase it for get-togethers.
—**SHARON SKILDUM** MAPLE GROVE, MN

PREP: 20 MIN. • **COOK:** 25 MIN.
MAKES: 2 SERVINGS

- ½ **teaspoon chili powder**
- ½ **teaspoon ground cumin**
- ¼ **to ½ teaspoon salt**
- ⅛ **teaspoon cayenne pepper**
- 1 **turkey breast tenderloin (½ pound)**
- 3 **teaspoons olive oil, divided**
- ¼ **cup chicken broth**
- 2 **tablespoons lime juice**
- 3 **tablespoons chopped onion**
- 2 **tablespoons chopped jalapeno pepper**
- 1 **cup canned black beans, rinsed and drained**
- ½ **cup frozen corn, thawed**
- 3 **tablespoons chopped fresh tomato**
- 4 **teaspoons picante sauce**
- 1 **tablespoon minced fresh cilantro**
- 2 **lime wedges**

1. In a small bowl, combine the chili powder, cumin, salt and cayenne. Sprinkle half of the spice mixture over turkey. In a skillet, brown turkey in 2 teaspoons oil for 3-4 minutes on each side. Add broth and lime juice to skillet. Reduce heat; cover and simmer for 15-18 minutes or until turkey juices run clear and a thermometer reads 170°, turning once.
2. In a small skillet, saute the onion and jalapeno in the remaining oil until crisp-tender. Transfer to a bowl. Add the beans, corn, tomato, picante sauce, cilantro and remaining spice mixture. Slice turkey; serve with onion mixture and lime wedges.
NOTE *Wear disposable gloves when cutting hot peppers; the oils can burn skin. Avoid touching your face.*
PER SERVING *1 serving equals 342 cal., 9 g fat (1 g sat. fat), 56 mg chol., 767 mg sodium, 32 g carb., 7 g fiber, 35 g pro. Diabetic Exchanges: 3 lean meat, 2 starch, 1½ fat.*

This salad is a welcome alternative to the usual post-Thanksgiving fare. It's a tasty main dish loaded with good-for-you protein. —**LILY JULOW** LAWRENCEVILLE, GA

TURKEY PINTO BEAN SALAD WITH SOUTHERN MOLASSES DRESSING

Turkey Pinto Bean Salad with Southern Molasses Dressing

PREP: 35 MIN. + CHILLING
MAKES: 6 SERVINGS

- ½ **cup oil-packed sun-dried tomatoes**
- 1 **garlic clove, peeled and halved**
- ½ **cup molasses**
- 3 **tablespoons cider vinegar**
- 1 **teaspoon prepared mustard**
- ½ **teaspoon salt**
- ¼ **teaspoon coarsely ground pepper**
- 3 **cups cubed cooked turkey breast**
- 2 **cans (15 ounces each) pinto beans, rinsed and drained**
- 1 **medium green pepper, diced**
- 2 **celery ribs, diced**
- 1 **cup chopped sweet onion**
- ¼ **cup minced fresh parsley**

1. Drain the tomatoes, reserving 2 tablespoons oil. Place the garlic and tomatoes in a food processor; cover and process until chopped. Add the molasses, vinegar, mustard, salt, pepper and reserved oil. Cover and process until smooth.
2. In a large bowl, combine the turkey, beans, green pepper, celery, onion and parsley. Add dressing and toss to coat. Cover and refrigerate salad for at least 2 hours.
PER SERVING *1⅓ cups equals 379 cal., 7 g fat (1 g sat. fat), 60 mg chol., 483 mg sodium, 49 g carb., 7 g fiber, 29 g pro. Diabetic Exchanges: 4 lean meat, 2½ starch, 1 vegetable, 1 fat.*

Turkey Verde Lettuce Wraps C FAST FIX

I think this dish is a clever pairing of low-fat food with high-end flavor. It'll certainly satisfy your cravings for a spicy and fun, quick-to-prepare dish.

—STEPHANIE BARRON LAKE ORION, MI

START TO FINISH: 25 MIN.
MAKES: 6 SERVINGS

- 2 packages (17.6 ounces each) turkey breast cutlets, cut into 1-inch strips
- 4 teaspoons olive oil
- 1 teaspoon garlic salt
- ¼ teaspoon pepper
- 1 cup salsa verde
- 12 romaine leaves

In a large bowl, combine the turkey, oil, garlic salt and pepper. Heat a large skillet over medium-high heat. Add the turkey in batches; cook and stir for 2-4 minutes or until no longer pink. Return all turkey to pan. Stir in salsa; heat through. Serve in romaine.

PER SERVING *2 lettuce wraps equals 229 cal., 4 g fat (1 g sat. fat), 103 mg chol., 617 mg sodium, 3 g carb., 1 g fiber, 42 g pro.* **Diabetic Exchanges:** *5 lean meat, ½ fat.*

Turkey Sausage-Stuffed Acorn Squash

Finding healthy recipes the family will eat is a challenge. This elegant squash is one we love, and it works with pork, turkey and chicken sausage.

—MELISSA PELKEY-HASS WALESKA, GA

PREP: 30 MIN. • **BAKE:** 50 MIN.
MAKES: 8 SERVINGS

- 4 medium acorn squash (about 1½ pounds each)
- 1 cup cherry tomatoes, halved
- 1 pound Italian turkey sausage links, casings removed
- ½ pound sliced fresh mushrooms
- 1 medium apple, peeled and finely chopped
- 1 small onion, finely chopped
- 2 teaspoons fennel seeds
- 2 teaspoons caraway seeds
- ½ teaspoon dried sage leaves
- 3 cups fresh baby spinach
- 1 tablespoon minced fresh thyme
- ¼ teaspoon salt
- ⅛ teaspoon pepper
- 8 ounces fresh mozzarella cheese, chopped
- 1 tablespoon red wine vinegar

1. Preheat oven to 400°. Cut squash lengthwise in half; remove and discard seeds. Using a sharp knife, cut a thin slice from bottom of each half to allow them to lie flat. Place the squash in a shallow roasting pan, hollow side down; add ¼ in. of hot water and the halved tomatoes. Bake, uncovered, for 45 minutes.

2. Meanwhile, in a large skillet, cook sausage, mushrooms, apple, onion and dried seasonings over medium heat 8-10 minutes or until the sausage is no longer pink, breaking up sausage into crumbles; drain. Add the spinach, thyme, salt and pepper; cook and stir 2 minutes. Remove from heat.

3. Carefully remove squash from the roasting pan. Drain the cooking liquid, reserving tomatoes. Return squash to pan, hollow side up.

4. Stir cheese, vinegar and reserved tomatoes into the sausage mixture. Spoon into squash cavities. Bake for 5-10 minutes or until heated through and the squash is easily pierced with a fork.

PER SERVING *1 stuffed squash half equals 302 cal., 10 g fat (5 g sat. fat), 43 mg chol., 370 mg sodium, 42 g carb., 7 g fiber, 15 g pro.* **Diabetic Exchanges:** *2½ starch, 2 medium-fat meat.*

TURKEY SAUSAGE-STUFFED ACORN SQUASH

Southwest-Style Shepherd's Pie

I was born in Montreal and lived in New England and the Southwest, so I've merged these influences into recipes like this hearty shepherd's pie made with turkey, corn and green chilies.

—LYNN PRICE MILLVILLE, MA

PREP: 20 MIN. • **BAKE:** 25 MIN.
MAKES: 6 SERVINGS

- 1¼ pounds lean ground turkey
- 1 small onion, chopped
- 2 garlic cloves, minced
- ½ teaspoon salt, divided
- 1 can (14¾ ounces) cream-style corn
- 1 can (4 ounces) chopped green chilies
- 1 to 2 tablespoons chipotle hot pepper sauce, optional
- 2⅔ cups water
- 2 tablespoons butter
- 2 tablespoons half-and-half cream
- ½ teaspoon pepper
- 2 cups mashed potato flakes

1. Preheat oven to 425°. In a large skillet, cook turkey, onion, garlic and ¼ teaspoon salt over medium heat for 8-10 minutes or until turkey is no longer pink and the onion is tender, breaking up turkey into crumbles. Stir in corn, green chilies and, if desired, pepper sauce. Transfer to a greased 8-in. square baking dish.

2. Meanwhile, in a saucepan, bring the water, butter, cream, pepper and remaining salt to a boil. Remove from heat. Stir in potato flakes. Spoon over the turkey mixture, spreading to cover. Bake 25-30 minutes or until bubbly and potatoes are light brown.

PER SERVING *1 cup equals 312 cal., 12 g fat (5 g sat. fat), 78 mg chol., 583 mg sodium, 31 g carb., 3 g fiber, 22 g pro.* **Diabetic Exchanges:** *3 lean meat, 2 starch, 1 fat.*

I make this salad when pears are in season. It's a great way to use leftover turkey, chicken or deli meat.

—NANCY HEISHMAN LAS VEGAS, NV

Turkey Salad with Pear Dressing FAST FIX ▶

START TO FINISH: 25 MIN.
MAKES: 4 SERVINGS

- 3 tablespoons olive oil
- 2 tablespoons lemon juice
- 1 tablespoon honey
- ¼ teaspoon salt
- ¼ teaspoon ground ginger
- 2 medium ripe pears, divided

SALAD

- 8 cups fresh arugula or baby spinach
- 2 cups cubed cooked turkey
- ½ cup pomegranate seeds
- ¼ cup chopped pecans, toasted
- ¼ cup dried cranberries
- 2 green onions, sliced
  Coarsely ground pepper

1. For dressing, place the first five ingredients in a blender. Peel, halve and core one pear; add to the blender. Cover and process until smooth.

2. Peel, core and thinly slice the remaining pear. Divide arugula among four plates; top with turkey, sliced pear, pomegranate seeds, pecans, cranberries and green onions. Drizzle with dressing; sprinkle with pepper. Serve immediately.

NOTE *To toast nuts, bake in a shallow pan in a 350° oven for 5-10 minutes or cook in a skillet over low heat until lightly browned, stirring occasionally.*

PER SERVING *1 serving equals 364 cal., 18 g fat (3 g sat. fat), 71 mg chol., 232 mg sodium, 31 g carb., 5 g fiber, 23 g pro.* **Diabetic Exchanges:** *3 lean meat, 3 fat, 2 vegetable, ½ fruit.*

SOUTHWEST-STYLE SHEPHERD'S PIE

TURKEY SALAD WITH PEAR DRESSING

154

150

153

Pork, Ham & More

66My family loves pork tenderloin, so I created this hearty meal. This slightly sweet preparation is one of our favorites. It's also an impressive dish for company.99

—JOYCE MOYNIHAN LAKEVILLE, MN
about her recipe, Apple & Spice Pork Tenderloin, on page 149

Molasses-Glazed Pork Chops S FAST FIX

How can you go wrong with these savory chops that only call for a handful of ingredients? Best of all, they're impressive enough to serve guests!

—ANGELA SPENGLER TAMPA, FL

START TO FINISH: 30 MIN.
MAKES: 4 SERVINGS

- ¼ cup molasses
- 1 tablespoon Worcestershire sauce
- 1½ teaspoons brown sugar
- 4 boneless pork loin chops (¾-inch thick and 5 ounces each)

1. In a small bowl, combine molasses, Worcestershire sauce and brown sugar. Reserve 3 tablespoons sauce for serving.
2. Grill pork, covered, over medium heat or broil 4 in. from the heat for 4-5 minutes on each side or until a thermometer reads 145°, brushing with remaining sauce during the last 3 minutes of cooking. Let stand 5 minutes before serving. Serve with reserved sauce.

PER SERVING *1 pork chop with about 2 teaspoons sauce equals 256 cal., 8 g fat (3 g sat. fat), 68 mg chol., 89 mg sodium, 17 g carb., 0 fiber, 27 g pro.* **Diabetic Exchanges:** *4 lean meat, 1 starch.*

PORK & VEGETABLE SPRING ROLLS

MOLASSES-GLAZED PORK CHOPS

Pork & Vegetable Spring Rolls FAST FIX

I thought rice paper wrappers would be a quick, fun way to put salad ingredients into a hand-held snack or meal. I also make this with shrimp or add in cranberries. Go ahead, experiment!

—MARLA STRADER OZARK, MO

START TO FINISH: 30 MIN.
MAKES: 4 SERVINGS

- 2 cups thinly sliced romaine
- 1½ cups cubed cooked pork
- 1 cup thinly sliced fresh spinach
- ¾ cup julienned carrot
- ⅓ cup thinly sliced celery
- ⅓ cup dried cherries, coarsely chopped
- 1 tablespoon sesame oil
- 12 round rice paper wrappers (8 inches)
- ¼ cup sliced almonds
- ¼ cup wasabi-coated green peas
  Sesame ginger salad dressing

1. In a large bowl, combine the first six ingredients. Drizzle with oil; toss to coat.
2. Fill a large shallow dish partway with water. Dip a rice paper wrapper into water just until pliable, about 45 seconds (do not soften completely); allow excess water to drip off.
3. Place wrapper on a flat surface. Layer some salad mixture, almonds and peas across bottom third of the wrapper. Fold in both ends of wrapper; fold bottom side over filling, then roll up tightly. Place on a serving plate, seam side down. Repeat with the remaining ingredients. Serve with salad dressing.

PER SERVING *3 spring rolls (calculated without salad dressing) equals 255 cal., 12 g fat (3 g sat. fat), 48 mg chol., 91 mg sodium, 19 g carb., 3 g fiber, 18 g pro.* **Diabetic Exchanges:** *3 lean meat, 1 starch, 1 vegetable, 1 fat.*

Apple & Spice Pork Tenderloin C FAST FIX

My family loves pork tenderloin, so I created this hearty meal. This slightly sweet preparation is one of our favorites. It's also an impressive dish for company.
—JOYCE MOYNIHAN LAKEVILLE, MN

START TO FINISH: 30 MIN.
MAKES: 4 SERVINGS

- ¾ teaspoon poultry seasoning
- ½ teaspoon garlic salt
- ½ teaspoon pepper
- ¼ teaspoon ground nutmeg
- ¼ teaspoon salt
- 1 pork tenderloin (1 pound)
- 1 tablespoon butter
- 1 medium tart apple, sliced
- 1 tablespoon canola oil
- ½ cup reduced-sodium chicken broth
- ½ cup white wine or additional reduced-sodium chicken broth
- 1 tablespoon cornstarch
- 3 tablespoons thawed apple juice concentrate
  Chopped fresh parsley, optional

1. Mix first five ingredients. Cut the pork crosswise into eight slices; pound with a meat mallet to ½-in. thickness. Sprinkle with seasoning mixture.
2. In a large nonstick skillet, heat butter over medium heat. Add apple; cook and stir 3-4 minutes or until crisp-tender. Remove from pan.
3. In same pan, heat oil over medium-high heat. Brown pork in batches on both sides; remove from the pan. Add the broth and wine to pan, stirring to loosen browned bits. Mix cornstarch and apple juice concentrate until smooth; stir into the broth mixture. Return to a boil, stirring constantly; cook and stir for 1-2 minutes or until thickened.
4. Return the pork and apple to pan. Reduce the heat; simmer, covered, 4-6 minutes or until a thermometer inserted into pork reads 145°. Let stand for 5 minutes before serving. If desired, sprinkle with parsley.
PER SERVING *3 ounces cooked pork with ⅓ cup apple mixture equals 260 cal., 10 g fat (3 g sat. fat), 71 mg chol., 413 mg sodium, 14 g carb., 1 g fiber, 23 g pro.* **Diabetic Exchanges:** *3 lean meat, 1½ fat, 1 starch.*

Lemon-Garlic Pork Chops C FAST FIX

START TO FINISH: 20 MIN.
MAKES: 4 SERVINGS

- 2 tablespoons lemon juice
- 2 garlic cloves, minced
- 1 teaspoon salt
- 1 teaspoon paprika
- ½ teaspoon pepper
- ¼ teaspoon cayenne pepper
- 4 boneless pork loin chops (6 ounces each)

1. Preheat broiler. In a small bowl, mix the first six ingredients; brush over pork chops. Place in a 15x10x1-in. baking pan.
2. Broil 4-5 in. from heat 4-5 minutes on each side or until a thermometer reads 145°. Let chops stand 5 minutes before serving.
PER SERVING *1 pork chop equals 233 cal., 10 g fat (4 g sat. fat), 82 mg chol., 638 mg sodium, 2 g carb., trace fiber, 33 g pro.* **Diabetic Exchange:** *5 lean meat.*

My son James created these zesty chops spiced with paprika and cayenne. He keeps the spice rub in a jar to use with chops or chicken. Try them on the grill in warm weather. —MOLLY SEIDEL EDGEWOOD, NM

LEMON-GARLIC PORK CHOPS

CRANBERRY SWEET-AND-SOUR PORK

Cranberry Sweet-and-Sour Pork FAST FIX

This fresh take on the beloved Asian-style dish is sure to cause excitement at the dinner table.
—**GERT SNYDER** WEST MONTROSE, ON

START TO FINISH: 20 MIN.
MAKES: 6 SERVINGS

- 1 tablespoon cornstarch
- ½ cup unsweetened pineapple juice
- 1 cup whole-berry cranberry sauce
- ½ cup barbecue sauce
- 1½ pounds pork tenderloin, cut into ½-inch cubes
- 1 tablespoon canola oil
- ½ teaspoon salt
- ¼ teaspoon pepper
- 1 medium green pepper, cut into strips
- ¾ cup pineapple tidbits
  Hot cooked rice, chow mein noodles or crispy wonton strips

1. In a small bowl, combine the cornstarch and pineapple juice until smooth. Stir in the cranberry and barbecue sauces; set aside.
2. In a large skillet, stir-fry pork in oil for 3 minutes or until meat is no longer pink. Sprinkle with salt and pepper. Remove from the pan and keep warm.
3. Add green pepper and pineapple to pan; stir-fry for 2 minutes. Stir the cornstarch mixture and add to pan. Bring to a boil. Cook and stir for 2 minutes or until thickened. Add the pork; heat through. Serve with rice, noodles or wonton strips.

FREEZE OPTION *Place cooled meat mixture in freezer containers. To use, partially thaw in the refrigerator overnight. Heat through slowly in a covered skillet, stirring occasionally and adding a little water if necessary.*
PER SERVING *1¼ cups (calculated without rice) equals 268 cal., 7 g fat (2 g sat. fat), 63 mg chol., 444 mg sodium, 28 g carb., 1 g fiber, 23 g pro.*

Pan-Roasted Pork Chops & Potatoes

A shortcut marinade gives these chops plenty of flavor, and the crumb coating packs on the crunch. For color, I like to tuck in a few handfuls of Brussels sprouts.
—**CHAR OUELLETTE** COLTON, OR

PREP: 20 MIN. + MARINATING
BAKE: 40 MIN. • **MAKES:** 4 SERVINGS

- 4 boneless pork loin chops (6 ounces each)
- ½ cup plus 2 tablespoons reduced-fat Italian salad dressing, divided
- 4 small potatoes (about 1½ pounds)
- ½ pound fresh Brussels sprouts, trimmed and halved
- ½ cup soft bread crumbs
- 1 tablespoon minced fresh parsley
- ¼ teaspoon salt
- ⅛ teaspoon pepper
- 2 teaspoons butter, melted

1. Place pork chops and ½ cup salad dressing in a large resealable plastic bag; seal the bag and turn to coat. Refrigerate 8 hours or overnight. Refrigerate remaining salad dressing.
2. Preheat oven to 400°. Cut each potato lengthwise into 12 wedges. Arrange potatoes and Brussels sprouts in a 15x10x1-in. baking pan coated with cooking spray. Drizzle vegetables with remaining salad dressing; toss to coat. Roast 20 minutes.
3. Drain pork, discarding marinade. Pat pork dry with paper towels. Stir vegetables; place pork chops over top. Roast 15-20 minutes longer or until a thermometer inserted into pork reads 145°. Preheat broiler.
4. In a small bowl, combine bread crumbs, parsley, salt and pepper; stir in butter. Top pork with crumb mixture. Broil 4-6 in. from heat 1-2 minutes or until bread crumbs are golden brown. Let stand 5 minutes.

NOTE *To make soft bread crumbs, tear bread into pieces and place in a food processor or blender. Cover and pulse until crumbs form. One slice of bread yields ½ to ¾ cup crumbs.*
PER SERVING *1 pork chop with 1 cup vegetables equals 451 cal., 16 g fat (5 g sat. fat), 87 mg chol., 492 mg sodium, 38 g carb., 5 g fiber, 38 g pro.* ***Diabetic Exchanges:*** *5 lean meat, 2½ starch, 2 fat.*

PAN-ROASTED PORK CHOPS & POTATOES

Braised Pork Stew FAST FIX ▶

Pork tenderloin is a treat in this hearty stew. It's fantastic for a winter night.

—**NELLA PARKER** HERSEY, MI

START TO FINISH: 30 MIN.
MAKES: 4 SERVINGS

- 1 **pound pork tenderloin, cut into 1-inch cubes**
- ½ **teaspoon salt**
- ½ **teaspoon pepper**
- 5 **tablespoons all-purpose flour, divided**
- 1 **tablespoon olive oil**
- 1 **package (16 ounces) frozen vegetables for stew**
- 1½ **cups reduced-sodium chicken broth**
- 2 **garlic cloves, minced**
- 2 **teaspoons stone-ground mustard**
- 1 **teaspoon dried thyme**
- 2 **tablespoons water**

1. Sprinkle pork with salt and pepper; add 3 tablespoons flour and toss to coat. In a large skillet, brown the pork in oil over medium heat. Stir in the vegetables, broth, garlic, mustard and thyme. Bring to a boil. Reduce heat; simmer, covered, 10-15 minutes or until pork and vegetables are tender.
2. Mix remaining flour and water until smooth; stir into stew. Return to a boil, stirring constantly; cook and stir 1-2 minutes or until thickened.
PER SERVING *1 cup equals 275 cal., 8 g fat (2 g sat. fat), 63 mg chol., 671 mg sodium, 24 g carb., 1 g fiber, 26 g pro.*
***Diabetic Exchanges:** 3 lean meat, 1½ starch, ½ fat.*

HOW TO

PREPARE STEW

❶ Season the meat and coat with flour. Brown in batches if necessary to avoid overcrowding.
❷ Add the remaining ingredients. Stir stew until it comes to a boil to prevent lumps.

BRAISED PORK STEW

ROSEMARY-THYME LAMB CHOPS

Rosemary-Thyme Lamb Chops C FAST FIX

My father loves lamb, so I make this dish whenever he visits. It's the perfect main course for holidays or get-togethers.
—**KRISTINA MITCHELL** CLEARWATER, FL

START TO FINISH: 30 MIN.
MAKES: 4 SERVINGS

- 8 lamb loin chops (3 ounces each), trimmed
- ½ teaspoon pepper
- ¼ teaspoon salt
- 3 tablespoons Dijon mustard
- 1 tablespoon minced fresh rosemary
- 1 tablespoon minced fresh thyme
- 3 garlic cloves, minced

1. Sprinkle lamb chops with pepper and salt. In a small bowl, mix mustard, rosemary, thyme and garlic.
2. Moisten a paper towel with cooking oil; using long-handled tongs, rub on grill rack to coat lightly. Grill chops, covered, over medium heat 6 minutes. Turn and spread the herb mixture over the chops. Grill for 6-8 minutes longer or until meat reaches the desired doneness (for medium-rare, a thermometer should read 145°; medium, 160°; well-done, 170°).
PER SERVING *2 lamb chops equals 231 cal., 9 g fat (4 g sat. fat), 97 mg chol., 493 mg sodium, 3 g carb., trace fiber, 32 g pro.* **Diabetic Exchange:** *4 lean meat.*

Spice-Brined Pork Roast C

This brined and barbecued pork roast is unbelievably tender. Adding seasonings to the coals produces an awesome aroma that draws guests to the grill!
—**LORRAINE SCHROEDER** ALBANY, OR

PREP: 15 MIN. + CHILLING
GRILL: 1½ HOURS • **MAKES:** 10 SERVINGS

- 2 quarts water
- 8 orange peel strips (1 to 3 inches)
- ½ cup sugar
- ¼ cup salt
- 3 tablespoons fennel seed, crushed
- 2 tablespoons dried thyme
- 2 tablespoons whole peppercorns
- 1 boneless rolled pork loin roast (4 pounds)

SPICE-BRINED PORK ROAST

1. In a large saucepan, combine the first seven ingredients. Bring to a boil; cook and stir until salt and sugar are dissolved. Remove from the heat; cool to room temperature.
2. Place a large heavy-duty resealable plastic bag inside a second large resealable plastic bag; add pork roast. Carefully pour cooled brine into the bag. Squeeze out as much air as possible; seal bags and turn to coat. Refrigerate for 12-24 hours, turning several times. Strain brine; discard liquid and set aside seasonings.
3. Moisten a paper towel with cooking oil; using long-handled tongs, lightly coat the grill rack. Prepare grill for indirect heat, using a drip pan. Add reserved seasonings to coals. Place pork over drip pan and grill, covered, over indirect medium heat for 1½-2 hours or until a thermometer reads 160°. Let stand for 5 minutes before slicing.
PER SERVING *6 ounces cooked pork equals 225 cal., 8 g fat (3 g sat. fat), 90 mg chol., 75 mg sodium, trace carb., 0 fiber, 35 g pro.* **Diabetic Exchange:** *6 lean meat.*

HAM PASTA TOSS

Cuban-Style Pork Chops c

These are like Cuban sandwiches without the bread, so they're a bit more elegant. Let your family customize theirs with pickles, mustard and other condiments.

—ERICA ALLEN TUCKERTON, NJ

PREP: 15 MIN. + MARINATING
GRILL: 10 MIN. • **MAKES:** 4 SERVINGS

- 1 tablespoon Dijon mustard
- 1 tablespoon lime juice
- 1 teaspoon adobo seasoning
- 4 boneless pork loin chops (4 ounces each)
- 4 slices deli ham (about 3 ounces)
- 4 slices Swiss cheese
- 2 tablespoons chopped fresh cilantro
  Optional ingredients: mayonnaise, additional Dijon mustard and thinly sliced dill pickles

1. Mix mustard, lime juice and adobo seasoning. Lightly pound pork chops with a meat mallet to ½-in. thickness; spread both sides with the mustard mixture. Refrigerate pork, covered, 3-4 hours.

2. Grill pork, covered, over medium heat 3 minutes. Turn pork and top with ham; grill 2 minutes longer. Top with cheese and cilantro; grill, covered, 30-60 seconds longer or until cheese is melted and a thermometer inserted in chops reads 145°. Let stand 5 minutes before serving. If desired, serve with mayonnaise, mustard and pickles.

PER SERVING *1 serving (calculated without optional ingredients) equals 247 cal., 12 g fat (5 g sat. fat), 84 mg chol., 700 mg sodium, 2 g carb., trace fiber, 31 g pro. **Diabetic Exchanges:** 4 lean meat, ½ fat.*

Ham Pasta Toss FAST FIX ▶

This is my favorite meal to make when I'm short on time. You can also use different meats or vegetables depending on what you have on hand.

—SHARON GERST NORTH LIBERTY, IA

START TO FINISH: 25 MIN.
MAKES: 6 SERVINGS

- 12 ounces uncooked whole wheat spaghetti
- 3 tablespoons butter
- 2 cups shredded or cubed fully cooked ham
- 2 garlic cloves, minced
- 3 cups frozen peas (about 12 ounces), thawed
- 2 tablespoons minced fresh parsley
- ¼ cup grated Parmesan cheese

1. Cook the spaghetti according to package directions; drain. Meanwhile, in a large skillet, heat the butter over medium heat. Add ham; cook and stir 2-4 minutes or until browned. Add garlic; cook 1 minute longer.

2. Stir in spaghetti, peas and parsley; heat through. Sprinkle with cheese; toss to combine.

PER SERVING *1⅓ cups equals 374 cal., 10 g fat (5 g sat. fat), 46 mg chol., 738 mg sodium, 52 g carb., 10 g fiber, 23 g pro.*

CUBAN-STYLE PORK CHOPS

GRILLED PORK NOODLE SALAD

3. Cook rice noodles according to package directions. Drain and rinse in cold water; drain well. In a small bowl, whisk dressing ingredients. Divide the rice noodles among six serving bowls. Top with the pork and remaining ingredients. Drizzle with dressing and serve immediately.

NOTE *Wear disposable gloves when cutting hot peppers; the oils can burn skin. Avoid touching your face.*

PER SERVING *1 serving equals 315 cal., 4 g fat (1 g sat. fat), 64 mg chol., 708 mg sodium, 40 g carb., 3 g fiber, 27 g pro.* **Diabetic Exchanges:** *3 lean meat, 2 starch, 1 vegetable.*

Pork Fried Rice FAST FIX ▶

My husband and I love pork roast, but we know there will always be leftovers. I like to use them up in this fast-to-fix stir-fry.

—JOYCE KRAMER DONALSONVILLE, GA

START TO FINISH: 30 MIN.
MAKES: 2 SERVINGS

- 1 tablespoon canola oil
- 1 large egg, lightly beaten
- ¾ cup cubed cooked pork
- ¼ cup finely chopped onion
- ¼ cup canned bean sprouts
- 2 cups cold cooked long grain rice
- ¼ cup chicken broth
- 1 tablespoon reduced-sodium soy sauce
- 1 green onion, sliced
- ¼ teaspoon sugar
  Dash pepper

1. In a large skillet or wok, heat oil over medium-high heat; add egg. As egg sets, lift edges, letting uncooked portion flow underneath. When egg is completely cooked, remove to a plate and keep warm.
2. In the same pan, stir-fry the pork, onion and bean sprouts 2-3 minutes or until onion is tender. Add rice and broth; cover and cook for 1-2 minutes or until heated through.
3. Chop egg into small pieces; add to rice mixture. Stir in the soy sauce, green onion, sugar and pepper.

PER SERVING *1¾ cup equals 433 cal., 15 g fat (3 g sat. fat), 154 mg chol., 502 mg sodium, 49 g carb., 2 g fiber, 24 g pro.*

Grilled Pork Noodle Salad

The only complex thing about my easy salad is the amazing flavor! With smoky barbecued pork and a variety of fresh herbs and vegetables, this is a tasty home-cooked meal.

—ROSALYN NGUYEN ASTORIA, NY

PREP: 40 MIN. + MARINATING • **GRILL:** 5 MIN.
MAKES: 6 SERVINGS

- 1 jalapeno pepper, seeded and minced
- 3 tablespoons lime juice
- 2 tablespoons fish sauce or soy sauce
- 2 teaspoons brown sugar
- 1½ pounds pork tenderloin, cut into ½-inch slices
- 1 package (8.8 ounces) vermicelli-style thin rice noodles

DRESSING
- ¼ cup water
- 2 tablespoons lime juice
- 1 tablespoon fish sauce or soy sauce
- ½ teaspoon brown sugar

SALAD
- 2 cups shredded lettuce
- 2 plum tomatoes, sliced
- 1 medium cucumber, julienned
- 2 medium carrots, julienned
- ½ cup coarsely chopped fresh cilantro
- ¼ cup loosely packed fresh mint leaves

1. In a large resealable plastic bag, combine the jalapeno, lime juice, fish sauce and brown sugar. Add pork; seal bag and turn to coat. Refrigerate for 3 hours or overnight.
2. Drain pork, discarding marinade. Moisten a paper towel with cooking oil; using long-handled tongs, rub on grill rack to coat lightly. Grill the pork, covered, over medium heat for 1-2 minutes on each side or until a thermometer reads 145°.

Grilled Dijon Pork Roast

I created this recipe one day when I was scrambling to find ingredients for dinner. My husband absolutely loved it. Now it's the only way I make pork!

—CYNDI LACY-ANDERSEN

WOODINVILLE, WA

PREP: 10 MIN. + MARINATING
GRILL: 1 HOUR + STANDING
MAKES: 12 SERVINGS

- ⅓ cup balsamic vinegar
- 3 tablespoons Dijon mustard
- 1 tablespoon honey
- 1 teaspoon salt
- 1 boneless pork loin roast (3 to 4 pounds)

1. In a large resealable plastic bag, whisk the vinegar, mustard, honey and salt. Add the pork; seal bag and turn to coat. Refrigerate at least 8 hours or overnight.

2. Prepare grill for indirect heat, using a drip pan. Moisten a paper towel with cooking oil; using long-handled tongs, rub on grill rack to coat lightly.

3. Drain pork, discarding marinade. Place pork over the drip pan and grill, covered, over indirect medium heat 1-1½ hours or until a thermometer reads 145°, turning occasionally. Let stand 10 minutes before slicing.

PER SERVING *3 ounces cooked pork equals 149 cal., 5 g fat (2 g sat. fat), 56 mg chol., 213 mg sodium, 2 g carb., trace fiber, 22 g pro.* **Diabetic Exchange:** *3 lean meat.*

DID YOU KNOW?

A good rule of thumb for calculating your daily protein need is to multiply your body weight in pounds by 0.4 gram. For example, a 150-pound person needs about 60 grams of protein daily. Three ounces (a serving the size of a deck of cards) of cooked sirloin steak, pork loin, tuna, chicken or turkey breast provides about 25 grams of protein.

GRILLED DIJON PORK ROAST

Parmesan Pork Chops with Spinach Salad C FAST FIX

My pork chops needed a change, and I stumbled across this pan-fry method. With a few small changes, we transformed them into a yummy spinach salad.

—LAUREL DALZELL MANTECA, CA

START TO FINISH: 30 MIN.
MAKES: 4 SERVINGS

- 3 medium tomatoes, seeded and chopped
- 1 tablespoon olive oil
- 1 tablespoon lemon juice
- 1 small garlic clove, minced
- ½ teaspoon salt, divided
- ¼ teaspoon pepper, divided
- 2 large egg whites
- 1 tablespoon Dijon mustard
- ½ teaspoon dried oregano
- ½ cup dry bread crumbs
- 3 tablespoons grated Parmesan cheese
- 4 thin boneless pork loin chops (½-inch thick and 3 ounces each)
- 4 cups fresh baby spinach

1. In a large bowl, combine tomatoes, oil, lemon juice, garlic, ¼ teaspoon of salt and ⅛ teaspoon pepper; toss to combine.

2. In a shallow bowl, whisk egg whites, mustard, oregano and the remaining salt and pepper until blended. In another shallow bowl, mix the bread crumbs with cheese. Dip pork chops in egg white mixture, then coat with bread crumb mixture.

3. Place a large nonstick skillet coated with cooking spray over medium heat. Add pork chops; cook 2-3 minutes on each side or until golden brown and pork is tender.

4. Add spinach to tomato mixture; toss to combine. Serve with the pork chops.

PER SERVING *1 pork chop with 1 cup salad equals 223 cal., 10 g fat (3 g sat. fat), 43 mg chol., 444 mg sodium, 12 g carb., 2 g fiber, 22 g pro.* **Diabetic Exchanges:** *3 lean meat, 2 vegetable, 1 fat.*

Pork Tenderloin with Fennel and Cranberries

PREP: 25 MIN. • **BAKE:** 20 MIN.
MAKES: 8 SERVINGS

- 1 teaspoon kosher salt
- 1 teaspoon fennel seeds, crushed
- 1 teaspoon paprika
- ¼ teaspoon cayenne pepper
- 2 pork tenderloins (1 pound each)
- 2 tablespoons olive oil, divided
- 2 medium fennel bulbs, halved and thinly sliced
- 2 shallots, thinly sliced
- 3 garlic cloves, minced
- 1½ cups dry white wine or chicken broth
- 1 cup dried cranberries
- 2 tablespoons minced fresh rosemary or 2 teaspoons dried rosemary, crushed
  Fennel fronds, optional

1. Preheat oven to 425°. In a small bowl, mix the salt, fennel seeds, paprika and cayenne. Rub seasoning over pork.

2. In a large skillet, heat 1 tablespoon oil over medium-high heat. Brown pork on all sides. Transfer to a rack in a shallow roasting pan. Roast pork for 20-25 minutes or until a thermometer reads 145°. Remove tenderloins from the oven; tent with foil. Let stand for 5 minutes before slicing.

3. Meanwhile, in the same skillet, heat remaining oil over medium-high heat. Add fennel and shallots; cook and stir 4-6 minutes or until tender. Add garlic; cook 1 minute longer.

4. Stir in the wine, cranberries and rosemary. Bring to a boil. Reduce heat; simmer, uncovered, 5-10 minutes.

5. To serve, spoon the fennel mixture onto a serving platter. Top with the tenderloin slices and, if desired, fennel fronds.

PER SERVING *3 ounces cooked pork with ½ cup fennel mixture equals 273 cal., 7 g fat (2 g sat. fat), 63 mg chol., 374 mg sodium, 20 g carb., 3 g fiber, 24 g pro.* **Diabetic Exchanges:** *3 lean meat, 1 starch, 1 vegetable, 1 fat.*

This delicious entree is quick to make at home and transport to a potluck. The combination of rosemary, fennel and sweet and tart cranberries makes for an elegant dinner. —JUDY ARMSTRONG PRAIRIEVILLE, LA

PORK TENDERLOIN WITH FENNEL AND CRANBERRIES

Spicy Tomato Pork Chops C FAST FIX

Sprinkle some garlic powder or Creole seasoning over the chops before browning to give them even more pop.

—HOLLY NEUHARTH MESA, AZ

START TO FINISH: 30 MIN.
MAKES: 4 SERVINGS

- 1 tablespoon olive oil
- 4 boneless pork loin chops (5 ounces each)
- 1 large onion, chopped
- 1 can (8 ounces) tomato sauce
- ¼ cup water
- 2 teaspoons chili powder
- 1 teaspoon dried oregano
- 1 teaspoon Worcestershire sauce
- ½ teaspoon sugar
- ½ teaspoon crushed red pepper flakes

1. In a large skillet, heat oil over medium heat. Brown pork chops on both sides. Remove; keep warm. In the same skillet, cook and stir onion until tender. Stir in remaining ingredients.
2. Return pork to skillet. Bring to a boil. Reduce heat; simmer, covered, 15-20 minutes or until tender. Let stand for 5 minutes before serving. Serve with sauce.
PER SERVING *1 pork chop with ⅓ cup sauce equals 257 cal., 12 g fat (3 g sat. fat), 68 mg chol., 328 mg sodium, 8 g carb., 2 g fiber, 29 g pro.* **Diabetic Exchanges:** *4 lean meat, 1 vegetable, 1 fat.*

Pork served with a luscious raspberry glaze is fancy enough for company. We bring it to the table with wild rice pilaf and steamed veggies.

—TRISHA KRUSE EAGLE, ID

RASPBERRY PORK MEDALLIONS

SPICY TOMATO PORK CHOPS

Raspberry Pork Medallions C FAST FIX

START TO FINISH: 25 MIN.
MAKES: 4 SERVINGS

- 1 pork tenderloin (1 pound)
- 1 tablespoon canola oil
- 2 tablespoons reduced-sodium soy sauce
- 1 garlic clove, minced
- ½ teaspoon ground ginger
- 1 cup fresh raspberries
- 2 tablespoons seedless raspberry spreadable fruit
- 2 teaspoons minced fresh basil
- ½ teaspoon minced fresh mint, optional

1. Cut tenderloin crosswise into eight slices; pound each with a meat mallet to ½-in. thickness. In a large skillet, heat oil over medium-high heat. Add pork; cook 3-4 minutes on each side or until a thermometer reads 145°. Remove from pan; keep warm.
2. Reduce heat to medium-low; add the soy sauce, garlic and ginger to pan, stirring to loosen browned bits. Add raspberries, spreadable fruit, basil and, if desired, mint; cook and stir mixture for 2-3 minutes or until slightly thickened. Serve with pork.
PER SERVING *3 ounces cooked pork with 3 tablespoons sauce equals 206 cal., 8 g fat (2 g sat. fat), 64 mg chol., 333 mg sodium, 10 g carb., 2 g fiber, 24 g pro.* **Diabetic Exchanges:** *3 lean meat, ½ starch, ½ fat.*

Maple-Pecan Glazed Ham

This ham with maple reduction is a holiday keeper. The nuts take on a candied flavor, and the baste seeps into the scored areas, so you taste maple in every bite.

—NANCY MUELLER MENOMONEE FALLS, WI

PREP: 10 MIN.
BAKE: 2½ HOURS + STANDING
MAKES: 15 SERVINGS

- 1 **fully cooked bone-in ham (7 to 9 pounds)**
- 1 **cup maple syrup**
- ⅓ **cup finely chopped pecans**
- 1 **tablespoon Dijon mustard**
- 2 **teaspoons grated orange peel**
- ½ **teaspoon ground allspice**

1. Trim off the skin of the ham and about ¼ in. of fat. Score the surface of the ham, making diamond shapes ¼-in. deep. Place the ham, fat side up, on a rack in a shallow roasting pan. Bake, uncovered, at 325° for 2 hours.
2. In a small saucepan, bring syrup to a boil. Reduce heat; simmer, uncovered, until reduced to ¾ cup. Remove from heat. Stir in the pecans, mustard, orange peel and allspice.
3. Baste ham with some of the glaze; bake 30-60 minutes longer or until a thermometer reads 140°, basting occasionally with the remaining glaze. Let the ham stand for 15 minutes before slicing.
PER SERVING *4 ounces cooked ham equals 252 cal., 7 g fat (2 g sat. fat), 93 mg chol., 1,135 mg sodium, 16 g carb., trace fiber, 31 g pro.*

Pork & Mango Stir-Fry FAST FIX

A recipe is special when everyone in your family raves about it. My finicky eaters all give thumbs-up to this hearty, nutty stir-fry meal.

—KATHY SPECHT CLINTON, MT

PREP/TOTAL: 25 MIN.
MAKES: 4 SERVINGS

- 1 **pork tenderloin (1 pound)**
- 1 **tablespoon plus 2 teaspoons canola oil, divided**
- ¼ **teaspoon salt**
- ½ **teaspoon crushed red pepper flakes, optional**
- 6 **ounces uncooked multigrain angel hair pasta**
- 1 **package (8 ounces) fresh sugar snap peas**
- 1 **medium sweet red pepper, cut into thin strips**
- ⅓ **cup reduced-sugar orange marmalade**
- ¼ **cup reduced-sodium teriyaki sauce**
- 1 **tablespoon packed brown sugar**
- 2 **garlic cloves, minced**
- 1 **cup chopped peeled mango**
- ¼ **cup lightly salted cashews, coarsely chopped**

1. Cut tenderloin lengthwise in half; cut each half crosswise into thin slices. Toss pork with 1 tablespoon oil, salt and, if desired, pepper flakes. Cook pasta according to package directions.
2. Place a large nonstick skillet over medium-high heat. Add half of the pork; stir-fry 2-3 minutes or just until browned. Remove from pan; repeat with remaining pork.
3. Stir-fry snap peas and red pepper in remaining oil 2-3 minutes or just until crisp-tender. Stir in the marmalade, teriyaki sauce, brown sugar and garlic; cook 1-2 minutes longer. Return pork to pan and add mango and cashews; heat through, stirring to combine. Serve with pasta.
PER SERVING *1½ cups pork mixture with ¾ cup pasta equals 515 cal., 16 g fat (3 g sat. fat), 64 mg chol., 553 mg sodium, 58 g carb., 6 g fiber, 36 g pro.*

PORK & MANGO STIR-FRY

GRILLED PORK WITH SPICY PINEAPPLE SALSA

Grilled Pork with Spicy Pineapple Salsa FAST FIX ▶

Here in Michigan, the outdoor grilling season is pretty short, so I often broil these chops. The salsa is equally good on chicken or shrimp.

—DIANE NEMITZ LUDINGTON, MI

START TO FINISH: 30 MIN.
MAKES: 8 SERVINGS (2 CUPS SALSA)

- 1 jar (16 ounces) chunky salsa
- 1 can (8 ounces) unsweetened crushed pineapple
- ½ cup port wine or grape juice
- ¼ cup packed brown sugar
- ¼ cup lime juice
- ¼ cup thawed orange juice concentrate
- 2 tablespoons Worcestershire sauce
- 1 teaspoon garlic powder
- ¼ teaspoon cayenne pepper
PORK
- 1 teaspoon ground cumin
- ½ teaspoon pepper
- ¼ teaspoon cayenne pepper
- 2 pork tenderloins (1 pound each)
  Lime wedges

1. In a large saucepan, combine the first nine ingredients. Bring to a boil; cook 20-25 minutes or until mixture is reduced by half, stirring occasionally.

2. Meanwhile, for pork, mix spices; rub over tenderloins. Moisten a paper towel with cooking oil; using long-handled tongs, rub on grill rack to coat lightly. Grill tenderloins, covered, over medium heat or broil 4 in. from heat 18-22 minutes or until a thermometer reads 145°, turning occasionally.

3. Let pork chops stand for 5 minutes before slicing. Serve with salsa and lime wedges.

PER SERVING *3 ounces cooked pork with ¼ cup salsa equals 220 cal., 4 g fat (1 g sat. fat), 63 mg chol., 318 mg sodium, 22 g carb., 1 g fiber, 23 g pro. Diabetic Exchanges: 3 lean meat, 1½ starch.*

Pizzaiola Chops C FAST FIX ▶

My favorite cousin shared this recipe, and I tweaked it for our family. Taste as you go, and try the Italian trick of sprinkling on some oregano to give it that extra "something."

—LORRAINE CALAND SHUNIAH, ON

START TO FINISH: 30 MIN.
MAKES: 4 SERVINGS

- 2 tablespoons olive oil, divided
- 4 boneless pork loin chops (6 ounces each)
- 1 teaspoon salt, divided
- ¼ teaspoon pepper, divided
- 1½ cups sliced baby portobello mushrooms
- 1 medium sweet yellow pepper, coarsely chopped
- 1 medium sweet red pepper, coarsely chopped
- 2 large tomatoes, chopped
- ½ cup white wine or chicken broth
- 1 tablespoon minced fresh oregano or ½ teaspoon dried oregano
- 2 garlic cloves, minced
  Hot cooked rice, optional

1. In a large skillet, heat 1 tablespoon oil over medium-high heat. Season pork chops with ½ teaspoon salt and ⅛ teaspoon pepper. Brown chops on both sides. Remove from pan.

2. In same pan, heat the remaining oil over medium-high heat. Add the mushrooms and peppers; cook and stir 3-4 minutes or until mushrooms are tender. Add tomatoes, wine, oregano, garlic and the remaining salt and pepper. Bring to a boil. Reduce heat; simmer, uncovered, 2 minutes.

3. Return pork chops to the pan. Cook, covered, 5-7 minutes or until a thermometer inserted in pork reads 145°. Let stand 5 minutes; if desired, serve with rice.

PER SERVING *1 pork chop and 1 cup vegetable mixture (calculated without rice) equals 351 cal., 17 g fat (5 g sat. fat), 82 mg chol., 647 mg sodium, 10 g carb., 2 g fiber, 35 g pro. Diabetic Exchanges: 5 lean meat, 1½ fat, 1 vegetable.*

PIZZAIOLA CHOPS

PORK CHOPS & MUSHROOMS

Pork Chops & Mushrooms C FAST FIX

My mother-in-law gave me this recipe years ago, and I have used it ever since. My family loves the sweetness with a little kick.
—**HILARY RIGO** WICKENBURG, AZ

START TO FINISH: 25 MIN.
MAKES: 4 SERVINGS

- 4 boneless pork loin chops (6 ounces each)
- ¾ teaspoon salt, divided
- ⅛ teaspoon white pepper
- 3 teaspoons butter, divided
- ¾ pound sliced fresh mushrooms
- ½ cup dry white wine or reduced-sodium chicken broth
- ½ teaspoon dried tarragon

1. Sprinkle pork with ½ teaspoon salt and white pepper. In a large nonstick skillet coated with cooking spray, heat 2 teaspoons butter over medium heat. Add pork chops; cook 5-6 minutes on each side or until a thermometer reads 145°. Remove from pan.
2. In same skillet, heat the remaining butter over medium-high heat. Add mushrooms; cook and stir 6-8 minutes or until tender. Add the wine, tarragon and remaining salt, stirring to loosen browned bits from pan. Bring to a boil; cook until liquid is reduced by half. Return chops to pan; heat through.
PER SERVING *1 pork chop with ⅓ cup mushrooms equals 299 cal., 13 g fat (5 g sat. fat), 89 mg chol., 515 mg sodium, 4 g carb., 1 g fiber, 35 g pro. Diabetic Exchanges: 5 lean meat, 1 vegetable, ½ fat.*

Apple Roasted Pork with Cherry Balsamic Glaze

I added roasted apples, cherries and onions to turn ordinary pork roast into a breakaway dish, and I haven't turned back since. There is a short time frame between caramelized onions and burnt ones, so pay close attention once they start cooking.
—**JOSH DOWNEY** MCHENRY, IL

PREP: 30 MIN. • **BAKE:** 50 MIN.+ STANDING
MAKES: 8 SERVINGS

- 1 boneless pork loin roast (3 pounds)
- 1½ teaspoons salt, divided
- ¾ teaspoon pepper, divided
- ¼ cup olive oil, divided
- 3 medium apples, sliced
- 1½ cups unsweetened apple juice
- 6 medium onions, sliced (about 5 cups)
- 3 tablespoons balsamic vinegar
- 1½ cups frozen pitted dark sweet cherries
- ½ cup cherry juice

1. Preheat oven to 350°. Sprinkle pork roast with 1 teaspoon salt and ½ teaspoon pepper. In an ovenproof Dutch oven, heat 2 tablespoons oil over medium-high heat; brown roast on all sides. Add apples and apple juice to pan. Bake, uncovered, 50-60 minutes or until a thermometer inserted into pork reads 145°, basting occasionally with pan juices.
2. Meanwhile, in a large skillet, heat remaining oil over medium heat. Add onions and the remaining salt and pepper; cook and stir for 8-10 minutes or until softened. Reduce heat to medium-low; cook 35-40 minutes or until onions are deep golden brown, stirring occasionally. Keep warm.
3. Remove the roast and apples to a serving plate; tent with foil. Let roast stand 10 minutes before slicing.
4. Skim fat from pork juices. Place pan over medium-high heat; add vinegar and cook 1 minute, stirring to loosen browned bits from pan. Stir in cherries and cherry juice. Bring to a boil; cook for 10-15 minutes or until mixture is reduced to about 1 cup. Serve pork, apples and onions with cherry glaze.
PER SERVING *1 serving equals 387 cal., 15 g fat (4 g sat. fat), 85 mg chol., 498 mg sodium, 29 g carb., 3 g fiber, 34 g pro.*

APPLE ROASTED PORK WITH CHERRY BALSAMIC GLAZE

Hearty Pork Chops ⓒ

Just six ingredients are required for the tasty mix that is used to marinate these well-seasoned chops. Whip up the combination, marinate the pork overnight and you'll have dinner on the table in no time tomorrow.

—*TASTE OF HOME* TEST KITCHEN

PREP: 15 MIN. + MARINATING
GRILL: 10 MIN. • **MAKES:** 6 SERVINGS

- ⅔ cup diet lemon-lime soda
- ½ cup reduced-sodium soy sauce
- ¼ cup honey
- 1 teaspoon dried thyme
- ¾ teaspoon dried rosemary, crushed
- ¼ teaspoon pepper
- 6 bone-in pork loin chops (¾-inch thick and 7 ounces each)

1. In a large resealable plastic bag, combine the first six ingredients. Add pork chops; seal bag and turn to coat. Refrigerate 4 hours or overnight.
2. Drain pork, discarding marinade. Moisten a paper towel with cooking oil; using long-handled tongs, rub on grill rack to coat lightly.
3. Grill pork, covered, over medium heat or broil 4 in. from the heat for 4-5 minutes on each side or until a thermometer reads 145°. Let stand for 5 minutes.

FREEZE OPTION *Freeze pork with marinade in a resealable plastic freezer bag. To use, thaw in the refrigerator overnight. Drain pork, discarding marinade. Grill as directed.*

PER SERVING *1 pork chop equals 227 cal., 8 g fat (3 g sat. fat), 86 mg chol., 387 mg sodium, 5 g carb., trace fiber, 31 g pro.* **Diabetic Exchange:** *4 lean meat.*

HEARTY PORK CHOPS

Jalapeno jelly makes a fabulous glaze. The chops have a beautiful golden color, and my husband says they're good enough to keep everyone quiet at the dinner table.
—**SHANNON BRUCE** MOORESVILLE, IN

JALAPENO JELLY-GLAZED PORK CHOPS

Jalapeno Jelly-Glazed Pork Chops FAST FIX ▶

START TO FINISH: 25 MIN.
MAKES: 4 SERVINGS

- 1 pound fresh green beans, trimmed
- 2 teaspoons olive oil
- ¾ teaspoon salt, divided
- ⅛ teaspoon plus ¼ teaspoon pepper, divided
- 4 boneless pork loin chops (¾-inch thick and 6 ounces each)
- 4 tablespoons jalapeno pepper jelly, divided

1. Preheat oven to 425°. Place green beans in a 15x10x1-in. baking pan coated with cooking spray; toss with oil, ¼ teaspoon salt and ⅛ teaspoon pepper. Roast 15-20 minutes or until tender and lightly browned, stirring occasionally.
2. Meanwhile, sprinkle pork chops with the remaining salt and pepper. Place a large nonstick skillet coated with cooking spray over medium heat. Add the pork chops; cook, uncovered, 4 minutes. Turn chops over; spread tops with half of the jalapeno jelly.
3. Cook, uncovered, 2-3 minutes longer or until a thermometer reads 145°. Turn chops over; spread tops with remaining jelly. Let stand for 5 minutes. Serve with green beans.

PER SERVING *1 serving equals 328 cal., 10 g fat (4 g sat. fat), 82 mg chol., 354 mg sodium, 27 g carb., trace fiber, 33 g pro.* **Diabetic Exchanges:** *4 lean meat, 1 starch, 1 vegetable, ½ fat.*

Orange-Glazed Pork with Sweet Potatoes

When it's chilly outside, I like to roast pork tenderloin with sweet potatoes, apples and an orange. The sweetness and spices make any evening cozy.

—DANIELLE LEE BOYLES WESTON, WI

PREP: 20 MIN. • **BAKE:** 55 MIN. + STANDING
MAKES: 6 SERVINGS

- 1 **pound sweet potatoes (about 2 medium)**
- 2 **medium apples**
- 1 **medium orange**
- 1 **teaspoon salt**
- ½ **teaspoon pepper**
- 1 **cup orange juice**
- 2 **tablespoons brown sugar**
- 2 **teaspoons cornstarch**
- 1 **teaspoon ground cinnamon**
- 1 **teaspoon ground ginger**
- 2 **pork tenderloins (about 1 pound each)**

1. Preheat oven to 350°. Peel sweet potatoes; core apples. Cut potatoes, apples and orange crosswise into ¼-in.-thick slices. Arrange on a foil-lined 15x10x1-in. baking pan coated with cooking spray; sprinkle with salt and pepper. Roast 10 minutes.
2. Meanwhile, in a microwave-safe bowl, mix orange juice, brown sugar, cornstarch, cinnamon and ginger. Microwave, covered, on high for 1-2 minutes or until thickened, stirring every 30 seconds. Stir until smooth.
3. Place pork over sweet potato mixture; drizzle with orange juice mixture. Roast 45-55 minutes longer or until a thermometer inserted into pork reads 145° and sweet potatoes and apples are tender. Remove from oven; tent with foil. Let pork stand for 10 minutes before slicing.
PER SERVING *4 ounces cooked pork with about ¾ cup sweet potato mixture equals 325 cal., 5 g fat (2 g sat. fat), 85 mg chol., 467 mg sodium, 36 g carb., 3 g fiber, 32 g pro.* **Diabetic Exchanges:** *4 lean meat, 2 starch.*

ORANGE-GLAZED PORK WITH SWEET POTATOES

172

174

177

Fish & Seafood

❝I had a similar meal during a tropical vacation, and I knew I had to re-create it. My quick recipe is a healthier version with the same taste.❞

—LAUREN KATZ ASHBURN, VA
about her recipe, Caribbean Shrimp & Rice Bowl, on page 166

Caribbean Shrimp & Rice Bowl FAST FIX

I had a similar meal during a tropical vacation, and I knew I had to re-create it. My quick recipe is a healthier version with the same taste.

—**LAUREN KATZ** ASHBURN, VA

START TO FINISH: 20 MIN.
MAKES: 4 SERVINGS

- 1 can (15 ounces) black beans, rinsed and drained
- 1 can (8 ounces) unsweetened crushed pineapple, undrained
- 1 medium mango, peeled and chopped
- ½ cup salsa
- 1 package (8.8 ounces) ready-to-serve brown rice
- 1 medium ripe avocado, peeled
- ⅓ cup reduced-fat sour cream
- ¼ teaspoon salt
- 1 pound uncooked shrimp (31-40 per pound), peeled and deveined
- 1 teaspoon Caribbean jerk seasoning
- 1 tablespoon canola oil
- 2 green onions, sliced
  Lime wedges, optional

1. In a small saucepan, combine beans, pineapple, mango and salsa; cook and stir 4-6 minutes or until heated through.

2. Prepare rice according to package directions. In a small bowl, mash avocado with sour cream and salt until blended. Sprinkle shrimp with jerk seasoning. In a large skillet, heat oil over medium-high heat. Add shrimp; cook and stir 2-3 minutes or until shrimp turn pink.

3. Divide rice among four bowls; layer with bean mixture, shrimp and avocado mixture. Sprinkle with green onions. If desired, serve with lime wedges.

PER SERVING *1 serving equals 498 cal., 14 g fat (2 g sat. fat), 145 mg chol., 698 mg sodium, 62 g carb., 9 g fiber, 29 g pro.*

I serve these as full-size burgers on kaiser rolls, too. The fresh flavors of the salmon and herbs are just unbeatable.

—**MARGEE BERRY** WHITE SALMON, WA

GARLIC-HERB SALMON SLIDERS

Garlic-Herb Salmon Sliders

PREP: 25 MIN. • **GRILL:** 10 MIN.
MAKES: 4 SERVINGS

- ⅓ cup panko (Japanese) bread crumbs
- 4 teaspoons finely chopped shallot
- 2 teaspoons snipped fresh dill
- 1 tablespoon prepared horseradish
- 1 large egg, beaten
- ¼ teaspoon salt
- ⅛ teaspoon pepper
- 1 pound salmon fillet, skin removed, cut into 1-inch cubes
- 8 whole wheat dinner rolls, split and toasted
- ¼ cup reduced-fat garlic-herb spreadable cheese
- 8 small lettuce leaves

1. In a large bowl, combine the first seven ingredients. Place salmon in food processor; pulse until coarsely chopped and add to bread crumb mixture. Mix lightly but thoroughly. Shape into eight ½-in.-thick patties.

2. Moisten a paper towel with cooking oil; using long-handled tongs, rub on grill rack to coat lightly. Grill burgers, covered, over medium heat or broil 4 in. from heat 3-4 minutes on each side or until a thermometer reads 160°. Serve on rolls with spreadable cheese and lettuce.

PER SERVING *2 sliders equals 442 cal., 17 g fat (5 g sat. fat), 119 mg chol., 676 mg sodium, 42 g carb., 6 g fiber, 30 g pro.* **Diabetic Exchanges:** *3 starch, 3 lean meat, 1 fat.*

Sole Fillets in Lemon Butter C FAST FIX

This is such a speedy, no-fuss and delicious way to prepare fish! My son started requesting this "fish with crackers" as a little boy, and he still asks for it as an adult today.

—BARB SHARON PLYMOUTH, WI

START TO FINISH: 20 MIN.
MAKES: 4 SERVINGS

- 4 sole fillets (4 ounces each)
- ¼ teaspoon salt
- ⅛ teaspoon pepper
- 3 tablespoons butter, melted
- ½ cup minced fresh parsley
- 1 tablespoon lemon juice
- ¼ cup crushed Ritz crackers
- ½ teaspoon paprika

1. Place the sole fillets in an ungreased microwave-safe 11x7-in. dish; sprinkle with salt and pepper. Cover and microwave on high for 3-4 minutes.
2. In a small bowl, combine the butter, parsley and lemon juice; pour over fillets. Sprinkle with cracker crumbs.
3. Microwave fish, uncovered, for 3-4 minutes longer or until fish just begins to flake easily with a fork. Sprinkle with paprika.
NOTE *This recipe was tested in a 1,100-watt microwave.*
PER SERVING *1 fillet equals 213 cal., 11 g fat (6 g sat. fat), 77 mg chol., 377 mg sodium, 5 g carb., trace fiber, 22 g pro.* **Diabetic Exchanges:** *3 lean meat, 2 fat.*

Coconut-Mango Tilapia S

Friends always request this recipe with its intriguing tropical taste. A sweet mango puree nicely complements the couscous and fish.

—JESSIE APFE BERKELEY, CA

PREP: 20 MIN. + MARINATING
GRILL: 10 MIN. • **MAKES:** 4 SERVINGS

- ½ cup light coconut milk
- 2 tablespoons lime juice
- 2 large mangoes, peeled and diced
- 3 tablespoons brown sugar
- 4½ teaspoons minced fresh gingerroot
- 4 tilapia fillets (4 ounces each)
- **COUSCOUS**
- ¾ cup light coconut milk
- 1½ teaspoons minced fresh gingerroot
- ⅔ cup uncooked couscous
- 2 tablespoons minced fresh cilantro

1. Place the first five ingredients in a blender; cover and process until smooth. Pour 1 cup mixture into a large resealable plastic bag. Add fish; seal bag and turn to coat. Refrigerate at least 2 hours. Cover and refrigerate remaining mixture for sauce.
2. Drain fish, discarding marinade in bag. Moisten a paper towel with cooking oil; using long-handled tongs, rub on grill rack to coat lightly. Grill fish, covered, over high heat or broil 3-4 in. from heat 3-5 minutes or until the fish just begins to flake easily with a fork.
3. Meanwhile, in a small saucepan, bring coconut milk and ginger to a boil. Stir in couscous. Remove from heat; let stand, covered, 5-10 minutes or until liquid is absorbed. Add cilantro; fluff with a fork. Serve fish with couscous and reserved sauce.

PER SERVING *1 fillet with ½ cup couscous and about 1 tablespoon sauce equals 350 cal., 10 g fat (7 g sat. fat), 55 mg chol., 72 mg sodium, 40 g carb., 2 g fiber, 25 g pro.* **Diabetic Exchanges:** *3 lean meat, 2 starch, 1½ fat, ½ fruit.*

COCONUT-MANGO TILAPIA

ASIAN SNAPPER WITH CAPERS

Tilapia with Fiesta Rice F FAST FIX

I often use my husband's fresh-caught bass or catfish for this recipe, but tilapia, salmon and even chicken will do.

—**TARIN HAUCK** MINNEAPOLIS, KS

START TO FINISH: 25 MIN.
MAKES: 4 SERVINGS

- 4 tilapia fillets (6 ounces each)
- ½ teaspoon chili powder
- ⅛ teaspoon salt
- ⅛ teaspoon ground cumin
- ⅛ teaspoon pepper
- 1 package (8.8 ounces) ready-to-serve brown rice
- 1 can (15 ounces) black beans, rinsed and drained
- 1½ cups frozen corn, thawed
- 1½ cups salsa

1. Place tilapia in a 15x10x1-in. baking pan. Mix chili powder, salt, cumin and pepper; sprinkle over fish. Broil 3-4 in. from heat 10-12 minutes or until fish just begins to flake easily with a fork.

2. Meanwhile, prepare rice according to package directions. Transfer to a microwave-safe bowl; stir in beans, corn and salsa. Microwave, covered, on high for 2-3 minutes or until heated through, stirring once. Serve with fish.

PER SERVING *1 fillet with ¾ cup rice mixture equals 424 cal., 3 g fat (1 g sat. fat), 83 mg chol., 874 mg sodium, 53 carb., 7 g fiber, 41 g pro.*

Asian Snapper with Capers FAST FIX

Here's a simple sauteed snapper with lots of flavor. It takes very little time and effort to prepare. Asian flavors really makes this dish exciting.

—**MARY ANN LEE** CLIFTON PARK, NY

START TO FINISH: 20 MIN.
MAKES: 4 SERVINGS

- 4 red snapper fillets (6 ounces each)
- 4½ teaspoons Mongolian Fire oil or sesame oil
- ¼ cup apple jelly
- 3 tablespoons ketchup
- 2 tablespoons capers, drained
- 1 tablespoon lemon juice
- 1 tablespoon reduced-sodium soy sauce
- 1 teaspoon grated fresh gingerroot

1. In a large skillet, cook fillets in oil over medium heat for 3-5 minutes on each side or until fish flakes easily with a fork; remove and keep warm.

2. Stir the jelly, ketchup, capers, lemon juice, soy sauce and grated ginger into the skillet. Cook and stir for 2-3 minutes or until slightly thickened; serve with red snapper.

PER SERVING *1 fish fillet with 2 tablespoons sauce equals 275 cal., 7 g fat (1 g sat. fat), 60 mg chol., 494 mg sodium, 17 g carb., trace fiber, 34 g pro.* **Diabetic Exchanges:** *4 lean meat, 1 starch, 1 fat.*

TILAPIA WITH FIESTA RICE

Tuna Veggie Kabobs C

This is such a quick and easy summer meal! My children love to help cut up the veggies and assemble the skewers. I serve it over brown rice cooked in low-salt chicken broth and garnish it with parsley and lemon wedges.
—**LYNN CARUSO** SAN JOSE, CA

PREP: 30 MIN. + MARINATING
GRILL: 10 MIN. • **MAKES:** 8 KABOBS

- 2 pounds tuna steaks, cut into 1½-inch cubes
- 16 large fresh mushrooms
- 3 medium green peppers, seeded and cut into 2-inch pieces
- 3 medium ears sweet corn, cut into 2-inch pieces
- 3 medium zucchini, cut into 1-inch slices
- ¼ cup olive oil
- 2 tablespoons lemon juice
- 2 tablespoons finely chopped shallot
- 1 tablespoon rice vinegar
- 1 tablespoon minced garlic
- 1 teaspoon salt
- 1 teaspoon dried rosemary, crushed
- 1 teaspoon dried thyme
- ½ teaspoon pepper

1. Place tuna in a large resealable plastic bag; place the vegetables in another large resealable plastic bag. In a small bowl, combine the remaining ingredients. Place half of the marinade in each bag. Seal bags and turn to coat; refrigerate for 1 hour.
2. Drain and discard marinade. On eight metal or soaked wooden skewers, alternately thread tuna and vegetables. Moisten a paper towel with cooking oil; using long-handled tongs, lightly coat the grill rack.
3. Grill tuna, covered, over medium heat or broil 4 in. from the heat for 10-12 minutes for medium-rare or until fish is slightly pink in the center and vegetables are crisp-tender, turning occasionally.
PER SERVING *1 kabob equals 253 cal., 9 g fat (1 g sat. fat), 51 mg chol., 348 mg sodium, 15 g carb., 3 g fiber, 30 g pro. Diabetic Exchanges: 4 lean meat, 1 vegetable, 1 fat, ½ starch.*

GRILLED SHRIMP & TOMATO SALAD

Grilled Shrimp & Tomato Salad C

Make this a main-dish salad, or put it in an appetizer buffet for extra-good grazing. I always serve it with little bowls of chili sauce for dipping.
—**MARUJA HUGHES** TORONTO, ON

PREP: 25 MIN. + MARINATING
GRILL: 10 MIN. • **MAKES:** 12 SERVINGS

- ½ cup lemon juice
- ½ cup lime juice
- 3 pounds uncooked jumbo shrimp, peeled and deveined
- 24 cherry tomatoes
- ½ cup chili sauce
- 2 teaspoons canola oil
- 1 teaspoon red wine vinegar
- 3 medium ripe avocados, peeled and sliced
  Minced fresh parsley, optional

1. In a large resealable plastic bag, combine lemon and lime juices. Add shrimp; seal bag and turn to coat. Refrigerate 30 minutes.
2. Drain shrimp, discarding marinade. On 12 metal or soaked wooden skewers, alternately thread shrimp and tomatoes. Moisten a paper towel with cooking oil; using long-handled tongs, rub on grill rack to coat lightly. Grill kabobs, covered, over medium heat 8-10 minutes or until shrimp turn pink, turning occasionally and basting frequently with chili sauce.
3. In a small bowl, combine oil and vinegar. Arrange avocados on a large platter; top with shrimp and tomatoes. If desired, sprinkle with parsley. Drizzle with oil mixture.
PER SERVING *1 serving equals 177 cal., 8 g fat (1 g sat. fat), 138 mg chol., 293 mg sodium, 8 g carb., 3 g fiber, 19 g pro. Diabetic Exchanges: 3 lean meat, 1½ fat.*

Lime-Cilantro Tilapia C FAST FIX

I have so much fun serving this Mexican-inspired tilapia at summer parties. Finish it off with a side of rice and a salad loaded with sliced avocados and tomatoes.
—**NADINE MESCH** MOUNT HEALTHY, OH

START TO FINISH: 25 MIN.
MAKES: 4 SERVINGS

- ⅓ cup all-purpose flour
- ¾ teaspoon salt
- ½ teaspoon pepper
- ½ teaspoon ground cumin, divided
- 4 tilapia fillets (6 ounces each)
- 1 tablespoon olive oil
- ½ cup reduced-sodium chicken broth
- 2 tablespoons minced fresh cilantro
- 1 teaspoon grated lime peel
- 2 tablespoons lime juice

1. In a shallow bowl, mix flour, salt, pepper and ¼ teaspoon cumin. Dip fillets in flour mixture to coat both sides; shake off excess.

2. In a large nonstick skillet, heat oil over medium heat. Add fillets; cook, uncovered, 3-4 minutes on each side or until fish flakes easily with a fork. Remove and keep warm.

3. To the same pan, add broth, cilantro, lime peel, lime juice and remaining cumin; bring to a boil. Reduce heat; simmer, uncovered, 2-3 minutes or until slightly thickened. Serve with tilapia.

PER SERVING *1 fish fillet with 2 tablespoons sauce equals 198 cal., 5 g fat (1 g sat. fat), 83 mg chol., 398 mg sodium, 6 g carb., trace fiber, 33 g pro.* **Diabetic Exchanges:** *4 lean meat, ½ starch, ½ fat.*

This lightened-up British favorite gets a zesty treatment of horseradish, panko and Worcestershire. Try it with any white fish, too, like cod, haddock and flounder.
—**LINDA SCHEND** KENOSHA, WI

Crispy Fish & Chips FAST FIX

START TO FINISH: 30 MIN.
MAKES: 4 SERVINGS

- 4 cups frozen steak fries
- 4 salmon fillets (6 ounces each)
- 1 to 2 tablespoons prepared horseradish
- 1 tablespoon grated Parmesan cheese
- 1 tablespoon Worcestershire sauce
- 1 teaspoon Dijon mustard
- ¼ teaspoon salt
- ½ cup panko (Japanese) bread crumbs
  Cooking spray

1. Preheat oven to 450°. Arrange the steak fries in a single layer on a baking sheet. Bake fries on the lowest oven rack for 18-20 minutes or until light golden brown.

2. Meanwhile, place salmon on a foil-lined baking sheet coated with cooking spray. In a small bowl, mix horseradish, cheese, Worcestershire sauce, mustard and salt; stir in panko. Press mixture onto fillets. Spritz tops with cooking spray.

3. Bake salmon on middle oven rack 8-10 minutes or until fish just begins to flake easily with a fork. Serve with steak fries.

PER SERVING *1 fillet with 1 cup fries equals 419 cal., 20 g fat (4 g sat. fat), 86 mg chol., 695 mg sodium, 26 g carb., 2 g fiber, 32 g pro.* **Diabetic Exchanges:** *5 lean meat, 1½ starch.*

LIME-CILANTRO TILAPIA

Scallops with Chipotle-Orange Sauce C FAST FIX

Tender scallops with a sprinkle of paprika and ground chipotle make this recipe a surefire way to warm up dinnertime.

—JAN JUSTICE CATLETTSBURG, KY

START TO FINISH: 15 MIN. • **MAKES:** 2 SERVINGS

- ¾ pound sea scallops
- ¼ teaspoon paprika
- ¼ teaspoon salt, divided
- 2 teaspoons butter
- ¼ cup orange juice
- ¼ teaspoon ground chipotle pepper
  Hot cooked linguine, optional
- 2 tablespoons thinly sliced green onion

1. Sprinkle scallops with paprika and ⅛ teaspoon salt. In a nonstick skillet coated with cooking spray, melt butter over medium heat. Add scallops; cook for 3-4 minutes on each side or until firm and opaque.

2. Add orange juice and remaining salt to the pan; bring to a boil. Remove from the heat; stir in chipotle pepper.

3. Serve over linguine if desired. Garnish with green onion.

PER SERVING *1 serving (calculated without linguine) equals 200 cal., 5 g fat (3 g sat. fat), 66 mg chol., 608 mg sodium, 8 g carb., trace fiber, 29 g pro.* **Diabetic Exchanges:** *4 lean meat, 1 fat.*

SHRIMP WITH GINGER-CHILI SAUCE

Shrimp with Ginger-Chili Sauce FAST FIX

Sweet and peppery ginger complements spicy chili sauce in this cook-friendly shrimp dish. It's ideal for nights when you want something a little different, but also quick.

—CAROLE RESNICK CLEVELAND, OH

START TO FINISH: 30 MIN. • **MAKES:** 6 SERVINGS

- 1½ pounds uncooked large shrimp, peeled and deveined
- 1 tablespoon cornstarch
- ¼ cup orange juice
- 2 tablespoons reduced-sodium soy sauce
- 2 tablespoons honey
- 1 tablespoon rice vinegar
- ¼ to ½ teaspoon Sriracha Asian hot chili sauce or ⅛ to ¼ teaspoon hot pepper sauce
- 2 garlic cloves, minced
- 2 teaspoons minced fresh gingerroot
- 2 tablespoons canola oil
- 4 green onions, finely chopped, divided
- 3 cups hot cooked rice

1. Pat shrimp dry with paper towels. In a large bowl, combine shrimp and cornstarch. In a small bowl, combine the orange juice, soy sauce, honey, vinegar and chili sauce; set aside.

2. In a wok or large skillet, stir-fry garlic and ginger in oil for 30 seconds. Add shrimp; stir-fry for 3 minutes. Stir half of the onions into the orange juice mixture; add to the pan.

3. Bring to a boil; cook and stir for 2 minutes or until sauce is thickened and shrimp turn pink. Sprinkle with remaining onions. Serve with rice.

PER SERVING *½ cup shrimp with ½ cup rice equals 269 cal., 6 g fat (1 g sat. fat), 168 mg chol., 405 mg sodium, 32 g carb., 1 g fiber, 21 g pro.* **Diabetic Exchanges:** *3 lean meat, 2 starch, 1 fat.*

SCALLOPS WITH CHIPOTLE ORANGE SAUCE

Orzo-Tuna Salad with Tomatoes FAST FIX ▶

START TO FINISH: 25 MIN. • **MAKES:** 4 SERVINGS

- ¾ cup uncooked whole wheat orzo pasta
- 4 large tomatoes, sliced
- 16 small fresh basil leaves
- 1 pouch (11 ounces) light tuna in water
- 1 cup cubed part-skim mozzarella cheese
- 3 tablespoons minced fresh basil
- 2 tablespoons olive oil
- 2 tablespoons balsamic vinegar
- ⅛ teaspoon salt
- ⅛ teaspoon pepper

1. Cook orzo pasta according to the package directions. Arrange sliced tomatoes on a serving plate and top with whole basil leaves.

2. Drain pasta; rinse with cold water and place in a large bowl. Add tuna, cheese and minced basil. In a small bowl, whisk oil, vinegar, salt and pepper; drizzle over pasta mixture and toss to combine. Spoon over tomatoes.

PER SERVING *1 serving equals 392 cal., 15 g fat (5 g sat. fat), 41 mg chol., 523 mg sodium, 31 g carb., 7 g fiber, 34 g pro.* ***Diabetic Exchanges:*** *4 lean meat, 1½ starch, 1½ fat, 1 vegetable.*

QUICK NICOISE SALAD

> Stuffed tomatoes provide endless options when you add meat, cheese, veggies, rice or, in this case, orzo.
> —**JENNI DISE** PHOENIX, AZ

ORZO-TUNA SALAD WITH TOMATOES

Quick Nicoise Salad FAST FIX ▶

Like the French, I pack my classic Nicoise salad with veggies, potatoes, tuna and eggs. Cooking the potato and beans together helps build it fast.
—**VALERIE BELLEY** ST. LOUIS, MO

START TO FINISH: 25 MIN. • **MAKES:** 4 SERVINGS (½ CUP DRESSING)

- 1 pound red potatoes (about 2 large), cubed
- ¼ pound fresh green beans, trimmed
- ½ cup oil and vinegar salad dressing
- ½ teaspoon grated lemon peel
- ¼ teaspoon freshly ground pepper
- 6 cups torn romaine
- 4 hard-cooked large eggs, sliced
- 3 pouches (2½ ounces each) light tuna in water
- 2 medium tomatoes, chopped

1. Place potatoes in a large saucepan; add water to cover. Bring to a boil. Reduce heat; cook, uncovered, 8-10 minutes or until tender, adding green beans during the last 3 minutes of cooking. Drain the potatoes and beans; immediately drop into ice water. Drain and pat dry.

2. In a small bowl, combine salad dressing, lemon peel and pepper. Divide the romaine among four plates; arrange potatoes, green beans, eggs, tuna and tomatoes over the romaine. Serve with dressing mixture.

PER SERVING *1 serving equals 327 cal., 15 g fat (2 g sat. fat), 206 mg chol., 691 mg sodium, 27 g carb., 5 g fiber, 21 g pro.* ***Diabetic Exchanges:*** *3 lean meat, 2 vegetable, 2 fat, 1 starch.*

CILANTRO SHRIMP & RICE

Cilantro Shrimp & Rice FAST FIX

I created this one-dish wonder for my son, who has the pickiest palate. The aroma of fresh herbs is so appetizing, even my son can't resist!
—**NIBEDITA DAS** FORT WORTH, TX

START TO FINISH: 30 MIN.
MAKES: 8 SERVINGS

- 2 packages (8½ ounces each) ready-to-serve basmati rice
- 2 tablespoons olive oil
- 2 cups frozen corn, thawed
- 2 medium zucchini, quartered and sliced
- 1 large sweet red pepper, chopped
- ½ teaspoon crushed red pepper flakes
- 3 garlic cloves, minced
- 1 pound peeled and deveined cooked large shrimp, tails removed
- ½ cup chopped fresh cilantro
- 1 tablespoon grated lime peel
- 2 tablespoons lime juice
- ¾ teaspoon salt
  Lime wedges, optional

1. Prepare the rice according to package directions.
2. Meanwhile, in a large skillet, heat oil over medium-high heat. Add corn, zucchini, red pepper and pepper flakes; cook and stir 3-5 minutes or until zucchini is crisp-tender. Add garlic; cook 1 minute longer. Add shrimp; heat through.
3. Stir in rice, cilantro, lime peel, lime juice and salt. If desired, serve with lime wedges.

PER SERVING *1½ cups equals 243 cal., 6 g fat (1 g sat. fat), 86 mg chol., 324 mg sodium, 28 g carb., 3 g fiber, 16 g pro.* **Diabetic Exchanges:** *2 lean meat, 1½ starch, ½ fat.*

Poached Salmon with Dill & Turmeric FAST FIX

This is among my husband's favorites because it's always moist, tender, juicy and delicious. It's a quick, simple way to prepare salmon, and the robust turmeric doesn't overpower the taste of the fish.
—**EVELYN BANKER** ELMHURST, NY

START TO FINISH: 30 MIN.
MAKES: 4 SERVINGS

- 1 tablespoon canola oil
- ¼ teaspoon cumin seeds
- 1 pound Yukon Gold potatoes (about 2 medium), finely chopped
- 1¼ teaspoons salt, divided
- ⅛ teaspoon plus ¼ teaspoon ground turmeric, divided
- 2 tablespoons chopped fresh dill, divided
- 4 salmon fillets (1 inch thick and 4 ounces each)
- 8 fresh dill sprigs
- 2 teaspoons grated lemon peel
- 2 tablespoons lemon juice
- 1 cup (8 ounces) reduced-fat plain yogurt
- ¼ teaspoon pepper

1. In a large skillet, heat oil and cumin over medium heat 1-2 minutes or until seeds are toasted, stirring occasionally. Stir in potatoes, ½ teaspoon salt and ⅛ teaspoon turmeric. Cook, covered, on medium-low 10-12 minutes or until tender. Stir in 1 tablespoon chopped dill; cook, uncovered, for 1 minute. Remove from heat.
2. Meanwhile, place salmon, skin side down, in a large skillet with high sides. Add dill sprigs, lemon peel, lemon juice, ½ teaspoon salt, remaining turmeric and enough water to cover salmon. Bring just to a boil. Adjust heat to maintain a gentle simmer. Cook, uncovered, for 7-9 minutes or until fish just begins to flake easily with a fork.
3. In a small bowl, mix yogurt, pepper and the remaining 1 tablespoon chopped dill and ¼ teaspoon salt. Serve with salmon and potatoes.

PER SERVING *3 ounces cooked salmon with ½ cup potatoes and ¼ cup sauce equals 350 cal., 15 g fat (3 g sat. fat), 61 mg chol., 704 mg sodium, 27 g carb., 2 g fiber, 25 g pro.* **Diabetic Exchanges:** *3 lean meat, 2 starch, 1 fat.*

POACHED SALMON WITH DILL & TURMERIC

COZUMEL RED SNAPPER VERACRUZ

Salmon with Balsamic Orange Sauce C FAST FIX

Dinner for eight? This salmon recipe imparts sweet orange flavor into every fillet and bakes in no time at all. Serve with roasted veggies and a side of rice for a no-stress meal.
—*TASTE OF HOME* TEST KITCHEN

START TO FINISH: 30 MIN.
MAKES: 8 SERVINGS

- 8 salmon fillets (6 ounces each), skin removed
- 4 teaspoons grated orange peel
- 4 teaspoons balsamic vinegar
- 4 teaspoons honey
- 1 teaspoon salt

SAUCE
- 1 teaspoon cornstarch
- 1 cup orange juice
- 2 teaspoons honey
- 1 teaspoon balsamic vinegar
- ¼ teaspoon salt

1. Preheat oven to 425°. Place salmon in a greased 15x10x1-in. baking pan. In a small bowl, mix orange peel, vinegar, honey and salt; spread over fillets.
2. Roast 15-18 minutes or until fish just begins to flake easily with a fork. Meanwhile, in a small saucepan, mix cornstarch and orange juice. Bring to a boil; cook and stir 1 minute or until thickened. Stir in honey, vinegar and salt; serve with salmon.
PER SERVING *1 salmon fillet with 2 tablespoons sauce equals 299 cal., 16 g fat (3 g sat. fat), 85 mg chol., 455 mg sodium, 9 g carb., trace fiber, 29 g pro. **Diabetic Exchanges:** 4 lean meat, ½ starch.*

Cozumel Red Snapper Veracruz C

Cozumel, Mexico, boasts magnificent Veracruz-style red snapper. It features traditional olives, capers and whole tomatoes. You can't bring it home, so create your own!
—**BARB MILLER** OAKDALE, MN

PREP: 25 MIN. • **BAKE:** 35 MIN.
MAKES: 4 SERVINGS

- 4 red snapper fillets (6 ounces each)
- ½ teaspoon salt
- ¼ teaspoon pepper
- ¼ cup white wine or chicken stock
- 2 large tomatoes, seeded and chopped
- 1 medium onion, chopped
- ⅓ cup pitted green olives, chopped
- 1 jalapeno pepper, seeded and minced
- 2 tablespoons capers, drained
- 2 garlic cloves, minced
- 2 tablespoons olive oil
  Hot cooked Israeli couscous and chopped fresh cilantro, optional

1. Preheat oven to 375°. Sprinkle fillets with salt and pepper. Place in a greased 13x9-in. baking dish; drizzle with wine. Top with tomatoes, onion, olives, jalapeno, capers and garlic; drizzle with olive oil.
2. Bake for 35-40 minutes or until fish flakes easily with a fork. If desired, serve fish with couscous and sprinkle with cilantro.
NOTE *Wear disposable gloves when cutting hot peppers; the oils can burn skin. Avoid touching your face.*
PER SERVING *1 fillet (calculated without couscous and cilantro) equals 285 cal., 11 g fat (1 g sat. fat), 60 mg chol., 741 mg sodium, 9 g carb., 2 g fiber, 35 g pro.*

SALMON WITH BALSAMIC ORANGE SAUCE

Parsley-Crusted Cod C FAST FIX

Looking to increase your family's fish servings? You'll appreciate this easy cod with staple ingredients. The flavors are mild and delicious, so even picky eaters won't complain.

—**JUDY GREBETZ** RACINE, WI

START TO FINISH: 30 MIN.
MAKES: 4 SERVINGS

- ¾ cup dry bread crumbs
- 1 tablespoon minced fresh parsley
- 2 teaspoons grated lemon peel
- 1 garlic clove, minced
- ¼ teaspoon kosher salt
- ¼ teaspoon pepper
- 2 tablespoons olive oil
- 4 cod fillets (6 ounces each)

1. In a shallow bowl, combine the first six ingredients. Brush oil over one side of fillets; gently press into bread crumb mixture.

2. Place crumb side up in a 13x9-in. baking dish coated with cooking spray. Bake at 400° for 15-20 minutes or until fish flakes easily with a fork.

PER SERVING *1 fillet equals 215 cal., 8 g fat (1 g sat. fat), 65 mg chol., 194 mg sodium, 6 g carb., trace fiber, 28 g pro.* **Diabetic Exchanges:** *5 lean meat, 1½ fat, ½ starch.*

PARSLEY-CRUSTED COD

When I was in second grade, my class put together a cookbook. I saw this recipe from one of my friends, and I thought my mom would like it. I was right!
—**PEGGY ROOS** MINNEAPOLIS, MN

GRILLED SHRIMP SCAMPI

Grilled Shrimp Scampi C

PREP: 15 MIN. + MARINATING
GRILL: 10 MIN. • **MAKES:** 6 SERVINGS

- 2 tablespoons olive oil
- 2 tablespoons lemon juice
- 3 garlic cloves, minced
- ¼ teaspoon salt
- ¼ teaspoon pepper
- 1½ pounds uncooked jumbo shrimp, peeled and deveined
  Hot cooked jasmine rice
  Minced fresh parsley

1. In a large bowl, whisk the first five ingredients. Add shrimp; toss to coat. Refrigerate, covered, 30 minutes.

2. Thread shrimp onto six metal or soaked wooden skewers. Grill, covered, over medium heat or broil 4 in. from heat 6-8 minutes or until shrimp turn pink, turning once. Serve with rice; sprinkle with parsley.

PER SERVING *1 skewer (calculated without rice) equals 118 cal., 4 g fat (1 g sat. fat), 138 mg chol., 184 mg sodium, 1 g carb., trace fiber, 18 g pro.* **Diabetic Exchanges:** *2 meat, ½ fat.*

Teriyaki Salmon C FAST FIX

For this delectable glaze, I blend maple syrup with teriyaki sauce. It makes the salmon tender and delicious.

—LENITA SCHAFER ORMOND BEACH, FL

START TO FINISH: 30 MIN.
MAKES: 4 SERVINGS

- ¾ cup reduced-sodium teriyaki sauce
- ½ cup maple syrup
- 4 salmon fillets (6 ounces each)
  Mixed salad greens, optional

1. In a small bowl, whisk teriyaki sauce and syrup. Pour 1 cup marinade into a large resealable plastic bag. Add salmon; seal bag and turn to coat. Refrigerate 15 minutes. Cover and refrigerate remaining marinade.
2. Drain salmon, discarding marinade in bag. Moisten a paper towel with cooking oil; using long-handled tongs, rub on grill rack to coat lightly.
3. Place the salmon on grill rack, skin side down. Grill, covered, over medium heat or broil 4 in. from heat 8-12 minutes or until fish just begins to flake easily with a fork, basting frequently with reserved marinade. If desired, serve over lettuce salad.

PER SERVING 1 fillet equals 362 cal., 18 g fat (4 g sat. fat), 100 mg chol., 422 mg sodium, 12 g carb., 0 fiber, 35 g pro. **Diabetic Exchanges:** 5 lean meat, 1 starch.

LEMON PARSLEY SWORDFISH

TERIYAKI SALMON

Lemon Parsley Swordfish C FAST FIX

This dish looks impressive and it's easy to prepare—a winner in my book! I like that it comes together fast enough for a family weeknight meal, but it's special enough to serve guests for Sunday dinner.

—NATHAN LEOPOLD MECHANICSBURG, PA

START TO FINISH: 25 MIN.
MAKES: 4 SERVINGS

- 4 swordfish steaks (7 ounces each)
- ½ teaspoon salt
- ½ cup minced fresh parsley, divided
- ⅓ cup olive oil
- 1 tablespoon lemon juice
- 2 teaspoons minced garlic
- ¼ teaspoon crushed red pepper flakes

1. Preheat oven to 425°. Place fish in a greased 13x9-in. baking dish; sprinkle with salt. In a small bowl, combine ¼ cup parsley, oil, lemon juice, garlic and pepper flakes; spoon over fish.
2. Bake, uncovered, 15-20 minutes or until fish flakes easily with a fork, basting occasionally. Sprinkle with remaining parsley.

PER SERVING 1 swordfish steak equals 390 cal., 26 g fat (5 g sat. fat), 72 mg chol., 171 mg sodium, 1 g carb., trace fiber, 37 g pro.

SPEEDY SALMON STIR-FRY

Speedy Salmon Stir-Fry FAST FIX ▶

Salmon is a staple where I live, so I tried it in a stir-fry. My recipe has an orange glaze, but I like it with lime, too.
—JONI HILTON ROCKLIN, CA

START TO FINISH: 30 MIN.
MAKES: 4 SERVINGS

- ¼ cup reduced-fat honey mustard salad dressing
- 2 tablespoons orange juice
- 1 tablespoon minced fresh gingerroot
- 1 tablespoon reduced-sodium soy sauce
- 1 tablespoon molasses
- 1 teaspoon grated orange peel
- 4 teaspoons canola oil, divided
- 1 pound salmon fillets, skin removed and cut into 1-inch pieces
- 1 package (16 ounces) frozen stir-fry vegetable blend
- 2⅔ cups hot cooked brown rice
- 1 tablespoon sesame seeds, toasted

1. In a small bowl, whisk the first six ingredients. In a large skillet, heat 2 teaspoons oil over medium-high heat. Add salmon; cook and gently stir 3-4 minutes or until fish just begins to flake easily with a fork. Remove from the pan.

2. In same pan, heat remaining oil. Add vegetable blend; stir-fry until crisp-tender. Add salad dressing mixture. Return salmon to skillet. Gently combine; heat through. Serve with rice; sprinkle with sesame seeds.
PER SERVING 1 cup stir-fry with ⅔ cup rice equals 498 cal., 19 g fat (3 g sat. fat), 57 mg chol., 394 mg sodium, 54 g carb., 5 g fiber, 26 g pro.

Tilapia & Veggies with Red Pepper Sauce F C FAST FIX ▶

The impressive look and taste of this dish are delectably deceiving. Only the cook needs to know how quickly the saucy fish and sauteed veggies come together.
—HELEN CONWELL PORTLAND, OR

START TO FINISH: 30 MIN.
MAKES: 6 SERVINGS

- ½ cup dry white wine or chicken broth
- ¼ cup water
- 1 tablespoon lemon juice
- 1 teaspoon salt, divided
- 6 tilapia fillets (4 ounces each)
- 2 small yellow summer squash, cut into ¼-inch slices
- 1 medium zucchini, cut into ¼-inch slices
- 1 medium onion, halved and sliced
- 1 tablespoon olive oil
- 1 garlic clove, minced
- ¼ teaspoon pepper
- ⅓ cup roasted sweet red peppers, drained
- 1 tablespoon white balsamic vinegar

1. In a large skillet, bring wine, water, lemon juice and ½ teaspoon salt to a boil. Reduce heat; add tilapia. Poach, uncovered, for 5-10 minutes or until fish flakes easily with a fork, turning once. Remove and keep warm.

2. Bring the poaching liquid to a boil; cook until reduced to about ½ cup. Meanwhile, in another skillet, saute the yellow squash, zucchini and onion in oil until tender. Add garlic; cook 1 minute longer. Sprinkle with pepper and remaining salt.

3. In a blender, combine the reduced liquid, roasted peppers and vinegar; cover and process until smooth. Serve with fish and vegetables.
PER SERVING 1 fillet with ½ cup vegetables and 2 tablespoons sauce equals 163 cal., 3 g fat (1 g sat. fat), 55 mg chol., 490 mg sodium, 7 g carb., 2 g fiber, 23 g pro. **Diabetic Exchanges:** 3 lean meat, 1 vegetable, ½ fat.

TILAPIA & VEGGIES WITH RED PEPPER SAUCE

SHRIMP LETTUCE WRAPS

Cod Delight C FAST FIX

I used to make this in the oven, but then I discovered that the microwave lets me enjoy it even faster. It's a pretty dish to serve company. In fact, many of my friends and family now cook this at home.
—**NANCY DAUGHERTY** CORTLAND, OH

START TO FINISH: 15 MIN.
MAKES: 4 SERVINGS

- 1 **small tomato, chopped**
- ⅓ **cup finely chopped onion**
- 2 **tablespoons water**
- 2 **tablespoons canola oil**
- 4 **to 5 teaspoons lemon juice**
- 1 **teaspoon dried parsley flakes**
- ½ **teaspoon dried basil**
- 1 **small garlic clove, minced**
- ⅛ **teaspoon salt**
- 4 **cod fillets (4 ounces each)**
- 1 **teaspoon seafood seasoning**

In a small bowl, combine the first nine ingredients. Place cod in an 11x7-in. baking dish; top with tomato mixture. Sprinkle with seafood seasoning. Microwave, covered, on high for 5-6 minutes or until the fish just begins to flake easily with a fork.
NOTE *This recipe was tested in a 1,100-watt microwave.*
PER SERVING *1 serving equals 154 cal., 8 g fat (1 g sat. fat), 43 mg chol., 304 mg sodium, 3 g carb., 1 g fiber, 18 g pro. Diabetic Exchanges: 3 lean meat, 1 fat.*

Shrimp Lettuce Wraps FAST FIX

Lettuce forms a crispy shell that's full of possibilities, depending on what's in your fridge. Swap shrimp for cooked chicken, pork or tofu. Mix in any veggies you want: Carrots, broccoli, snow peas and chopped zucchini are all fantastic add-ins.
—*TASTE OF HOME* **TEST KITCHEN**

START TO FINISH: 30 MIN.
MAKES: 4 SERVINGS

- ¼ **cup reduced-sodium soy sauce**
- 3 **tablespoons lime juice**
- 2 **tablespoons plus 1 teaspoon apricot preserves**
- 2 **tablespoons water**
- 2 **garlic cloves, minced**
- ¼ **teaspoon ground ginger**
- 2 **medium carrots**
- 6 **green onions**
- 3 **teaspoons olive oil, divided**
- 1 **pound uncooked medium shrimp, peeled and deveined**
- 1 **large sweet red pepper, chopped**
- 2 **cups hot cooked rice**
- 8 **large lettuce leaves**

1. In a small bowl, mix the first six ingredients. Using a vegetable peeler, shave carrots lengthwise into very thin strips. Slice white parts of green onions; cut the green tops in half lengthwise.

2. In a large skillet, heat 2 teaspoons oil over medium-high heat. Add the shrimp; stir-fry until shrimp turn pink. Remove from pan.

3. Stir-fry pepper and carrots in remaining oil 4 minutes. Add white parts of onions; stir-fry 1-2 minutes longer or until the vegetables are crisp-tender.

4. Add ⅓ cup soy sauce mixture to pan. Bring to a boil. Add shrimp; heat through. Place ¼ cup rice on each lettuce leaf; top with ½ cup shrimp mixture. Drizzle with remaining soy sauce mixture and roll up. Tie with green onion strips.
PER SERVING *2 lettuce wraps equals 306 cal., 5 g fat (1 g sat. fat), 138 mg chol., 777 mg sodium, 41 g carb., 3 g fiber, 23 g pro.* **Diabetic Exchanges:** *3 lean meat, 2 starch, 1 vegetable, ½ fat.*

COD DELIGHT

PESTO GRILLED SALMON

Pesto Grilled Salmon C FAST FIX ▶

Made with just a few ingredients, this fresh and easy summertime dish is sure to become a family favorite.

—**SONYA LABBE** WEST HOLLYWOOD, CA

START TO FINISH: 30 MIN.
MAKES: 12 SERVINGS

- 1 **salmon fillet (3 pounds)**
- ½ **cup prepared pesto**
- 2 **green onions, finely chopped**
- ¼ **cup lemon juice**
- 2 **garlic cloves, minced**

1. Moisten a paper towel with cooking oil; using long-handled tongs, lightly coat the grill rack. Place salmon, skin side down, on grill rack. Grill, covered, over medium heat or broil 4 in. from heat for 5 minutes.

2. In a small bowl, combine pesto, onions, lemon juice and garlic. Spoon some of the mixture over salmon. Grill 15-20 minutes longer or until fish flakes easily with a fork, basting occasionally with remaining mixture.

PER SERVING *3 ounces cooked salmon equals 262 cal., 17 g fat (4 g sat. fat), 70 mg chol., 147 mg sodium, 1 g carb., trace fiber, 25 g pro.* **Diabetic Exchanges:** *3 lean meat, 3 fat.*

HOW TO

GRILL A SALMON FILLET

❶ Prepare salmon according to the recipe, leaving the skin on (this makes it easier to remove the fish from the grill). Lightly oil the hot grill to prevent sticking. Place the whole fillet, skin side down, onto grill. Cover and cook until done. There is no need to turn the fillet during cooking.

❷ With a spatula, gently remove the salmon to a serving platter. The cooked fish easily separates from the skin, which makes serving up portions of the fillet quite simple.

Basil Crab Cakes [C]

I love crabmeat any way it's served, especially in these crab cakes. If you don't have fresh basil, you can substitute 2 teaspoons of dried basil.

—PRISCILLA GILBERT
INDIAN HARBOUR BEACH, FL

PREP: 15 MIN. + CHILLING
COOK: 10 MIN./BATCH
MAKES: 4 SERVINGS

- 1 large egg white
- ¼ cup mayonnaise
- 2 tablespoons minced fresh basil
- 2 teaspoons Dijon mustard
- 2 teaspoons Worcestershire sauce
- ¼ teaspoon salt
- ¼ teaspoon pepper
- 2 drops hot pepper sauce
- ½ pound lump crabmeat, drained
- 6 saltines, finely crushed
- 1 tablespoon canola oil
  Seafood cocktail sauce, optional

1. In a small bowl, combine the first eight ingredients. Stir in the crab and cracker crumbs. Refrigerate for at least 30 minutes.

2. Shape mixture into four patties. In a large skillet, cook crab cakes in oil in batches for 3-4 minutes on each side or until golden brown. Serve with cocktail sauce if desired.

PER SERVING *1 crab cake (calculated without cocktail sauce) equals 214 cal., 16 g fat (2 g sat. fat), 55 mg chol., 568 mg sodium, 4 g carb., trace fiber, 13 g pro.* **Diabetic Exchanges:** *2½ fat, 2 lean meat.*

BASIL CRAB CAKES

> I typically serve this succulent pasta with French bread and asparagus. Cook it the next time you have company, and guests will beg for the recipe.
> **—HOLLY BAUER** WEST BEND, WI

SHRIMP PICCATA

Shrimp Piccata `FAST FIX`

START TO FINISH: 25 MIN.
MAKES: 4 SERVINGS

- ½ pound uncooked angel hair pasta
- 2 shallots, finely chopped
- 2 garlic cloves, minced
- 2 tablespoons olive oil
- 1 pound uncooked large shrimp, peeled and deveined
- 1 teaspoon dried oregano
- ⅛ teaspoon salt
- 1 cup chicken broth
- 1 cup white wine or additional chicken broth
- 4 teaspoons cornstarch
- ⅓ cup lemon juice
- ¼ cup capers, drained
- 3 tablespoons minced fresh parsley

1. Cook the pasta according to package directions.

2. Meanwhile, in a large skillet, saute shallots and garlic in oil for 1 minute. Add the shrimp, oregano and salt; cook and stir until shrimp turn pink. In small bowl, combine the broth, wine and cornstarch; gradually stir into pan. Bring to a boil; cook and stir for 2 minutes or until thickened. Remove from the heat.

3. Drain pasta. Add the pasta, lemon juice, capers and parsley to the skillet; toss to coat.

PER SERVING *1½ cups equals 295 cal., 9 g fat (1 g sat. fat), 139 mg chol., 715 mg sodium, 27 g carb., 2 g fiber, 22 g pro.* **Diabetic Exchanges:** *3 lean meat, 1½ starch, 1 fat.*

187

195

189

Meatless Mains

66 As the head cook at a girls camp, I have to make a vegetarian option for each meal. This one is a favorite! 99

—DEBBIE FLEENOR MONTEREY, TN
about her recipe, Curried Rice & Noodles, on page 185

Mushroom Burgers M FAST FIX

Even the most stubborn meat-and-potatoes people have a change of heart when they bite into one of these cheddary mushroom burgers.
—**DENISE HOLLEBEKE** PENHOLD, AB

START TO FINISH: 25 MIN.
MAKES: 4 SERVINGS

- 2 **cups finely chopped fresh mushrooms**
- 2 **large eggs, lightly beaten**
- ½ **cup dry bread crumbs**
- ½ **cup shredded cheddar cheese**
- ½ **cup finely chopped onion**
- ¼ **cup all-purpose flour**
- ½ **teaspoon salt**
- ¼ **teaspoon dried thyme**
- ¼ **teaspoon pepper**
- 1 **tablespoon canola oil**
- 4 **whole wheat hamburger buns, split**
- 4 **lettuce leaves**

1. In a large bowl, combine the first nine ingredients. Shape into four ¾-in.-thick patties.
2. In a large skillet, heat oil over medium heat. Add the burgers; cook 3-4 minutes on each side or until crisp and lightly browned. Serve on buns with lettuce.

PER SERVING *1 burger with bun equals 330 cal., 13 g fat (5 g sat. fat), 121 mg chol., 736 mg sodium, 42 g carb., 5 g fiber, 14 g pro.* **Diabetic Exchanges:** *3 starch, 1 medium-fat meat, ½ fat.*

STRAWBERRY-QUINOA SPINACH SALAD

MUSHROOM BURGERS

Strawberry-Quinoa Spinach Salad M FAST FIX

We make quinoa with spinach and strawberries year-round, but it's most fun when we go to the farmers market to get the season's first berries.
—**SARAH JOHNSON** INDIANAPOLIS, IN

START TO FINISH: 30 MIN.
MAKES: 4 SERVINGS

- 2 **cups water**
- 1 **cup quinoa, rinsed**
- 6 **cups torn fresh spinach (about 5 ounces)**
- 2 **cups sliced fresh strawberries**
- ½ **cup chopped walnuts, toasted**
- ½ **cup reduced-fat red wine vinaigrette**
- ¼ **cup shredded Dubliner or Parmesan cheese**
- ¼ **teaspoon freshly ground pepper**

1. In a small saucepan, bring water to a boil. Add quinoa. Reduce heat; simmer, covered, 12-15 minutes or until water is absorbed. Remove from heat; fluff with a fork. Cool slightly.
2. In a large bowl, combine spinach, strawberries, walnuts and quinoa. Drizzle with vinaigrette; toss to coat. Sprinkle with cheese and pepper.
NOTE *To toast nuts, bake in a shallow pan in a 350° oven for 5-10 minutes or cook in a skillet over low heat until lightly browned, stirring occasionally.*
PER SERVING *2 cups equals 355 cal., 18 g fat (3 g sat. fat), 4 mg chol., 444 mg sodium, 41 g carb., 7 g fiber, 12 g pro.*

Curried Rice & Noodles M FAST FIX

As the head cook at a girls camp, I have to make a vegetarian option for each meal. This one is a favorite!

—DEBBIE FLEENOR MONTEREY, TN

START TO FINISH: 30 MIN.
MAKES: 4 SERVINGS

- 2 ounces uncooked multigrain angel hair pasta, broken into 1- to 2-inch pieces
- 2 large eggs, lightly beaten
- 1 tablespoon canola oil
- 1 yellow summer squash, sliced
- 1 small sweet red pepper, chopped
- 2 garlic cloves, minced
- 2 teaspoons curry powder
- ½ teaspoon ground ginger
- ¼ teaspoon crushed red pepper flakes
- 1 package (8½ ounces) ready-to-serve basmati rice
- 2 tablespoons reduced-sodium soy sauce
- 1 tablespoon lime juice
- 1 teaspoon sesame oil
- 2 green onions, thinly sliced
- ½ cup chopped cashews

1. In a small saucepan, cook pasta according to package directions; drain and cool.
2. Meanwhile, place a large nonstick skillet coated with cooking spray over medium heat. Pour in eggs; cook and stir until eggs are thickened and no liquid egg remains. Remove from pan.
3. In the same skillet, heat canola oil over medium-high heat. Add the squash, red pepper and garlic; stir-fry 2-3 minutes or until squash is crisp-tender. Stir in curry powder, ginger and pepper flakes.
4. Add rice and pasta; drizzle with soy sauce, lime juice and sesame oil. Heat through, tossing to combine. Stir in the green onions, cashews and cooked eggs.

PER SERVING 1 serving equals 360 cal., 17 g fat (3 g sat. fat), 93 mg chol., 449 mg sodium, 38 g carb., 4 g fiber, 12 g pro. **Diabetic Exchanges:** 2½ starch, 2 fat, 1 medium-fat meat.

Portobello Fajitas M FAST FIX

I serve portobello fajitas family-style so everyone can build his or her own. Just pass the tortillas and garnishes like salsa, cheese, guacamole and sour cream.

—CAROLYN BUTTERFIELD

LAKE STEVENS, WA

START TO FINISH: 30 MIN.
MAKES: 4 SERVINGS

- 3 large portobello mushrooms (about ½ pound)
- 1 large sweet red pepper, cut into strips
- ½ large sweet onion, sliced
- ½ cup fat-free Italian salad dressing
- 2 tablespoons lime juice
- 4 flour tortillas (8 inches), warmed
- ½ cup shredded cheddar cheese
  Optional toppings: salsa, guacamole and sour cream

1. Remove and discard stems from mushrooms; with a spoon, scrape and remove gills. Cut into ½-in. slices and place in a large bowl. Add pepper and onion; drizzle with salad dressing and toss to coat. Let stand 10 minutes.
2. Transfer vegetables to a lightly greased grill wok or grill basket; place on grill rack. Grill, covered, over medium-high heat 10-12 minutes or until tender, stirring occasionally. Drizzle with lime juice.
3. Serve vegetables with tortillas, cheese and toppings as desired.

NOTE If you do not have a grill wok or basket, use a disposable foil pan. Poke holes in the bottom of the pan with a meat fork to allow liquid to drain.

PER SERVING 1 portobello fajita (calculated without the optional toppings) equals 282 cal., 8 g fat (4 g sat. fat), 15 mg chol., 664 mg sodium, 40 g carb., 4 g fiber, 10 g pro. **Diabetic Exchanges:** 2 starch, 1 medium-fat meat, 1 vegetable.

PORTOBELLO FAJITAS

SPICY ORANGE QUINOA

Spicy Orange Quinoa Ⓜ

A creative way to serve quinoa, this recipe combines the flavors of fresh citrus and crunchy Brazil nuts with veggies, garlic, saffron and spicy cayenne.

—KATHY PATALSKY NEW YORK, NY

PREP: 30 MIN. • **COOK:** 25 MIN.
MAKES: 4 SERVINGS

- 1 serrano pepper, halved and seeded
- 1½ cups vegetable broth
- ¼ cup orange juice
- ¼ teaspoon cayenne pepper
- ¼ teaspoon saffron threads or 1 teaspoon ground turmeric
- 1 cup quinoa, rinsed
- 1 tablespoon olive oil
- 1 tablespoon buttery spread
- 1 large onion, chopped
- 1 cup chopped fresh mushrooms
- ½ cup plus 2 tablespoons chopped Brazil nuts, divided
- 2 bay leaves
- 1 package (16 ounces) frozen mixed vegetables, thawed
- 7 garlic cloves, minced
- 1 medium orange, sectioned and chopped
- 3 tablespoons lemon juice
- 2 teaspoons grated lemon peel
- 2 teaspoons grated orange peel
- ½ teaspoon pepper
- ¼ teaspoon salt

1. Broil serrano pepper halves 4 in. from the heat until skin blisters, about 10 minutes. Finely chop the pepper; set aside.

2. In a large saucepan, bring broth, orange juice, cayenne and saffron to a boil. Add quinoa. Reduce heat; simmer, covered, 12-15 minutes or until liquid is absorbed. Remove from heat; fluff with a fork.

3. Meanwhile, in a Dutch oven, heat oil and buttery spread over medium-high heat. Add onion, mushrooms, ½ cup nuts and bay leaves; cook and stir until onion is tender. Add mixed vegetables, garlic and serrano pepper; cook 4-5 minutes longer. Stir in the orange, lemon juice, peels, pepper and salt.

4. Gently stir quinoa into vegetable mixture; discard bay leaves. Sprinkle with remaining Brazil nuts.

NOTE *Look for quinoa in the cereal, rice or organic food aisle.*

PER SERVING *1¾ cups equals 480 cal., 23 g fat (5 g sat. fat), 0 chol., 583 mg sodium, 60 g carb., 11 g fiber, 14 g pro.*

Mushroom Bolognese with Whole Wheat Pasta Ⓜ

A traditional Bolognese sauce is meat-based with everything from pork to pancetta. Skipping the meat, I load mine with baby portobellos and veggies.

—AMBER MASSEY ARGYLE, TX

PREP: 10 MIN. • **COOK:** 35 MIN.
MAKES: 6 SERVINGS

- 1 tablespoon olive oil
- 1 large sweet onion, finely chopped
- 2 medium carrots, finely chopped
- 1 large zucchini, finely chopped
- ½ pound baby portobello mushrooms, finely chopped
- 3 garlic cloves, minced
- ½ cup dry red wine or reduced-sodium chicken broth
- 1 can (28 ounces) crushed tomatoes, undrained
- 1 can (14½ ounces) diced tomatoes, undrained
- ½ cup grated Parmesan cheese
- ½ teaspoon dried oregano
- ½ teaspoon pepper
- ⅛ teaspoon crushed red pepper flakes
  Dash ground nutmeg
- 4½ cups uncooked whole wheat rigatoni

1. In a 6-qt. stockpot coated with cooking spray, heat oil over medium-high heat. Add onion and carrots; cook and stir until tender. Add zucchini, mushrooms and garlic; cook and stir until tender. Stir in wine; bring to a boil; cook until the liquid is almost evaporated.

2. Stir in the crushed and diced tomatoes, cheese and seasonings; bring to a boil. Reduce heat; simmer, covered, for 25-30 minutes or until slightly thickened.

3. Cook rigatoni according to package directions; drain. Serve with sauce.

PER SERVING *1⅓ cups sauce with 1 cup pasta equals 369 cal., 6 g fat (2 g sat. fat), 6 mg chol., 483 mg sodium, 65 g carb., 12 g fiber, 17 g pro.*

MUSHROOM BOLOGNESE WITH WHOLE WHEAT PASTA

Mushroom-Bean Bourguignon Ⓜ

A French baguette goes well with this meatless version of a dish that's been a staple in our family for generations.
—**SONYA LABBE** WEST HOLLYWOOD, CA

PREP: 15 MIN. • **COOK:** 1¼ HOURS
MAKES: 10 SERVINGS (2½ QUARTS)

- 4 **tablespoons olive oil, divided**
- 5 **medium carrots, cut into 1-inch pieces**
- 2 **medium onions, halved and sliced**
- 2 **garlic cloves, minced**
- 8 **large portobello mushrooms, cut into 1-inch pieces**
- 1 **tablespoon tomato paste**
- 1 **bottle (750 milliliters) dry red wine**
- 2 **cups mushroom broth or vegetable broth, divided**
- 1 **teaspoon salt**
- 1 **teaspoon minced fresh thyme or ½ teaspoon dried thyme**
- ½ **teaspoon pepper**
- 2 **cans (15½ ounces each) navy beans, rinsed and drained**
- 1 **package (14.4 ounces) frozen pearl onions**
- 3 **tablespoons all-purpose flour**

1. In a Dutch oven, heat 2 tablespoons oil over medium-high heat. Add carrots and onions; cook and stir 8-10 minutes or until the onions are tender. Add garlic; cook 1 minute longer. Remove from pan.

2. In same pan, heat 1 tablespoon oil. Add half of mushrooms; cook until lightly browned. Remove from the pan; cook remaining mushrooms in remaining oil.

3. Return mushrooms to pan. Add tomato paste; cook and stir 1 minute. Add wine, 1½ cups broth, seasonings and carrot mixture. Simmer, covered, for 25 minutes.

4. Add beans and pearl onions; cook 30 minutes longer. In a small bowl, whisk flour and remaining broth until smooth; stir into pan. Bring to a boil; cook and stir for 2 minutes or until slightly thickened.

PER SERVING *1 cup equals 234 cal., 6 g fat (1 g sat. fat), 0 chol., 613 mg sodium, 33 g carb., 7 g fiber, 9 g pro. Diabetic Exchanges: 2 starch, 2 vegetable, 1 lean meat, 1 fat.*

As a vegan, I'm always looking for easy, delicious dishes to share. A touch of peanut butter (or almond butter) gives these loaded sweet potatoes a special flavor. —**KAYLA CAPPER** OJAI, CA

SWEET POTATOES WITH CILANTRO BLACK BEANS

Sweet Potatoes with Cilantro Black Beans Ⓜ FAST FIX

START TO FINISH: 20 MIN.
MAKES: 4 SERVINGS

- 4 **medium sweet potatoes (about 8 ounces each)**
- 1 **tablespoon olive oil**
- 1 **small sweet red pepper, chopped**
- 2 **green onions, chopped**
- 1 **can (15 ounces) black beans, rinsed and drained**
- ½ **cup salsa**
- ¼ **cup frozen corn**
- 2 **tablespoons lime juice**
- 1 **tablespoon creamy peanut butter**
- 1 **teaspoon ground cumin**
- ¼ **teaspoon garlic salt**
- ¼ **cup minced fresh cilantro**
  Additional minced fresh cilantro, optional

1. Scrub sweet potatoes; pierce several times with a fork. Place on a microwave-safe plate. Microwave, uncovered, on high 6-8 minutes or until tender, turning once.

2. Meanwhile, in a large skillet, heat oil over medium-high heat. Add the pepper and green onions; cook and stir 3-4 minutes or until tender. Stir in beans, salsa, corn, lime juice, peanut butter, cumin and garlic salt; heat through. Stir in cilantro.

3. With a sharp knife, cut an "X" in each sweet potato. Fluff pulp with a fork. Spoon bean mixture over sweet potatoes. If desired, sprinkle with additional cilantro.

PER SERVING *1 potato with ½ cup black bean mixture equals 400 cal., 6 g fat (1 g sat. fat), 0 chol., 426 mg sodium, 77 g carb., 12 g fiber, 11 g pro.*

GARDEN HARVEST SPAGHETTI SQUASH

Garden Harvest Spaghetti Squash M

I was in the grocery store and spotted a perfectly ripe spaghetti squash. I knew I had to try it, so I cooked it according to the label. I topped it with my favorite vegetables for pasta, and it was an instant family favorite.

—**VERONICA MCCANN** COLUMBUS, OH

PREP: 30 MIN. • **BAKE:** 35 MIN.
MAKES: 4 SERVINGS

- 1 **medium spaghetti squash (about 4 pounds)**
- 1 **medium sweet red pepper, chopped**
- 1 **medium red onion, chopped**
- 1 **small zucchini, chopped**
- 1 **cup chopped fresh mushrooms**
- ½ **cup chopped leek (white portion only)**
- ½ **cup shredded carrots**
- 1 **tablespoon olive oil**
- 1 **garlic clove, minced**
- 1 **can (14½ ounces) stewed tomatoes**
- ½ **cup tomato paste**
- ¼ **cup V8 juice**
- 1 **teaspoon pepper**
- ½ **teaspoon salt**
- 2 **cups fresh baby spinach**
- 1 **tablespoon minced fresh basil**
- 2 **teaspoons minced fresh oregano**
- 2 **teaspoons minced fresh thyme**
- 1 **teaspoon minced fresh rosemary**
- ¼ **cup grated Parmesan and Romano cheese blend**

1. Cut the squash in half lengthwise; discard seeds. Place squash cut side down in a 15x10x1-in. baking pan; add ½ in. of hot water. Bake, uncovered, at 375° for 30-40 minutes. Drain water from pan; turn squash cut side up. Bake 5 minutes longer or until the squash is tender.

2. Meanwhile, in a Dutch oven, saute the red pepper, onion, zucchini, mushrooms, leek and carrots in oil until tender. Add garlic; cook 1 minute longer. Add the stewed tomatoes, tomato paste, V8 juice, pepper and salt; bring to a boil. Reduce heat; cover and simmer for 15 minutes. Stir in spinach and herbs; heat through.

3. When squash is cool enough to handle, use a fork to separate strands. Serve with sauce; sprinkle with cheese.

PER SERVING *1 cup squash with 1 cup sauce equals 270 cal., 8 g fat (2 g sat. fat), 8 mg chol., 751 mg sodium, 47 g carb., 10 g fiber, 10 g pro.* **Diabetic Exchanges:** *3 starch, 1½ fat.*

Ricotta-Stuffed Portobello Mushrooms C M FAST FIX ▶

These mushrooms are rich, creamy and bright-tasting at the same time because of the fresh herbs and tomato. I especially like them served with grilled asparagus.

—TRE BALCHOWSKY SAUSALITO, CA

START TO FINISH: 30 MIN.
MAKES: 6 SERVINGS

- ¾ cup reduced-fat ricotta cheese
- ¾ cup grated Parmesan cheese, divided
- ½ cup shredded part-skim mozzarella cheese
- 2 tablespoons minced fresh parsley
- ⅛ teaspoon pepper
- 6 large portobello mushrooms
- 6 slices large tomato
- ¾ cup fresh basil leaves
- 3 tablespoons slivered almonds or pine nuts, toasted
- 1 small garlic clove
- 2 tablespoons olive oil
- 2 to 3 teaspoons water

1. In a small bowl, mix ricotta cheese, ¼ cup Parmesan cheese, mozzarella cheese, parsley and pepper. Remove and discard stems from mushrooms; with a spoon, scrape and remove gills. Fill caps with ricotta mixture. Top with tomato slices.

2. Grill, covered, over medium heat for 8-10 minutes or until mushrooms are tender. Remove from grill with a metal spatula.

3. Meanwhile, place basil, almonds and garlic in a small food processor; pulse until chopped. Add remaining Parmesan cheese; pulse just until blended. While processing, gradually add oil and enough water to reach desired consistency. Spoon over stuffed mushrooms before serving.

NOTE *To toast nuts, bake in a shallow pan in a 350° oven for 5-10 minutes or cook in a skillet over low heat until lightly browned, stirring occasionally.*

PER SERVING *1 stuffed portobello mushroom equals 201 cal., 13 g fat (4 g sat. fat), 22 mg chol., 238 mg sodium, 9 g carb., 2 g fiber, 12 g pro.* **Diabetic Exchanges:** *1½ fat, 1 medium-fat meat, 1 vegetable.*

Vegetarian Bean Tacos M FAST FIX ▶

I love Mexican food but was looking for a healthier option to share. My family devours these tasty tacos whenever I make them.

—AMANDA PETRUCELLI PLYMOUTH, IN

START TO FINISH: 25 MIN.
MAKES: 4 SERVINGS

- 1 tablespoon canola oil
- 1 medium onion, chopped
- 1 jalapeno pepper, seeded and finely chopped
- 2 garlic cloves, minced
- 1 tablespoon chili powder
- 2 teaspoons ground cumin
- 1 teaspoon ground coriander
- 1 can (16 ounces) refried beans
- 1 can (15 ounces) black beans, rinsed and drained
- 1 can (14½ ounces) no-salt-added diced tomatoes, drained
- 4 whole wheat tortillas (8 inches), warmed

Optional toppings: shredded lettuce, shredded cheddar cheese, cubed avocado, sour cream and salsa

1. In a large nonstick skillet coated with cooking spray, heat oil over medium heat. Add chopped onion and jalapeno; cook and stir until tender. Add garlic and seasonings; cook 1 minute longer. Stir in beans and diced tomatoes; heat through.

2. Serve bean mixture in tortillas with toppings as desired.

NOTE *Wear disposable gloves when cutting hot peppers; the oils can burn skin. Avoid touching your face.*

PER SERVING *1 taco (calculated without optional toppings) equals 413 cal., 9 g fat (1 g sat. fat), 9 mg chol., 774 mg sodium, 66 g carb., 16 g fiber, 17 g pro.*

VEGETARIAN BEAN TACOS

TOMATO & GARLIC BUTTER BEAN DINNER

Tomato & Garlic Butter Bean Dinner M FAST FIX

For those days when I get home late and just want a warm meal, I stir up this dish of tomatoes, garlic and butter beans.
—**JESSICA MEYERS** AUSTIN, TX

START TO FINISH: 15 MIN.
MAKES: 4 SERVINGS

- 1 tablespoon olive oil
- 2 garlic cloves, minced
- 2 cans (14½ ounces) no-salt-added petite diced tomatoes, undrained
- 1 can (16 ounces) butter beans, rinsed and drained
- 6 cups fresh baby spinach (about 6 ounces)
- ½ teaspoon Italian seasoning
- ¼ teaspoon pepper
  Hot cooked pasta and grated Parmesan cheese, optional

1. In a large skillet, heat oil over medium-high heat. Add garlic; cook and stir 30-45 seconds or until tender.
2. Add tomatoes, beans, spinach, Italian seasoning and pepper; cook until spinach is wilted, stirring occasionally. If desired, serve with pasta and cheese.
FREEZE OPTION *Freeze cooled bean mixture in freezer containers. To use, partially thaw in refrigerator overnight. Heat through in a saucepan, stirring occasionally and adding a little water if necessary.*
PER SERVING *1¼ cups (calculated without pasta and cheese) equals 147 cal., 4 g fat (1 g sat. fat), 0 chol., 353 mg sodium, 28 g carb., 9 g fiber, 8 g pro.* **Diabetic Exchanges:** *2 starch, ½ fat.*

Whole Wheat Orzo Salad M FAST FIX

START TO FINISH: 30 MIN.
MAKES: 8 SERVINGS

- 2½ cups uncooked whole wheat orzo pasta (about 1 pound)
- 1 can (15 ounces) white kidney or cannellini beans, rinsed and drained
- 3 medium tomatoes, finely chopped
- 1 English cucumber, finely chopped
- 2 cups (8 ounces) crumbled feta cheese
- 1¼ cups pitted Greek olives (about 6 ounces), chopped
- 1 medium sweet yellow pepper, finely chopped
- 1 medium green pepper, finely chopped
- 1 cup fresh mint leaves, chopped
- ½ medium red onion, finely chopped
- ¼ cup lemon juice
- 2 tablespoons olive oil
- 1 tablespoon grated lemon peel
- 3 garlic cloves, minced
- ½ teaspoon pepper

1. Cook orzo according to package directions. Drain orzo; rinse well with cold water.
2. Meanwhile, in a large bowl, combine remaining ingredients. Stir in orzo. Refrigerate until serving.
PER SERVING *1¾ cups equals 411 cal., 17 g fat (4 g sat. fat), 15 mg chol., 740 mg sodium, 51 g carb., 13 g fiber, 14 g pro.*

In only 30 minutes, I can put together this hearty salad of pasta, white beans and veggies—and it feeds a crowd.
—**MYA ZERONIS** PITTSBURGH, PA

WHOLE WHEAT ORZO SALAD

STACKED VEGETABLES AND RAVIOLI

Stacked Vegetables and Ravioli M

Yellow squash, zucchini and basil meet ricotta and ravioli in this crowd-pleasing entree with delicious summer flavors. One bite and you'll know—this is what summer tastes like.

—*TASTE OF HOME* TEST KITCHEN

PREP: 20 MIN. • **BAKE:** 30 MIN. + STANDING
MAKES: 6 SERVINGS

- 2 **yellow summer squash**
- 2 **medium zucchini**
- 1 **package (9 ounces) refrigerated cheese ravioli**
- 1 **cup ricotta cheese**
- 1 **large egg**
- ½ **teaspoon garlic salt**
- 1 **jar (24 ounces) marinara or spaghetti sauce**
- 10 **fresh basil leaves, divided**
- ¾ **cup shredded Parmesan cheese**

1. Preheat oven to 350°. Using a vegetable peeler, cut squash and zucchini into very thin lengthwise strips. In a Dutch oven, cook ravioli according to package directions, adding vegetable strips during last 3 minutes of cooking.

2. Meanwhile, in a small bowl, combine the ricotta cheese, egg and garlic salt; set aside. Drain ravioli and vegetables.

3. Spread ½ cup marinara sauce into a greased 11x7-in. baking dish. Layer with half of the ravioli and vegetables, half of the ricotta mixture, seven basil leaves and 1 cup marinara sauce. Layer with remaining ravioli, vegetables and marinara sauce. Dollop remaining ricotta mixture over the top; sprinkle with Parmesan cheese.

4. Cover and bake for 25 minutes. Uncover and bake 5-10 minutes longer or until cheese is melted. Let stand 10 minutes before cutting. Thinly slice remaining basil; sprinkle over top.

PER SERVING *1 piece equals 323 cal., 11 g fat (6 g sat. fat), 76 mg chol., 779 mg sodium, 39 g carb., 4 g fiber, 19 g pro.* **Diabetic Exchanges:** *2 starch, 2 medium-fat meat, 1 vegetable.*

Arugula & Brown Rice Salad M FAST FIX

When we have company, arugula with brown rice is always on the menu. It's my go-to pick for the potluck and party circuit, and I'm always sharing the recipe.

—**MINDY OSWALT** WINNETKA, CA

START TO FINISH: 25 MIN.
MAKES: 4 SERVINGS

- 1 **package (8.8 ounces) ready-to-serve brown rice**
- 7 **cups fresh arugula or baby spinach (about 5 ounces)**
- 1 **can (15 ounces) garbanzo beans or chickpeas, rinsed and drained**
- 1 **cup (4 ounces) crumbled feta cheese**
- ¾ **cup loosely packed basil leaves, torn**
- ½ **cup dried cherries or cranberries**

DRESSING

- ¼ **cup olive oil**
- ¼ **teaspoon grated lemon peel**
- 2 **tablespoons lemon juice**
- ¼ **teaspoon salt**
- ⅛ **teaspoon pepper**

1. Heat rice according to package directions. Transfer to a large bowl; cool slightly.

2. Stir the arugula, beans, cheese, basil and cherries into rice. In a small bowl, whisk dressing ingredients. Drizzle over salad; toss to coat. Serve immediately.

PER SERVING *2 cups equals 473 cal., 22 g fat (5 g sat. fat), 15 mg chol., 574 mg sodium, 53 g carb., 7 g fiber, 13 g pro.*

ARUGULA & BROWN RICE SALAD

BLACK BEAN CHIP & DIP BURGERS

Black Bean Chip & Dip Burgers ⓕ Ⓜ

I tried to create a healthy veggie burger that wasn't dry and crumbly or really boring. These amazing burgers taste like chips and dip—and even my grandkids prefer them over regular burgers!

—KT REHRIG ALLENTOWN, PA

PREP: 30 MIN. • **GRILL:** 10 MIN.
MAKES: 8 SERVINGS

- ⅔ **cup water**
- ⅓ **cup quinoa, rinsed**
- 1 **can (15 ounces) black beans, rinsed and drained**
- 1 **jar (16 ounces) salsa, divided**
- 1 **cup crushed baked tortilla chip scoops**
- 2 **tablespoons reduced-sodium taco seasoning**
- 8 **whole wheat hamburger buns, split**
- 8 **lettuce leaves**
- 8 **slices tomato**
- 8 **slices red onion**

1. In a small saucepan, bring water to a boil. Add quinoa. Reduce heat; simmer, covered, 12-15 minutes or until liquid is absorbed. Remove from heat; fluff with a fork.

2. In a large bowl, mash black beans. Add 1 cup salsa, chips, taco seasoning and cooked quinoa; mix well. Shape into eight ¼-in.-thick patties.

3. Grill, covered, over medium heat 5-6 minutes on each side or until heated through. Serve on buns with veggies and remaining salsa.

TO BAKE PATTIES *Preheat oven to 350°. Place patties on a baking sheet coated with cooking spray. Bake for 25-30 minutes or until heated through, turning once.*

PER SERVING *1 burger equals 247 cal., 3 g fat (1 g sat. fat), 0 chol., 700 mg sodium, 47 g carb., 7 g fiber, 8 g pro.*

DID YOU KNOW?

Quinoa (pronounced KEEN-wah), an ancient South American grain, is called "the perfect grain" because it offers a complete protein. Quinoa is an excellent choice for vegetarian and vegan meals, which tend to be low in protein.

My from-scratch pizza has a whole wheat crust flavored with beer. Top it with spinach, artichoke hearts and tomatoes, then add sliced fresh basil.

—RAYMONDE BOURGEOIS SWASTIKA, ON

SPINACH & ARTICHOKE PIZZA

Spinach & Artichoke Pizza Ⓜ

PREP: 25 MIN. • **BAKE:** 20 MIN.
MAKES: 6 SLICES

- 1½ to 1¾ **cups white whole wheat flour**
- 1½ **teaspoons baking powder**
- ¼ **teaspoon salt**
- ¼ **teaspoon each dried basil, oregano and parsley flakes**
- ¾ **cup beer or nonalcoholic beer**

TOPPINGS

- 1½ **teaspoons olive oil**
- 1 **garlic clove, minced**
- 2 **cups (8 ounces) shredded Italian cheese blend**
- 2 **cups fresh baby spinach**
- 1 **can (14 ounces) water-packed quartered artichoke hearts, drained and coarsely chopped**
- 2 **medium tomatoes, seeded and coarsely chopped**
- 2 **tablespoons thinly sliced fresh basil**

1. Preheat oven to 425°. In a large bowl, whisk 1½ cups flour, baking powder, salt and dried herbs until blended. Add beer, stirring just until moistened.

2. Turn dough onto a well-floured surface; knead gently 6-8 times, adding additional flour if needed. Press dough to fit a greased 12-in. pizza pan. Pinch edge to form a rim. Bake 8 minutes or until edge is lightly browned.

3. Mix oil and garlic; spread over crust. Sprinkle with ½ cup cheese; layer with spinach, artichoke hearts and tomatoes. Sprinkle with the remaining cheese. Bake 8-10 minutes or until crust is golden and cheese is melted. Sprinkle with fresh basil.

PER SERVING *1 slice equals 290 cal., 10 g fat (6 g sat. fat), 27 mg chol., 654 mg sodium, 32 g carb., 5 g fiber, 14 g pro.* **Diabetic Exchanges:** *2 starch, 1 medium-fat meat, 1 vegetable.*

Brown Rice Chutney Salad M

After tasting a stellar rice salad at my favorite cafe, I created my own at home. This Indian-inspired dish is packed full of interesting textures, flavors and colors. To fire things up, mix in a small amount of hot chili oil, tasting carefully as you go.

—BROOKE MARTIN GREENFIELD, MN

PREP: 30 MIN. + CHILLING • **MAKES:** 8 SERVINGS

- 8 cups cooked brown rice, cooled
- 3 medium carrots, shredded
- ¾ cup dried cranberries
- 1 small sweet red pepper, chopped
- 3 green onions, sliced
- ½ cup mango chutney
- 3 tablespoons olive oil
- 2 tablespoons red wine vinegar
- 2 teaspoons curry powder
- ½ teaspoon salt
- ½ teaspoon garam masala
- 3 cups fresh baby spinach, chopped if desired
- 1 medium apple, chopped
- 1 cup salted cashews

1. In a large bowl, combine the first five ingredients. In a small bowl, whisk the chutney, oil, vinegar, curry powder, salt and garam masala. Pour over rice mixture; toss to coat. Refrigerate for several hours.

2. Just before serving, add spinach and apple; toss to combine. Sprinkle with cashews.

NOTE *Look for garam masala in the spice aisle.*

PER SERVING *1½ cups equals 469 cal., 17 g fat (3 g sat. fat), 0 chol., 314 mg sodium, 72 g carb., 7 g fiber, 9 g pro.*

BROWN RICE CHUTNEY SALAD

PINTO BEAN TOSTADAS

Pinto Bean Tostadas M FAST FIX ▶

Ready-to-go pinto beans and crispy corn tortillas prove how easy it is to make a healthy meal. Sometimes I add some chopped leftover meat to the tostadas, but they're equally satisfying just as they are.

—LILY JULOW LAWRENCEVILLE, GA

START TO FINISH: 30 MIN. • **MAKES:** 6 SERVINGS

- ¼ cup sour cream
- ¾ teaspoon grated lime peel
- ¼ teaspoon ground cumin
- ½ teaspoon salt, divided
- 2 tablespoons canola oil, divided
- 2 garlic cloves, minced
- 2 cans (15 ounces each) pinto beans, rinsed and drained
- 1 to 2 teaspoons hot pepper sauce
- 1 teaspoon chili powder
- 6 corn tortillas (6 inches)
- 2 cups shredded lettuce
- ½ cup salsa
- ¾ cup crumbled feta cheese or queso fresco
  Lime wedges

1. In a small bowl, mix sour cream, lime peel, cumin and ¼ teaspoon salt. In a large saucepan, heat 1 tablespoon oil over medium heat. Add garlic; cook and stir just until fragrant, about 45 seconds. Stir in beans, pepper sauce, chili powder and remaining salt; heat through, stirring occasionally. Keep warm.

2. Brush both sides of tortillas with remaining oil. Place a large skillet over medium-high heat. Add tortillas in two batches; cook 2-3 minutes on each side or until lightly browned and crisp.

3. To serve, arrange beans and lettuce over tostada shells; top with salsa, sour cream mixture and cheese. Serve with lime wedges.

PER SERVING *1 tostada equals 291 cal., 10 g fat (3 g sat. fat), 14 mg chol., 658 mg sodium, 38 g carb., 8 g fiber, 11 g pro.*
***Diabetic Exchanges:** 2½ starch, 1 lean meat, 1 fat.*

Cheese Manicotti Ⓜ

PREP: 25 MIN. • **BAKE:** 1 HOUR • **MAKES:** 7 SERVINGS

- 1 carton (15 ounces) reduced-fat ricotta cheese
- ½ cup shredded part-skim mozzarella cheese
- 1 small onion, finely chopped
- 1 large egg, lightly beaten
- 2 tablespoons minced fresh parsley
- ½ teaspoon pepper
- ¼ teaspoon salt
- 1 cup grated Parmesan cheese, divided
- 4 cups marinara sauce
- ½ cup water
- 1 package (8 ounces) manicotti shells

1. Preheat oven to 350°. In a small bowl, mix the first seven ingredients; stir in ½ cup Parmesan cheese. In another bowl, mix marinara sauce and water; spread ¾ cup sauce onto bottom of a 13x9-in. baking dish coated with cooking spray. Fill uncooked manicotti shells with ricotta mixture; arrange over sauce. Top with remaining sauce.

2. Bake, covered, 50 minutes or until pasta is tender. Sprinkle with the remaining Parmesan cheese. Bake, uncovered, 10-15 minutes longer or until cheese is melted.

PER SERVING *2 stuffed manicotti equals 340 cal., 8 g fat (5 g sat. fat), 60 mg chol., 615 mg sodium, 46 g carb., 4 g fiber, 19 g pro.* **Diabetic Exchanges:** *3 starch, 2 lean meat, ½ fat.*

This is the first meal I ever cooked for my husband, and all these years later he still enjoys my manicotti!
—**JOAN HALLFORD** NORTH RICHLAND HILLS, TX

CHEESE MANICOTTI

MEDITERRANEAN VEGETABLE PITAS

Mediterranean Vegetable Pitas Ⓜ FAST FIX ▸

Craving a fast and healthy meal? This one packs tomato, onion, cucumber and olives. Add a touch of cayenne for a punch.
—**IVY ABBADESSA** LOXAHATCHEE, FL

START TO FINISH: 20 MIN. • **MAKES:** 4 SERVINGS

- ¼ cup olive oil
- 2 tablespoons balsamic vinegar
- 2 teaspoons grated lemon peel
- 2 teaspoons minced fresh oregano or ½ teaspoon dried oregano
- ½ teaspoon garlic powder
- ½ teaspoon pepper
- ⅛ teaspoon cayenne pepper, optional
- 1 large tomato, chopped
- 1 cup chopped seeded cucumber
- ½ cup chopped red onion
- 1 can (2¼ ounces) sliced ripe olives, drained
- 2 cups torn romaine
- 8 whole wheat pita pocket halves
- ½ cup crumbled feta cheese

1. In a large bowl, whisk the first six ingredients until blended; if desired, stir in cayenne. Add tomato, cucumber, onion and olives; toss to coat. Refrigerate until serving.

2. To serve, add lettuce to vegetables; toss to combine. Spoon into pita halves; sprinkle with cheese.

PER SERVING *2 filled pita halves equals 354 cal., 19 g fat (4 g sat. fat), 8 mg chol., 580 mg sodium, 39 g carb., 7 g fiber, 9 g pro.*

BOW TIE & SPINACH SALAD

Black Beans with Bell Peppers & Rice M FAST FIX

My entire family falls hard for this vegetarian dish every time I make it. It's pretty and quick, and it has an awesome flavor. For my children, the more cheese I add, the better.

—STEPHANIE LAMBERT MOSELEY, VA

START TO FINISH: 30 MIN.
MAKES: 6 SERVINGS

- 1 tablespoon olive oil
- 1 each medium sweet yellow, orange and red pepper, chopped
- 1 large onion, chopped
- 2 garlic cloves, minced
- 2 cans (15 ounces each) black beans, rinsed and drained
- 1 package (8.8 ounces) ready-to-serve brown rice
- 1½ teaspoons ground cumin
- ½ teaspoon dried oregano
- 1½ cups (6 ounces) shredded Mexican cheese blend, divided
- 3 tablespoons minced fresh cilantro

1. In a large skillet, heat oil over medium-high heat. Add peppers, onion and garlic; cook and stir 6-8 minutes or until tender. Add beans, rice, cumin and oregano; heat through.
2. Stir in 1 cup cheese; sprinkle with remaining cheese. Remove from the heat. Let stand, covered, 5 minutes or until cheese is melted. Sprinkle with fresh cilantro.
PER SERVING *1 cup equals 347 cal., 12 g fat (6 g sat. fat), 25 mg chol., 477 mg sodium, 40 g carb., 8 g fiber, 15 g pro.* **Diabetic Exchanges:** *2½ starch, 2 lean meat, 1 fat.*

BLACK BEANS WITH BELL PEPPERS & RICE

Bow Tie & Spinach Salad M FAST FIX

With pasta salad, it's easy to change up ingredients. We like to add pine nuts, and sometimes we change the garbanzo beans to black beans.

—JULIE KIRKPATRICK BILLINGS, MT

START TO FINISH: 30 MIN.
MAKES: 6 SERVINGS

- 2 cups uncooked multigrain bow tie pasta
- 1 can (15 ounces) garbanzo beans or chickpeas, rinsed and drained
- 6 cups fresh baby spinach (about 6 ounces)
- 2 cups fresh broccoli florets
- 2 plum tomatoes, chopped
- 1 medium sweet red pepper, chopped
- ½ cup cubed part-skim mozzarella cheese
- ½ cup pitted Greek olives, halved
- ¼ cup minced fresh basil
- ⅓ cup reduced-fat sun-dried tomato salad dressing
- ¼ teaspoon salt
- ¼ cup chopped walnuts, toasted

1. Cook bow tie pasta according to package directions. Drain; transfer to a large bowl.
2. Add beans, vegetables, cheese, olives and basil to pasta. Drizzle with dressing and sprinkle with salt; toss to coat. Sprinkle with walnuts.
NOTE *To toast nuts, bake in a shallow pan in a 350° oven for 5-10 minutes or cook in a skillet over low heat until lightly browned, stirring occasionally.*
PER SERVING *2 cups equals 319 cal., 13 g fat (2 g sat. fat), 6 mg chol., 660 mg sodium, 39 g carb., 7 g fiber, 14 g pro.* *Diabetic Exchanges: 2 starch, 2 fat, 1 lean meat, 1 vegetable.*

HERB GARDEN LASAGNAS

until al dente. Place one-fifth of the noodle in bottom of a prepared dish; top with 1 tablespoon ricotta mixture and 2 tablespoons tomato. Fold noodle back to cover filling; repeat three times, topping and folding the noodle each time.

6. Sprinkle lasagnas with remaining queso fresco and tomatoes. Bake, covered, 30-35 minutes or until heated through. If desired, sprinkle with additional herbs.

PER SERVING *1 individual lasagna equals 363 cal., 13 g fat (6 g sat. fat), 135 mg chol., 343 mg sodium, 44 g carb., 3 g fiber, 19 g pro. **Diabetic Exchanges:** 2½ starch, 2 medium-fat meat, 1 vegetable, ½ fat.*

HOW TO

MAKE LASAGNAS

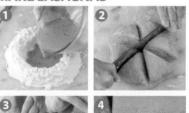

1 On a clean counter, make a well in the dry ingredients. Add eggs and mix as recipe directs.
2 Easily portion the dough by shaping into a ball, then cutting it into six wedges.
3 Shape each portion into a ball; cover dough to keep it from drying out. Rest dough as recipe directs.
4 Roll each portion into a noodle, keeping remaining dough covered until ready to use. Boil as directed.
5 Gently fold noodle into prepared dish and layer with ingredients as recipe directs.

Herb Garden Lasagnas Ⓜ

I love the taste and texture of these homemade noodles and the beautiful lasagnas they make. A healthy dose of fresh herbs gives this dish its unique flavor.
—**KATHRYN CONRAD** MILWAUKEE, WI

PREP: 45 MIN. + STANDING • **BAKE:** 30 MIN.
MAKES: 6 SERVINGS

- 2 large eggs
- 1 large egg yolk
- ¼ cup water
- 1 tablespoon olive oil
- ½ teaspoon coarsely ground pepper
- ¼ teaspoon salt
- 1½ cups all-purpose flour
- ½ cup semolina flour

FILLING

- 1 cup whole-milk ricotta cheese
- 1 large egg white, lightly beaten
- 2 tablespoons shredded carrot
- 1 tablespoon minced fresh basil
- 1 tablespoon thinly sliced green onion
- 1 teaspoon minced fresh mint
- ¼ teaspoon salt
- 1 cup crumbled queso fresco or feta cheese, divided
- 4 cups chopped tomatoes (about 6 medium), divided

Optional toppings: thinly sliced green onion, fresh basil and fresh mint

1. In a small bowl, whisk the first six ingredients. On a clean work surface, mix all-purpose and semolina flours; form into a mound. Make a large well in the center. Pour egg mixture into well. Using a fork or fingers, gradually mix flour mixture into egg mixture, forming a soft dough (dough will be soft and slightly sticky).

2. Lightly dust work surface with flour; knead dough gently five times. Divide into six portions; cover with plastic wrap. Let rest 30 minutes.

3. In a small bowl, mix the first seven filling ingredients; stir in ½ cup queso fresco. Grease six individual 12-oz. au gratin dishes; place on baking sheets. Preheat oven to 350°.

4. Fill a Dutch oven three-fourths full with salted water; bring to a boil. On a floured surface, roll each portion of dough into a 20x4-in. rectangle, dusting with additional all-purpose flour as needed.

5. For each lasagna, add one noodle to boiling water; cook 1-2 minutes or

204

210

203

The Bread Basket

Old-Fashioned Buttermilk Biscuits M FAST FIX

My family gobbles up these biscuits, which are low in fat, cholesterol and sugar. I almost always make these now instead of my old shortening-based recipe.

—**WENDY MASTERS** GRAND VALLEY, ON

START TO FINISH: 20 MIN.
MAKES: 8 BISCUITS

- 1¾ cups all-purpose flour
- 2 teaspoons baking powder
- ½ teaspoon baking soda
- ½ teaspoon sugar
- ¼ teaspoon salt
- ⅔ cup buttermilk
- 2 tablespoons canola oil
- 1 tablespoon reduced-fat sour cream

1. In a large bowl, combine the flour, baking powder, baking soda, sugar and salt. Combine the buttermilk, oil and sour cream; stir into flour mixture just until moistened. Turn onto a lightly floured surface; knead 8-10 times.

2. Pat or roll out to ½-in. thickness; cut with a floured 2½-in. biscuit cutter. Place biscuits 2 in. apart on an ungreased baking sheet. Bake at 400° for 8-12 minutes or until lightly golden brown. Serve warm.

PER SERVING *1 biscuit equals 142 cal., 4 g fat (trace sat. fat), 1 mg chol., 276 mg sodium, 22 g carb., 1 g fiber, 4 g pro.* **Diabetic Exchanges:** *1½ starch, 1 fat.*

OLD-FASHIONED BUTTERMILK BISCUITS

GRILLED GARDEN VEGGIE FLATBREAD

Grilled Garden Veggie Flatbread M FAST FIX

Grilled flatbread is a tasty way to put fresh garden vegetables to use. It's so versatile; simply change up the vegetables and cheese to suit your family's taste. It also works well indoors, cooked on a grill pan with a lid.

—**CARLY CURTIN** ELLICOTT CITY, MD

START TO FINISH: 20 MIN.
MAKES: 8 SERVINGS

- 2 whole grain naan flatbreads
- 2 teaspoons olive oil
- 1 medium yellow or red tomato, thinly sliced
- ¼ cup thinly sliced onion
- ½ cup shredded part-skim mozzarella cheese
- 2 tablespoons shredded Parmesan cheese
- 1 tablespoon minced fresh basil
- ½ teaspoon garlic powder
- 1 teaspoon balsamic vinegar
- ½ teaspoon coarse sea salt

1. Grill flatbreads, covered, over indirect medium heat 2-3 minutes or until bottoms are lightly browned.

2. Remove from grill. Brush grilled sides with oil; top with tomato and onion to within ½ in. of edges. In a small bowl, toss cheeses with basil and garlic powder; sprinkle over vegetables. Drizzle with vinegar; sprinkle with salt. Return to grill; cook, covered, 2-3 minutes longer or until cheese is melted. Cut into wedges.

PER SERVING *1 wedge equals 132 cal., 5 g fat (2 g sat. fat), 8 mg chol., 390 mg sodium, 16 g carb., 2 g fiber, 5 g pro.* **Diabetic Exchanges:** *1 starch, 1 fat.*

Double Berry Quick Bread M

Healthy, fast and easy! This bread is a favorite of mine when prep time is tight and I have small amounts of different kinds of berries on hand.

—JENNIFER CODUTO KENT, OH

PREP: 15 MIN. • **BAKE:** 50 MIN. + COOLING
MAKES: 1 LOAF (12 SLICES)

- 1½ cups all-purpose flour
- ½ cup whole wheat flour
- ½ cup sugar
- 1½ teaspoons baking powder
- ½ teaspoon salt
- ¼ teaspoon baking soda
- 2 large egg whites
- 1 large egg
- ½ cup fat-free milk
- ½ cup reduced-fat sour cream
- ¼ cup unsweetened applesauce
- ¼ cup canola oil
- 2 teaspoons vanilla extract
- 1 cup fresh raspberries
- 1 cup fresh blackberries

1. In a large bowl, whisk the first six ingredients. In another bowl, whisk egg whites, egg, milk, sour cream, applesauce, oil and vanilla until blended. Add to flour mixture; stir just until moistened. Gently fold in berries.
2. Transfer to a 9x5-in. loaf pan coated with cooking spray. Bake at 375° for 50-60 minutes or until a toothpick inserted in center comes out clean. Cool in pan for 10 minutes before removing to a wire rack to cool.
PER SERVING *1 slice equals 188 cal., 6 g fat (1 g sat. fat), 19 mg chol., 201 mg sodium, 28 g carb., 2 g fiber, 5 g pro. Diabetic Exchanges: 2 starch, 1 fat.*

Herb & Olive Oil Corn Bread M

PREP: 25 MIN. • **BAKE:** 15 MIN.
MAKES: 8 SERVINGS

- ¾ cup cornmeal
- ½ cup all-purpose flour
- 1 tablespoon sugar
- 1 tablespoon grated Parmesan cheese
- 1½ teaspoons baking powder
- 1 teaspoon minced fresh rosemary or ¼ teaspoon dried rosemary, crushed
- 1 teaspoon minced fresh thyme or ¼ teaspoon dried thyme
- ½ teaspoon salt
- 1 large egg
- ¾ cup buttermilk
- 3 tablespoons olive oil, divided
- ½ cup plus 2 tablespoons shredded Italian cheese blend, divided

1. Preheat oven to 425°. Place an 8-in. cast-iron skillet in the oven; heat skillet 10 minutes.
2. Meanwhile, in a large bowl, whisk the first eight ingredients. In another bowl, whisk the egg, buttermilk and 2 tablespoons oil until blended. Add to cornmeal mixture; stir just until moistened. Stir in ½ cup cheese.
3. Carefully remove hot skillet from oven. Add remaining oil to skillet; tilt pan to coat bottom and sides. Add the batter, spreading evenly. Sprinkle with remaining cheese.
4. Bake 12-15 minutes or until golden brown and a toothpick inserted in the center comes out clean. Cut corn bread into wedges; serve warm.
PER SERVING *1 wedge equals 183 cal., 8 g fat (2 g sat. fat), 31 mg chol., 352 mg sodium, 21 g carb., 1 g fiber, 6 g pro. Diabetic Exchanges: 1½ starch, 1½ fat.*

Olive oil helps showcase the flavor of fresh herbs in this fragrant corn bread. It's always a huge hit with my family and friends! —MARY LISA SPEER PALM BEACH, FL

HERB & OLIVE OIL CORN BREAD

PEANUT BUTTER & JAM MUFFINS

Peanut Butter & Jam Muffins M

Selling youngsters on bran muffins is a breeze when PB&J are key ingredients. Delicious and easy to freeze, they make a fast and portable breakfast food or anytime snack.

—JUDY VAN HEEK CROFTON, NE

PREP: 20 MIN. • **BAKE:** 15 MIN.
MAKES: 1 DOZEN

- 1 cup all-purpose flour
- 1 cup oat bran
- ½ cup packed brown sugar
- 2 teaspoons baking powder
- ½ teaspoon salt
- ¼ teaspoon baking soda
- 1 cup 2% milk
- ½ cup unsweetened applesauce
- ⅓ cup peanut butter
- 1 large egg white
- 2 tablespoons honey
- ¼ cup seedless strawberry jam

1. In a large bowl, combine the flour, oat bran, brown sugar, baking powder, salt and baking soda. In a small bowl, beat the milk, applesauce, peanut butter, egg white and honey on low speed until smooth; stir into the dry ingredients just until moistened.

2. Fill greased or foil-lined muffin cups half full. Drop 1 teaspoon jam into the center of each muffin; cover with remaining batter.

3. Bake at 400° for 15-20 minutes or until a toothpick inserted in muffin comes out clean. Cool for 5 minutes before removing from pan to a wire rack. Serve warm.

PER SERVING *1 muffin equals 161 cal., 5 g fat (1 g sat. fat), 2 mg chol., 244 mg sodium, 29 g carb., 2 g fiber, 5 g pro.* **Diabetic Exchanges:** *2 starch, ½ fat.*

Chocolate Chip-Cranberry Scones M FAST FIX ▶

START TO FINISH: 30 MIN.
MAKES: 1 DOZEN

- 2 cups all-purpose flour
- 3 tablespoons brown sugar
- 2 teaspoons baking powder
- 1 teaspoon grated orange peel
- ½ teaspoon salt
- ½ teaspoon baking soda
- ¼ cup cold butter
- 1 cup (8 ounces) plain yogurt
- 1 large egg yolk
- ½ cup dried cranberries
- ½ cup semisweet chocolate chips

1. Preheat oven to 400°. In a large bowl, whisk the first six ingredients. Cut in cold butter until the mixture resembles coarse crumbs. In another bowl, whisk the yogurt and egg yolk; stir into crumb mixture just until moistened. Stir in cranberries and chocolate chips.

2. Turn onto a floured surface; knead gently 10 times. Pat dough into an 8-in. circle. Cut into 12 wedges. Place wedges on a baking sheet coated with cooking spray. Bake 10-12 minutes or until golden brown. Serve warm.

FREEZE OPTION *Freeze cooled scones in resealable plastic freezer bags. To use, thaw at room temperature or, if desired, microwave each scone on high for 20-30 seconds or until heated through.*

PER SERVING *1 scone equals 189 cal., 7 g fat (4 g sat. fat), 28 mg chol., 264 mg sodium, 29 g carb., 1 g fiber, 3 g pro.* **Diabetic Exchanges:** *2 starch, 1 fat.*

My daughter started making these as a healthier alternative to cookies, since we seem to like cookies of any kind. For a more citrusy flavor, use orange-flavored cranberries. —NICHOLE JONES IDAHO FALLS, ID

CHOCOLATE CHIP-CRANBERRY SCONES

Pumpkin Egg Braid F S M

I developed this bread to celebrate our two favorite holidays, Thanksgiving and Hanukkah. Try it with flavored butters, and use the leftovers for amazing French toast.
—**SARA MELLAS** HARTFORD, CT

PREP: 30 MIN. + RISING • **BAKE:** 20 MIN.
MAKES: 1 LOAF (12 SLICES)

- 1 package (¼ ounce) active dry yeast
- 3 tablespoons warm water (110° to 115°)
- ½ cup canned pumpkin
- 1 large egg
- 2 tablespoons light brown sugar
- 2 tablespoons butter, softened
- 1 teaspoon pumpkin pie spice
- ½ teaspoon salt
- 2 to 2½ cups bread flour

EGG WASH
- 1 large egg
- 1 tablespoon water

1. In a small bowl, dissolve yeast in warm water. In a large bowl, combine pumpkin, egg, brown sugar, butter, pie spice, salt, yeast mixture and 1 cup flour; beat on medium speed until smooth. Stir in enough remaining flour to form a soft dough (dough will be sticky).

2. Turn dough onto a floured surface; knead until smooth and elastic, about 6-8 minutes. Place in a greased bowl, turning once to grease the top. Cover with plastic wrap and let rise in a warm place until doubled, about 1 hour.

3. Punch down dough. Turn onto a lightly floured surface; divide into thirds. Roll each into a 16-in. rope. Place ropes on a greased baking sheet and braid. Pinch the ends to seal; tuck ends under.

4. Cover with a kitchen towel; let rise in a warm place until almost doubled, about 45 minutes.

5. Preheat oven to 350°. Whisk egg and water until blended; brush over loaf. Bake 20-25 minutes or until golden brown. Remove from pan to a wire rack to cool.

PER SERVING *1 slice equals 126 cal., 3 g fat (2 g sat. fat), 36 mg chol., 129 mg sodium, 20 g carb., 1 g fiber, 4 g pro.*
***Diabetic Exchanges:** 1 starch, ½ fat.*

PUMPKIN EGG BRAID

Herb & Sun-Dried Tomato Muffins M

Mom often served these muffins instead of bread or buns. Now I bake them to serve with soup or chili.
—**BETSY KING** DULUTH, MN

PREP: 20 MIN. • **BAKE:** 20 MIN.
MAKES: 1 DOZEN

- 2 **cups all-purpose flour**
- 2 **teaspoons baking powder**
- 1 **teaspoon snipped fresh dill or**
  ¼ teaspoon dill weed
- 1 **teaspoon minced fresh thyme or**
  ¼ teaspoon dried thyme
- ½ **teaspoon baking soda**
- ½ **teaspoon salt**
- ½ **teaspoon pepper**
- 1 **large egg**
- 1¼ **cups 2% milk**
- ¼ **cup olive oil**
- ½ **cup shredded cheddar cheese**
- ½ **cup oil-packed sun-dried**
  tomatoes, finely chopped

1. Preheat oven to 375°. In a large bowl, mix the first seven ingredients. In another bowl, whisk egg, milk and oil. Add to flour mixture; stir just until moistened. Fold in the cheese and tomatoes.

2. Fill greased muffin cups three-fourths full. Bake 18-20 minutes or until a toothpick inserted in center comes out clean. Cool for 5 minutes before removing from pan to a wire rack. Serve warm.

PER SERVING *1 muffin equals 161 cal., 8 g fat (2 g sat. fat), 25 mg chol., 277 mg sodium, 18 g carb., 1 g fiber, 5 g pro. Diabetic Exchanges: 1½ fat, 1 starch.*

Crusty Homemade Bread F M

Crackling homemade bread turns an average day into extraordinary. Enjoy this beautiful loaf as is, or stir in a few favorites like cheese, garlic, herbs or dried fruits.
—**MEGUMI GARCIA** MILWAUKEE, WI

PREP: 20 MIN. + RISING
BAKE: 50 MIN. + COOLING
MAKES: 1 LOAF (16 SLICES)

- 1½ **teaspoons active dry yeast**
- 1¾ **cups water (70° to 75°)**
- 3½ **cups plus 1 tablespoon all-purpose**
  flour, divided

CRUSTY HOMEMADE BREAD

- 2 **teaspoons salt**
- 1 **tablespoon cornmeal or additional**
  flour

1. In a small bowl, dissolve yeast in water. In a large bowl, mix 3½ cups flour and salt. Using a rubber spatula, stir in yeast mixture to form a soft, sticky dough. Do not knead. Cover with plastic wrap; let rise at room temperature 1 hour.

2. Punch down dough. Turn onto a lightly floured surface; pat into a 9-in. square. Fold square into thirds, forming a 9x3-in. rectangle. Fold rectangle into thirds, forming a 3-in. square. Turn dough over; place in a greased bowl. Cover with plastic wrap; let rise at room temperature until almost doubled, about 1 hour.

3. Punch down dough and repeat folding process. Return dough to bowl; refrigerate, covered, overnight.

4. Dust bottom of a disposable foil roasting pan with cornmeal. Turn dough onto a floured surface. Knead gently 6-8 times; shape into a 6-in. round loaf. Place in prepared pan; dust top with remaining 1 tablespoon flour. Cover pan with plastic wrap; let loaf rise at room temperature until the dough expands to a 7½-in. loaf, about 1¼ hours.

5. Preheat oven to 500°. Using a sharp knife, make a slash (¼ in. deep) across top of loaf. Cover pan tightly with foil. Bake on lowest oven rack 25 minutes.

6. Reduce oven setting to 450°. Remove foil; bake bread 25-30 minutes longer or until bread is deep golden brown. Remove to a wire rack to cool.

FOR CHEDDAR CHEESE BREAD
Prepare dough as directed. After refrigerating dough overnight, knead in 4 ounces diced sharp cheddar cheese before shaping.

FOR RUSTIC CRANBERRY & ORANGE BREAD *Prepare dough as directed. After refrigerating dough overnight, knead in 1 cup dried cranberries and 4 teaspoons grated orange peel before shaping.*

FOR GARLIC & OREGANO BREAD
Prepare dough as directed. After refrigerating dough overnight, microwave ½ cup peeled and quartered garlic cloves with ¼ cup 2% milk on high for 45 seconds. Drain garlic, discarding milk; knead garlic and 2 tablespoons minced fresh oregano into dough before shaping.

PER SERVING *1 slice (calculated without add-ins) equals 105 cal., trace fat (trace sat. fat), 0 chol., 296 mg sodium, 22 g carb., 1 g fiber, 3 g pro.*

Favorite Banana Chip Muffins M

These muffins are one of the first things my husband, U.S. Army Major John Duda Jr., gets hungry for when he's home from deployment. I make sure to have the overripe bananas ready.

—KIMBERLY DUDA SANFORD, NC

PREP: 20 MIN. • **BAKE:** 20 MIN.
MAKES: 1 DOZEN

- 1½ **cups all-purpose flour**
- ⅔ **cup sugar**
- 1 **teaspoon baking soda**
- ¼ **teaspoon ground cinnamon**
- ⅛ **teaspoon salt**
- 1 **large egg**
- 1⅓ **cups mashed ripe bananas (about 3 medium)**
- ⅓ **cup butter, melted**
- 1 **teaspoon vanilla extract**
- ½ **cup semisweet chocolate chips**

1. Preheat oven to 375°. In a large bowl, whisk flour, sugar, baking soda, cinnamon and salt. In another bowl, whisk egg, bananas, melted butter and vanilla until blended. Add to the flour mixture; stir just until moistened. Fold in chocolate chips.

2. Fill greased or paper-lined muffin cups three-fourths full. Bake muffins 17-20 minutes or until a toothpick inserted in center comes out clean. Cool 5 minutes before removing from pan to a wire rack. Serve warm.

PER SERVING *1 muffin equals 207 cal., 8 g fat (5 g sat. fat), 31 mg chol., 172 mg sodium, 33 g carb., 2 g fiber, 3 g pro. Diabetic Exchanges: 2 starch, 1½ fat.*

FAVORITE BANANA CHIP MUFFINS

GLUTEN-FREE ANADAMA BREAD

Gluten-Free Anadama Bread S M

Anadama bread has been a New England mainstay for generations. This version substitutes gluten-free flour but keeps the loaf's traditional slightly sweet flavor and hearty texture.

—DORIS KINNEY MERRIMACK, NH

PREP: 25 MIN. + RISING
BAKE: 30 MIN. + COOLING
MAKES: 1 LOAF (12 SLICES)

- 1 **package (¼ ounce) active dry yeast**
- 1 **tablespoon sugar**
- 1 **cup warm water (110° to 115°)**
- 2 **large eggs**
- 3 **tablespoons canola oil**
- 1 **tablespoon molasses**
- 1 **teaspoon white vinegar**
- 1½ **cups gluten-free all-purpose baking flour**
- ¾ **cup cornmeal**
- 1½ **teaspoons xanthan gum**
- ½ **teaspoon salt**

1. Grease an 8x4-in. loaf pan and sprinkle it with gluten-free flour; set aside.

2. In a small bowl, dissolve yeast and sugar in warm water. In bowl of a stand mixer with a paddle attachment, combine eggs, oil, molasses, vinegar and yeast mixture. Gradually beat in the flour, cornmeal, xanthan gum and salt. Beat on low speed for 1 minute. Beat on medium speed for 2 minutes. (Dough will be softer than a yeast bread dough that contains gluten.)

3. Transfer to the prepared pan. Smooth the top with a wet spatula. Cover and let rise in a warm place until dough reaches top of pan, about 40 minutes.

4. Bake at 375° for 20 minutes; cover loosely with foil. Bake 10-15 minutes longer or until golden brown. Turn oven off. Leave bread in oven with door ajar for 15 minutes. Remove from pan to a wire rack to cool.

NOTE *Read all ingredient labels for possible gluten content prior to use. Ingredient formulas can change, and production facilities vary among brands. If you're concerned that your brand may contain gluten, contact the company.*

PER SERVING *1 slice equals 136 cal., 5 g fat (1 g sat. fat), 35 mg chol., 115 mg sodium, 21 g carb., 3 g fiber, 4 g pro. Diabetic Exchanges: 1½ starch, ½ fat.*

DARK CHOCOLATE CHIP ZUCCHINI BREAD

Dark Chocolate Chip Zucchini Bread Ⓜ

A colleague brought this in one day for someone's birthday. I grow zucchini in my garden so I've had a lot of opportunities to experiment with the recipe. My mother-in-law loves it, and she doesn't even know that it's also pretty good for you.

—**SALLY NEWTON** SMETHPORT, PA

PREP: 20 MIN. • **BAKE:** 55 MIN. + COOLING
MAKES: 2 LOAVES (12 SLICES EACH)

- 2 cups all-purpose flour
- 1 cup whole wheat flour
- 2 cups sugar
- 3 tablespoons baking cocoa
- 2 teaspoons ground cinnamon
- 1 teaspoon baking soda
- 1 teaspoon salt
- ½ teaspoon baking powder
- 2 large eggs
- 2 large egg whites
- ½ cup buttermilk
- ⅓ cup canola oil
- 2 teaspoons vanilla extract
- 2 cups shredded zucchini
- ⅔ cup dark chocolate chips
- ½ cup chopped walnuts, toasted

1. Preheat oven to 350°. Coat two 8x4-in. loaf pans with cooking spray; dust with flour, tapping out extra.
2. In a large bowl, whisk the first eight ingredients. In another bowl, whisk eggs, egg whites, buttermilk, oil and vanilla until blended. Add to flour mixture; stir just until moistened. Fold in the zucchini, chocolate chips and walnuts.
3. Transfer to prepared pans. Bake 55-65 minutes or until a toothpick inserted in center comes out clean. Loosen sides from pans with a knife. Cool in pans 10 minutes before removing to a wire rack to cool.
NOTE *To toast nuts, bake in a shallow pan in a 350° oven for 5-10 minutes or cook in a skillet over low heat until lightly browned, stirring occasionally.*
PER SERVING *1 slice equals 209 cal., 7 g fat (2 g sat. fat), 16 mg chol., 183 mg sodium, 34 g carb., 2 g fiber, 4 g pro.* ***Diabetic Exchanges:** 2 starch, 1½ fat.*

Perfect Pizza Crust F M

I've spent years trying different recipes and techniques in a search for the perfect pizza crust recipe, and this is it!
—LESLI DUSTIN NIBLEY, UT

PREP: 20 MIN. + RISING • **BAKE:** 10 MIN.
MAKES: 8 SERVINGS

- 1 tablespoon active dry yeast
- 1½ cups warm water (110° to 115°)
- 2 tablespoons sugar
- ½ teaspoon salt
- 2 cups bread flour
- 1½ cups whole wheat flour
- Cornmeal
- Pizza toppings of your choice

1. In a large bowl, dissolve yeast in warm water. Add the sugar, salt, 1 cup bread flour and the whole wheat flour. Beat until smooth. Stir in enough remaining bread flour to form a soft dough (dough will be sticky).
2. Turn onto a floured surface; knead dough until smooth and elastic, about 6-8 minutes. Place in a greased bowl, turning once to grease the top. Cover dough and let rise in a warm place until doubled, about 1 hour.
3. Punch dough down; roll into a 15-in. circle. Grease a 14-in. pizza pan and sprinkle with cornmeal. Transfer dough to prepared pan; build up edges slightly. Add toppings of your choice.
4. Bake at 425° for 10-15 minutes or until crust is golden brown and top is lightly browned and heated through.

PER SERVING *1 slice (calculated without toppings) equals 193 cal., trace fat (trace sat. fat), 0 chol., 149 mg sodium, 42 g carb., 4 g fiber, 8 g pro.*

DID YOU KNOW?

Frozen pizza can be high in trans fat, which raises LDL (the "bad" cholesterol). The crust is the culprit: Manufacturers often add hydrogenated oils to pizza crusts, refrigerated doughs and the buns of grab-and-go sandwiches to extend shelf life or to improve flavor and texture. Half of Americans' consumption of trans fat comes from processed foods; the rest is naturally occurring in meat and dairy.

LEMON MERINGUE MUFFINS

Lemon Meringue Muffins S M

These muffins taste like a favorite pie of mine, and the meringue adds a little height and a lot of fun.
—NANCY KEARNEY MASSILLON, OH

PREP: 25 MIN. • **BAKE:** 25 MIN.
MAKES: 1 DOZEN

- 6 tablespoons butter, softened
- 1 cup sugar, divided
- 2 large eggs
- ½ cup plain yogurt
- 2 tablespoons lemon juice
- 1 tablespoon grated lemon peel
- ¼ teaspoon lemon extract
- 1⅓ cups all-purpose flour
- ½ teaspoon baking powder
- ½ teaspoon baking soda
- 2 large egg whites

1. Preheat oven to 350°. In a large bowl, cream butter and ⅔ cup sugar until light and fluffy. Add eggs, one at a time, beating well after each addition. Beat in the yogurt, lemon juice, peel and extract.
2. In another bowl, whisk flour, baking powder and baking soda. Add to creamed mixture; stir just until moistened. Fill greased or paper-lined muffin cups three-fourths full. Bake 17-19 minutes or until a toothpick inserted in center comes out clean. Remove from the oven. Increase oven setting to 400°.
3. Meanwhile, in a small bowl, beat egg whites on medium speed until soft peaks form. Gradually add remaining sugar, 1 tablespoon at a time, beating on high after each addition until sugar is dissolved. Continue beating until stiff glossy peaks form.
4. Spread or pipe meringue onto muffins. Bake 6-8 minutes longer or until meringue is golden brown.
5. Cool 5 minutes before removing from pan to a wire rack. Serve warm. Refrigerate leftovers.

PER SERVING *1 muffin equals 188 cal., 7 g fat (4 g sat. fat), 52 mg chol., 135 mg sodium, 28 g carb., trace fiber, 4 g pro.* **Diabetic Exchanges:** *2 starch, 1 fat.*

kernels and, if desired, wheat germ. Bake 35-45 minutes or until dark golden brown. Cool in pans 5 minutes. Remove to a wire rack to cool.

PER SERVING *1 slice (calculated without wheat germ) equals 142 cal., 4 g fat (1 g sat. fat), 4 mg chol., 205 mg sodium, 23 g carb., 2 g fiber, 4 g pro.* **Diabetic Exchanges:** *1½ starch, ½ fat.*

Rustic Oatmeal Scones M

My family loves scones, but traditional recipes contain excessive fat and calories. After lots of experimentation, I came up with this alternative recipe. The effort is well worth it for the delicious flavor, amazing texture and nutrient density of these scones.

—GAIL D'URSO CARLISLE, PA

PREP: 20 MIN. • **BAKE:** 15 MIN.
MAKES: 16 SCONES

- 1½ **cups all-purpose flour**
- ½ **cup whole wheat flour**
- ½ **cup sugar**
- 2 **teaspoons baking powder**
- 1 **teaspoon baking soda**
- ¾ **teaspoon salt**
- ¼ **cup cold butter, cubed**
- 2 **cups quick-cooking oats**
- 1 **cup dried blueberries or raisins**
- 1 **cup (8 ounces) plain yogurt**
- 3 **tablespoons fat-free milk, divided**
  Coarse sugar

1. Preheat oven to 400°. In a large bowl, whisk the first six ingredients. Cut in butter until mixture resembles coarse crumbs. Stir in the oats and blueberries. In another bowl, whisk yogurt and 1 tablespoon milk until blended; stir into crumb mixture just until moistened.

2. Turn onto a lightly floured surface; knead gently 10 times. Divide dough in half; pat each into a 7-in. circle. Cut each into eight wedges. Place wedges on a baking sheet coated with cooking spray. Brush tops with remaining milk. Sprinkle with coarse sugar.

3. Bake 13-15 minutes or until golden brown. Serve warm.

PER SERVING *1 scone (calculated without coarse sugar) equals 186 cal., 4 g fat (2 g sat. fat), 11 mg chol., 273 mg sodium, 32 g carb., 3 g fiber, 4 g pro.* **Diabetic Exchanges:** *2 starch, 1 fat.*

I loved skipping the boring school cafeteria meals and going to my grandma's house for lunch. She spent most of her life in northeastern Minnesota, which is reflected in this bread's ingredients. Now my family uses this for our holiday stuffing. —**CRYSTAL SCHLUETER** NORTHGLENN, CO

WILD RICE BREAD WITH SUNFLOWER SEEDS

Wild Rice Bread with Sunflower Seeds M

PREP: 35 MIN. + RISING • **BAKE:** 35 MIN.
MAKES: 2 LOAVES (16 SLICES EACH)

- 2 **packages (¼ ounce each) active dry yeast**
- 1 **cup warm water (110° to 115°)**
- 1 **package (8.8 ounces) ready-to-serve long grain and wild rice**
- 1 **cup plus 1 tablespoon unsalted sunflower kernels, divided**
- 1 **cup warm fat-free milk (110° to 115°)**
- ⅓ **cup honey or molasses**
- ¼ **cup butter, softened**
- 2 **tablespoons ground flaxseed**
- 2 **teaspoons salt**
- 3 **cups whole wheat flour**
- 2¾ to 3¼ **cups all-purpose flour**
- 1 **large egg white, lightly beaten**
- 1 **tablespoon toasted wheat germ, optional**

1. In a small bowl, dissolve yeast in warm water. In a large bowl, combine rice, 1 cup sunflower kernels, milk, honey, butter, flaxseed, salt, yeast mixture, whole wheat flour and 1 cup all-purpose flour; beat on medium speed until combined. Stir in enough remaining flour to form a stiff dough (dough will be sticky).

2. Turn dough onto a floured surface; knead until elastic, about 6-8 minutes. Place in a greased bowl, turning once to grease the top. Cover with plastic wrap and let rise in a warm place until doubled, about 1¼ hours.

3. Punch down dough. Turn onto a lightly floured surface; divide in half. Roll each half into a 12x8-in. rectangle. Roll up jelly-roll style, starting with a short side; pinch seam and ends to seal. Place each portion in a 9x5-in. loaf pan coated with cooking spray, seam side down.

4. Cover with kitchen towels; let rise in a warm place until almost doubled, about 45 minutes. Preheat oven to 375°.

5. Brush loaves with egg white; sprinkle with remaining sunflower

RUSTIC OATMEAL SCONES

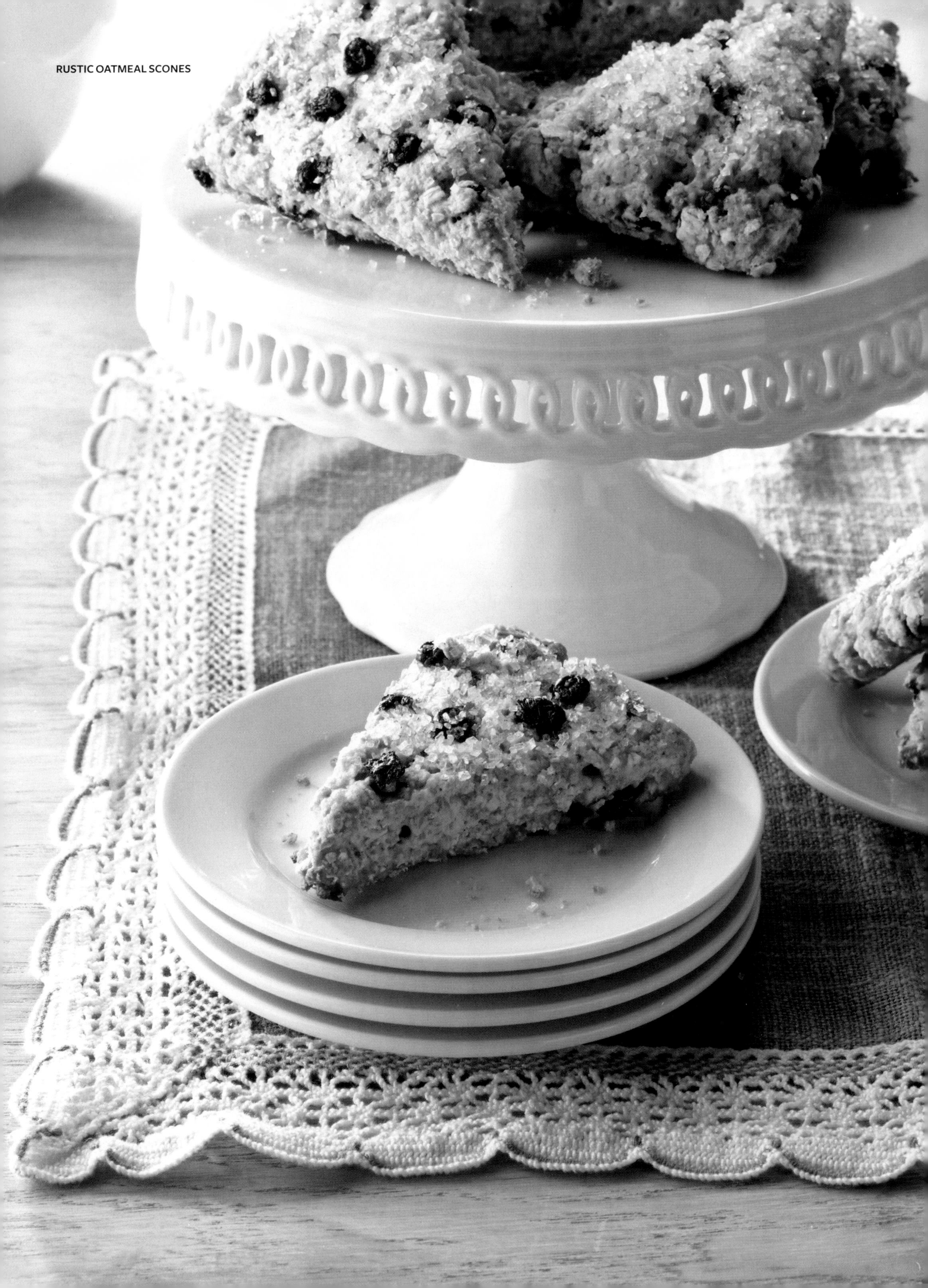

HONEY SPICE BREAD

Honey Spice Bread S M

The texture of this bread is almost like a cake, so I often serve it for dessert. Plus, the loaf looks so festive with the glaze drizzled on top.

—GAYE O'DELL BINGHAMTON, NY

PREP: 20 MIN. • **BAKE:** 55 MIN. + COOLING
MAKES: 1 LOAF (12 SLICES)

- ⅔ **cup packed brown sugar**
- ⅓ **cup 2% milk**
- 2 **cups all-purpose flour**
- 1½ **teaspoons baking powder**
- ½ **teaspoon ground cinnamon**
- ½ **teaspoon ground nutmeg**
- ⅛ **teaspoon ground cloves**
- 2 **large eggs**
- ½ **cup honey**
- ⅓ **cup canola oil**

GLAZE
- ⅓ **cup confectioners' sugar**
- 2 **teaspoons 2% milk**

1. Preheat oven to 350°. In a small saucepan, combine brown sugar and milk. Cook and stir over low heat until sugar is dissolved. Remove from heat.
2. In a large bowl, whisk the flour, baking powder, cinnamon, nutmeg and cloves. In another bowl, whisk eggs, honey, oil and brown sugar mixture until blended. Add to flour mixture; stir just until moistened.
3. Transfer to a greased 8x4-in. loaf pan. Bake 55-60 minutes or until a

toothpick inserted in center comes out clean (cover top loosely with foil if needed to prevent overbrowning).
4. Cool in pan 10 minutes before removing to a wire rack to cool completely. Stir glaze ingredients until smooth; drizzle over bread.
FREEZE OPTION *Securely wrap and freeze cooled loaf in plastic wrap and foil. To use, thaw at room temperature. Glaze as directed.*
PER SERVING *1 slice equals 187 cal., 6 g fat (1 g sat. fat), 27 mg chol., 53 mg sodium, 33 g carb., 1 g fiber, 3 g pro. Diabetic Exchanges: 2 starch, 1 fat.*

No-Knead Harvest Bread F M

This loaf allows you to enjoy homemade bread without all the work. Fresh-baked slices are seriously irresistible.

—TASTE OF HOME TEST KITCHEN

PREP: 30 MIN. + RISING
BAKE: 30 MIN. + COOLING
MAKES: 1 LOAF (16 SLICES)

- ½ **cup whole wheat flour**
- ½ **cup cornmeal**
- ½ **cup assorted seeds, such as sesame seeds, flaxseed, sunflower kernels and/or poppy seeds, divided**
- 1¾ **teaspoons salt**
- ¼ **teaspoon active dry yeast**
- 3 **cups bread flour, divided**

2¼ **cups cool water (55° to 65°)**
- 2 **tablespoons molasses**
   Additional cornmeal

1. In a large bowl, combine the whole wheat flour, cornmeal, ⅓ cup seeds, salt, yeast and 2½ cups bread flour. Stir in water and molasses until blended; dough will be wet and sticky.
2. Cover with plastic wrap and let stand at room temperature until more than doubled in size and bubbles are present on surface, 12 to 18 hours. Stir in remaining bread flour.
3. Grease a baking sheet and sprinkle well with additional cornmeal; turn dough onto prepared baking sheet. Gently shape with a spatula into a 9-in. round loaf. Cover and let rise at room temperature for 2 hours or until dough holds an indentation when gently pressed (loaf will slightly increase in size).
4. Arrange one oven rack at lowest rack setting; place second rack in middle of oven. Place an oven-safe skillet on bottom oven rack; preheat oven and skillet to 475°. Meanwhile, in a small saucepan, bring 2 cups water to a boil.
5. Gently press remaining seeds onto top of loaf. Wearing oven mitts, place bread on top rack. Pull bottom rack out by 6-8 in.; add boiling water to skillet. (Work quickly and carefully, pouring water away from you. Don't worry if some water is left in the saucepan.) Carefully slide bottom rack back into place; quickly close door to trap steam in oven.
6. Reduce heat to 425°; bake for 10 minutes. Remove skillet from oven; bake bread 20-25 minutes longer or until deep golden brown and bread sounds hollow when center is tapped. Cool on a wire rack.
NOTE *This recipe was tested with a cast-iron skillet. If using a different type of pan, confirm that it is oven-safe to 450°.*
PER SERVING *1 slice equals 134 cal., 2 g fat (trace sat. fat), 0 chol., 265 mg sodium, 26 g carb., 2 g fiber, 5 g pro. Diabetic Exchange: 1½ starch.*

Cranberry-Walnut Toasting Bread Ⓜ

Looking for a delicious bread to start your day? My multigrain loaf is fabulous toasted. It's also good for sandwiches or served warm with dinner.

—**TISH STEVENSON** WYOMING, MI

PREP: 30 MIN. + RISING • **BAKE:** 45 MIN.
MAKES: 2 LOAVES (12 SLICES EACH)

- 6 to 6½ cups all-purpose flour
- 1 cup old-fashioned oats
- ½ cup whole wheat flour
- ⅓ cup packed brown sugar
- 2 teaspoons salt
- 1 package (¼ ounce) active dry yeast
- 2½ cups water
- 2 tablespoons butter
- 1¼ cups dried cranberries or cherries
- ¾ cup chopped walnuts, toasted

1. In a large bowl, combine 3 cups all-purpose flour, oats, whole wheat flour, brown sugar, salt and yeast. In a small pan, heat water and butter to 120°-130°. Beat into dry ingredients just until moistened. Stir in dried cranberries, toasted walnuts and enough remaining all-purpose flour to form a soft dough.

2. Turn onto a floured surface; knead until smooth and elastic, about 6-8 minutes. Place in a greased bowl, turning once to grease the top. Cover and let rise in a warm place until doubled, about 1 hour.

3. Punch dough down; divide in half. Shape into loaves; place in two greased 9x5-in. loaf pans. Cover and let rise until doubled, about 45 minutes. Bake at 350° for 45-50 minutes or until golden brown. Remove to wire racks to cool. Cut into thick slices and toast.

PER SERVING *1 slice equals 198 cal., 4 g fat (1 g sat. fat), 3 mg chol., 206 mg sodium, 37 g carb., 2 g fiber, 5 g pro.*

DID YOU KNOW?

Salt plays many roles in yeast bread. It slows the yeast's growth, allowing the dough to develop more complex flavors and a stronger structure. It also contributes to the bread's flavor, crust color and shelf life.

These puffy dinner rolls take on rich color when you add squash to the dough. Any squash variety works, and I've even used cooked carrots.
—**MARCIA WHITNEY** GAINESVILLE, FL

HONEY-SQUASH DINNER ROLLS

Honey-Squash Dinner Rolls Ⓜ

PREP: 40 MIN. + RISING • **BAKE:** 20 MIN.
MAKES: 2 DOZEN

- 2 packages (¼ ounce each) active dry yeast
- 2 teaspoons salt
- ¼ teaspoon ground nutmeg
- 6 to 6½ cups all-purpose flour
- 1¼ cups 2% milk
- ½ cup butter, cubed
- ½ cup honey
- 1 package (12 ounces) frozen mashed winter squash, thawed (about 1⅓ cups)
- 1 large egg, lightly beaten
   Poppy seeds, sesame seeds, or salted pumpkin seeds or pepitas

1. In a large bowl, mix yeast, salt, nutmeg and 3 cups flour. In a small saucepan, heat milk, butter and honey to 120°-130°. Add to dry ingredients; beat on medium speed 2 minutes. Add squash; beat on high 2 minutes. Stir in enough remaining flour to form a soft dough (dough will be sticky).

2. Turn dough onto a floured surface; knead until smooth and elastic, about 6-8 minutes. Place in a greased bowl, turning once to grease the top. Cover the dough with plastic wrap and let rise in a warm place until doubled, about 1 hour.

3. Punch down dough. Turn dough onto a lightly floured surface; divide and shape into 24 balls. Divide between two greased 9-in. round baking pans. Cover with kitchen towels; let rise in a warm place until doubled, about 45 minutes.

4. Preheat oven to 375°. Brush tops with beaten egg; sprinkle with seeds. Bake 20-25 minutes or until dark golden brown. Cover loosely with foil during the last 5-7 minutes if needed to prevent overbrowning. Remove from pans to wire racks; serve warm.

PER SERVING *1 roll equals 186 cal., 5 g fat (3 g sat. fat), 19 mg chol., 238 mg sodium, 32 g carb., 1 g fiber, 4 g pro.*
Diabetic Exchanges: 2 starch, 1 fat.

223

216

221

Cakes & Pies

"This sweet tooth-satisfying dessert has a unique taste, plus fewer calories and less fat than traditional key lime pie."

—SAMARA DONALD REDMOND, WA
about her recipe, Lime Basil Pie, on page 215

Gran's Apple Cake ⓜ

My grandmother occasionally brought over this wonderful cake warm from the oven. The spicy apple flavor combined with the sweet cream cheese frosting made this dessert a treasured recipe. Even though I've lightened it up, it's still a family favorite.

—**LAURIS CONRAD** TURLOCK, CA

PREP: 30 MIN. • **BAKE:** 35 MIN. + COOLING
MAKES: 18 SERVINGS

- 1⅔ cups sugar
- 2 large eggs
- ½ cup unsweetened applesauce
- 2 tablespoons canola oil
- 2 teaspoons vanilla extract
- 2 cups all-purpose flour
- 2 teaspoons baking soda
- 2 teaspoons ground cinnamon
- ¾ teaspoon salt
- 6 cups chopped peeled tart apples
- ½ cup chopped pecans

FROSTING

- 4 ounces reduced-fat cream cheese
- 2 tablespoons butter, softened
- 1 teaspoon vanilla extract
- 1 cup confectioners' sugar

1. In a bowl, combine the sugar, eggs, applesauce, oil and vanilla. Beat for 2 minutes on medium speed. Combine the flour, baking soda, cinnamon and salt; add to applesauce mixture and beat until combined. Fold in apples and pecans.

2. Transfer to a 13x9-in. baking dish coated with cooking spray. Bake at 350° for 35-40 minutes or until top is golden brown and a toothpick inserted near the center comes out clean. Cool on a wire rack.

3. For frosting, combine cream cheese, butter and vanilla in a small bowl until smooth. Gradually beat in confectioners' sugar (mixture will be soft). Spread over cooled cake.

PER SERVING *1 piece equals 241 cal., 8 g fat (2 g sat. fat), 32 mg chol., 283 mg sodium, 42 g carb., 2 g fiber, 3 g pro.*

CARROT CUPCAKES WITH CREAM CHEESE FROSTING

Carrot Cupcakes with Cream Cheese Frosting ⓜ

I love to serve healthy desserts that will satisfy those with a sweet tooth. I make these every Christmas Eve, but they're great anytime of the year.

—**SARA PLESO** SPARTA, TN

PREP: 20 MIN. • **BAKE:** 15 MIN. + COOLING
MAKES: 1 DOZEN

- ¾ cup packed brown sugar
- ½ cup unsweetened applesauce
- 2 large eggs
- ¼ cup canola oil
- ½ teaspoon vanilla extract
- ¾ cup whole wheat flour
- ½ cup all-purpose flour
- 1 teaspoon baking soda
- ¼ teaspoon salt
- ¼ teaspoon ground cinnamon
- ¼ teaspoon ground nutmeg
- 1½ cups shredded carrots (about 3 medium)
- ¼ cup chopped walnuts

FROSTING

- 4 ounces reduced-fat cream cheese
- ¾ cup confectioners' sugar
- ½ teaspoon lemon juice

1. Preheat the oven to 350°. Line 12 muffin cups with paper or foil liners.
2. In a large bowl, beat the first five ingredients until well blended. In another bowl, whisk flours, baking soda, salt, cinnamon and nutmeg; gradually beat into brown sugar mixture. Stir in carrots and walnuts.
3. Fill prepared cups two-thirds full. Bake for 15-20 minutes or until a toothpick inserted in center comes out clean. Cool in pan 10 minutes before removing to a wire rack to cool completely.
4. In a small bowl, beat the frosting ingredients until smooth. Spread over cupcakes. Refrigerate leftovers.

PER SERVING *1 cupcake equals 229 cal., 9 g fat (2 g sat. fat), 38 mg chol., 220 mg sodium, 34 g carb., 2 g fiber, 4 g pro.* **Diabetic Exchanges:** *2 starch, 1½ fat.*

Lime Basil Pie M

This sweet tooth-satisfying dessert has a unique taste, plus fewer calories and less fat than traditional key lime pie.
—SAMARA DONALD REDMOND, WA

PREP: 15 MIN. • **BAKE:** 15 MIN. + CHILLING
MAKES: 8 SERVINGS

- 1 package (8 ounces) reduced-fat cream cheese
- 1 can (14 ounces) fat-free sweetened condensed milk
- 1 tablespoon grated lime peel
- ½ cup lime juice
- 2 large egg yolks
- ¼ cup minced fresh basil
- 1 reduced-fat graham cracker crust (8 inches)
  Sweetened whipped cream or creme fraiche, optional

1. Preheat oven to 325°. In a large bowl, beat cream cheese until smooth; gradually beat in milk. Add lime peel, juice and egg yolks; beat just until blended. Stir in basil. Pour into crust.
2. Bake 15-18 minutes or until center is set. Cool 1 hour on a wire rack. Refrigerate at least 2 hours before serving. If desired, serve with whipped cream.
PER SERVING *1 piece (calculated without whipped cream) equals 328 cal., 10 g fat (5 g sat. fat), 72 mg chol., 268 mg sodium, 49 g carb., trace fiber, 9 g pro.*

Rosy Rhubarb Upside-Down Cake M

PREP: 35 MIN. • **BAKE:** 35 MIN. + COOLING
MAKES: 9 SERVINGS

- 3 cups cubed (1-inch pieces) fresh or frozen rhubarb (about 8 stalks)
- ¾ cup sugar
- ¾ cup water
- 1 tablespoon lemon juice
- ½ teaspoon ground cinnamon
- ¼ teaspoon ground nutmeg

CAKE
- 3 tablespoons butter, melted
- ¼ cup packed brown sugar
- 1 cup all-purpose flour
- 1 teaspoon baking powder
- ¼ teaspoon salt
- 2 large eggs
- ⅔ cup sugar
- 1 teaspoon lemon extract

1. Preheat oven to 350°. In a large saucepan, combine the first six ingredients; bring to a boil. Reduce heat; simmer, uncovered, for 6-8 minutes or until rhubarb is crisp-tender, stirring to dissolve sugar. Drain, reserving 6 tablespoons cooking liquid.
2. Pour butter into an 8-in. square baking dish. Sprinkle with brown sugar; top with drained rhubarb. Sift the flour, baking powder and salt together twice.
3. In a large bowl, beat eggs on high speed 3 minutes. Gradually add sugar, beating until thick and lemon-colored. Beat in extract and reserved cooking liquid. Fold in flour mixture. Pour over rhubarb. Bake 35-40 minutes or until top springs back when lightly touched.
4. Cool 10 minutes before inverting onto a serving plate. Serve warm.
PER SERVING *1 piece equals 257 cal., 5 g fat (3 g sat. fat), 57 mg chol., 157 mg sodium, 50 g carb., 1 g fiber, 3 g pro.*

Here's a cake that gets its rosy hue from the rhubarb topping. It's moist on top and light as a feather on the bottom.
—DAWN E. LOWENSTEIN HUNTINGDON VALLEY, PA

ROSY RHUBARB UPSIDE-DOWN CAKE

BANANA-PINEAPPLE CREAM PIES

Sue's Chocolate Zucchini Cake M

Our family absolutely loves zucchini, especially when we grow it ourselves. We've found many ways to use it, including this spiced cake that's super moist and chocolaty.

—SUE FALK WARREN, MI

PREP: 20 MIN. • **BAKE:** 25 MIN. + COOLING
MAKES: 15 SERVINGS

- 2 cups all-purpose flour
- 2 cups sugar
- ½ cup dark baking cocoa
- 1½ teaspoons ground cinnamon
- 1 teaspoon baking powder
- 1 teaspoon baking soda
- 1 teaspoon salt
- 2 large eggs
- ¾ cup reduced-fat plain yogurt
- ¼ cup canola oil
- 2 teaspoons vanilla extract
- 2 cups shredded zucchini
  Confectioners' sugar, optional

1. Preheat oven to 350°. Grease a 13x9-in. baking pan.
2. In a large bowl, whisk the first seven ingredients. In another bowl, whisk eggs, yogurt, oil and vanilla until blended. Add to flour mixture; stir just until moistened. Stir in zucchini.
3. Transfer batter to prepared pan. Bake 25-30 minutes or until top springs back when lightly touched.
4. Cool completely in pan on a wire rack. If desired, dust with confectioner's sugar before serving.
PER SERVING *1 piece equals 227 cal., 5 g fat (1 g sat. fat), 25 mg chol., 287 mg sodium, 43 g carb., 1 g fiber, 4 g pro.*

SUE'S CHOCOLATE ZUCCHINI CAKE

Banana-Pineapple Cream Pies S M

My mother gave me this simple and delicious recipe years ago. The recipe makes two pies, so it's perfect for a potluck. I've never met anyone who didn't like it!

—ROBYN APPENZELLER PORTSMOUTH, VA

PREP: 15 MIN. + CHILLING
MAKES: 2 PIES (8 SERVINGS EACH)

- ¼ cup cornstarch
- ¼ cup sugar
- 1 can (20 ounces) unsweetened crushed pineapple, undrained
- 3 medium bananas, sliced
  Two 9-inch graham cracker crusts (about 6 ounces each)
- 1 carton (8 ounces) frozen whipped topping, thawed

1. In a large saucepan, combine cornstarch and sugar. Stir in pineapple until blended. Bring to a boil; cook and stir 1-2 minutes or until thickened.
2. Arrange the bananas over the bottom of each crust; spread pineapple mixture over tops. Refrigerate for at least 1 hour before serving. Top with whipped topping.
PER SERVING *1 piece equals 205 cal., 8 g fat (3 g sat. fat), 0 chol., 122 mg sodium, 33 g carb., 1 g fiber, 1 g pro.*
Diabetic Exchanges: 2 starch, 1½ fat.

Pumpkin Chip Cake with Walnuts

My grandmother gave me this family recipe. After a few changes, I made the treat even healthier and tastier. Holidays wouldn't be the same without it!

—AMY BRIDGEWATER AZTEC, NM

PREP: 20 MIN. • **BAKE:** 50 MIN. + COOLING
MAKES: 16 SERVINGS

- 3 **cups all-purpose flour**
- 1¼ **cups sugar**
- 2 **teaspoons baking powder**
- 1 **teaspoon baking soda**
- 2 **teaspoons ground cinnamon**
- ¾ **teaspoon salt**
- ½ **teaspoon ground cloves**
- ¼ **teaspoon ground allspice**
- 4 **large eggs**
- 1 **can (15 ounces) solid-pack pumpkin**
- 1 **cup unsweetened applesauce**
- ¼ **cup canola oil**
- ¼ **teaspoon maple flavoring, optional**
- ½ **cup miniature semisweet chocolate chips**
- ½ **cup chopped walnuts, toasted**
  Confectioners' sugar

1. Preheat oven to 350°. Grease and flour a 10-in. fluted tube pan.

2. In a large bowl, whisk the first eight ingredients. In another bowl, whisk eggs, pumpkin, applesauce, oil and, if desired, flavoring until blended. Add to flour mixture; stir just until moistened. Fold in chocolate chips and walnuts.

3. Transfer to prepared pan. Bake 50-60 minutes or until a toothpick inserted in center comes out clean. Cool cake in the pan for 10 minutes before removing to a wire rack to cool completely. Dust the top with confectioners' sugar.

NOTE *To remove cakes easily, use solid shortening to grease plain and fluted tube pans. To toast nuts, bake in a shallow pan in a 350° oven for 5-10 minutes or cook in a skillet over low heat until lightly browned, stirring occasionally.*

PER SERVING *1 slice equals 261 cal., 9 g fat (2 g sat. fat), 47 mg chol., 260 mg sodium, 42 g carb., 2 g fiber, 5 g pro.*

PUMPKIN CHIP CAKE WITH WALNUTS

Lemon Blueberry Cornmeal Cake M

I lightened up this quick and easy dessert by making a few substitutions. Because the treat is so sweet, no one will know it's healthy, too.

—ROXANNE CHAN ALBANY, CA

PREP: 20 MIN. • **BAKE:** 30 MIN.
MAKES: 8 SERVINGS

- 2 **large egg whites**
- 1 **large egg**
- ½ **cup lemon yogurt**
- ⅓ **cup honey**
- ¼ **cup canola oil**
- 1 **teaspoon grated lemon peel**
- ¼ **teaspoon almond extract**
- ¾ **cup all-purpose flour**
- ½ **cup yellow cornmeal**
- 1 **teaspoon baking powder**
- ¼ **teaspoon salt**
- 1 **cup fresh or frozen blueberries**
- 3 **tablespoons slivered almonds**
- ¼ **cup reduced-sugar orange marmalade, warmed**

1. Preheat oven to 350°. Coat a 9-in. fluted tart pan with removable bottom with cooking spray. In a large bowl, beat egg whites, egg, yogurt, honey, oil, lemon peel and extract until well blended. In another bowl, whisk flour, cornmeal, baking powder and salt; gradually beat into yogurt mixture.

2. Transfer batter to prepared pan; top with blueberries and almonds. Bake 30-35 minutes or until a toothpick inserted in center comes out clean. Drizzle marmalade over warm cake. Cool on a wire rack; serve warm or at room temperature.

PER SERVING *1 slice equals 250 cal., 9 g fat (1 g sat. fat), 24 mg chol., 156 mg sodium, 37 g carb., 2 g fiber, 5 g pro.*

BLACKBERRY NECTARINE PIE

Blackberry Nectarine Pie S M

Blackberries are a big crop in our area, so I've made this pretty double-fruit pie many times. I can always tell when my husband wants me to make it because he brings home berries that he picked behind his office.

—LINDA CHINN ENUMCLAW, WA

PREP: 25 MIN. + CHILLING
MAKES: 8 SERVINGS

- ¼ **cup cornstarch**
- 1 **can (12 ounces) frozen apple juice concentrate, thawed**
- 2 **cups fresh blackberries, divided**
- 5 **medium nectarines, peeled and coarsely chopped**
- 1 **reduced-fat graham cracker crust (8 inches)**
  Reduced-fat whipped topping, optional

1. In a small saucepan, mix cornstarch and apple juice concentrate until smooth. Bring to a boil. Add ½ cup blackberries; cook and stir 2 minutes or until thickened. Remove from heat.

2. In a large bowl, toss nectarines with remaining blackberries; transfer to crust. Pour apple juice mixture over fruit (crust will be full). Refrigerate, covered, 8 hours or overnight. If desired, serve with whipped topping.

PER SERVING *1 piece (calculated without whipped topping) equals 240 cal., 4 g fat (1 g sat. fat), 0 chol., 106 mg sodium, 50 g carb., 4 g fiber, 3 g pro.*

LEMON BLUEBERRY CORNMEAL CAKE

Chocolate-Glazed Cupcakes M

Because I have a dairy allergy, I'm always on the search for treats I can eat. I prepare these cupcakes with dairy-free chocolate chips and vanilla coconut milk instead of cream.

—KIRSTIN TURNER RICHLANDS, NC

PREP: 25 MIN. • **BAKE:** 15 MIN. + COOLING
MAKES: 16 CUPCAKES

- 1½ cups all-purpose flour
- ¾ cup sugar
- ⅓ cup baking cocoa
- 1 teaspoon baking soda
- ¾ teaspoon salt
- 1 cup water
- ¼ cup unsweetened applesauce
- ¼ cup canola oil
- 1 tablespoon white vinegar
- 1 teaspoon vanilla extract
- ⅔ cup semisweet chocolate chips, optional

GLAZE
- ½ cup semisweet chocolate chips
- ¼ cup half-and-half cream
  White nonpareils, optional

1. Preheat oven to 350°. Line 16 muffin cups with foil liners.
2. In a large bowl, whisk the first five ingredients. In another bowl, whisk water, applesauce, oil, vinegar and vanilla until blended. Add to flour mixture; stir just until moistened. If desired, stir in chocolate chips.
3. Fill prepared muffin cups three-fourths full. Bake 14-16 minutes or until a toothpick inserted in center comes out clean. Cool 5 minutes before removing from pans to wire racks; cool completely.
4. For glaze, in a small saucepan, combine chocolate chips and cream; cook and stir over low heat 3-5 minutes or until smooth. Remove from heat. Cool at room temperature until glaze is slightly thickened, stirring occasionally, about 30 minutes. Dip tops of cupcakes into glaze. If desired, sprinkle with nonpareils.

PER SERVING *1 cupcake (calculated without optional ingredients) equals 148 cal., 6 g fat (1 g sat. fat), 2 mg chol., 192 mg sodium, 23 g carb., 1 g fiber, 2 g pro.* **Diabetic Exchanges:** *1½ starch, 1 fat.*

Cranberry-Orange Snack Cake S M

This recipe contains some of my favorite flavors: cranberry, orange and pecans. The cream cheese icing really takes it over the top.

—LISA VARNER EL PASO, TX

PREP: 30 MIN. • **BAKE:** 20 MIN. + COOLING
MAKES: 24 SERVINGS

- 1 cup packed light brown sugar
- ½ cup butter, melted
- ½ cup egg substitute
- ½ cup unsweetened applesauce
- 2 teaspoons grated orange peel, divided
- 1 teaspoon vanilla extract
- 2 cups all-purpose flour
- 1½ teaspoons baking powder
- ⅛ teaspoon salt
- ½ cup dried cranberries
- ½ cup white baking chips
- 8 ounces reduced-fat cream cheese
- 1 cup confectioners' sugar
- ½ cup chopped pecans

1. Preheat the oven to 350°. Coat a 13x9-in. baking pan with cooking spray.
2. In a large bowl, beat brown sugar, melted butter, egg substitute, applesauce, 1 teaspoon orange peel and vanilla until well blended. In another bowl, whisk flour, baking powder and salt; gradually beat into brown sugar mixture. Stir in cranberries and baking chips.
3. Transfer cake batter to prepared pan. Bake 20-25 minutes or until a toothpick inserted in center comes out clean. Cool completely on a wire rack.
4. In a small bowl, beat cream cheese and confectioners' sugar until blended. Beat in remaining orange peel. Spread over cake. Sprinkle with pecans. Refrigerate leftovers.

PER SERVING *1 piece equals 198 cal., 9 g fat (5 g sat. fat), 17 mg chol., 122 mg sodium, 27 g carb., 1 g fiber, 3 g pro.* **Diabetic Exchanges:** *2 starch, 1½ fat.*

CHOCOLATE-GLAZED CUPCAKES

APPLE RHUBARB CRUMB PIE

Apple Rhubarb Crumb Pie M

My family and friends always request this pie for birthdays and get-togethers. Everyone loves the unexpected flavor that the rhubarb adds.

—**SHERRI MOON** DECATUR, IN

PREP: 25 MIN. • **BAKE:** 50 MIN. + COOLING
MAKES: 8 SERVINGS

- 1 **refrigerated pie pastry**
FILLING
- 5 **cups thinly sliced peeled Fuji apples (about 5 medium)**
- 2 **cups sliced fresh or frozen rhubarb (½ inch thick), thawed**
- ½ **cup sugar**
- 3 **tablespoons all-purpose flour**
- ½ **teaspoon ground cinnamon**
TOPPING
- ⅓ **cup all-purpose flour**
- ¼ **cup sugar**
- ¼ **cup quick-cooking oats**
- ⅛ **teaspoon salt**
- ⅛ **teaspoon ground cinnamon**
- 2 **tablespoons butter**

1. Preheat oven to 375°. Unroll the pastry sheet into a 9-in. pie plate; flute edge. Refrigerate while preparing filling and topping.

2. In a large bowl, combine apples and rhubarb. In a small bowl, mix sugar, flour and cinnamon; add to apple mixture and toss to coat. In a small bowl, mix the first five topping ingredients; cut in the butter until crumbly. Transfer filling to crust and sprinkle with topping.

3. Bake for 50-60 minutes or until topping is lightly browned and filling is bubbly. Cover edge loosely with foil during the last 20 minutes if needed to prevent overbrowning. Remove foil. Cool on a wire rack.

NOTE *If using frozen rhubarb, measure rhubarb while still frozen, then thaw completely. Drain in a colander, but do not press liquid out.*

PER SERVING *1 piece equals 297 cal., 10 g fat (5 g sat. fat), 13 mg chol., 161 mg sodium, 50 g carb., 2 g fiber, 3 g pro.*

Raspberry Peach Tart S M

There's no shortage of fresh peaches and raspberries where I live. I use the fruit I grow to bake up this sweet and special fruit tart.

—**MARY ANN REMPEL** SOUTHOLD, NY

PREP: 15 MIN. + STANDING
BAKE: 25 MIN. + COOLING
MAKES: 8 SERVINGS

- 2⅔ **cups sliced peeled peaches (about 4 medium)**
- 1 **cup fresh raspberries**
- 1 **tablespoon lemon juice**
- ½ **cup sugar**
- 5 **teaspoons quick-cooking tapioca**
- ½ **teaspoon ground cinnamon**
- 1 **sheet refrigerated pie pastry**
- 1 **tablespoon butter**
- 1 **large egg white, lightly beaten**
- 1 **tablespoon coarse sugar**

1. Preheat oven to 425°. In a large bowl, combine peaches, raspberries and lemon juice. In another bowl, combine sugar, tapioca and cinnamon. Gently stir into fruit mixture; let stand 15 minutes.

2. Unroll pastry sheet onto a parchment paper-lined 15x10x1-in. baking pan. Spoon filling over pastry to within 2 in. of edge; dot with butter. Fold pastry edge over filling, pleating as you go and leaving a 6-in. opening in the center. Brush folded pastry with egg white; sprinkle with sugar. Bake 25-30 minutes on a lower oven rack or until crust is golden and filling is bubbly. Transfer tart to a wire rack to cool.

PER SERVING *1 slice equals 227 cal., 9 g fat (4 g sat. fat), 9 mg chol., 119 mg sodium, 36 g carb., 2 g fiber, 2 g pro.*

RASPBERRY PEACH TART

Pear-Cranberry Gingerbread Cake Ⓢ Ⓜ

I love the warm, spicy flavors and festive fall fruits in this upside-down gingerbread cake. It could have a special place at any holiday buffet.

—**CHRISTINA METKE** CALGARY, AB

PREP: 25 MIN. • **BAKE:** 35 MIN. + COOLING
MAKES: 24 SERVINGS

- ¾ cup butter, melted, divided
- ⅔ cup packed brown sugar, divided
- 3 medium pears, sliced
- 2 cups fresh or frozen cranberries, thawed
- ¾ cup brewed chai tea
- ½ cup sugar
- ½ cup molasses
- 1 large egg
- 2 cups all-purpose flour
- 1 teaspoon ground ginger
- 1 teaspoon ground cinnamon
- ½ teaspoon salt
- ½ teaspoon baking soda
- ½ teaspoon ground cloves
- ¼ teaspoon ground nutmeg

1. Pour ¼ cup melted butter into a 13x9-in. baking dish; sprinkle with ⅓ cup brown sugar. Arrange pears and cranberries in a single layer over brown sugar.
2. In a small bowl, beat the brewed tea, sugar, molasses, egg and the remaining butter and brown sugar until well blended.
3. Combine flour, ginger, cinnamon, salt, baking soda, cloves and nutmeg; gradually beat into the tea mixture until blended.
4. Spoon over pears. Bake at 350° for 35-45 minutes or until a toothpick inserted near the center comes out clean. Cool for 10 minutes before inverting onto a serving plate. Serve warm.
PER SERVING *1 piece equals 166 cal., 6 g fat (4 g sat. fat), 24 mg chol., 124 mg sodium, 27 g carb., 1 g fiber, 2 g pro.* **Diabetic Exchanges:** *1½ starch, 1 fat.*

PUMPKIN GINGERSNAP ICE CREAM PIE

Pumpkin Gingersnap Ice Cream Pie Ⓜ

My family and I always try new desserts during the holidays. This one was a clear winner at our Christmas party, so we now make it for all occasions!

—**PATRICIA NESS** LA MESA, CA

PREP: 25 MIN. + FREEZING
MAKES: 8 SERVINGS

- 1½ cups crushed gingersnap cookies (about 30 cookies)
- 2 tablespoons ground walnuts
- 1 tablespoon canola oil

FILLING

- 4 cups reduced-fat vanilla ice cream, softened if necessary
- 1 cup canned pumpkin pie filling
  Pumpkin pie spice

1. Preheat oven to 350°. In a small bowl, mix crushed cookies and walnuts; stir in oil. Press onto bottom and up sides of an ungreased 9-in. pie plate. Bake 8-10 minutes or until set. Cool completely on a wire rack.
2. In a large bowl, mix ice cream and pie filling until blended. Spread into prepared crust; sprinkle with pie spice. Freeze, covered, 8 hours or overnight.
PER SERVING *1 piece equals 304 cal., 9 g fat (3 g sat. fat), 21 mg chol., 233 mg sodium, 50 g carb., 2 g fiber, 6 g pro.*

Blackberry-Topped Sponge Cakes [F] [M] FAST FIX

The recipe for my blackberry cakes is easy to play with. You can replace the sponge cake with angel food, pound cake or ladyfingers. And any fruit that has liquor with the same flavor can be used.

—**KAREN ROBINSON** WOODBURY, CT

START TO FINISH: 25 MIN.
MAKES: 6 SERVINGS

- 6 **individual round sponge cakes**
- 4 **cups fresh blackberries**
- ¼ **cup blackberry brandy**
- 1¼ **teaspoons sugar**
  Whipped cream, optional

1. Place sponge cakes on serving plates. Top each with three blackberries. Place remaining blackberries in a food processor; process until pureed. Strain and discard seeds and pulp.

2. Transfer the puree to a small saucepan. Stir in brandy and sugar. Bring to a boil; cook until liquid is reduced by half, stirring occasionally. Pour over berries. If desired, top with whipped cream.

PER SERVING *1 fruit-topped sponge cake (calulated without whipped cream) equals 141 cal., 2 g fat (1 g sat. fat), 28 mg chol., 181 mg sodium, 26 g carb., 5 g fiber, 3 g pro.* **Diabetic Exchanges:** *1 starch, 1 fruit.*

HOW TO

BAKE FOAM CAKES

❶ Foam cakes are done when the top springs back when touched and the cracks at the top of the cake look and feel dry.

❷ If your tube pan has legs, invert the pan onto its legs until the cake is completely cool. If your tube pan does not have legs, place the pan over a funnel or the neck of a narrow bottle until the cake is completely cool.

Angel food cake is my favorite blank slate for making awesome desserts. Serve it with a simple glaze, or pile on fresh fruit, chocolate sauce or nutty sprinkles.

—**LEAH REKAU** MILWAUKEE, WI

VANILLA ANGEL FOOD CAKE

Vanilla Angel Food Cake [F] [S] [M]

PREP: 30 MIN. • **BAKE:** 45 MIN. + COOLING
MAKES: 16 SERVINGS

- 12 **large egg whites (about 1⅔ cups)**
- 1 **cup cake flour**
- 1½ **cups sugar, divided**
- 1 **teaspoon vanilla extract**
- ½ **teaspoon cream of tartar**
- ¼ **teaspoon salt**

GLAZE
- 2 **cups confectioners' sugar**
- 1 **teaspoon vanilla extract**
- 3 **to 4 tablespoons 2% milk**

1. Place egg whites in a large bowl; let stand at room temperature 30 minutes.

2. Preheat oven to 325°. In a small bowl, mix the flour and ¾ cup sugar until blended.

3. Add vanilla, cream of tartar and salt to egg whites. Beat on medium speed until soft peaks form. Gradually add the remaining ¾ cup sugar, 1 tablespoon at a time, beating on high after each addition until sugar is dissolved. Continue beating until soft glossy peaks form. Gradually fold in flour mixture, about ½ cup at a time.

4. Gently transfer batter to an ungreased 10-in. tube pan. Cut through batter with a knife to remove air pockets. Bake on the lowest oven rack for 45-55 minutes or until top springs back when lightly touched. Immediately invert the pan; cool completely in pan, about 1½ hours.

5. Run a knife around the sides and center tube of the pan. Remove cake to a serving plate.

6. For glaze, in a small bowl, mix confectioners' sugar, vanilla and enough milk to reach desired consistency. Spread glaze over cake, allowing some to drip down sides.

PER SERVING *1 slice equals 177 cal., trace fat (trace sat. fat), trace chol., 80 mg sodium, 41 g carb., trace fiber, 3 g pro.*

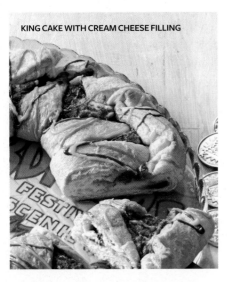

KING CAKE WITH CREAM CHEESE FILLING

King Cake with Cream Cheese Filling Ⓜ

Round out your Mardi Gras celebration with a king cake—a colorful ring-shaped pastry drizzled with green, gold and purple icing. This stunning cake has become the holiday's signature dessert.

—**ALICE LEJEUNE** VILLE PLATTE, LA

PREP: 25 MIN. • **BAKE:** 20 MIN.
MAKES: 16 SERVINGS

- 2 **tubes (8 ounces each) refrigerated reduced-fat crescent rolls**
- 4 **ounces reduced-fat cream cheese**
- 2 **tablespoons confectioners' sugar**
- 1 **teaspoon vanilla extract**
- ⅓ **cup light brown sugar**
- 2 **tablespoons butter, softened**
- 3 **teaspoons ground cinnamon**

ICING

- 1 **cup confectioners' sugar**
- ½ **teaspoon vanilla extract**
- 1 **to 2 tablespoons 2% milk**
  Red, blue, yellow and green food coloring

1. Unroll both tubes of crescent dough and separate into triangles. Place triangles on a greased 12-in. pizza pan, forming a ring with pointed ends facing toward the center and wide ends overlapping. Lightly press wide ends together.
2. In a small bowl, beat the cream cheese, confectioners' sugar and vanilla until smooth. Spoon over wide ends of ring. In another bowl, stir the brown sugar, butter and cinnamon until crumbly. Sprinkle over cream cheese mixture.

3. Fold points over filling and fold wide ends over points to seal. Bake at 350° for 20-25 minutes or until golden brown. Cool for 5 minutes.
4. Combine confectioners' sugar, vanilla and enough milk to achieve desired consistency. Divide the icing among three bowls. Using red and blue food coloring, tint one portion purple. Tint another portion yellow and the remaining portion green. Drizzle over cake. Serve warm.

PER SERVING *1 piece equals 184 cal., 8 g fat (3 g sat. fat), 9 mg chol., 275 mg sodium, 26 g carb., trace fiber, 3 g pro. Diabetic Exchanges: 1½ starch, 1½ fat.*

Rustic Pear Tart Ⓢ Ⓜ

This recipe is simplicity itself—you use refrigerated pastry, top with filling and fold! It's ideal for inexperienced pie bakers and a wonderful dessert for fall.

—**LISA VARNER** EL PASO, TX

PREP: 20 MIN. • **BAKE:** 35 MIN. + COOLING
MAKES: 8 SERVINGS

- 1 **sheet refrigerated pie pastry**
- 4 **cups thinly sliced peeled fresh pears**
- ¼ **cup dried cherries**
- 1 **teaspoon vanilla extract**
- 4 **tablespoons sugar, divided**
- 4 **teaspoons cornstarch**
- 1 **teaspoon ground cinnamon**
- ½ **teaspoon ground ginger**
- ¼ **cup chopped walnuts**
- 1 **large egg white**
- 1 **tablespoon water**

1. On a lightly floured surface, roll out pastry into a 14-in. circle. Transfer to a parchment paper-lined baking sheet; set aside.
2. In a large bowl, combine pears, cherries and vanilla. Combine 3 tablespoons sugar, cornstarch, cinnamon and ginger; sprinkle over pear mixture and stir gently to combine. Spoon over pastry to within 2 in. of edges; sprinkle with walnuts. Fold edges of pastry over filling, leaving center uncovered.
3. Beat egg white and water; brush over folded pastry. Sprinkle with remaining sugar. Bake at 375° for 35-40 minutes or until crust is golden and filling is bubbly. Using parchment paper, slide the tart onto a wire rack to cool.

PER SERVING *1 piece equals 239 cal., 10 g fat (3 g sat. fat), 5 mg chol., 107 mg sodium, 37 g carb., 2 g fiber, 3 g pro.*

RUSTIC PEAR TART

CHOCOLATE EGGNOG PIE

Chocolate Eggnog Pie S M

An easy chocolate-walnut crust perfectly complements this pretty layered pie.

—KERI WHITNEY CASTRO VALLEY, CA

PREP: 45 MIN. + CHILLING
MAKES: 8 SERVINGS

- ½ cup all-purpose flour
- ⅓ cup ground walnuts
- 3 tablespoons brown sugar
- 1 tablespoon baking cocoa
- ¼ cup reduced-fat butter, melted

FILLING

- ½ cup sugar
- 2 tablespoons cornstarch
- 2 cups reduced-fat eggnog
- 2½ teaspoons unflavored gelatin
- ½ cup cold water, divided
- 2 tablespoons baking cocoa
- ¾ teaspoon rum extract
- 2 cups reduced-fat whipped topping
  Additional reduced-fat whipped topping, optional
  Ground nutmeg, optional

1. Preheat oven to 375°. In a small bowl, mix flour, walnuts, brown sugar and cocoa; stir in butter. Lightly coat hands with cooking spray; press mixture into an ungreased 9-in. pie plate. Bake 8-10 minutes or until set. Cool completely on a wire rack.

2. For filling, in a small heavy saucepan, mix sugar and cornstarch. Whisk in eggnog. Cook and stir over medium heat until thickened and bubbly. Reduce heat to low; cook and stir 2 minutes longer. Remove from heat.

3. In a microwave-safe bowl, sprinkle gelatin over ¼ cup cold water; let stand 1 minute. Microwave on high for 20 seconds. Stir and let stand 1 minute or until gelatin is completely dissolved. Stir into eggnog mixture.

4. Divide mixture in half. In a small bowl, whisk cocoa and remaining water until blended; stir into half of the eggnog mixture. Stir rum extract into the remaining half. Refrigerate both mixtures, covered, until they are partially set.

5. Fold 2 cups whipped topping into rum-flavored portion; spoon into crust. Gently spread chocolate portion over top. Refrigerate, covered, at least 2 hours before serving. If desired, top with additional whipped topping and sprinkle with nutmeg.

PER SERVING *1 piece (calculated without additional whipped topping) equals 259 cal., 10 g fat (5 g sat. fat), 56 mg chol., 90 mg sodium, 39 g carb., 1 g fiber, 5 g pro.*

Orange Pound Cake with Cranberry Compote M

My husband and I enjoy dessert but not all of the fat and calories that go with it. This pound cake is made lighter with Greek yogurt. You will never miss that extra fat in taste or texture.

—ANN GONCHEROSKI WILKES BARRE, PA

PREP: 30 MIN. • **BAKE:** 55 MIN. + COOLING
MAKES: 16 SERVINGS

- ½ cup butter, softened
- 1 cup sugar
- 3 large eggs
- 1 tablespoon grated orange peel
- 1½ teaspoons vanilla extract
- ¾ cup fat-free plain Greek yogurt
- ¼ cup orange juice
- 2 cups all-purpose flour
- 1 teaspoon baking powder
- ¼ teaspoon salt

COMPOTE

- 1 cup fresh or frozen cranberries
- 1 cup orange juice
- ½ cup sugar
- 2 teaspoons grated orange peel
- 1 cinnamon stick (3 inches), optional

1. Preheat oven to 325°. Coat a 9x5-in. loaf pan with cooking spray.

2. In a large bowl, beat butter and sugar until blended. Add eggs, one at a time, beating well after each addition. Beat in orange peel and vanilla. Mix yogurt and orange juice. In another bowl, whisk flour, baking powder and salt; add to sugar mixture alternately with yogurt mixture, beating after each addition just until combined.

3. Transfer to prepared pan. Bake 55-65 minutes or until a toothpick inserted in center comes out clean. Cool in pan 10 minutes before removing to a wire rack to cool.

4. Meanwhile, in a small saucepan, combine compote ingredients; bring to a boil. Reduce the heat; simmer, uncovered, for 12-15 minutes or until compote is slightly thickened, stirring occasionally. Discard cinnamon stick if necessary. Serve warm with cake.

PER SERVING *1 slice with 1 tablespoon compote equals 216 cal., 7 g fat (4 g sat. fat), 50 mg chol., 129 mg sodium, 35 g carb., 1 g fiber, 4 g pro.* **Diabetic Exchanges:** *2 starch, 1½ fat.*

Grilled Angel Food Cake with Strawberries Ⓜ FAST FIX

START TO FINISH: 15 MIN.
MAKES: 8 SERVINGS

- 2 **cups sliced fresh strawberries**
- 2 **teaspoons sugar**
- 3 **tablespoons butter, melted**
- 2 **tablespoons balsamic vinegar**
- 8 **slices angel food cake (about 1 ounce each)**
  Reduced-fat vanilla ice cream and blueberry syrup, optional

1. In a small bowl, toss strawberries with sugar. In another bowl, mix butter and vinegar; brush over cut sides of cake.

2. Moisten a paper towel with cooking oil; using long-handled tongs, rub on grill rack to coat lightly. Grill the cake, uncovered, over medium heat for 1-2 minutes on each side or until golden brown. Serve the cake with strawberries and, if desired, ice cream and blueberry syrup.

PER SERVING *1 cake slice with ¼ cup strawberries (calculated without ice cream and blueberry syrup) equals 132 cal., 5 g fat (3 g sat. fat), 11 mg chol., 247 mg sodium, 22 g carb., 1 g fiber, 2 g pro.* **Diabetic Exchanges:** *1½ starch, 1 fat.*

One night I accidentally used the balsamic butter I save for grilling chicken on my pound cake. What a delicious mistake! For a patriotic look, add a drizzle of blueberry syrup.
—MOIRA MCGARRY PARKMAN, ME

GRILLED ANGEL FOOD CAKE WITH STRAWBERRIES

Spiced Butternut Squash Pie Ⓜ

My mom always made this dessert with her homegrown squash. It was my dad's favorite after-dinner treat. I continue to make it to this day.
—JOHNNA POULSON CELEBRATION, FL

PREP: 20 MIN. • **BAKE:** 40 MIN. + COOLING
MAKES: 8 SERVINGS

- 1 **refrigerated pie pastry**
- 3 **large eggs**
- 1½ **cups mashed cooked butternut squash**
- 1 **cup fat-free milk**
- ⅔ **cup fat-free evaporated milk**
- ¾ **cup sugar**
- ½ **teaspoon salt**
- 1 **teaspoon ground cinnamon**
- ½ **teaspoon ground ginger**
- ¼ **teaspoon ground nutmeg**
- ¼ **teaspoon ground cloves**
  Sweetened whipped cream, optional

1. Preheat oven to 450°. Unroll pastry sheet into a 9-in. pie plate; flute edge. Place eggs, squash, milks, sugar, salt and spices in a food processor; process until smooth. Pour into crust. Bake on a lower oven rack 10 minutes.

2. Reduce oven setting to 350°. Bake 30-40 minutes longer or until a knife inserted near the center comes out clean. Cool on a wire rack; serve or refrigerate within 2 hours. If desired, serve with whipped cream.

PER SERVING *1 piece (calculated without whipped cream) equals 266 cal., 9 g fat (4 g sat. fat), 76 mg chol., 313 mg sodium, 41 g carb., 2 g fiber, 7 g pro.*

TOP TIP

The microwave oven does a quick job of cooking butternut squash. Cut squash in half and remove seeds; place cut side down in a microwave-safe dish. Add 2 to 3 tablespoons of water; cover and microwave on high for 9-12 minutes or until tender, turning once. Let stand for 5 minutes before handling.

SPICED BUTTERNUT SQUASH PIE

235

243

236

Treat Yourself

❝Eat these as-is, or crush them into a bowl of strawberries and whipped cream. Readers of my blog, utry.it, went nuts when I posted that idea!❞

—AMY TONG ANAHEIM, CA
about her recipe, Chocolate-Dipped Strawberry Meringue Roses, on page 231

Must-Have Tiramisu S M

This is the perfect guilt-free version of a classic delectable dessert. My friends even say that they prefer my healthy recipe over other tiramisu.

—**ALE GAMBINI** BEVERLY HILLS, CA

PREP: 25 MIN. + CHILLING
MAKES: 9 SERVINGS

- ½ **cup heavy whipping cream**
- 2 **cups (16 ounces) vanilla yogurt**
- 1 **cup fat-free milk**
- ½ **cup brewed espresso or strong brewed coffee**
- 1 **package (7 ounces) crisp ladyfinger cookies**
  Baking cocoa
  Fresh raspberries, optional

1. In a small bowl, beat cream until stiff peaks form; fold in yogurt. Spread ½ cup cream mixture onto bottom of an 8-in. square baking dish.

2. In a shallow dish, mix milk and espresso until blended. Quickly dip 12 ladyfingers into coffee mixture, allowing excess to drip off. Arrange in a single layer in dish, breaking as needed to fit. Top with half of the remaining cream mixture; dust with cocoa. Repeat layers.

3. Refrigerate, covered, for at least 2 hours before serving. If desired, top with raspberries before serving.

PER SERVING *1 piece (calculated without raspberries) equals 178 cal., 6 g fat (4 g sat. fat), 45 mg chol., 82 mg sodium, 25 g carb., 0 fiber, 5 g pro.* **Diabetic Exchanges:** *1 starch, 1 fat, ½ fat-free milk.*

MUST-HAVE TIRAMISU

One summer, my mother-in-law made us grilled peaches basted with a sweet and tangy sauce. These are so good, I'm always tempted to eat the whole batch.

—**KRISTIN VAN DYKEN** KENNEWICK, WA

GRILLED HONEY-BALSAMIC FRUIT

Grilled Honey-Balsamic Fruit F S M FAST FIX

START TO FINISH: 25 MIN.
MAKES: 6 SERVINGS (½ CUP GLAZE)

- ½ **cup balsamic vinegar**
- ½ **cup honey**
  Dash salt
- 6 **medium peaches or nectarines, halved and pitted**
  Vanilla ice cream, optional

1. In a small saucepan, combine the vinegar, honey and salt; cook and stir over low heat 2-3 minutes or until blended. Reserve ⅓ cup of mixture for brushing peaches as they grill. Bring the remaining mixture to a boil over medium heat; cook and stir 4-6 minutes or just until mixture begins to thicken slightly (do not overcook). Remove from heat.

2. Moisten a paper towel with cooking oil; using long-handled tongs, rub on grill rack to coat lightly. Brush the peaches with some of the reserved balsamic mixture.

3. Grill the peaches, covered, over medium heat 6-8 minutes on each side or until caramelized, brushing occasionally with remaining reserved balsamic mixture. Serve with glaze and, if desired, ice cream.

PER SERVING *1 serving (calculated without ice cream) equals 164 cal., trace fat (trace sat. fat), 0 chol., 26 mg sodium, 43 g carb., 2 g fiber, 1 g pro.*

Chocolate-Dipped Strawberry Meringue Roses F S C

Eat these as-is, or crush them into a bowl of strawberries and whipped cream. Readers of my blog, utry.it, went nuts when I posted that idea!

—AMY TONG ANAHEIM, CA

PREP: 25 MIN. • **BAKE:** 40 MIN. + COOLING
MAKES: 3½ DOZEN

- 3 **large egg whites**
- ¼ **cup sugar**
- ¼ **cup freeze-dried strawberries**
- 1 **package (3 ounces) strawberry gelatin**
- ½ **teaspoon vanilla extract, optional**
- 1 **cup 60% cacao bittersweet chocolate baking chips, melted**

1. Place the egg whites in a large bowl; allow to stand at room temperature 30 minutes. Preheat oven to 225°.
2. Place sugar and strawberries in a food processor; process until powdery. Add gelatin; pulse to blend.
3. Beat egg whites on medium speed until foamy, adding vanilla if desired. Gradually add the gelatin mixture, 1 tablespoon at a time, beating on high after each addition until sugar is dissolved. Continue beating until stiff glossy peaks form.
4. Cut a small hole in the tip of a pastry bag or in a corner of a food-safe plastic bag; insert a #1M star tip. Transfer meringue to bag. Pipe 2-in. roses 1½ in. apart onto parchment paper-lined baking sheets.
5. Bake 40-45 minutes or until set and dry. Turn off oven (do not open oven door); leave meringues in oven for 1½ hours. Remove from oven; cool completely on baking sheets.
6. Remove meringues from paper. Dip bottoms in melted chocolate; allow excess to drip off. Place cookies on waxed paper; let stand until set, about 45 minutes. Store in an airtight container at room temperature.
PER SERVING *1 cookie equals 33 cal., 1 g fat (1 g sat. fat), 0 chol., 9 mg sodium, 6 g carb., trace fiber, 1 g pro.*
Diabetic Exchange: *½ starch.*

Frozen Greek Vanilla Yogurt F S

It's simple and easy to make your own frozen Greek yogurt—you might even want to get the kids in on the fun.

—TASTE OF HOME TEST KITCHEN

PREP: 15 MIN. + CHILLING
PROCESS: 15 MIN. + FREEZING
MAKES: 2½ CUPS

- 3 **cups reduced-fat plain Greek yogurt**
- ¾ **cup sugar**
- 1½ **teaspoons clear vanilla extract**
- 1 **tablespoon cold water**
- 1 **tablespoon lemon juice**
- 1 **teaspoon unflavored gelatin**

1. Line a strainer or colander with four layers of cheesecloth or one coffee filter; place over a bowl. Place yogurt in prepared strainer; cover yogurt with sides of cheesecloth. Refrigerate for 2-4 hours.
2. Remove yogurt from cheesecloth to a bowl; discard strained liquid. Add sugar and vanilla to yogurt, stirring until sugar is dissolved.
3. In a small microwave-safe bowl, combine cold water and lemon juice; sprinkle with gelatin and let stand 1 minute. Microwave on high for 30 seconds. Stir and let mixture stand 1 minute or until the gelatin is completely dissolved.
4. Pour yogurt mixture into cylinder of ice cream freezer; freeze according to the manufacturer's directions, adding gelatin mixture during the last 10 minutes of processing.
5. Transfer frozen yogurt to a freezer container. Freeze 2-4 hours or until firm enough to scoop.
PER SERVING *½ cup equals 225 cal., 3 g fat (2 g sat. fat), 8 mg chol., 57 mg sodium, 36 g carb., trace fiber, 14 g pro.*

FROZEN GREEK VANILLA YOGURT

Raspberry Sorbet F S M

With an abundant crop of fresh raspberries from the backyard, it's no wonder that I rely on this recipe for a tasty, no-fuss frozen dessert.

—**KAREN BAILEY** GOLDEN, CO

PREP: 5 MIN. + FREEZING
MAKES: 6 SERVINGS

- ¼ cup plus 1½ teaspoons fresh lemon juice
- 3¾ cups fresh or frozen unsweetened raspberries
- 2¼ cups confectioners' sugar

Place all ingredients in a blender or food processor; cover and process until smooth. Transfer to a freezer container; freeze until firm.

PER SERVING *1 serving equals 216 cal., trace fat (trace sat. fat), 0 chol., 1 mg sodium, 55 g carb., 5 g fiber, 1 g pro.*

Crunchy Apricot-Coconut Balls S C M FAST FIX

My mom gave me this no-bake cookie recipe years ago when she had them on her Christmas buffet. I can't believe how simple they are to make.

—**JANE WHITTAKER** PENSACOLA, FL

START TO FINISH: 30 MIN.
MAKES: 2 DOZEN

- 1¼ cups flaked coconut
- 1 cup dried apricots, finely chopped
- ⅔ cup chopped pecans
- ½ cup fat-free sweetened condensed milk
- ½ cup confectioners' sugar

1. In a small bowl, combine coconut, apricots and pecans. Add condensed milk; mix well (mixture will be sticky).
2. Shape into 1¼-in. balls and roll in confectioners' sugar. Store in an airtight container in the refrigerator.

PER SERVING *1 ball equals 87 cal., 4 g fat (2 g sat. fat), 1 mg chol., 19 mg sodium, 12 g carb., 1 g fiber, 1 g pro.*

RASPBERRY SORBET

Cardamom Yogurt Pudding with Honeyed Oranges F S

I live near Florida, and the holiday season ushers in the new citrus crop there. My favorite citrus is navel oranges, so I added them to an easy pudding to create a special dessert.

—LILY JULOW LAWRENCEVILLE, GA

PREP: 25 MIN. + CHILLING
COOK: 15 MIN. + COOLING
MAKES: 4 SERVINGS

- 1 teaspoon unflavored gelatin
- 2 tablespoons cold water
- 2 cups reduced-fat plain Greek yogurt
- ⅓ cup sugar
- 1 teaspoon vanilla extract
- ½ teaspoon ground cardamom
- 4 medium navel oranges, divided
- ¼ cup orange blossom honey
- ¼ teaspoon ground cinnamon

1. In a small saucepan, sprinkle gelatin over cold water; let stand 1 minute. Heat and stir over low heat until gelatin is completely dissolved.
2. In a small bowl, whisk yogurt, sugar, vanilla and cardamom until sugar is dissolved. Whisk in gelatin mixture. Refrigerate, covered, about 2 hours or until soft-set.
3. Meanwhile, place a small strainer over a bowl. Cut a thin slice from the top and bottom of two oranges; stand oranges upright on a cutting board. With a knife, cut off peel and outer membrane from each orange. Working over strainer, cut along the membrane of each segment to remove fruit. Place orange sections in strainer.
4. Squeeze juice from remaining oranges; transfer to a small saucepan. Stir in honey, cinnamon and juice drained from orange sections. Bring to a boil, stirring occasionally. Reduce the heat; simmer, uncovered, 9-12 minutes or until syrupy. Remove from the heat; gently stir in orange sections. Cool mixture completely.
5. To serve, alternately layer the orange and yogurt mixtures into four dessert dishes.

PER SERVING *1 serving equals 290 cal., 3 g fat (1 g sat. fat), 7 mg chol., 50 mg sodium, 57 g carb., 3 g fiber, 13 g pro.*

BAKED ELEPHANT EARS

Baked Elephant Ears S M

My mother-in-law handed down this recipe from her mother. They're a special treat—even better, I think, than those at a carnival or festival.

—DELORES BAETEN DOWNERS GROVE, IL

PREP: 35 MIN. + CHILLING • **BAKE:** 10 MIN.
MAKES: 2 DOZEN

- 1 package (¼ ounce) active dry yeast
- ¼ cup warm water (110° to 115°)
- 2 cups all-purpose flour
- 4½ teaspoons sugar
- ½ teaspoon salt
- ⅓ cup cold butter, cubed
- ⅓ cup fat-free milk
- 1 large egg yolk

FILLING
- 2 tablespoons butter, softened
- ½ cup sugar
- 2 teaspoons ground cinnamon

CINNAMON SUGAR
- ½ cup sugar
- ¾ teaspoon ground cinnamon

1. In a small bowl, dissolve yeast in warm water. In a large bowl, mix flour, sugar and salt; cut in butter until crumbly. Stir milk and egg yolk into yeast mixture; add to flour mixture, stirring to form a stiff dough (dough will be sticky). Cover with plastic wrap and refrigerate 2 hours.
2. Preheat oven to 375°. Turn dough onto a lightly floured surface; roll into an 18x10-in. rectangle. Spread with softened butter to within ¼ in. of edges. Mix sugar and cinnamon; sprinkle over butter. Roll up jelly-roll style, starting with a long side; pinch seam to seal. Cut crosswise into 24 slices. Cover slices with plastic wrap until ready to flatten.
3. In a small bowl, mix ingredients for cinnamon sugar. Place a 6-in. square piece of waxed paper on a work surface; sprinkle with ½ teaspoon cinnamon sugar. Top with one slice of dough; sprinkle dough with an additional ½ teaspoon cinnamon sugar. Roll dough to a 4-in. circle. Using waxed paper, flip dough onto a baking sheet coated with cooking spray. Repeat with remaining ingredients, placing slices 2 in. apart. Bake 7-9 minutes or until golden brown. Cool on wire racks.

PER SERVING *1 elephant ear equals 109 cal., 4 g fat (2 g sat. fat), 18 mg chol., 76 mg sodium, 18 g carb., trace fiber, 1 g pro.* **Diabetic Exchanges:** *1 starch, ½ fat.*

Date Oat Bars S M

My mother found this recipe many years ago. I love the citrusy taste of these treats just as much today as I did back then.

—JOYCE EASTMAN GARDEN GROVE, CA

PREP: 30 MIN. • **BAKE:** 30 MIN. + COOLING
MAKES: 3 DOZEN

- 1¾ cups chopped dates
- ½ cup water
- 2 tablespoons brown sugar
- 1 teaspoon grated orange peel
- 2 tablespoons orange juice
- 1 teaspoon lemon juice

CRUST

- 1½ cups all-purpose flour
- 1 teaspoon baking powder
- ½ teaspoon baking soda
- ¼ teaspoon salt
- 1 cup cold butter
- 1½ cups old-fashioned oats
- 1 cup packed brown sugar

1. In a small saucepan, combine the dates, water, brown sugar and orange peel. Cook and stir over medium heat until mixture comes to a boil, about 4 minutes. Cook and stir 3 minutes longer or until liquid is absorbed. Remove from the heat. Stir in orange and lemon juices. Cool to room temperature.

2. In a large bowl, combine the flour, baking powder, baking soda and salt. Cut in butter until crumbly. Add oats and brown sugar; mix well. Set aside half for the topping. Press remaining crumb mixture into a greased 13x9-in. baking pan.

3. Drop the date mixture by small spoonfuls onto crust. Sprinkle with reserved crumb mixture; press down gently. Bake at 325° for 30-35 minutes or until golden brown. Cool on a wire rack. Cut into bars.

PER SERVING *1 bar equals 126 cal., 5 g fat (3 g sat. fat), 14 mg chol., 100 mg sodium, 19 g carb., 1 g fiber, 1 g pro.*
Diabetic Exchanges: *1 starch, 1 fat.*

SKILLET BLUEBERRY SLUMP

Skillet Blueberry Slump F M

My mother-in-law made a slump of wild blueberries with dumplings and served it warm with a pitcher of farm cream. We've been eating slump for nearly 60 years!

—ELEANORE EBELING BREWSTER, MN

PREP: 25 MIN. • **BAKE:** 20 MIN.
MAKES: 6 SERVINGS

- 4 cups fresh or frozen blueberries
- ½ cup sugar
- ½ cup water
- 1 teaspoon grated lemon peel
- 1 tablespoon lemon juice
- 1 cup all-purpose flour
- 2 tablespoons sugar
- 2 teaspoons baking powder
- ½ teaspoon salt
- 1 tablespoon butter
- ½ cup 2% milk
  Vanilla ice cream

1. Preheat oven to 400°. In a 10-in. ovenproof skillet, combine the first five ingredients; bring to a boil. Reduce heat; simmer, uncovered, 9-11 minutes or until slightly thickened, stirring occasionally.

2. Meanwhile, in a small bowl, whisk flour, sugar, baking powder and salt. Cut in butter until mixture resembles coarse crumbs. Add the milk; stir just until moistened.

3. Drop batter in six portions on top of the simmering blueberry mixture. Transfer to oven. Bake, uncovered, 17-20 minutes or until the dumplings are golden brown. Serve warm with ice cream.

PER SERVING *1 serving (calculated without ice cream) equals 239 cal., 3 g fat (2 g sat. fat), 7 mg chol., 355 mg sodium, 52 g carb., 3 g fiber, 4 g pro.*

Fruit & Granola Crisp with Yogurt [F] [S] [M] [FAST FIX] ►

Here's an easy dessert you can feel good about serving. Blueberries and peaches are such a delightful flavor combination.

—SUE SCHMIDTKE ORO VALLEY, AZ

START TO FINISH: 10 MIN.
MAKES: 4 SERVINGS

- 3 cups fresh or frozen sliced peaches, thawed
- 1 cup fresh or frozen blueberries, thawed
- 4 tablespoons hot caramel ice cream topping
- 4 tablespoons granola without raisins
- 2 cups low-fat frozen yogurt

Divide the peaches and blueberries among four 8-oz. ramekins. Top each with caramel and granola. Microwave, uncovered, on high for 1-2 minutes or until bubbly. Serve with frozen yogurt.

PER SERVING *1 serving equals 251 cal., 3 g fat (1 g sat. fat), 5 mg chol., 133 mg sodium, 54 g carb., 4 g fiber, 7 g pro.*

Pear Sorbet [F] [S] [M]

A touch of sweet white wine and citrus makes this lovely pear sorbet so refreshing. You can use canned pears when fresh ones aren't available. And lime juice is a nice substitute for lemon.

—DEIRDRE COX KANSAS CITY, MO

PREP: 20 MIN. + FREEZING
MAKES: 4 SERVINGS

- 5 small pears, peeled and sliced
- ¾ cup sweet white wine or apple juice
- ⅓ cup sugar
- 4½ teaspoons lemon juice

1. In a large saucepan, combine all ingredients. Bring to a boil. Reduce the heat; simmer, uncovered, for 8-10 minutes or until the pears are tender. Cool slightly.
2. Pour into a food processor; cover and process for 1-2 minutes or until smooth. Transfer to a 13x9-in. dish. Cover and freeze for 4 hours or until firm.
3. Just before serving, process again in a food processor for 1-2 minutes or until smooth. Spoon sorbet into dessert dishes.

PER SERVING *½ cup equals 198 cal., 1 g fat (trace sat. fat), 0 chol., 2 mg sodium, 44 g carb., 4 g fiber, 1 g pro.*

Rhubarb Strawberry Granita [F] [S] [M]

Fresh rhubarb and strawberries make this sweet and icy dessert such a treat. You'll love how quickly it comes together and that it's prepared without any special equipment.

—CHRISTEN ROYE WEATHERFORD, TX

PREP: 15 MIN. + FREEZING
MAKES: 8 SERVINGS

- 3 cups water
- 1 cup plus 2 tablespoons sugar
- 1 cup diced fresh or frozen rhubarb, thawed
- ½ cup halved fresh strawberries
- 2 tablespoons orange liqueur or orange juice
  Fresh mint leaves and orange peel strips, optional

1. In a large saucepan, bring the water, sugar, rhubarb and strawberries to a boil. Cook and stir until sugar is dissolved. Strain; discard the pulp and seeds.
2. Transfer syrup to an 8-in. square dish. Stir in orange liqueur; cool to room temperature. Freeze for 1 hour; stir with a fork. Freeze 2-3 hours longer or until completely frozen, stirring every 30 minutes. Stir granita with a fork just before serving; spoon into dessert dishes. Garnish with mint and orange peel if desired.
NOTE *If using frozen rhubarb, measure rhubarb while still frozen, then thaw completely. Drain in a colander, but do not press liquid out.*
PER SERVING *1 serving equals 128 cal., trace fat (trace sat. fat), 0 chol., 1 mg sodium, 31 g carb., trace fiber, trace pro.*

RHUBARB STRAWBERRY GRANITA

Cream Cheese Swirl Brownies M

I'm a chocolate lover, and this treat has satisfied my cravings many times. No one guesses the brownies are lower in fat, because their chewy texture and rich chocolate taste can't be beat.

—**HEIDI JOHNSON** WORLAND, WY

PREP: 20 MIN. • **BAKE:** 25 MIN.
MAKES: 1 DOZEN

- 3 **large eggs**
- 6 **tablespoons reduced-fat butter, softened**
- 1 **cup sugar, divided**
- 3 **teaspoons vanilla extract**
- ½ **cup all-purpose flour**
- ¼ **cup baking cocoa**
- 1 **package (8 ounces) reduced-fat cream cheese**

1. Preheat oven to 350°. Separate two eggs, putting each white in a separate bowl (discard yolks or save for another use); set aside. In a small bowl, beat butter and ¾ cup sugar until crumbly. Beat in the whole egg, one egg white and vanilla until well combined. Combine flour and cocoa; gradually add to egg mixture until blended. Pour into a 9-in. square baking pan coated with cooking spray; set aside.

2. In a small bowl, beat cream cheese and remaining sugar until smooth. Beat in the second egg white. Drop by rounded tablespoonfuls over the batter; cut through batter with a knife to swirl.

3. Bake 25-30 minutes or until set and edges pull away from sides of pan. Cool on a wire rack.

PER SERVING *1 brownie equals 172 cal., 8 g fat (5 g sat. fat), 36 mg chol., 145 mg sodium, 23 g carb., trace fiber, 4 g pro.* **Diabetic Exchanges:** *1½ starch, 1½ fat.*

FROZEN YOGURT FRUIT POPS

> My grandson, Patrick, who's now in high school, was "Grammy's Helper" for years. We made these frozen pops for company and everyone, including the adults, loved them. They're delicious and good for you!
> —**JUNE DICKENSON** PHILIPPI, WV

Frozen Yogurt Fruit Pops F S C M

PREP: 15 MIN. + FREEZING
MAKES: 1 DOZEN

- 2¼ **cups (18 ounces) raspberry yogurt**
- 2 **tablespoons lemon juice**
- 2 **medium ripe bananas, cut into chunks**
- 12 **freezer pop molds or 12 paper cups (3 ounces each) and wooden pop sticks**

1. Place yogurt, lemon juice and bananas in a blender; cover and process until smooth, stopping to stir if necessary.

2. Pour mixture into molds or paper cups. Top molds with holders. If using cups, top with foil and insert sticks through foil. Freeze until firm.

PER SERVING *1 fruit pop equals 60 cal., 1 g fat (trace sat. fat), 2 mg chol., 23 mg sodium, 13 g carb., 1 g fiber, 2 g pro.* **Diabetic Exchange:** *1 starch.*

DID YOU KNOW?

Most vanilla comes from Madagascar and Reunion Island—formerly known as the Bourbon Islands—off the southeast coast of Africa. Bourbon vanilla is celebrated for its strong, clear vanilla flavor and creamy finish.

CREAM CHEESE SWIRL BROWNIES

WARM CHOCOLATE MELTING CUPS

Warm Chocolate Melting Cups S M

Described as over-the-top delicious, these rich, chocolaty desserts are surprisingly smooth and creamy. But what's even more surprising is that each one has fewer than 200 calories and only 6 grams of fat.

—**KISSA VAUGHN** TROY, TX

PREP: 20 MIN. • **BAKE:** 20 MIN.
MAKES: 10 SERVINGS

- 1¼ cups sugar, divided
- ½ cup baking cocoa
- 2 tablespoons all-purpose flour
- ⅛ teaspoon salt
- ¾ cup water
- ¾ cup plus 1 tablespoon semisweet chocolate chips
- 1 tablespoon brewed coffee
- 1 teaspoon vanilla extract
- 2 large eggs
- 1 large egg white
- 10 fresh strawberry halves, optional

1. In a small saucepan, combine ¾ cup sugar, cocoa, flour and salt. Gradually stir in water. Bring to a boil; cook and stir for 2 minutes or until thickened. Remove from the heat; stir in the chocolate chips, coffee and vanilla until smooth. Transfer to a large bowl.

2. In another bowl, beat the eggs and egg white until slightly thickened. Gradually add the remaining sugar, beating until thick and lemon-colored. Fold into the chocolate mixture.

3. Transfer to ten 4-oz. ramekins coated with cooking spray. Place ramekins in a baking pan; add 1 in. of boiling water to the pan. Bake, uncovered, at 350° for 20-25 minutes or just until centers are set. Garnish with strawberry halves if desired. Serve immediately.

PER SERVING *1 each equals 197 cal., 6 g fat (3 g sat. fat), 42 mg chol., 51 mg sodium, 37 g carb., 2 g fiber, 3 g pro.*

Banana Boats F S FAST FIX

This recipe, given to me years ago by a good friend, is a favorite with my family when we go camping. It's quick, fun to make and scrumptious!

—**BRENDA LOVELESS** GARLAND, TX

START TO FINISH: 20 MIN.
MAKES: 4 SERVINGS

- 4 medium unpeeled ripe bananas
- 4 teaspoons miniature chocolate chips
- 4 tablespoons miniature marshmallows

1. Cut banana peel lengthwise about ½ in. deep, leaving ½ in. at both ends. Open peel wider to form a pocket. Fill each with 1 teaspoon chocolate chips and 1 tablespoon marshmallows. Crimp and shape four pieces of heavy-duty foil (about 12 in. square) around bananas, forming boats.

2. Grill bananas, covered, over medium heat for 5-10 minutes or until marshmallows melt and are golden brown.

PER SERVING *1 banana boat equals 136 cal., 2 g fat (1 g sat. fat), 0 chol., 3 mg sodium, 32 g carb., 3 g fiber, 1 g pro.*

TOP TIP

Been making these for 50 years. We also add a sprinkle of brown sugar in the bottom and use Hershey's chocolate bars broken into pieces. You can also add peanut butter.

—**JLBARHORST** TASTEOFHOME.COM

BANANA BOATS

This silky, smooth dessert captures the essence and elegance of fall. I came up with the recipe myself, aiming to make something both luscious and light.
—CHARLES INSLER SILVER SPRING, MD

PUMPKIN FLANS

Pumpkin Flans F M

PREP: 45 MIN. • **BAKE:** 30 MIN. + CHILLING
MAKES: 6 SERVINGS

- 1 cup sugar, divided
- ¼ cup water
- 1½ cups fat-free evaporated milk
- 3 large eggs
- 1 egg white
- ¼ teaspoon salt
- ¼ teaspoon each ground cinnamon, cloves and ginger
- 1 cup canned pumpkin
- 1 teaspoon vanilla extract
  Additional ground cinnamon, optional

1. In a small heavy skillet over medium-low heat, combine ⅓ cup sugar and water. Cook, stirring occasionally, until sugar begins to melt. Cook without stirring until amber, about 20 minutes. Quickly pour into six ungreased 6-oz. ramekins or custard cups, tilting to coat bottom of dishes. Let stand for 10 minutes.

2. In a small saucepan, heat milk until bubbles form around sides of saucepan. In a small bowl, whisk the eggs, egg white, salt, spices and remaining sugar. Remove milk from the heat; stir a small amount of hot milk into egg mixture. Return all to pan, stirring constantly. Stir in pumpkin and vanilla. Slowly pour into prepared ramekins.

3. Place in a baking pan; add ¾ in. of boiling water to pan. Bake, uncovered, at 325° for 30-35 minutes or until centers are just set (mixture will jiggle). Remove ramekins from water bath; cool for 10 minutes. Cover and refrigerate for at least 4 hours.

4. Carefully run a knife around edges of ramekins to loosen; invert each dish onto a rimmed serving dish. Sprinkle with additional cinnamon if desired. Serve immediately.

PER SERVING *1 serving equals 233 cal., 3 g fat (1 g sat. fat), 108 mg chol., 218 mg sodium, 44 g carb., 2 g fiber, 9 g pro.*

Saucy Spiced Pears S M FAST FIX ▶

We serve these tangy, saucy pears over angel food cake, pound cake or with a little yogurt or vanilla ice cream. Sprinkle with a favorite topping.
—JOY ZACHARIA CLEARWATER, FL

START TO FINISH: 20 MIN.
MAKES: 4 SERVINGS

- ½ cup orange juice
- 2 tablespoons butter
- 2 tablespoons sugar
- 2 teaspoons lemon juice
- 1 teaspoon vanilla extract
- 1 teaspoon ground ginger
- ¼ teaspoon ground cinnamon
- ⅛ teaspoon salt
- ⅛ teaspoon ground allspice
- ⅛ teaspoon cayenne pepper, optional
- 3 large Bosc pears (about 1¾ pounds), cored, peeled and sliced
  Thinly sliced fresh mint leaves, optional

1. In a large skillet, combine the first nine ingredients and, if desired, cayenne. Cook over medium-high heat 1-2 minutes or until butter is melted, stirring occasionally.

2. Add pears; bring to a boil. Reduce heat to medium; cook, uncovered, 3-4 minutes or until sauce is slightly thickened and pears are crisp-tender, stirring occasionally. Cool slightly. If desired, top with mint.

PER SERVING *¾ cup equals 192 cal., 6 g fat (4 g sat. fat), 15 mg chol., 130 mg sodium, 36 g carb., 5 g fiber, 1 g pro.* ***Diabetic Exchanges:*** *1 starch, 1 fruit, 1 fat.*

SAUCY SPICED PEARS

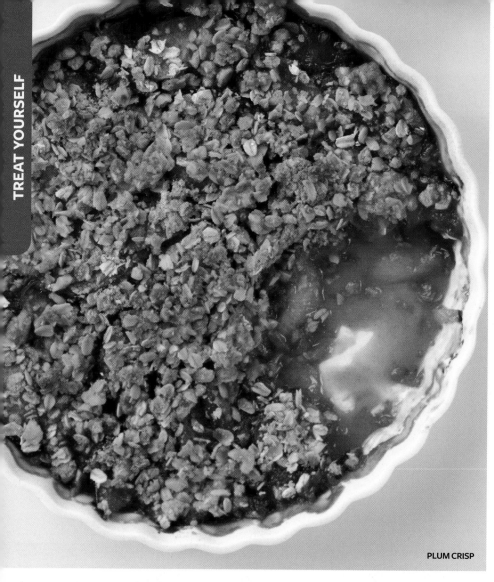

PLUM CRISP

Gluten-Free Chocolate Cake Cookies F S C M

I need to avoid gluten, so I've tried transforming my favorite recipes to fit my diet. I came up with these cakelike cookies, and no one ever guesses that they're gluten-free.

—**BECKI DIMERCURIO** MARTINEZ, CA

PREP: 30 MIN.
BAKE: 10 MIN./BATCH + COOLING
MAKES: 2 DOZEN

- 2 cups confectioners' sugar
- ½ cup plus 3 tablespoons Dutch process cocoa powder
- 2¼ teaspoons cornstarch
- ¼ teaspoon salt
- 2 egg whites
- 2½ teaspoons Kahlua coffee liqueur
- 1 cup chopped walnuts, toasted
  Additional confectioners' sugar

1. In a large bowl, combine the confectioners' sugar, cocoa powder, cornstarch and salt. Stir in egg whites and coffee liqueur until batter resembles frosting. Add walnuts.
2. Drop by tablespoonfuls 3 in. apart onto parchment paper-lined baking sheets. Bake at 300° for 10-14 minutes or until set. Cool for 2 minutes before removing from pans to wire racks to cool completely. Dust with additional confectioners' sugar.

NOTE *Read all ingredient labels for possible gluten content prior to use. Ingredient formulas can change, and production facilities vary among brands. If you're concerned that your brand may contain gluten, contact the company.*

PER SERVING *1 cookie equals 82 cal., 3 g fat (trace sat. fat), 0 chol., 29 mg sodium, 12 g carb., 1 g fiber, 2 g pro.* **Diabetic Exchanges:** *1 starch, ½ fat.*

DID YOU KNOW?

Dutch process cocoa has been treated with an alkaline solution in its manufacture. It has a smoother, richer flavor and darker color than regular cocoa. Baked goods made with it are a more intense chocolate brown color than those made with regular cocoa.

Plum Crisp S M

Made with fresh plums and a crunchy oat topping, this crisp is a lighter alternative to classic fruit pie. It goes over well with the women in my church group.

—**DEIDRE KOBEL** BOULDER, CO

PREP: 25 MIN. + STANDING • **BAKE:** 40 MIN.
MAKES: 8 SERVINGS

- ¾ cup old-fashioned oats
- ⅓ cup all-purpose flour
- ¼ cup plus 2 tablespoons sugar, divided
- ¼ cup packed brown sugar
- ¼ teaspoon salt
- ¼ teaspoon ground cinnamon
- ¼ teaspoon ground nutmeg
- 3 tablespoons butter, softened
- ¼ cup chopped walnuts
- 5 cups sliced fresh plums (about 2 pounds)
- 1 tablespoon quick-cooking tapioca
- 2 teaspoons lemon juice

1. In a small bowl, combine the oats, flour, ¼ cup sugar, brown sugar, salt, cinnamon and nutmeg. With clean hands, work butter into sugar mixture until well combined. Add nuts; toss to combine. Refrigerate for 15 minutes.
2. Meanwhile, in a large bowl, combine the plums, tapioca, lemon juice and remaining sugar. Transfer to a greased 9-in. pie plate. Let stand for 15 minutes. Sprinkle topping over plum mixture.
3. Bake at 375° for 40-45 minutes or until topping is golden brown and plums are tender. Serve warm.

PER SERVING *1 serving equals 233 cal., 8 g fat (3 g sat. fat), 11 mg chol., 107 mg sodium, 40 g carb., 3 g fiber, 3 g pro.*

GRILLED APPLE PIZZA

Grilled Apple Pizza M FAST FIX ▶

Here's a dessert that will make you go *"Mmm!"* Start with this basic apple pizza, then dress it up any way you like using the ideas at the end of the recipe.

—**R. SANDLIN** PRESCOTT VALLEY, AZ

START TO FINISH: 25 MIN.
MAKES: 2 PIZZAS (4 PIECES EACH)

- 5 medium tart apples, peeled and sliced
- 4 tablespoons butter, divided
- ½ cup packed brown sugar
- 1 teaspoon ground cinnamon
- 1 tube (13.8 ounces) refrigerated pizza crust

1. In a large skillet, saute apples in 3 tablespoons butter until crisp-tender. Stir in brown sugar and cinnamon; keep warm.

2. Unroll the pizza crust and cut lengthwise in half. In a microwave, melt remaining butter; brush onto both sides of crust.

3. Grill, covered, over medium heat for 1-3 minutes on each side or until lightly browned, rotating halfway through cooking to ensure an evenly browned crust. Remove from the grill. Top with apples and desired topping ingredients.

AMERICAN WAY *Sprinkle with arugula, cooked chopped bacon and shredded cheddar cheese.*

FRUIT AND CREAM *Sprinkle with dried cranberries; drizzle with cream cheese frosting.*

FRENCH *Top with sliced Brie cheese and fresh thyme.*

TURTLE STYLE *Sprinkle with chopped toasted pecans; drizzle with caramel sauce.*

PER SERVING *1 piece equals 271 cal., 8 g fat (4 g sat. fat), 15 mg chol., 372 mg sodium, 47 g carb., 2 g fiber, 4 g pro.*

Cherry Dumplings S M

This is my mom's recipe, and I'm happy to share it. The dumplings are out of this world, and they complement the tart cherries.

—GAIL HALE FILLMORE, NY

PREP: 10 MIN. • **COOK:** 30 MIN.
MAKES: 8 SERVINGS

- 1 can (14½ ounces) pitted tart cherries, undrained
- 1 cup sugar, divided
- ½ cup water
- 1 cup all-purpose flour
- 1 teaspoon baking powder
- ½ teaspoon grated lemon peel
  Dash salt
- ⅓ cup milk
- 3 tablespoons butter, melted

1. In a large saucepan, combine the cherries with juice, ¾ cup sugar and water; bring to a boil. Reduce heat; cover and simmer.

2. Meanwhile, in a small bowl, combine the flour, baking powder, lemon peel, salt and remaining sugar. Stir in milk and butter just until moistened.

3. Drop by tablespoonfuls onto simmering cherry mixture. Cover and simmer for 20 minutes or until a toothpick inserted in a dumpling comes out clean (do not lift the cover while simmering).

PER SERVING *1 serving equals 216 cal., 5 g fat (3 g sat. fat), 12 mg chol., 107 mg sodium, 42 g carb., 1 g fiber, 2 g pro.*

Peppermint Meringues F S C M

Green and red swirls set these whimsical delights apart from any other meringue recipe. They look like they came straight from Candy Land! Each melt-in-your-mouth bite packs just the right amount of refreshing peppermint flavor to perfectly balance the bottom layer of chocolate.

—TASTE OF HOME TEST KITCHEN

PREP: 45 MIN. + STANDING
BAKE: 40 MIN. + STANDING
MAKES: 6 DOZEN

- 4 large egg whites
- ½ teaspoon cream of tartar
- ½ teaspoon peppermint extract

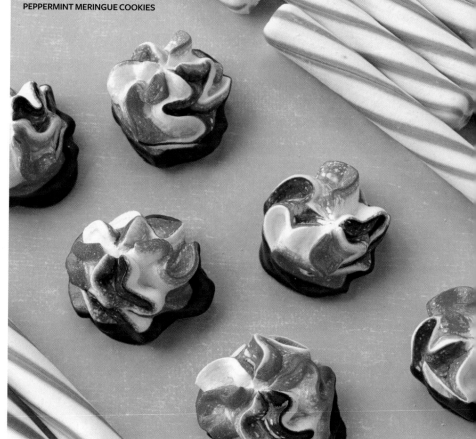

PEPPERMINT MERINGUE COOKIES

- ¼ teaspoon salt
- 1 cup sugar
  Red and green paste food coloring, optional
- 6 ounces dark chocolate candy coating, chopped

1. Place egg whites in a large bowl; let stand at room temperature for 30 minutes. Add the cream of tartar, peppermint extract and salt; beat on medium speed until soft peaks form. Gradually add sugar, 1 tablespoon at a time, beating on high until stiff glossy peaks form and sugar is dissolved.

2. If desired, using a new small paintbrush, paint four alternating red and green stripes inside a pastry bag fitted with a #2D star tip. Fill bag with meringue. Pipe 1½-in.-diameter cookies onto parchment paper-lined baking sheets, repainting the stripes if necessary.

3. Bake at 250° for 40-45 minutes or until set and dry. Turn oven off; leave meringues in oven for 1½ hours. Carefully remove meringues from parchment paper.

4. In a microwave, melt candy coating; stir until smooth. Dip bottoms of meringues into melted coating, allowing excess to drip off. Place on waxed paper; let stand until set. Store in an airtight container.

PER SERVING *1 cookie equals 24 cal., 1 g fat (1 g sat. fat), trace chol., 11 mg sodium, 4 g carb., 0 fiber, trace pro.*

HOW TO

TEST FOR STIFF PEAKS

Stiff peaks are achieved when the egg whites stand up in points, rather than curling over. If you tilt the bowl, the whites shouldn't move. Sugar is dissolved when the mixture feels silky smooth between your fingers.

Vanilla Meringue Cookies F S C M

PREP: 20 MIN. • **BAKE:** 40 MIN. + STANDING
MAKES: ABOUT 5 DOZEN

- 3 **large egg whites**
- 1½ **teaspoons clear or regular vanilla extract**
- ¼ **teaspoon cream of tartar**
  Dash salt
- ⅔ **cup sugar**

1. Place egg whites in a small bowl; let stand at room temperature for 30 minutes.

2. Preheat oven to 250°. Add vanilla, cream of tartar and salt to egg whites; beat on medium speed until foamy. Gradually add sugar, 1 tablespoon at a time, beating on high after each addition until sugar is dissolved. Continue beating until stiff glossy peaks form, about 7 minutes.

3. Cut a small hole in the tip of a pastry bag or in a corner of a food-safe plastic bag; insert a #32 star tip. Transfer meringue to the bag. Pipe 1¼-in.-diameter cookies 2 in. apart onto parchment paper-lined baking sheets.

4. Bake 40-45 minutes or until firm to the touch. Turn off oven (do not open oven door); leave meringues in oven 1 hour. Remove from oven; cool completely on baking sheets. Remove meringues from paper; store in an airtight container at room temperature.

PER SERVING *1 cookie equals 10 cal., trace fat (0 sat. fat), 0 chol., 5 mg sodium, 2 g carb., 0 fiber, trace pro.*
Diabetic Exchange: *Free food.*

Peanut Butter Snack Bars S M

Store-bought granola bars are full of sugar, so I came up with this nutritious version that my kids love. We like to bring these snacks on road trips.

—**NETTIE HOGAN** WADSWORTH, OH

PREP: 25 MIN. + COOLING
MAKES: 3 DOZEN

- 3¼ **cups Kashi Heart to Heart honey toasted oat cereal**
- 2¾ **cups old-fashioned oats**
- 1 **cup unblanched almonds**
- ½ **cup sunflower kernels**
- ¼ **cup ground flaxseed**
- ¼ **cup uncooked oat bran cereal**
- ¼ **cup wheat bran**
- ¼ **cup whole flaxseed**
- 3 **tablespoons sesame seeds**
- 2 **cups creamy peanut butter**
- 1½ **cups honey**
- 1 **teaspoon vanilla extract**

1. In a large bowl, combine the first nine ingredients. In a small saucepan, combine peanut butter and honey. Cook over medium heat until peanut butter is melted, stirring occasionally. Remove from the heat. Stir in vanilla. Pour over cereal mixture; mix well.

2. Transfer to a greased 15x10x1-in. baking pan; gently press into pan. Cool completely. Cut into bars. Store in an airtight container.

NOTE *Look for uncooked oat bran cereal near the hot cereals or in the natural foods section.*

PER SERVING *1 bar equals 215 cal., 12 g fat (2 g sat. fat), 0 chol., 87 mg sodium, 24 g carb., 3 g fiber, 7 g pro.*
Diabetic Exchanges: *1½ starch, 1 high-fat meat.*

PEANUT BUTTER SNACK BARS

General Recipe Index

This index lists every recipe by food category, major ingredient and/or cooking method, so you can easily locate recipes that suit your needs.

• *Table-ready in 30 minutes or less.*

APPETIZERS & SNACKS

•Artichoke Hummus, 17
Avocado Endive Cups with Salsa, 10
Balsamic-Cranberry Potato Bites, 19
•Blueberry Salsa, 13
Cilantro Shrimp Cups, 15
•Crab Rangoon Canapes, 12
•Crabbie Phyllo Cups, 13
Curried Chicken Meatball Wraps, 17
Festive Cherry Tomatoes, 18
•Garlicky Herbed Shrimp, 16
•Grilled Chicken, Mango &
    Blue Cheese Tortillas, 12
Grilled Leek Dip, 8
•Homemade Guacamole, 18
Meatballs in Cherry Sauce, 9
•Mocha Pumpkin Seeds, 14
Pea Soup Shooters, 14
Roasted Grape Crostini, 16
Sesame-Beef Pot Stickers, 8
•Spring Pea Crostini, 19
Thyme-Sea Salt Crackers, 15
•Tomato-Squash Appetizer Pizza, 10
Tropical Island Shrimp Kabobs, 9
•Wicked Deviled Eggs, 13

APPLES

•Apple & Spice Pork Tenderloin, 149
Apple Pie Oatmeal Dessert, 91
Apple Rhubarb Crumb Pie, 221
Apple Roasted Pork with Cherry
    Balsamic Glaze, 161
•Broccoli & Apple Salad, 41
Caramel Apple Coffee Cake with
    Walnuts, 71
•Ginger-Kale Smoothies, 80
Gran's Apple Cake, 214
•Grilled Apple Pizza, 241
Maple Apple Baked Oatmeal, 76
Orange-Glazed Pork with Sweet
    Potatoes, 163
•Waldorf Turkey Salad, 132
•Wendy's Apple Pomegranate
    Salad, 49

ARTICHOKES

•Artichoke Hummus, 17
Artichoke Ratatouille Chicken, 117
Spinach & Artichoke Pizza, 193

ARUGULA

•Arugula & Brown Rice Salad, 191

•Arugula Salad with Shaved
    Parmesan, 46
•Summer Squash & Watermelon
    Salad, 51

ASPARAGUS

Fresh Asparagus Soup, 29
•Honey-Tarragon Grilled
    Asparagus, 57
•Poached Eggs with Tarragon
    Asparagus, 77
•Roasted Asparagus with Feta, 65
Rosemary Roasted Potatoes and
    Asparagus, 61

AVOCADOS

Avocado Endive Cups with Salsa, 10
•Chipotle Lime Avocado Salad, 44
Festive Cherry Tomatoes, 18
•Homemade Guacamole, 18

BACON & PANCETTA

Balsamic-Cranberry Potato Bites, 19
•Broccoli with Garlic, Bacon &
    Parmesan, 64
Hearty Vegetable Lentil Soup, 33
Roasted Balsamic Brussels Sprouts
    with Pancetta, 59

BANANAS

•Banana Boats, 238
Banana-Pineapple Cream Pies, 216
•Brown Sugar & Banana Oatmeal, 81
Favorite Banana Chip Muffins, 205
•Fluffy Banana Pancakes, 69
Frozen Yogurt Fruit Pops, 236

BARS & BROWNIES

Cream Cheese Swirl Brownies, 236
Date Oat Bars, 234
Peanut Butter Snack Bars, 243

BEANS

•Artichoke Hummus, 17
•Arugula & Brown Rice Salad, 191
Balsamic Three-Bean Salad, 39
Black Bean Chip & Dip Burgers, 193
Black Bean-Tomato Chili, 30
Black Bean Turkey Enchiladas, 137
•Black Beans with Bell Peppers
    & Rice, 196
•Bow Tie & Spinach Salad, 196

•Jalapeno Jelly-Glazed Pork
    Chops, 162
Moroccan Chickpea Stew, 35
Mushroom-Bean Bourguignon, 187
•Pinto Bean Tostadas, 194
Sausage & Greens Soup, 25
Slow-Cooked Chicken Chili, 87
Spiced Turkey Tenderloin, 142
Spicy Sweet Potato Kale Soup, 31
•Sweet Potatoes with Cilantro Black
    Beans, 187
•Tomato & Garlic Butter Bean
    Dinner, 190
Turkey Pinto Bean Salad with
    Southern Molasses Dressing, 142
•Vegetarian Bean Tacos, 189
•Whole Wheat Orzo Salad, 190

BEEF (ALSO SEE GROUND BEEF)

Main Dishes
All-Day Brisket with Potatoes, 88
Easy & Elegant Tenderloin Roast, 96
Easy Marinated Flank Steak, 103
•Fajita Skillet, 104
•Feta Steak Tacos, 105
Grilled Southwestern Steak
    Salad, 107
Italian Crumb-Crusted Beef
    Roast, 103
Mexican Shredded Beef Wraps, 90
•Open-Faced Roast Beef
    Sandwiches, 99
•Pepper Steak with Potatoes, 103
Slow Cooker French Dip
    Sandwiches, 90
Spicy Beef & Pepper Stir-Fry, 99
Spring Herb Roast, 85
Steaks with Poblano Relish, 102
•Sublime Lime Beef, 98
Teriyaki Beef Stew, 89
Vegetable Steak Kabobs, 106
Soup
Hearty Beef & Sweet Potato Stew, 34

BEVERAGES

•Apple Spiced Tea, 70
•Blackberry Smoothies, 80
•Ginger-Kale Smoothies, 80

BLACKBERRIES

Blackberry Nectarine Pie, 218
•Blackberry Smoothies, 80

•Blackberry-Topped Sponge
Cakes, 223
Double Berry Quick Bread, 201

BLUEBERRIES
•Blueberry Salsa, 13
•Fruit & Granola Crisp with
Yogurt, 235
Lemon Blueberry Cornmeal
Cake, 218
Skillet Blueberry Slump, 234

BREADS (SEE CORN BREAD &
CORNMEAL; MUFFINS; QUICK BREADS
& BISCUITS; YEAST BREADS & ROLLS)

BREAKFAST & BRUNCH
(ALSO SEE BEVERAGES)
Breads
•Bagel with a Veggie Schmear, 74
Cranberry-Walnut Toasting
Bread, 211
Cereals
•Brown Sugar & Banana Oatmeal, 81
Cool Summertime Oatmeal, 68
Get-Up-and-Go Granola, 78
Maple Apple Baked Oatmeal, 76
Coffee Cakes
Caramel Apple Coffee Cake with
Walnuts, 71
Cinnamon-Sugar Coffee Cake, 69
King Cake with Cream Cheese
Filling, 224
Egg Dishes
Basil Vegetable Strata, 75
Beef, Potato & Egg Bake, 79
•Curry Scramble, 74
•English Muffin Egg Sandwich, 70
•Fiesta Time Omelet, 76
Mini Italian Frittatas, 77
•Poached Eggs with Tarragon
Asparagus, 77
•Potato-Cheddar Frittata, 80
Sausage-Egg Burritos, 72
•Sausage-Sweet Potato Hash &
Eggs, 68
Fruit
Fresh Fruit Combo, 78
•Grapes with Lemon-Honey
Yogurt, 71
Meat
Turkey Sausage Patties, 81
Pancakes, Waffles & French Toast
•Cocoa Pancakes, 81
•Crisp Chocolate Chip Waffles, 79
•Crunchy French Toast, 75
•Fluffy Banana Pancakes, 69
Raspberry Peach Puff Pancake, 72

BROCCOLI
•Broccoli & Apple Salad, 41
•Broccoli & Potato Soup, 25
•Broccoli, Rice and Sausage
Dinner, 133
•Broccoli with Garlic, Bacon &
Parmesan, 64
•Sausage Orecchiette Pasta, 141

BRUSSELS SPROUTS
Roasted Balsamic Brussels Sprouts
with Pancetta, 59
•Shredded Gingered Brussels
Sprouts, 64

BURGERS
•BBQ Yumburgers, 105
Black Bean Chip & Dip Burgers, 193
Garlic-Herb Salmon Sliders, 166
•Mushroom Burgers, 184
Spinach & Feta Burgers, 98
Sun-Dried Tomato Burgers, 133
•Turkey Burgers with Peach
Mayo, 141

CABBAGE & COLE SLAW MIX
•Chinese Chicken Salad, 121
Thai Chicken and Slaw, 118
Zesty Coleslaw, 47

CAKES & CUPCAKES
•Blackberry-Topped Sponge
Cakes, 223
Carrot Cupcakes with Cream
Cheese Frosting, 214
Chocolate-Glazed Cupcakes, 219
Cranberry-Orange Snack Cake, 219
Gran's Apple Cake, 214
•Grilled Angel Food Cake with
Strawberries, 226
King Cake with Cream Cheese
Filling, 224
Lemon Blueberry Cornmeal
Cake, 218
Orange Pound Cake with Cranberry
Compote, 225
Pear-Cranberry Gingerbread
Cake, 222
Pumpkin Chip Cake with
Walnuts, 217
Rosy Rhubarb Upside-Down
Cake, 215
Sue's Chocolate Zucchini Cake, 216
Vanilla Angel Food Cake, 223

CARROTS
Carrot Cupcakes with Cream Cheese
Frosting, 214

•Honey & Ginger Glazed Carrots, 54
Mushroom-Bean Bourguignon, 187
Stovetop Tarragon Chicken, 126
Sunday Roast Chicken, 111

CAULIFLOWER
Cheddar Cauliflower Soup, 27
•Faux Potato Salad, 51
•Pumpkin & Cauliflower Garlic
Mash, 65
Roasted Cauliflower with Tahini
Yogurt Sauce, 62

CHEESE (ALSO SEE CREAM CHEESE)
•Arugula Salad with Shaved
Parmesan, 46
Black Bean Turkey Enchiladas, 137
•Broccoli with Garlic, Bacon &
Parmesan, 64
Cheddar Cauliflower Soup, 27
Cheese Manicotti, 195
•Cheesy Chive Potatoes, 54
Cuban-Style Pork Chops, 154
•Fiesta Time Omelet, 76
•Grilled Chicken, Mango &
Blue Cheese Tortillas, 12
Herb Garden Lasagnas, 197
•Italian Sausage and Provolone
Skewers, 128
•Italian Turkey Skillet, 138
Mini Italian Frittatas, 77
•Parmesan-Butternut Squash, 63
•Ricotta-Stuffed Portobello
Mushrooms, 189
•Roasted Asparagus with Feta, 65
Spinach & Artichoke Pizza, 193
Spinach & Feta Burgers, 98
Stacked Vegetables and Ravioli, 191
Turkey Sausage Zucchini Boats, 136
•Whole Wheat Orzo Salad, 190

CHERRIES
Cherry Dumplings, 242
Rustic Pear Tart, 224

CHICKEN & CHICKEN
SAUSAGE
Appetizers
Curried Chicken Meatball Wraps, 17
•Grilled Chicken, Mango &
Blue Cheese Tortillas, 12
Main Dishes
Apple-Marinated Chicken &
Vegetables, 115
Artichoke Ratatouille Chicken, 117
Asian Chicken Thighs, 125
•Balsamic Chicken with Roasted
Tomatoes, 118

CHICKEN & CHICKEN SAUSAGE

Main Dishes (continued)
Basil Chicken, 124
Caribbean Delight, 114
•Chicken & Garlic with Fresh Herbs, 123
Chicken Cordon Bleu Stroganoff, 116
•Chicken Sausages with Polenta, 119
•Chicken Strips Milano, 122
•Chicken with Mandarin Salsa, 124
•Chicken with Peach-Cucumber Salsa, 111
Chicken with Three-Citrus Topping, 127
•Chinese Chicken Salad, 121
•Fajita Skillet, 104
•Garlic Chicken Rigatoni, 114
Grilled Tomatillo Chicken for Two, 119
•Honey-Lemon Chicken Enchiladas, 121
•In-a-Pinch Chicken & Spinach, 126
•Italian Sausage and Provolone Skewers, 128
•Lime Chicken with Salsa Verde Sour Cream, 127
Mediterranean Baked Chicken with Lemon, 123
•Mediterranean Orzo Chicken Salad, 115
•Mushroom & Herb Chicken, 129
Oven-Fried Chicken Drumsticks, 112
Pan-Roasted Chicken and Vegetables, 113
Sausage & Pepper Pizza, 128
Sausage Chicken Jambalaya, 116
•Skillet Chicken with Olives, 110
Slow Cooker Mushroom Chicken & Peas, 92
•Speedy Chicken Marsala, 110
•Spicy Barbecued Chicken, 112
Spicy Roasted Sausage, Potatoes and Peppers, 125
•Spring Chicken and Pea Salad, 122
Stovetop Tarragon Chicken, 126
•Summer Splash Chicken Salad, 129
Sunday Roast Chicken, 111
Tangy Orange Chicken Thighs, 89
•Tapenade-Stuffed Chicken Breasts, 117
Thai Chicken and Slaw, 118
Soups
Andouille Sausage Soup, 30
Brown Rice Mulligatawny, 24
Ginger Chicken Noodle Soup, 93
Mediterranean Chicken Orzo Soup, 33
Slow-Cooked Chicken Chili, 87

CHILI

Black Bean-Tomato Chili, 30
Slow-Cooked Chicken Chili, 87

CHOCOLATE

•Banana Boats, 238
•Chocolate Chip-Cranberry Scones, 202
Chocolate-Dipped Strawberry Meringue Roses, 231
Chocolate Eggnog Pie, 225
Chocolate-Glazed Cupcakes, 219
•Cocoa Pancakes, 81
Cream Cheese Swirl Brownies, 236
•Crisp Chocolate Chip Waffles, 79
Dark Chocolate Chip Zucchini Bread, 206
Favorite Banana Chip Muffins, 205
•Mocha Pumpkin Seeds, 14
Pumpkin Chip Cake with Walnuts, 217
Slow Cooker Lava Cake, 85
Sue's Chocolate Zucchini Cake, 216
Warm Chocolate Melting Cups, 238

COCONUT & COCONUT MILK

Coconut Curry Vegetable Soup, 23
Coconut-Mango Tilapia, 167
•Crunchy Apricot-Coconut Balls, 232
Spicy Beef & Pepper Stir-Fry, 99

CONDIMENT

Sweet Onion & Red Bell Pepper Topping, 91

COOKIES

Chocolate-Dipped Strawberry Meringue Roses, 231
•Crunchy Apricot-Coconut Balls, 232
Gluten-Free Chocolate Cake Cookies, 240
Peppermint Meringues, 242
Vanilla Meringue Cookies, 243

CORN

•Cilantro Shrimp & Rice, 174
•Confetti Corn, 62
•Confetti Succotash, 65
Corn Chowder, 35
Layered Grilled Corn Salad, 38
Southwest-Style Shepherd's Pie, 144
•Spicy Pumpkin & Corn Soup, 22

CORN BREAD & CORNMEAL

Gluten-Free Anadama Bread, 205
Herb & Olive Oil Corn Bread, 201
Lemon Blueberry Cornmeal Cake, 218
No-Knead Harvest Bread, 210

CRANBERRIES

Balsamic-Cranberry Potato Bites, 19
•Chocolate Chip-Cranberry Scones, 202
Cranberry-Orange Snack Cake, 219
•Cranberry Sweet-and-Sour Pork, 150
Cranberry-Walnut Toasting Bread, 211
•Lemon Cranberry Quinoa Salad, 42
Orange Pound Cake with Cranberry Compote, 225
Pear-Cranberry Gingerbread Cake, 222
Pork Tenderloin with Fennel and Cranberries, 157
Turkey with Cranberry Sauce, 84

CREAM CHEESE

•Bagel with a Veggie Schmear, 74
Carrot Cupcakes with Cream Cheese Frosting, 214
•Crab Rangoon Canapes, 12
Cream Cheese Swirl Brownies, 236
Gran's Apple Cake, 214
King Cake with Cream Cheese Filling, 224
Lime Basil Pie, 215

CUCUMBERS

•Chicken with Peach-Cucumber Salsa, 111
•Crab Rangoon Canapes, 12
Crisp & Spicy Cucumber Salad, 44

DESSERTS (ALSO SEE BARS & BROWNIES; CAKES & CUPCAKES; COOKIES; PIES & TARTS)

Apple Pie Oatmeal Dessert, 91
Baked Elephant Ears, 233
•Banana Boats, 238
Cardamom Yogurt Pudding with Honeyed Oranges, 233
Cherry Dumplings, 242
Frozen Greek Vanilla Yogurt, 231
Frozen Yogurt Fruit Pops, 236
•Fruit & Granola Crisp with Yogurt, 235
•Grilled Apple Pizza, 241
•Grilled Honey-Balsamic Fruit, 230
Must-Have Tiramisu, 230
Pear Sorbet, 235
Plum Crisp, 240
Pumpkin Flans, 239
Raspberry Sorbet, 232
Rhubarb Strawberry Granita, 235
•Saucy Spiced Pears, 239
Skillet Blueberry Slump, 234
Slow Cooker Lava Cake, 85
Warm Chocolate Melting Cups, 238

EGGS

Basil Vegetable Strata, 75
Beef, Potato & Egg Bake, 79
•Crunchy French Toast, 75
•Curry Scramble, 74
•English Muffin Egg Sandwich, 70
•Fiesta Time Omelet, 76
Mini Italian Frittatas, 77
•Poached Eggs with Tarragon
    Asparagus, 77
•Potato-Cheddar Frittata, 80
Sausage-Egg Burritos, 72
•Sausage-Sweet Potato Hash &
    Eggs, 68
•Wicked Deviled Eggs, 13

FISH (ALSO SEE SEAFOOD)

•Asian Snapper with Capers, 168
Cioppino-Style Soup, 24
Coconut-Mango Tilapia, 167
•Cod Delight, 179
Cozumel Red Snapper Veracruz, 175
•Crispy Fish & Chips, 170
Garlic-Herb Salmon Sliders, 166
•Lemon Parsley Swordfish, 177
•Lime-Cilantro Tilapia, 170
•Orzo-Tuna Salad with Tomatoes, 173
•Parsley-Crusted Cod, 176
•Pesto Grilled Salmon, 180
•Poached Salmon with Dill &
    Turmeric, 174
•Quick Nicoise Salad, 173
•Salmon with Balsamic Orange
    Sauce, 175
•Sole Fillets in Lemon Butter, 167
•Speedy Salmon Stir-Fry, 178
•Teriyaki Salmon, 177
•Tilapia & Veggies with Red Pepper
    Sauce, 178
•Tilapia with Fiesta Rice, 168
Tuna Veggie Kabobs, 169

FRUIT (ALSO SEE SPECIFIC KINDS)

Blackberry Nectarine Pie, 218
Chicken with Three-Citrus
    Topping, 127
•Crunchy Apricot-Coconut
    Balls, 232
Date Oat Bars, 234
Fresh Fruit Combo, 78
Minted Fruit Salad, 47
Plum Crisp, 240
•Wendy's Apple Pomegranate
    Salad, 49

GRAPES

•Grapes with Lemon-Honey
    Yogurt, 71

Roasted Grape Crostini, 16
•Waldorf Turkey Salad, 132

GREEN BEANS

Balsamic Three-Bean Salad, 39
Garlic-Sesame Green Beans, 56
•Green Beans with Shallots, 62
Roasted Green Vegetable Medley, 58
•Sauteed Radishes with
    Green Beans, 55

GRILLED RECIPES

Appetizers
•Grilled Chicken, Mango &
    Blue Cheese Tortillas, 12
Grilled Leek Dip, 8

Bread
•Grilled Garden Veggie
    Flatbread, 200

Desserts
•Banana Boats, 238
•Grilled Angel Food Cake with
    Strawberries, 226
•Grilled Apple Pizza, 241
•Grilled Honey-Balsamic
    Fruit, 230

Main Dishes
Apple-Marinated Chicken &
    Vegetables, 115
Basil Chicken, 124
•BBQ Yumburgers, 105
Black Bean Chip & Dip Burgers, 193
Caribbean Delight, 114
•Chicken with Peach-Cucumber
    Salsa, 111
Chicken with Three-Citrus
    Topping, 127
Coconut-Mango Tilapia, 167
Cuban-Style Pork Chops, 154
Easy Marinated Flank Steak, 103
Garlic-Herb Salmon Sliders, 166
Grilled Beef Chimichangas, 100
Grilled Dijon Pork Roast, 156
Grilled Pork Noodle Salad, 155
•Grilled Pork with Spicy Pineapple
    Salsa, 160
Grilled Shrimp & Tomato Salad, 169
Grilled Shrimp Scampi, 176
Grilled Southwestern Steak
    Salad, 107
Grilled Tomatillo Chicken for
    Two, 119

GROUND BEEF

•BBQ Yumburgers, 105
Beef & Bulgur-Stuffed Zucchini
    Boats, 97
Beef, Potato & Egg Bake, 79

•Cajun Beef & Rice, 99
Garden Vegetable Beef Soup, 29
Gluten-Free Skillet Pasta, 104
Grilled Beef Chimichangas, 100
•Italian Beef and Shells, 100
•Korean Beef and Rice, 96
Meatballs in Cherry Sauce, 9
Mini Barbecue Meat Loaves, 100
Orange Beef Lettuce Wraps, 97
Power Lasagna, 102
Salisbury Steak Supreme, 107
Sesame-Beef Pot Stickers, 8
Spinach & Feta Burgers, 98
•Tasty Tacos, 96
•West Coast Snappy Joes, 106

HAM

•Ham Pasta Toss, 154
Maple-Pecan Glazed Ham, 159
Roasted Sweet Potato &
    Prosciutto Salad, 38
Slow Cooker Split Pea Soup, 88

HERBS

Basil
Basil Chicken, 124
Basil Crab Cakes, 181
Basil Vegetable Strata, 75
Brown Rice, Tomato &
    Basil Salad, 43
Layered Grilled Corn Salad, 38
Lime Basil Pie, 215

Cilantro
•Cilantro Shrimp & Rice, 174
Cilantro Shrimp Cups, 15
Curried Chicken Meatball Wraps, 17
•Homemade Guacamole, 18
•Lime-Cilantro Tilapia, 170
•Sweet Potatoes with Cilantro
    Black Beans, 187
Tropical Island Shrimp Kabobs, 9

Mint
•All-Spiced Up Raspberry and
    Mushroom Salad, 48
Minted Fruit Salad, 47
Pea Soup Shooters, 14

Other
•Artichoke Hummus, 17
•Cheesy Chive Potatoes, 54
Cherry Tomato Salad, 46
•Chicken & Garlic with
    Fresh Herbs, 123
Garlic-Herb Salmon Sliders, 166
•Garlicky Herbed Shrimp, 16
•Heirloom Tomato &
    Zucchini Salad, 50
Herb & Olive Oil Corn Bread, 201
Herb & Sun-Dried Tomato Muffins, 204

HERBS

Other (continued)
Herb Garden Lasagnas, 197
Herb-Rubbed Turkey, 138
Herbed Potato Packet, 57
•Honey-Tarragon Grilled
  Asparagus, 57
•Mushroom & Herb Chicken, 129
•Poached Eggs with Tarragon
  Asparagus, 77
•Pumpkin & Cauliflower Garlic
  Mash, 65
Roasted Green Vegetable Medley, 58
Rosemary Roasted Potatoes and
  Asparagus, 61
•Rosemary-Thyme Lamb
  Chops, 153
Thyme-Sea Salt Crackers, 15
•Tomato-Squash Appetizer Pizza, 10
Turkey-Thyme Stuffed Peppers, 139

Parsley
Cherry Tomato Salad, 46
•Lemon Parsley Swordfish, 177
•Parsley-Crusted Cod, 176
Parsley Smashed Potatoes, 93
•Spring Pea Crostini, 19
Honey Cardamom Yogurt Pudding
  with Honeyed Oranges, 233
Cool Summertime Oatmeal, 68
•Grapes with Lemon-Honey
  Yogurt, 71
•Grilled Honey-Balsamic Fruit, 230
•Honey & Ginger Glazed Carrots, 54
Honey-Ginger Turkey Kabobs, 139
•Honey-Lemon Chicken
  Enchiladas, 121
Honey Spice Bread, 210
Honey-Squash Dinner Rolls, 211
•Honey-Tarragon Grilled
  Asparagus, 57
Peanut Butter Snack Bars, 243
Tangy Lamb Tagine, 92

KALE
•Ginger-Kale Smoothies, 80
Spicy Sweet Potato Kale Soup, 31

LAMB
Tangy Lamb Tagine, 92

LEMON
Chicken with Three-Citrus
  Topping, 127

•Honey-Lemon Chicken
  Enchiladas, 121
Lemon Blueberry Cornmeal
  Cake, 218
•Lemon Cranberry Quinoa Salad, 42
•Lemon-Garlic Pork Chops, 149
Lemon Meringue Muffins, 207
•Lemon Parsley Swordfish, 177
Mediterranean Baked Chicken with
  Lemon, 123
Roasted Green Vegetable Medley, 58
•Sole Fillets in Lemon Butter, 167

LETTUCE (ALSO SEE ARUGULA)
•All-Spiced Up Raspberry and
  Mushroom Salad, 48
Curried Chicken Meatball Wraps, 17
•Mixed Greens with Orange-Ginger
  Vinaigrette, 40
Orange Beef Lettuce Wraps, 97
•Pinto Bean Tostadas, 194
•Shrimp Lettuce Wraps, 179
Southwest Shredded Pork Salad, 87
•Turkey Verde Lettuce Wraps, 143

LIME
•Chipotle Lime Avocado Salad, 44
•Feta Steak Tacos, 105
Lime Basil Pie, 215
•Lime Chicken with Salsa Verde
  Sour Cream, 127
•Lime-Cilantro Tilapia, 170
•Sublime Lime Beef, 98

LOW-CARB MAIN DISHES
•Apple & Spice Pork Tenderloin, 149
Artichoke Ratatouille Chicken, 117
Asian Chicken Thighs, 125
Basil Chicken, 124
Basil Crab Cakes, 181
Caribbean Delight, 114
•Chicken & Garlic with Fresh
  Herbs, 123
•Cod Delight, 179
Cozumel Red Snapper Veracruz, 175
Cuban-Style Pork Chops, 154
Easy & Elegant Tenderloin Roast, 96
Easy Marinated Flank Steak, 103
Grilled Dijon Pork Roast, 156
Grilled Shrimp & Tomato Salad, 169
Grilled Shrimp Scampi, 176
Grilled Tomatillo Chicken for
  Two, 119
Hearty Pork Chops, 162
Herbed-Rubbed Turkey, 138
•In-a-Pinch Chicken & Spinach, 126
Italian Crumb-Crusted Beef
  Roast, 103

•Italian Sausage and Provolone
  Skewers, 128
•Lemon-Garlic Pork Chops, 149
•Lemon Parsley Swordfish, 177
•Lime Chicken with Salsa Verde
  Sour Cream, 127
•Lime-Cilantro Tilapia, 170
Mediterranean Baked Chicken with
  Lemon, 123
Mini Barbecue Meat Loaves, 100
•Mushroom & Herb Chicken, 129
•Open-Faced Roast Beef
  Sandwiches, 99
Oven-Fried Chicken Drumsticks, 112
•Parmesan Pork Chops with
  Spinach Salad, 157
•Parsley-Crusted Cod, 176
•Pesto Grilled Salmon, 180
•Pizzaiola Chops, 160
•Pork Chops & Mushrooms, 161
•Raspberry Pork Medallions, 158
•Ricotta-Stuffed Portobello
  Mushrooms, 189
•Rosemary-Thyme Lamb
  Chops, 153
Salisbury Steak Supreme, 107
•Salmon with Balsamic Orange
  Sauce, 175
•Scallops with Chipotle-Orange
  Sauce, 172
•Skillet Chicken with Olives, 110
•Sole Fillets in Lemon Butter, 167
Southwest Shredded Pork Salad, 87
Spice-Brined Pork Roast, 153
•Spicy Barbecued Chicken, 112
Spicy Beef & Pepper Stir-Fry, 99
•Spicy Tomato Pork Chops, 158
•Spring Chicken and Pea Salad, 122
Spring Herb Roast, 85
Steaks with Poblano Relish, 102
Tangy Orange Chicken Thighs, 89
•Tapenade-Stuffed Chicken
  Breasts, 117
•Teriyaki Salmon, 177
•Tilapia & Veggies with Red Pepper
  Sauce, 178
Tuna Veggie Kabobs, 169
Turkey Sausage Zucchini Boats, 136
•Turkey Verde Lettuce Wraps, 143
Turkey with Cranberry Sauce, 84
Vegetable Steak Kabobs, 106

LOW-FAT MAIN DISHES
Black Bean Chip & Dip Burgers, 193
Chicken with Three-Citrus
  Topping, 127
•Tilapia & Veggies with Red Pepper
  Sauce, 178

•Tilapia with Fiesta Rice, 168
Turkey with Cranberry Sauce, 84

LOW-SODIUM MAIN DISHES
Coconut-Mango Tilapia, 167
Herbed-Rubbed Turkey, 138
•Molasses-Glazed Pork Chops, 148
•Pork & Vegetable Spring Rolls, 148
Vegetable Steak Kabobs, 106

MANGOES
Coconut-Mango Tilapia, 167
•Grilled Chicken, Mango &
    Blue Cheese Tortillas, 12
•Mango-Peach Smoothies, 79
•Pork & Mango Stir-Fry, 159
Tropical Island Shrimp Kabobs, 9

MEAT LOAVES & MEATBALLS
Curried Chicken Meatball Wraps, 17
Meatballs in Cherry Sauce, 9
Mini Barbecue Meat Loaves, 100

MEATLESS RECIPES
Burgers
Black Bean Chip & Dip Burgers, 193
•Mushroom Burgers, 184
Main Dishes
•Arugula & Brown Rice Salad, 191
•Black Beans with Bell Peppers &
    Rice, 196
•Bow Tie & Spinach Salad, 196
Brown Rice Chutney Salad, 194
Cheese Manicotti, 195
•Curried Rice & Noodles, 185
Garden Harvest Spaghetti
    Squash, 188
Herb Garden Lasagnas, 197
Mushroom-Bean Bourguignon, 187
Mushroom Bolognese with
    Whole Wheat Pasta, 186
•Pinto Bean Tostadas, 194
•Portobello Fajitas, 185
•Ricotta-Stuffed Portobello
    Mushrooms, 189
Spicy Orange Quinoa, 186
Spinach & Artichoke Pizza, 193
Stacked Vegetables and Ravioli, 191
•Strawberry-Quinoa Spinach
    Salad, 184
•Sweet Potatoes with Cilantro
    Black Beans, 187
•Tomato & Garlic Butter Bean
    Dinner, 190
•Vegetarian Bean Tacos, 189
•Whole Wheat Orzo Salad, 190
Sandwich
•Mediterranean Vegetable Pitas, 195

MELON
Minted Fruit Salad, 47
•Summer Squash & Watermelon
    Salad, 51
•Sunny Strawberry & Cantaloupe
    Salad, 41

MOLASSES
•Molasses-Glazed Pork Chops, 148
Pear-Cranberry Gingerbread
    Cake, 222
Turkey Pinto Bean Salad with
    Southern Molasses Dressing, 142

MUFFINS
Favorite Banana Chip Muffins, 205
Herb & Sun-Dried Tomato
    Muffins, 204
Lemon Meringue Muffins, 207
Peanut Butter & Jam Muffins, 202

MUSHROOMS
•All-Spiced Up Raspberry and
    Mushroom Salad, 48
Garden Harvest Spaghetti
    Squash, 188
Gluten-Free Skillet Pasta, 104
Hearty Beef & Sweet Potato Stew, 34
•Mushroom & Herb Chicken, 129
•Mushroom & Pea Rice Pilaf, 58
Mushroom-Bean Bourguignon, 187
Mushroom Bolognese with
    Whole Wheat Pasta, 186
•Mushroom Burgers, 184
•Pizzaiola Chops, 160
•Pork Chops & Mushrooms, 161
•Portobello Fajitas, 185
•Ricotta-Stuffed Portobello
    Mushrooms, 189
Salisbury Steak Supreme, 107
Slow Cooker Mushroom Chicken &
    Peas, 92
•Speedy Chicken Marsala, 110
Tuna Veggie Kabobs, 169
Vegetable Steak Kabobs, 106

NOODLES
Chicken Cordon Bleu Stroganoff, 116
Grilled Pork Noodle Salad, 155
•Mushroom & Herb Chicken, 129
Shrimp Pad Thai Soup, 28

NUTS
Brown Rice Chutney Salad, 194
Chocolate Eggnog Pie, 225
Cranberry-Walnut Toasting
    Bread, 211
•Crunchy Apricot-Coconut Balls, 232

Gluten-Free Chocolate Cake
    Cookies, 240
Maple-Pecan Glazed Ham, 159
Pumpkin Chip Cake with
    Walnuts, 217

OATS
Apple Pie Oatmeal Dessert, 91
•Brown Sugar & Banana
    Oatmeal, 81
Cool Summertime Oatmeal, 68
•Crunchy French Toast, 75
Date Oat Bars, 234
Get-Up-and-Go Granola, 78
Maple Apple Baked Oatmeal, 76
Rustic Oatmeal Scones, 208

OLIVES
•Mediterranean Orzo Chicken
    Salad, 115
•Mediterranean Vegetable Pitas, 195
•Skillet Chicken with Olives, 110
•Tapenade-Stuffed Chicken
    Breasts, 117
•Whole Wheat Orzo Salad, 190

ORANGE
Cardamom Yogurt Pudding with
    Honeyed Oranges, 233
•Chicken with Mandarin Salsa, 124
Chicken with Three-Citrus
    Topping, 127
Cranberry-Orange Snack Cake, 219
•Mixed Greens with Orange-Ginger
    Vinaigrette, 40
Orange-Glazed Pork with
    Sweet Potatoes, 163
Orange Pound Cake with Cranberry
    Compote, 225
•Salmon with Balsamic Orange
    Sauce, 175
•Scallops with Chipotle-Orange
    Sauce, 172
Spice-Brined Pork Roast, 153
Spicy Orange Quinoa, 186
Tangy Orange Chicken Thighs, 89

PASTA
Main Dishes
•Bow Tie & Spinach Salad, 196
•Chicken Strips Milano, 122
•Curried Rice & Noodles, 185
•Garlic Chicken Rigatoni, 114
Gluten-Free Skillet Pasta, 104
Gluten-Free Turkey Spaghetti, 135
Grilled Southwestern Steak
    Salad, 107
•Ham Pasta Toss, 154
Herb Garden Lasagnas, 197

PASTA

Main Dishes (*continued*)
- Italian Beef and Shells, 100
- Italian Turkey Skillet, 138
- Mediterranean Orzo Chicken Salad, 115

Mushroom Bolognese with Whole Wheat Pasta, 186
- Orzo-Tuna Salad with Tomatoes, 173
- Pork & Mango Stir-Fry, 159

Power Lasagna, 102
- Sausage Orecchiette Pasta, 141
- Shrimp Piccata, 181
- Speedy Chicken Marsala, 110

Stacked Vegetables and Ravioli, 191
- Turkey Lo Mein, 134
- Whole Wheat Orzo Salad, 190

Side Dishes

Creamy Roasted Garlic & Spinach Orzo, 61

Kasha Varnishkes, 56

Side Salads
- Chilled Shrimp Pasta Salad, 42
- Spring Greek Pasta Salad, 43

Soups

Ginger Chicken Noodle Soup, 93

Mediterranean Chicken Orzo Soup, 33

PEACHES
- Chicken with Peach-Cucumber Salsa, 111
- Fruit & Granola Crisp with Yogurt, 235
- Grilled Honey-Balsamic Fruit, 230

Raspberry Peach Puff Pancake, 72

Raspberry Peach Tart, 221

Slow-Cooked Peach Salsa, 84
- Turkey Burgers with Peach Mayo, 141

PEANUTS & PEANUT BUTTER

Peanut Butter & Jam Muffins, 202

Peanut Butter Snack Bars, 243

Shrimp Pad Thai Soup, 28

PEARS

Pear-Cranberry Gingerbread Cake, 222

Pear Sorbet, 235

Rustic Pear Tart, 224
- Saucy Spiced Pears, 239
- Turkey Salad with Pear Dressing, 144

PEAS

Festive Cherry Tomatoes, 18

Fresh Sugar Snap Pea Salad, 40
- Ham Pasta Toss, 154

- Mushroom & Pea Rice Pilaf, 58

Pea Soup Shooters, 14
- Pork & Mango Stir-Fry, 159

Slow Cooker Mushroom Chicken & Peas, 92

Slow Cooker Split Pea Soup, 88
- Spring Chicken and Pea Salad, 122
- Spring Pea Crostini, 19

Vibrant Black-Eyed Pea Salad, 50

PEPPERS
- Black Beans with Bell Peppers & Rice, 196

Spicy Roasted Sausage, Potatoes and Peppers, 125

Sweet Onion & Red Bell Pepper Topping, 91
- Turkey Lo Mein, 134

Turkey-Thyme Stuffed Peppers, 139

PIES & TARTS

Apple Rhubarb Crumb Pie, 221

Banana-Pineapple Cream Pies, 216

Blackberry Nectarine Pie, 218

Chocolate Eggnog Pie, 225

Lime Basil Pie, 215

Pumpkin Gingersnap Ice Cream Pie, 222

Raspberry Peach Tart, 221

Rustic Pear Tart, 224

Spiced Butternut Squash Pie, 226

PINEAPPLE

Banana-Pineapple Cream Pies, 216
- Caribbean Shrimp & Rice Bowl, 166
- Chinese Chicken Salad, 121
- Grilled Pork with Spicy Pineapple Salsa, 160

Honey-Ginger Turkey Kabobs, 139

Tropical Island Shrimp Kabobs, 9

PIZZAS
- Grilled Apple Pizza, 241

Perfect Pizza Crust, 207

Sausage & Pepper Pizza, 128

Spinach & Artichoke Pizza, 193
- Tomato-Squash Appetizer Pizza, 10

PORK (*ALSO SEE HAM*)

Appetizer

Meatballs in Cherry Sauce, 9

Main Dishes
- Apple & Spice Pork Tenderloin, 149

Apple Roasted Pork with Cherry Balsamic Glaze, 161
- Braised Pork Stew, 151
- Cranberry Sweet-and-Sour Pork, 150

Cuban-Style Pork Chops, 154

Grilled Dijon Pork Roast, 156

Grilled Pork Noodle Salad, 155
- Grilled Pork with Spicy Pineapple Salsa, 160

Hearty Pork Chops, 162
- Jalapeno Jelly-Glazed Pork Chops, 162
- Lemon-Garlic Pork Chops, 149
- Molasses-Glazed Pork Chops, 148

Orange-Glazed Pork with Sweet Potatoes, 163

Pan-Roasted Pork Chops & Potatoes, 150
- Parmesan Pork Chops with Spinach Salad, 157
- Pizzaiola Chops, 160
- Pork & Mango Stir-Fry, 159
- Pork & Vegetable Spring Rolls, 148
- Pork Chops & Mushrooms, 161
- Pork Fried Rice, 155

Pork Tenderloin with Fennel and Cranberries, 157
- Raspberry Pork Medallions, 158
- Rosemary-Thyme Lamb Chops, 153

Southwest Shredded Pork Salad, 87

Spice-Brined Pork Roast, 153
- Spicy Tomato Pork Chops, 158

POTATOES

All-Day Brisket with Potatoes, 88

Andouille Sausage Soup, 30

Balsamic-Cranberry Potato Bites, 19

Beef, Potato & Egg Bake, 79
- Broccoli & Potato Soup, 25
- Cheesy Chive Potatoes, 54

Corn Chowder, 35
- Curry-Roasted Turkey and Potatoes, 134

Garden Bounty Potato Salad, 48

Hearty Vegetable Lentil Soup, 33

Herbed Potato Packet, 57

Orange-Glazed Pork with Sweet Potatoes, 163

Pan-Roasted Chicken and Vegetables, 113

Pan-Roasted Pork Chops & Potatoes, 150

Parsley Smashed Potatoes, 93
- Pepper Steak with Potatoes, 103
- Poached Salmon with Dill & Turmeric, 174
- Potato-Cheddar Frittata, 80

Potato Kugel, 63
- Quick Nicoise Salad, 173

Rosemary Roasted Potatoes and Asparagus, 61

Spicy Roasted Sausage, Potatoes and
  Peppers, 125
•Sweet Potatoes with Cilantro Black
  Beans, 187
Two-Tone Potato Wedges, 55

PUMPKIN & PUMPKIN SEEDS
•Mocha Pumpkin Seeds, 14
•Pumpkin & Cauliflower Garlic
  Mash, 65
Pumpkin Chip Cake with Walnuts, 217
Pumpkin Egg Braid, 203
Pumpkin Flans, 239
Pumpkin Gingersnap Ice Cream
  Pie, 222
•Spicy Pumpkin & Corn Soup, 22

QUICK BREADS & BISCUITS
•Chocolate Chip-Cranberry
  Scones, 202
Dark Chocolate Chip Zucchini
  Bread, 206
Double Berry Quick Bread, 201
Honey Spice Bread, 210
•Old-Fashioned Buttermilk
  Biscuits, 200
Rustic Oatmeal Scones, 208

QUINOA
•Lemon Cranberry Quinoa Salad, 42
Spicy Orange Quinoa, 186
•Strawberry-Quinoa Spinach
  Salad, 184

RAISINS
Curried Chicken Meatball Wraps, 17
•Honey & Ginger Glazed Carrots, 54
•Waldorf Turkey Salad, 132

RASPBERRIES
•All-Spiced Up Raspberry and
  Mushroom Salad, 48
•Cocoa Pancakes, 81
Raspberry Peach Puff Pancake, 72
Raspberry Peach Tart, 221
•Raspberry Pork Medallions, 158
Raspberry Sorbet, 232

RHUBARB
Apple Rhubarb Crumb Pie, 221
Rhubarb Strawberry Granita, 235
Rosy Rhubarb Upside-Down Cake, 215

RICE
Bread
Wild Rice Bread with Sunflower
  Seeds, 208

Main Dishes
•Arugula & Brown Rice Salad, 191
•Black Beans with Bell Peppers &
  Rice, 196
•Broccoli, Rice and Sausage
  Dinner, 133
Brown Rice Chutney Salad, 194
•Cajun Beef & Rice, 99
•Caribbean Shrimp & Rice Bowl, 166
•Chicken with Mandarin Salsa, 124
•Cilantro Shrimp & Rice, 174
•Curried Rice & Noodles, 185
Grilled Shrimp Scampi, 176
Grilled Tomatillo Chicken for Two, 119
Honey-Ginger Turkey Kabobs, 139
•Korean Beef and Rice, 96
•Pork Fried Rice, 155
Sausage Chicken Jambalaya, 116
•Shrimp Lettuce Wraps, 179
•Shrimp with Ginger-Chili Sauce, 172
•Speedy Salmon Stir-Fry, 178
Spicy Orange Quinoa, 186
•Strawberry-Quinoa Spinach
  Salad, 184
•Tilapia with Fiesta Rice, 168
•Turkey Chop Suey, 137
Turkey-Thyme Stuffed Peppers, 139
Side Dishes
Butternut Squash with Whole Grain
  Pilaf, 91
•Mushroom & Pea Rice Pilaf, 58
Side Salad
Brown Rice, Tomato & Basil
  Salad, 43
Soup
Brown Rice Mulligatawny, 24

SALADS
Main Dishes
•Arugula & Brown Rice Salad, 191
•Bow Tie & Spinach Salad, 196
Brown Rice Chutney Salad, 194
•Chinese Chicken Salad, 121
Grilled Pork Noodle Salad, 155
Grilled Shrimp & Tomato Salad, 169
Grilled Southwestern Steak
  Salad, 107
•Mediterranean Orzo Chicken
  Salad, 115
•Orzo-Tuna Salad with
  Tomatoes, 173
•Quick Nicoise Salad, 173
Southwest Shredded Pork Salad, 87
•Spring Chicken and Pea Salad, 122
•Strawberry-Quinoa Spinach
  Salad, 184
•Summer Splash Chicken Salad, 129
Thai Chicken and Slaw, 118

Turkey Pinto Bean Salad with
  Southern Molasses Dressing, 142
•Turkey Salad with Pear
  Dressing, 144
•Waldorf Turkey Salad, 132
•Whole Wheat Orzo Salad, 190
Side Dishes
•All-Spiced Up Raspberry and
  Mushroom Salad, 48
•Arugula Salad with Shaved
  Parmesan, 46
Balsamic Three-Bean Salad, 39
•Broccoli & Apple Salad, 41
Brown Rice, Tomato & Basil Salad, 43
Cherry Tomato Salad, 46
•Chilled Shrimp Pasta Salad, 42
•Chipotle Lime Avocado Salad, 44
Crisp & Spicy Cucumber Salad, 44
•Faux Potato Salad, 51
Fresh Sugar Snap Pea Salad, 40
Garden Bounty Potato Salad, 48
•Heirloom Tomato & Zucchini
  Salad, 50
Layered Grilled Corn Salad, 38
•Lemon Cranberry Quinoa Salad, 42
Minted Fruit Salad, 47
•Mixed Greens with Orange-Ginger
  Vinaigrette, 40
•Rainbow Veggie Salad, 39
Roasted Sweet Potato & Prosciutto
  Salad, 38
•Spring Greek Pasta Salad, 43
•Summer Squash & Watermelon
  Salad, 51
•Sunny Strawberry & Cantaloupe
  Salad, 41
Vibrant Black-Eyed Pea Salad, 50
•Wendy's Apple Pomegranate
  Salad, 49
Zesty Coleslaw, 47

SALSA
Avocado Endive Cups with Salsa, 10
Black Bean Chip & Dip Burgers, 193
•Blueberry Salsa, 13
•Grilled Pork with Spicy Pineapple
  Salsa, 160
•In-a-Pinch Chicken & Spinach, 126
Slow-Cooked Peach Salsa, 84
•Tilapia with Fiesta Rice, 168

SANDWICHES
•Bagel with a Veggie Schmear, 74
•English Muffin Egg Sandwich, 70
•Mediterranean Vegetable Pitas, 195
Mexican Shredded Beef Wraps, 90
•Open-Faced Roast Beef
  Sandwiches, 99

SANDWICHES (CONTINUED)

- Quick & Easy Turkey Sloppy Joes, 135
- Slow Cooker French Dip Sandwiches, 90
- Turkey & Apricot Wraps, 132
- West Coast Snappy Joes, 106

SAUSAGE

- Andouille Sausage Soup, 30
- Broccoli, Rice and Sausage Dinner, 133
- Chicken Sausages with Polenta, 119
- Italian Sausage and Provolone Skewers, 128
- Sausage & Greens Soup, 25
- Sausage & Pepper Pizza, 128
- Sausage Chicken Jambalaya, 116
- Sausage-Egg Burritos, 72
- Sausage Orecchiette Pasta, 141
- Sausage-Sweet Potato Hash & Eggs, 68
- Spicy Roasted Sausage, Potatoes and Peppers, 125
- Turkey Sausage Patties, 81
- Turkey Sausage-Stuffed Acorn Squash, 143
- Turkey Sausage Zucchini Boats, 136

SEAFOOD (ALSO SEE FISH)

- Basil Crab Cakes, 181
- Caribbean Shrimp & Rice Bowl, 166
- Chilled Shrimp Pasta Salad, 42
- Cilantro Shrimp & Rice, 174
- Cilantro Shrimp Cups, 15
- Cioppino-Style Soup, 24
- Crab Rangoon Canapes, 12
- Crabbie Phyllo Cups, 13
- Garlicky Herbed Shrimp, 16
- Grilled Shrimp & Tomato Salad, 169
- Grilled Shrimp Scampi, 176
- Scallops with Chipotle-Orange Sauce, 172
- Shrimp Lettuce Wraps, 179
- Shrimp Pad Thai Soup, 28
- Shrimp Piccata, 181
- Shrimp with Ginger-Chili Sauce, 172
- Tropical Island Shrimp Kabobs, 9

SERVES ONE OR TWO

- Apple Spiced Tea, 70
- Fiesta Time Omelet, 76
- Ginger-Kale Smoothies, 80
- Gluten-Free Skillet Pasta, 104
- Grilled Tomatillo Chicken for Two, 119
- Pork Fried Rice, 155
- Scallops with Chipotle-Orange Sauce, 172
- Spiced Turkey Tenderloin, 142

- Squash Saute, 61
- Steaks with Poblano Relish, 102

SIDE DISHES

Grains

- Kasha Varnishkes, 56
- Mushroom & Pea Rice Pilaf, 58

Pasta

- Creamy Roasted Garlic & Spinach Orzo, 61
- Kasha Varnishkes, 56

Potatoes

- Cheesy Chive Potatoes, 54
- Herbed Potato Packet, 57
- Parsley Smashed Potatoes, 93
- Potato Kugel, 63
- Rosemary Roasted Potatoes and Asparagus, 61
- Two-Tone Potato Wedges, 55

Vegetables

- Broccoli with Garlic, Bacon & Parmesan, 64
- Butternut Squash with Whole Grain Pilaf, 91
- Confetti Corn, 62
- Confetti Succotash, 65
- Garlic-Sesame Green Beans, 56
- Green Beans with Shallots, 62
- Honey & Ginger Glazed Carrots, 54
- Honey-Tarragon Grilled Asparagus, 57
- Parmesan-Butternut Squash, 63
- Pumpkin & Cauliflower Garlic Mash, 65
- Roasted Asparagus with Feta, 65
- Roasted Balsamic Brussels Sprouts with Pancetta, 59
- Roasted Cauliflower with Tahini Yogurt Sauce, 62
- Roasted Green Vegetable Medley, 58
- Sauteed Radishes with Green Beans, 55
- Shredded Gingered Brussels Sprouts, 64
- Squash Saute, 61

SLOW COOKER RECIPES

- All-Day Brisket with Potatoes, 88
- Apple Pie Oatmeal Dessert, 91
- Butternut Squash with Whole Grain Pilaf, 91
- Ginger Chicken Noodle Soup, 93
- Mexican Shredded Beef Wraps, 90
- Parsley Smashed Potatoes, 93
- Slow-Cooked Chicken Chili, 87
- Slow-Cooked Peach Salsa, 84
- Slow Cooker French Dip Sandwiches, 90

- Slow Cooker Lava Cake, 85
- Slow Cooker Mushroom Chicken & Peas, 92
- Slow Cooker Split Pea Soup, 88
- Southwest Shredded Pork Salad, 87
- Spring Herb Roast, 85
- Sweet Onion & Red Bell Pepper Topping, 91
- Tangy Lamb Tagine, 92
- Tangy Orange Chicken Thighs, 89
- Teriyaki Beef Stew, 89
- Turkey with Cranberry Sauce, 84

SOUPS (ALSO SEE CHILI)

- Andouille Sausage Soup, 30
- Broccoli & Potato Soup, 25
- Brown Rice Mulligatawny, 24
- Cheddar Cauliflower Soup, 27
- Chunky Turkey Soup, 28
- Cioppino-Style Soup, 24
- Coconut Curry Vegetable Soup, 23
- Corn Chowder, 35
- Fresh Asparagus Soup, 29
- Garden Vegetable & Herb Soup, 26
- Garden Vegetable Beef Soup, 29
- Ginger Chicken Noodle Soup, 93
- Hearty Beef & Sweet Potato Stew, 34
- Hearty Vegetable Lentil Soup, 33
- Mediterranean Chicken Orzo Soup, 33
- Moroccan Chickpea Stew, 35
- Satisfying Tomato Soup, 27
- Sausage & Greens Soup, 25
- Shrimp Pad Thai Soup, 28
- Slow Cooker Split Pea Soup, 88
- Spicy Pumpkin & Corn Soup, 22
- Spicy Sweet Potato Kale Soup, 31
- Summer Squash Soup, 23
- Turkey Tortilla Soup, 22

SPINACH

- Bow Tie & Spinach Salad, 196
- Brown Rice Chutney Salad, 194
- Creamy Roasted Garlic & Spinach Orzo, 61
- Garden Harvest Spaghetti Squash, 188
- In-a-Pinch Chicken & Spinach, 126
- Pan-Roasted Chicken and Vegetables, 113
- Parmesan Pork Chops with Spinach Salad, 157
- Power Lasagna, 102
- Spicy Beef & Pepper Stir-Fry, 99
- Spinach & Artichoke Pizza, 193
- Spinach & Feta Burgers, 98
- Strawberry-Quinoa Spinach Salad, 184

• Tomato & Garlic Butter Bean
Dinner, 190
• Turkey Salad with Pear Dressing, 144
Turkey Sausage-Stuffed Acorn
Squash, 143

STRAWBERRIES
Chocolate-Dipped Strawberry
Meringue Roses, 231
• Grilled Angel Food Cake with
Strawberries, 226
Rhubarb Strawberry Granita, 235
• Strawberry-Quinoa Spinach
Salad, 184
• Sunny Strawberry & Cantaloupe
Salad, 41

SUNFLOWER SEEDS
Peanut Butter Snack Bars, 243
Wild Rice Bread with Sunflower
Seeds, 208

SWEET POTATOES
Hearty Beef & Sweet Potato Stew, 34
Roasted Sweet Potato & Prosciutto
Salad, 38
• Sausage-Sweet Potato Hash &
Eggs, 68
Spicy Sweet Potato Kale Soup, 31
Two-Tone Potato Wedges, 55

TOMATOES
Appetizers
Festive Cherry Tomatoes, 18
Slow-Cooked Peach Salsa, 84
• Tomato-Squash Appetizer Pizza, 10
Bread
Herb & Sun-Dried Tomato
Muffins, 204
Breakfast & Brunch
• Curry Scramble, 74
Main Dishes
• Balsamic Chicken with Roasted
Tomatoes, 118
Black Bean Turkey Enchiladas, 137
Cozumel Red Snapper Veracruz, 175
Grilled Shrimp & Tomato Salad, 169
Herb Garden Lasagnas, 197
• Italian Sausage and Provolone
Skewers, 128
• Italian Turkey Skillet, 138
• Mediterranean Orzo Chicken
Salad, 115
• Orzo-Tuna Salad with
Tomatoes, 173
Power Lasagna, 102
• Ricotta-Stuffed Portobello
Mushrooms, 189

• Spicy Tomato Pork Chops, 158
Sun-Dried Tomato Burgers, 133
• Tomato & Garlic Butter Bean
Dinner, 190
• Vegetarian Bean Tacos, 189
Side Salads
Brown Rice, Tomato & Basil
Salad, 43
Cherry Tomato Salad, 46
• Chipotle Lime Avocado Salad, 44
• Heirloom Tomato & Zucchini
Salad, 50
Soups
Black Bean-Tomato Chili, 30
• Satisfying Tomato Soup, 27
Slow-Cooked Chicken Chili, 87
Turkey Tortilla Soup, 22

TORTILLAS
Black Bean Turkey Enchiladas, 137
• Fajita Skillet, 104
• Feta Steak Tacos, 105
Grilled Beef Chimichangas, 100
• Grilled Chicken, Mango &
Blue Cheese Tortillas, 12
• Honey-Lemon Chicken
Enchiladas, 121
Mexican Shredded Beef Wraps, 90
• Pinto Bean Tostadas, 194
• Portobello Fajitas, 185
Sausage-Egg Burritos, 72
• Turkey & Apricot Wraps, 132
Turkey Tortilla Soup, 22
• Vegetarian Bean Tacos, 189

TURKEY & TURKEY SAUSAGE
Breakfast & Brunch
Sausage-Egg Burritos, 72
• Sausage-Sweet Potato Hash &
Eggs, 68
Turkey Sausage Patties, 81
Main Dishes
Black Bean Turkey Enchiladas, 137
• Broccoli, Rice and Sausage
Dinner, 133
• Curry-Roasted Turkey and
Potatoes, 134
Gluten-Free Turkey Spaghetti, 135
Herbed-Rubbed Turkey, 138
Honey-Ginger Turkey Kabobs, 139
• Italian Turkey Skillet, 138
• Quick & Easy Turkey Sloppy
Joes, 135
• Sausage Orecchiette Pasta, 141
Southwest-Style Shepherd's Pie, 144
Spiced Turkey Tenderloin, 142
Sun-Dried Tomato Burgers, 133
• Turkey & Apricot Wraps, 132

• Turkey Burgers with Peach
Mayo, 141
• Turkey Chop Suey, 137
• Turkey Lo Mein, 134
Turkey Pinto Bean Salad with
Southern Molasses Dressing, 142
• Turkey Salad with Pear
Dressing, 144
Turkey Sausage-Stuffed Acorn
Squash, 143
Turkey Sausage Zucchini Boats, 136
Turkey-Thyme Stuffed Peppers, 139
• Turkey Verde Lettuce Wraps, 143
Turkey with Cranberry Sauce, 84
• Waldorf Turkey Salad, 132
Soups
Chunky Turkey Soup, 28
Sausage & Greens Soup, 25
Turkey Tortilla Soup, 22

VEGETABLES
Appetizers
Avocado Endive Cups with Salsa, 10
Grilled Leek Dip, 8
Breakfast & Brunch
Basil Vegetable Strata, 75
English Muffin Egg Sandwich, 70
Condiment
Sweet Onion & Red Bell Pepper
Topping, 91
Main Dishes
Apple-Marinated Chicken &
Vegetables, 115
Artichoke Ratatouille Chicken, 117
Braised Pork Stew, 151
Grilled Tomatillo Chicken for
Two, 119
Mediterranean Vegetable Pitas, 195
Pan-Roasted Chicken and
Vegetables, 113
Pork & Vegetable Spring Rolls, 148
Pork Tenderloin with Fennel and
Cranberries, 157
Speedy Salmon Stir-Fry, 178
Spicy Orange Quinoa, 186
Stacked Vegetables and Ravioli, 191
Tangy Lamb Tagine, 92
Tilapia & Veggies with Red Pepper
Sauce, 178
Tuna Veggie Kabobs, 169
Vegetable Steak Kabobs, 106
Side Dishes
Roasted Green Vegetable Medley, 58
Sauteed Radishes with Green
Beans, 55
Side Salads
• Rainbow Veggie Salad, 39
Vibrant Black-Eyed Pea Salad, 50

VEGETABLES (CONTINUED)

Soups
Chunky Turkey Soup, 28
Garden Vegetable & Herb Soup, 26
Garden Vegetable Beef Soup, 29
Moroccan Chickpea Stew, 35
Sausage & Greens Soup, 25

WINTER SQUASH
Butternut Squash with Whole Grain
    Pilaf, 91
Garden Harvest Spaghetti
    Squash, 188
Honey-Squash Dinner Rolls, 211
•Parmesan-Butternut Squash, 63
Spiced Butternut Squash Pie, 226
Turkey Sausage-Stuffed Acorn
    Squash, 143

YEAST BREADS & ROLLS
Cranberry-Walnut Toasting
    Bread, 211
Crusty Homemade Bread, 204
Gluten-Free Anadama Bread, 205
•Grilled Garden Veggie
    Flatbread, 200
Honey-Squash Dinner Rolls, 211
No-Knead Harvest Bread, 210
Perfect Pizza Crust, 207
Pumpkin Egg Braid, 203
Wild Rice Bread with Sunflower
    Seeds, 208

ZUCCHINI & SUMMER
SQUASH
Apple-Marinated Chicken &
    Vegetables, 115
Beef & Bulgur-Stuffed Zucchini
    Boats, 97
Dark Chocolate Chip Zucchini
    Bread, 206
•Heirloom Tomato & Zucchini
    Salad, 50
•Italian Beef and Shells, 100
•Squash Saute, 61
Stacked Vegetables and Ravioli, 191
Sue's Chocolate Zucchini Cake, 216
•Summer Squash & Watermelon
    Salad, 51
Summer Squash Soup, 23
•Tilapia & Veggies with Red Pepper
    Sauce, 178
•Tomato-Squash Appetizer Pizza, 10
Turkey Sausage Zucchini Boats, 136

Alphabetical Index

This index lists every recipe alphabetically, so you can easily find the dishes you enjoy most.
•*Table-ready in 30 minutes or less.*

A
All-Day Brisket with Potatoes, 88
•All-Spiced Up Raspberry and
    Mushroom Salad, 48
Andouille Sausage Soup, 30
•Apple & Spice Pork Tenderloin, 149
Apple-Marinated Chicken &
    Vegetables, 115
Apple Pie Oatmeal Dessert, 91
Apple Rhubarb Crumb Pie, 221
Apple Roasted Pork with Cherry
    Balsamic Glaze, 161
•Apple Spiced Tea, 70
Artichoke Hummus, 17
Artichoke Ratatouille Chicken, 117
•Arugula & Brown Rice Salad, 191
•Arugula Salad with Shaved
    Parmesan, 46
Asian Chicken Thighs, 125
•Asian Snapper with Capers, 168
Avocado Endive Cups with Salsa, 10

B
•Bagel with a Veggie Schmear, 74
Baked Elephant Ears, 233
•Balsamic Chicken with Roasted
    Tomatoes, 118
Balsamic-Cranberry Potato Bites, 19
Balsamic Three-Bean Salad, 39
•Banana Boats, 238
Banana-Pineapple Cream Pies, 216
Basil Chicken, 124
Basil Crab Cakes, 181
Basil Vegetable Strata, 75
•BBQ Yumburgers, 105
Beef & Bulgur-Stuffed Zucchini
    Boats, 97
Beef, Potato & Egg Bake, 79
Black Bean Chip & Dip Burgers, 193
Black Bean-Tomato Chili, 30
Black Bean Turkey Enchiladas, 137
•Black Beans with Bell Peppers &
    Rice, 196
Blackberry Nectarine Pie, 218
•Blackberry Smoothies, 80
•Blackberry-Topped Sponge Cakes, 223
•Blueberry Salsa, 13
•Bow Tie & Spinach Salad, 196
•Braised Pork Stew, 151
•Broccoli & Apple Salad, 41
•Broccoli & Potato Soup, 25
•Broccoli, Rice and Sausage Dinner, 133
•Broccoli with Garlic, Bacon &
    Parmesan, 64

Brown Rice Chutney Salad, 194
Brown Rice Mulligatawny, 24
Brown Rice, Tomato & Basil Salad, 43
•Brown Sugar & Banana Oatmeal, 81
Butternut Squash with Whole Grain
    Pilaf, 91

C
•Cajun Beef & Rice, 99
Caramel Apple Coffee Cake with
    Walnuts, 71
Cardamom Yogurt Pudding with
    Honeyed Oranges, 233
Caribbean Delight, 114
•Caribbean Shrimp & Rice Bowl, 166
Carrot Cupcakes with Cream Cheese
    Frosting, 214
Cheddar Cauliflower Soup, 27
Cheese Manicotti, 195
•Cheesy Chive Potatoes, 54
Cherry Dumplings, 242
Cherry Tomato Salad, 46
•Chicken & Garlic with Fresh Herbs, 123
Chicken Cordon Bleu Stroganoff, 116
•Chicken Sausages with Polenta, 119
•Chicken Strips Milano, 122
•Chicken with Mandarin Salsa, 124
•Chicken with Peach-Cucumber
    Salsa, 111
Chicken with Three-Citrus Topping, 127
•Chilled Shrimp Pasta Salad, 42
•Chinese Chicken Salad, 121
•Chipotle Lime Avocado Salad, 44
•Chocolate Chip-Cranberry Scones, 202
Chocolate-Dipped Strawberry Meringue
    Roses, 231
Chocolate Eggnog Pie, 225
Chocolate-Glazed Cupcakes, 219
Chunky Turkey Soup, 28
•Cilantro Shrimp & Rice, 174
Cilantro Shrimp Cups, 15
Cinnamon-Sugar Coffee Cake, 69
Cioppino-Style Soup, 24
•Cocoa Pancakes, 81
Coconut Curry Vegetable Soup, 23
Coconut-Mango Tilapia, 167
•Cod Delight, 179
•Confetti Corn, 62
•Confetti Succotash, 65
Cool Summertime Oatmeal, 68
Corn Chowder, 35
Cozumel Red Snapper Veracruz, 175
•Crab Rangoon Canapes, 12
•Crabbie Phyllo Cups, 13
Cranberry-Orange Snack Cake, 219

•Cranberry Sweet-and-Sour Pork, 150
Cranberry-Walnut Toasting Bread, 211
Cream Cheese Swirl Brownies, 236
Creamy Roasted Garlic & Spinach
    Orzo, 61
Crisp & Spicy Cucumber Salad, 44
•Crisp Chocolate Chip Waffles, 79
•Crispy Fish & Chips, 170
•Crunchy Apricot-Coconut Balls, 232
•Crunchy French Toast, 75
Crusty Homemade Bread, 204
Cuban-Style Pork Chops, 154
Curried Chicken Meatball Wraps, 17
•Curried Rice & Noodles, 185
•Curry-Roasted Turkey and
    Potatoes, 134
•Curry Scramble, 74

D

Dark Chocolate Chip Zucchini
    Bread, 206
Date Oat Bars, 234
Double Berry Quick Bread, 201

E

Easy & Elegant Tenderloin Roast, 96
Easy Marinated Flank Steak, 103
•English Muffin Egg Sandwich, 70

F

•Fajita Skillet, 104
•Faux Potato Salad, 51
Favorite Banana Chip Muffins, 205
Festive Cherry Tomatoes, 18
•Feta Steak Tacos, 105
•Fiesta Time Omelet, 76
•Fluffy Banana Pancakes, 69
Fresh Asparagus Soup, 29
Fresh Fruit Combo, 78
Fresh Sugar Snap Pea Salad, 40
Frozen Greek Vanilla Yogurt, 231
Frozen Yogurt Fruit Pops, 236
•Fruit & Granola Crisp with Yogurt, 235

G

Garden Bounty Potato Salad, 48
Garden Harvest Spaghetti Squash, 188
Garden Vegetable & Herb Soup, 26
Garden Vegetable Beef Soup, 29
•Garlic Chicken Rigatoni, 114
Garlic-Herb Salmon Sliders, 166
Garlic-Sesame Green Beans, 56
•Garlicky Herbed Shrimp, 16
Get-Up-and-Go Granola, 78
Ginger Chicken Noodle Soup, 93
•Ginger-Kale Smoothies, 80
Gluten-Free Anadama Bread, 205
Gluten-Free Chocolate Cake
    Cookies, 240
Gluten-Free Skillet Pasta, 104
Gluten-Free Turkey Spaghetti, 135

Gran's Apple Cake, 214
•Grapes with Lemon-Honey Yogurt, 71
•Green Beans with Shallots, 62
•Grilled Angel Food Cake with
    Strawberries, 226
•Grilled Apple Pizza, 241
Grilled Beef Chimichangas, 100
•Grilled Chicken, Mango & Blue Cheese
    Tortillas, 12
Grilled Dijon Pork Roast, 156
•Grilled Garden Veggie Flatbread, 200
•Grilled Honey-Balsamic Fruit, 230
Grilled Leek Dip, 8
Grilled Pork Noodle Salad, 155
•Grilled Pork with Spicy Pineapple
    Salsa, 160
Grilled Shrimp & Tomato Salad, 169
Grilled Shrimp Scampi, 176
Grilled Southwestern Steak Salad, 107
Grilled Tomatillo Chicken for Two, 119

H

•Ham Pasta Toss, 154
Hearty Beef & Sweet Potato Stew, 34
Hearty Pork Chops, 162
Hearty Vegetable Lentil Soup, 33
•Heirloom Tomato & Zucchini Salad, 50
Herb & Olive Oil Corn Bread, 201
Herb & Sun-Dried Tomato Muffins, 204
Herb Garden Lasagnas, 197
Herbed Potato Packet, 57
Herb-Rubbed Turkey, 138
•Homemade Guacamole, 18
•Honey & Ginger Glazed Carrots, 54
Honey-Ginger Turkey Kabobs, 139
•Honey-Lemon Chicken Enchiladas, 121
Honey Spice Bread, 210
Honey-Squash Dinner Rolls, 211
•Honey-Tarragon Grilled Asparagus, 57

I

•In-a-Pinch Chicken & Spinach, 126
•Italian Beef and Shells, 100
Italian Crumb-Crusted Beef Roast, 103
•Italian Sausage and Provolone
    Skewers, 128
•Italian Turkey Skillet, 138

J

•Jalapeno Jelly-Glazed Pork Chops, 162

K

Kasha Varnishkes, 56
King Cake with Cream Cheese
    Filling, 224
•Korean Beef and Rice, 96

L

Layered Grilled Corn Salad, 38
Lemon Blueberry Cornmeal Cake, 218
•Lemon Cranberry Quinoa Salad, 42

•Lemon-Garlic Pork Chops, 149
Lemon Meringue Muffins, 207
•Lemon Parsley Swordfish, 177
Lime Basil Pie, 215
•Lime Chicken with Salsa Verde Sour
    Cream, 127
•Lime-Cilantro Tilapia, 170

M

•Mango-Peach Smoothies, 79
Maple Apple Baked Oatmeal, 76
Maple-Pecan Glazed Ham, 159
Meatballs in Cherry Sauce, 9
Mediterranean Baked Chicken with
    Lemon, 123
Mediterranean Chicken Orzo Soup, 33
•Mediterranean Orzo Chicken Salad, 115
•Mediterranean Vegetable Pitas, 195
Mexican Shredded Beef Wraps, 90
Mini Barbecue Meat Loaves, 100
Mini Italian Frittatas, 77
Minted Fruit Salad, 47
•Mixed Greens with Orange-Ginger
    Vinaigrette, 40
•Mocha Pumpkin Seeds, 14
•Molasses-Glazed Pork Chops, 148
Moroccan Chickpea Stew, 35
•Mushroom & Herb Chicken, 129
•Mushroom & Pea Rice Pilaf, 58
Mushroom-Bean Bourguignon, 187
Mushroom Bolognese with Whole
    Wheat Pasta, 186
•Mushroom Burgers, 184
Must-Have Tiramisu, 230

N

No-Knead Harvest Bread, 210

O

•Old-Fashioned Buttermilk
    Biscuits, 200
•Open-Faced Roast Beef Sandwiches, 99
Orange Beef Lettuce Wraps, 97
Orange-Glazed Pork with Sweet
    Potatoes, 163
Orange Pound Cake with Cranberry
    Compote, 225
•Orzo-Tuna Salad with Tomatoes, 173
Oven-Fried Chicken Drumsticks, 112

P

Pan-Roasted Chicken and
    Vegetables, 113
Pan-Roasted Pork Chops & Potatoes, 150
•Parmesan-Butternut Squash, 63
•Parmesan Pork Chops with Spinach
    Salad, 157
•Parsley-Crusted Cod, 176
Parsley Smashed Potatoes, 93
Pea Soup Shooters, 14
Peanut Butter & Jam Muffins, 202

Peanut Butter Snack Bars, 243
Pear-Cranberry Gingerbread Cake, 222
Pear Sorbet, 235
•Pepper Steak with Potatoes, 103
Peppermint Meringues, 242
Perfect Pizza Crust, 207
•Pesto Grilled Salmon, 180
•Pinto Bean Tostadas, 194
•Pizzaiola Chops, 160
Plum Crisp, 240
•Poached Eggs with Tarragon
    Asparagus, 77
•Poached Salmon with Dill &
    Turmeric, 174
•Pork & Mango Stir-Fry, 159
•Pork & Vegetable Spring Rolls, 148
•Pork Chops & Mushrooms, 161
•Pork Fried Rice, 155
Pork Tenderloin with Fennel and
    Cranberries, 157
•Portobello Fajitas, 185
•Potato-Cheddar Frittata, 80
Potato Kugel, 63
Power Lasagna, 102
•Pumpkin & Cauliflower Garlic Mash, 65
Pumpkin Chip Cake with Walnuts, 217
Pumpkin Egg Braid, 203
Pumpkin Flans, 239
Pumpkin Gingersnap Ice Cream Pie, 222

Q
•Quick & Easy Turkey Sloppy Joes, 135
•Quick Nicoise Salad, 173

R
•Rainbow Veggie Salad, 39
Raspberry Peach Puff Pancake, 72
Raspberry Peach Tart, 221
•Raspberry Pork Medallions, 158
Raspberry Sorbet, 232
Rhubarb Strawberry Granita, 235
•Ricotta-Stuffed Portobello
    Mushrooms, 189
•Roasted Asparagus with Feta, 65
Roasted Balsamic Brussels Sprouts with
    Pancetta, 59
Roasted Cauliflower with Tahini Yogurt
    Sauce, 62
Roasted Grape Crostini, 16
Roasted Green Vegetable Medley, 58
Roasted Sweet Potato & Prosciutto
    Salad, 38
Rosemary Roasted Potatoes and
    Asparagus, 61
•Rosemary-Thyme Lamb Chops, 153
Rosy Rhubarb Upside-Down Cake, 215
Rustic Oatmeal Scones, 208
Rustic Pear Tart, 224

S
Salisbury Steak Supreme, 107
•Salmon with Balsamic Orange
    Sauce, 175

•Satisfying Tomato Soup, 27
•Saucy Spiced Pears, 239
Sausage & Greens Soup, 25
Sausage & Pepper Pizza, 128
Sausage Chicken Jambalaya, 116
Sausage-Egg Burritos, 72
•Sausage Orecchiette Pasta, 141
•Sausage-Sweet Potato Hash & Eggs, 68
•Sauteed Radishes with Green Beans, 55
•Scallops with Chipotle-Orange
    Sauce, 172
Sesame-Beef Pot Stickers, 8
•Shredded Gingered Brussels
    Sprouts, 64
•Shrimp Lettuce Wraps, 179
Shrimp Pad Thai Soup, 28
•Shrimp Piccata, 181
•Shrimp with Ginger-Chili Sauce, 172
Skillet Blueberry Slump, 234
•Skillet Chicken with Olives, 110
Slow-Cooked Chicken Chili, 87
Slow-Cooked Peach Salsa, 84
Slow Cooker French Dip Sandwiches, 90
Slow Cooker Lava Cake, 85
Slow Cooker Mushroom Chicken &
    Peas, 92
Slow Cooker Split Pea Soup, 88
•Sole Fillets in Lemon Butter, 167
Southwest Shredded Pork Salad, 87
Southwest-Style Shepherd's Pie, 144
•Speedy Chicken Marsala, 110
•Speedy Salmon Stir-Fry, 178
Spice-Brined Pork Roast, 153
Spiced Butternut Squash Pie, 226
Spiced Turkey Tenderloin, 142
•Spicy Barbecued Chicken, 112
Spicy Beef & Pepper Stir-Fry, 99
Spicy Orange Quinoa, 186
•Spicy Pumpkin & Corn Soup, 22
Spicy Roasted Sausage, Potatoes and
    Peppers, 125
•Spicy Sweet Potato Kale Soup, 31
•Spicy Tomato Pork Chops, 158
Spinach & Artichoke Pizza, 193
Spinach & Feta Burgers, 98
•Spring Chicken and Pea Salad, 122
•Spring Greek Pasta Salad, 43
Spring Herb Roast, 85
•Spring Pea Crostini, 19
•Squash Saute, 61
Stacked Vegetables and Ravioli, 191
Steaks with Poblano Relish, 102
Stovetop Tarragon Chicken, 126
•Strawberry-Quinoa Spinach Salad, 184
•Sublime Lime Beef, 98
Sue's Chocolate Zucchini Cake, 216
•Summer Splash Chicken Salad, 129
•Summer Squash & Watermelon
    Salad, 51
Summer Squash Soup, 23
Sun-Dried Tomato Burgers, 133
Sunday Roast Chicken, 111
•Sunny Strawberry & Cantaloupe
    Salad, 41

Sweet Onion & Red Bell Pepper
    Topping, 91
•Sweet Potatoes with Cilantro Black
    Beans, 187

T
Tangy Lamb Tagine, 92
Tangy Orange Chicken Thighs, 89
•Tapenade-Stuffed Chicken Breasts, 117
•Tasty Tacos, 96
Teriyaki Beef Stew, 89
•Teriyaki Salmon, 177
Thai Chicken and Slaw, 118
Thyme-Sea Salt Crackers, 15
•Tilapia & Veggies with Red Pepper
    Sauce, 178
•Tilapia with Fiesta Rice, 168
•Tomato & Garlic Butter Bean
    Dinner, 190
•Tomato-Squash Appetizer Pizza, 10
Tropical Island Shrimp Kabobs, 9
Tuna Veggie Kabobs, 169
•Turkey & Apricot Wraps, 132
•Turkey Burgers with Peach Mayo, 141
•Turkey Chop Suey, 137
•Turkey Lo Mein, 134
Turkey Pinto Bean Salad with Southern
    Molasses Dressing, 142
•Turkey Salad with Pear Dressing, 144
Turkey Sausage Patties, 81
Turkey Sausage-Stuffed Acorn
    Squash, 143
Turkey Sausage Zucchini Boats, 136
Turkey-Thyme Stuffed Peppers, 139
Turkey Tortilla Soup, 22
•Turkey Verde Lettuce Wraps, 143
Turkey with Cranberry Sauce, 84
Two-Tone Potato Wedges, 55

V
Vanilla Angel Food Cake, 223
Vanilla Meringue Cookies, 243
Vegetable Steak Kabobs, 106
•Vegetarian Bean Tacos, 189
Vibrant Black-Eyed Pea Salad, 50

W
•Waldorf Turkey Salad, 132
Warm Chocolate Melting Cups, 238
•Wendy's Apple Pomegranate Salad, 49
•West Coast Snappy Joes, 106
•Whole Wheat Orzo Salad, 190
•Wicked Deviled Eggs, 13
Wild Rice Bread with Sunflower
    Seeds, 208

Z
Zesty Coleslaw, 47